Educational Restructuring in the Context of Globalization and National Policy

Educational Restructuring in the Context of Globalization and National Policy

EDITED BY HOLGER DAUN

RoutledgeFalmer
New York & London

Published in 2002 by
RoutledgeFalmer
29 West 35th Street
New York, NY 10001

Published in Great Britain by
RoutledgeFalmer
11 New Fetter Lane
London EC4P 4EE

RoutledgeFalmer is an imprint of the Taylor & Francis Group.

Library of Congress Cataloging-in Publication Data

Educational restructuring in the context of globalization and national policy
    / Holger Daun (ed.)
        p. cm. — (Reference books in international education)
        Includes bibliographical references and index.
        ISBN 0-8153-3941-0
        1. Education and state—Cross-cultural studies. 2. Educational
change—Cross-cultural studies. 3. Gloalization—Cross-cultural
studies. 4. International economic relations—Cross-cultural studies.
I. Daun Holger. II. Series.

10   9   8   7   6   5   4   3   2   1

TABLE OF CONTENTS

List of Tables

List of Figures and Appendices

Acknowledgments

This book is the product of several years of work, carried out to a large extent, within the framework of research projects funded by Sida/SAREC, and The Council for Humanistic and Social Research in Sweden.

I am grateful to many persons, all of whom cannot be mentioned here. Professor Martin Carnoy, Stanford University, and Professor William L. Boyd, Pennsylvania State University, USA, read and commented upon early versions of some of the chapters. Through long-term discussions and dialogues, I received direct or indirect input on my work, especially from: Professor Gustave Callewaert, Copenhagen University, Denmark; Dr. Luciana Benincasa, Yoannina University, Greece; MA Cynthia Vynnycky, Stockholm University, Sweden; Professor David N. Plank, Michigan State University, USA; MA Abdoulaye Sane, CONGAD, Senegal; MA Mario Cissoko, The National Institute for Educational Development, Guinea-Bissau. Cynthia Vynnycky also assisted me in improving the English. Stimulating discussions with the students at the Institute of International Education, Stockholm University, provided me with inspiration, as well as intelligent ideas on both particular and general aspects of education in the world. Together with Dr. Karen Sörensen, several students at the last mentioned institute contributed to the manuscript: Michiyo Kiwako Ôkuma, Dinah M'Baga Eurén, Wycliffe Odiwuor, Cresantus Biamba, and Reza Arjmand.

Last but not least, I want to thank my wife, Ulla Persson, and my children, Marlene, Andreas and Joakim, for their patience with my spending time on writing.

Foreword

It is widely believed that globalization is transforming the lives of people in the developed countries and most developing ones. Together with new information technology and the innovative processes it stimulates, globalization appears to be driving a revolution in the organization of work, the production of goods and services, relations among nations, and even local culture.

Because two of the main bases of globalization are knowledge intensive information and innovation, globalization should have a profound impact on education. Yet, education does not seem to have changed much at the classroom level—even in those nations most involved in the global economy and the information age. Beyond occasionally used computers in classrooms, teaching methods and national and local curricula remain largely intact. At first glance, this suggests that globalization is not as pervasive a phenomenon as some analysts claim. It implies that globalization might be mainly economic or at some level, political without touching deeply entrenched national institutions such as the formal educational system.

In this ambitious book, Holger Daun and his associates develop a very different case. They use a far-reaching, worldwide perspective to show that whereas classrooms may not be changing much, at a more macro level globalization is transforming educational systems. Not surprisingly, this transformation, like globalization itself, is driven mainly by financial forces, new patterns of economic growth, and market ideology.

Because global financial flows are so large, governments rely increasingly on foreign capital to finance economic growth. One way to attract finance capital is to provide a ready supply of skilled labor by increasing the average level of education in the labor force. Beyond that, the payoff to higher levels of education is rising worldwide as a result of the shifts of economic production to knowledge-intensive services and manufacturing. Rising relative incomes for higher educated labor increases the demand for university education, pushing governments to expand their higher education, and, correspondingly, to increase the number of secondary school graduates ready to attend post-secondary. In countries that were previously resistant to providing equal access to education for young women, the need for more highly educated low-cost labor tends to expand women's educational opportunities.

But another important variable in attracting finance capital is reduced public spending and the relative expansion of private sector investment. Financial forces pressure many governments—mainly those in developing countries—to reduce the growth of *public* spending on education and to find other sources of funding for the expected expansion of their educational systems. Thus, globalized capital pushes for more and better education at the same time as it argues for lower public spending to achieve it.

This is where market ideology comes in. Globalization is not just a set of new "objective" economic realities. It is also provides the context of a new round of ideological debates concerning market efficiency and market imperfections. Education is a major battleground in the debate. Market ideology argues that public bureaucracy forms a major impediment to delivering more and better education for the same amount of resources. It argues that public education is inherently inefficient for several reasons. Particularly when education is managed by a national bureaucracy, decision-makers are too distant from education users (pupils' parents) to be responsive to local needs and to be accountable for educational quality. Because public education tends to be a monopoly, it lacks the competition needed to promote efficiency. As a result, public schools can waste resources, produce poor quality education, and still be guaranteed students. And, finally, public education is often heavily influenced by teachers' unions that represent teachers' rather than students' interests.

These reasons eliminate the apparent contradiction between reducing public spending on education and increasing the quantity and quality of educational services. By decentralizing the management and finance of schooling, increasing competition in the education sector through greater school choice, including privatization, and diminishing the power of teachers' unions, educational systems can achieve large gains in efficiency and attract increasing private resources from families ready to pay for better schooling.

The argument claims that this can bring more students into better schools for the same level of public spending.

The main impact of globalization on education is exercised through the implementation of such "restructuring" of the world's public sectors and the way they deliver schooling. Economic and educational restructuring are twinned outcomes of the new globalization. "Objective" pressures to overcome financial crises and to attract foreign capital in the longer run with "correct" economic policies are accompanied by these reduced public spending formulas, educational decentralization, increased privatization, and, concomitantly, reduced influence of teachers' unions over educational policy.

This is not its only impact, however. Globalization is not without its critics or resistors. The most important are religious and ethnic/social movements that oppose the power of global market ideology. Globalized information networks means transformation of world culture. But globalization also means that many groups feel marginalized by the market values of this new culture. Such groups struggle against the globalized economy by asserting cultural values that may themselves be global (traditional fundamentalist religion on one hand, for example, and post-modern environmentalism and feminism, on the other), but are, at the same time, profoundly anti-market. This constitutes a new kind of struggle over the meaning and value of knowledge.

In Africa and Asia, Islam has posed itself as the major counter force to Euro-centric global capitalism. Islamic education emphasizes inner power through religious belief rather than material achievements and poses an alternative universal to the market. The chapters in this book on Africa and Central Asia suggest that in these regions the two philosophies are engaged in an epic struggle, and that in the new globalized context, schools are at the center of stuggles over the definition of what knowledge is valuable and how a society's culture should be defined in the new global environment.

Whether globalization in all these manifestations is "bad" or "good" for education remains to be seen. It appears that in many places, globalization has led to greater economic and social inequality, and that educational access has expanded but has also become more unequal in quality. Greater decentralization and privatization has generally not increased the quality of educational services and has produced more educational inequality. Neither has a greater emphasis on religious values in those nations or regions committed to combating the market system seemed to have much effect on educational equality unless the public sector has specifically stressed an equalization policy.

In the studies of the various parts of the world developed in this book, the trends outlined here are shown to play out in different forms. The chapters attempt to show how the recent economic and social history of each region has shaped educational reform and how these educational reforms reflect the pressures of a globalizing economy. Through these various pieces, a picture emerges of a world increasingly dominated by global market hegemony going through enormous changes at the regional level. In some regions, such as the former European socialist bloc, these changes have been sudden and almost overwhelming. In other regions, such as Latin America, they have been more gradual, but almost as powerful. The scope of this analysis of world economic and educational restructuring allows the reader to grasp both the variety of changes and their relationship to a larger whole.

The analysis of these different regions and the variety of responses to globalization they embrace indicates that governments—at least in theory—can respond to globalization in fundamentally different ways, and how governments respond is crucial to understanding the effect that globalization has on education. In practice, however, the approach governments take in educational reform, hence their educational response to globalization, depends on three key factors: their real financial situation, their *interpretation* of that situation, and their *ideological* position regarding the role of the public sector in education. These three elements are expressed through the way that countries "structurally adjust" their economies to the new globalized environment.

Perhaps the most important lesson to take away from the study is that the changes we are witnessing are both global and local. The social effects of globalization, are, after all, passed through the policy structures of national states. Although national states are increasingly being asked to devolve power over education to global market forces or ethnicity/religious-based regional and local movements, it is still these states (or sub-states) that ultimately decide how globalization affects national (regional) education.

Daun's own country of Sweden is an important example of a national state that has successfully ridden out economic adjustment without succumbing to pressures to reduce its commitment to economic and social equalization. True, Sweden is a highly developed country with a strong economic and human capital base. But Sweden is also a relatively small economy in the world system. It was able to adjust it economic structure to accommodate greater competition, increase economic growth, reduce unemployment, and, at the same time, preserve its public expenditure structure largely intact. Public educational spending continues to expand and is just as "incorporative" as in the past.

So Daun's analysis suggests that there may be much more political and even financial space for the public sector to choose alternatives for education than is usually admitted. It also suggests that when states abandon more equitable versions of knowledge production it is at least partly the result of ideological preference rather than helplessness in the face of globalization and the exigencies of finance capital.

Martin Carnoy
Stanford, California

Series Preface

This series of scholarly works in comparative and international education has grown well beyond the initial conception of a collection of reference books. Although retaining its original purpose of providing a resource to scholars, students, and a variety of other professionals who need to understand the role played by education in various societies or world regions, it also strives to provide accurate, relevant, and up-to-date information on a wide variety of selected educational issues, problems, and experiments within an international context.

Contributors to this series are well-known scholars who have devoted their professional lives to the study of their specializations. Without exception these men and women possess an intimate understanding of the subject of their research and writing. Without exception they have studied their subject not only in dusty archives, but have lived and traveled widely in their quest for knowledge. In short, they are "experts" in the best sense of that often overused word.

In our increasingly interdependent world, it is now widely understood that it is a matter of military, economic, and environmental survival that we understand better not only what makes other societies tick, but also how others, be they Japanese, Hungarian, South African, or Chilean, attempt to solve the same kinds of educational problems that we face in North America. As the late George Z. F. Bereday wrote more than three decades ago: "[E]ducation is a mirror held against the face of a people. Nations may put on blustering shows of strength to conceal public weakness, erect grand façades to conceal shabby backyards, and profess peace while secretly arming for conquest, but how they take care of their children tells unerringly who they are" (*Comparative Methods in Education*, New York: Holt, Rinehart and Winston, 1964, p. 5).

Perhaps equally important, however, is the valuable perspective that studying another education system (or its problems) provides us in understanding our own system (or its problems). When we step beyond our own limited experience and our commonly held assumptions about schools and learning in order to look back at our system in contrast to another, we see it in a very different light. To learn, for example, how China or Belgium handles the education of a multilingual society; how the French provide for the funding of public education; or how the Japanese control access to their universities enables us to better understand that there are reasonable alternatives to our own familiar way of doing things. Not that we can *borrow* directly from other societies. Indeed, educational arrangements are inevitably a reflection of deeply embedded political, economic, and cultural factors that are unique to a particular society. But a conscious recognition that there are other ways of doing things can serve to open our minds and provoke our imaginations in ways that can result in new experiments or approaches that we may not have otherwise considered.

Since this series is intended to be a useful research tool, the editor and contributors welcome suggestions for future volumes, as well as ways in which this series can be improved.

Edward R. Beauchamp
University of Hawaii

Introduction

This book is about the educational changes that are taking place around the world in the name of globalization, global competitiveness, "Education For All" and multiculturalism. Worldwide there is increasing surveillance of educational processes and penetration of the last remote and isolated areas of the world. The book makes an overview of principal changes of national societies and their educational systems, definitions and arrangements of educational restructuring and educational research. A review is made of educational changes in selected countries on each continent.

The Second World War was followed by a tremendous expansion of education. Educational reforms were made in relation to the requirements and conditions of the national framework; they were to correspond to the national economy and the national culture(s). Between the industrialized countries, some educational "borrowing" occurred but each country tended to construct its education system in accordance with its specific characteristics.

However, since the beginning of the 1980s, an almost uniform pattern of policy for compulsory or basic education has been formulated all over the world, from Chile to the United States, from Mozambique to Finland, and from Estonia to China. Most of them, with the exception of some Asian and Arab Gulf Countries, have formulated and made attempts to implement policies of educational restructuring. These policies imply decentralization/centralization, freedom of educational choice, application of market forces in education or systemic reforms, which includes these three measures plus piecemeal changes such as curriculum change, extension of compulsory education, change of teacher competence, teaching based on constructionist psychology, and so on.

This uniform policy pattern may be seen as a response to globalization processes, recommendations from international organizations such as OECD and the World Bank and the post-modern conditions as described by some researchers and ideologists.

Introduction

This book shows that:

(i) in its details the policy of educational restructuring is not as uniform and homogeneous as it generally seems to be;

(ii) the degree of implementation of the policies of restructuring varies to a large extent;

(iii) despite globalization and convergence, countries still differ economically, politically and culturally;

(iv) although the policies implemented resemble one another, the outcomes differ considerably;

(v) the drive for global competitiveness seems to make countries create a loose coupling of the education system to the central state and increase the degree of retroactive surveillance; and

(vi) although research has revealed that no firm conclusions can be drawn about the effects of educational restructuring on pupils' achievement, teacher autonomy, and parental involvement the changes to education systems continue in the same direction.

There is something of a paradox in that, while standardization and universalization of structures and administration of education systems are taking place, in some cases the content of the curricula and the languages of instruction are in fact becoming more diverse.

Efforts are made to highlight the encounters between the world model for education and the standardized policies emanating from this model, on the one hand, and the different cultural, economic, and contexts into which countries attempt to articulate and/or implement such policies. For this reason, the chapters differ in the issues being prioritized for presentation.

This book is divided into two parts, the first of which describes globalization theories and ideologies and the societal conditions in relation to which educational changes have taken place. Educational restructuring is then conceptualized. The features described in Part I (Chapters 1–3) are studied in different parts of the world in Part II (Chapters 4–10): the OECD countries, transition countries in Eastern Europe and Central Asia, China, the Arab countries, Africa and Latin America.

The globalization processes that started to accelerate rapidly with the economic recession and the almost worldwide liberalizations during the 1970s are described in Chapter 1. To begin with, some theoretical arguments are presented. Then follows a general overview that brings together thoughts about globalization that generally are dealt with separately in different disciplines: globalization economically, politically, culturally, educationally, and so on.

Chapter 2 gives an overview of the role of the nation-state in policy and research as well as the economic and educational changes after the Second World War. It shows that substantial economic differences exist amongst countries and in particular the category labelled the Third World. These differences were maintained 30–40 years later into the 1990s. The emergence of new social and cultural movements, the rediscovery of civil society, the changing role of the national state and the internationalization of educational research, all of which resulted from or coincided with globalization, are globalized.

In Chapter 3, educational restructuring is conceptualized as one type of reform that requires extensive involvement from school principals, teachers and parents for its implementation. Apart from defining restructuring, this chapter reviews different arrangements of decentralization/centralization, choice, private schooling and systemic reform. None of the reforms implemented is new *per se* but they are described in a new language borrowed from economics and the market forces that have entered the educational domain. This chapter also makes a review of current research on the effects and impact of decentralization, freedom of choice, privatization and systemic reform on costs, pupil achievement, and so on in different parts of the world. This review indicates that there are no systematic and clear findings concerning the effect and impact of the restructuring. Some results indicate positive effects, while others indicate negative effects. If the aim of the reforms is to improve quality of education and pupils' academic achievement, then research findings are able to indicate neither failure nor success. If, on the other hand, the aim is political and economical, that is, to increase accountability and parental involvement and to decrease educational costs, these areas have not been systematically studied. The effects of decentralization, for instance, have sometimes been such that authorities at higher levels have seen it as a necessity to re-centralize decision-making.

Chapter 4 describes and compares educational changes in a number of OECD countries. It is evident that structurally, convergence has taken place but in several other respects there are still many other differences between these countries. Educational change in transitional countries (Eastern Europe) is analyzed in Chapter 5. The educational systems in these countries were rather similar during the socialist period. Several countries show a contradictory policy pattern since 1990. Aspects of the pre-war education stand in contrast to the innovations of the same type as those decided upon in the OECD countries. Education has to deal with the demand for cultural diversity, on the one hand, and the requirements of a modern market economy on the other.

China has introduced market forces not only in the economy but also in education. Decentralization has been combined with an encouragement of the growth of private schools. In practice, education is now geared more toward growth and formation of human capital than toward equality and broader development. Chinese educational policy during the past two decades is presented in Chapter 6.

The Arab countries, especially those in the Gulf, started to modernize later than the other countries and have not adopted a policy of restructuring to the extent that others have. This may be due to their favorable economic situation and the strong cultural foundation of Islam. Chapter 7 describes educational development in four of these countries.

The transition countries in Central Asia have were influenced by China as well as the Arab countries before they became part of Soviet Union. The political, economic and educational changes are accounted for in Chapter 8. These countries had, in relation to their economic level, a highly developed education system that deteriorated during the 1990s. For instance, decentralization is implemented without a reinforcement of local resources so that districts and communities cannot respond to the new policy.

After independence, many countries in Sub-Saharan Africa (Chapter 9) experienced economic growth and a tremendous increase in literacy and primary and secondary school enrolment. However, the continent suffered severely during the world-wide economic recession. Many African countries had to implement structural adjustment programs and to restructure their education systems, principally in the form of decentralization and privatization. The contradiction between globalization forces and revival of local cultures is perhaps more obvious in Africa than in other parts of the world. Economic decline and marginalization have been accompanied by religious revival and a reinforcement of the informal sector. Since the beginning of the 1980s, there has also been a decline in most components of the education systems.

Educational restructuring has been extensive in Latin America. Many of the countries have implemented decentralization of different types. The past two decades of educational changes in Latin America are described in Chapter 10, the final chapter of the book.

Part I

Globalization and Educational Policies

CHAPTER 1

Globalization and National Education Systems
HOLGER DAUN

INTRODUCTION

Almost everywhere in the world, educational systems are now under the pressure to produce individuals for global competition, individuals who can themselves compete for their own positions in the global context, and who can legitimate the state and strengthen its global competitiveness. Although there is no consensus as to the nature and scope of globalization, nor its beginnings, the discourse since the 1980s continues to intensify and increase, and education is expected to respond. There is, however, agreement among politicians, researchers and others on the value of acquiring more education of all kinds, particularly in the lifelong perspective.[1] Since global processes are complex, nation states adopt a strategy combining demands for diversity and local initiatives, one the one hand, and increased surveillance of both pupils' acquisition of knowledge and the work of school directors and teachers.

GLOBALIZATION: THEORETICAL PERSPECTIVES

The scope and depth of globalization have increased rapidly since the 1970s. The economic liberalizations of the 1970s, cheaper transportation and the advent of information technology made globalization processes accelerate. New or more complex patterns of the flow of the global economy are emerging: flows of goods and services; flows of financial and other capital; and flows of ideas and messages (Waters, 1995).

The most prominent theories dealing with the "global" as an object of research are internationalization, globalization, and world system theory. The first two do not assume that the world can necessarily be characteristerized that as a system[2]. Globalization differs from internationalization in the fact that it is more than interaction between nation states. Both may be analyzed from a world system perspective but there are also "globalization theories" which do not use a systems theory.

The world system, globalization, and internationalization imply both structures and ideas. McGrew (1992) distinguishes three paradigms dealing with the world or the global. The realist and neo-realist paradigms focus on states as players in the global context and see their struggle for power as the most important factor in the emergence of a world system. According to the liberal-pluralist paradigm, economy and technology are the driving forces but many different groups struggle for their own interests. In the neo-Marxist paradigm, economic power is the principal force and states, classes and transnational corporations are the principal players in the world arena. McGrew (1992) summarizes the perspectives shown in table 1.1.

TABLE 1.1 THEORETICAL PERSPECTIVES ON WORLD SYSTEMS

	Realism and neo-realism	Liberal-pluralism	Neo-Marxism
Dominant actors	States.	Mixed-actor system, e.g. states, corporations, international organizations	States, classes, transnational corporations
Political process	Competition, conflict, bargaining, negotiation and diplomacy between states.	Polyarchy, issue areas, global policy processes, and consensual and authoritative decision-making.	Class conflict mediated through states. Conflict between national and transnational capital.
Global order	Balance of power Hegemonic powers. Structure of power. Society of states.	Global management International organization and regimes.	Global structure of production and exchange. Rule of capital
Dominant forms of power; processes of globalization	Military power. Struggle for hegemony between great powers.	Technological and economic progress. Technological and economic power.	Economic and ideological power. Transnational capitalism. Capitalist modernization

Source: McGrew (1992:22)

Sklair (1995) discusses five different "theories of the global system": (i) imperialist and neo-imperialist; (ii) modernization and neo-evolutionist; (iii) neo-Marxist (dependency theories, for instance); (iv) world system theory (the NIDL or New International Division of Labor theory); and (v) modes of production theory. Some of these theories deal primarily with the economy and its implications for other areas. Type (i) corresponds to what McGrew classifies as neo-realist or neo-Marxist, while types (iii)–(v) belong solely to the neo-Marxist category. Type (ii) is liberalist-pluralist.

Sklair (ibid.) herself employs a structuralist perspective for an analysis of the world system. She analyzes transnational practices used by different players on three levels: economic, political and cultural-ideological. All transnational players have the nation-state as their "spatial reference point" (p. 7).

The institutionalists use a world system theory according to which there exists, culturally, a model that is globalized (Meyer *et al.* 1997). It is the world polity. It does not exist as a body or institution but may be seen as a complex of cultural expectations that exists among national governments, international organizations and different categories of people. Governments everywhere in the world take for granted that they should implement the modern institutions and cultures indicated in this model. Internationalization can be seen as resulting from actions taken from within countries in relation to other countries, while globalization and world system processes take place rather independently from a single country's actions and frontiers.

Thus, the processes of globalization are complex, and Appadurai (1991) describes them in terms of five dimensions: (i) ethnoscapes (tourists, immigrants, refugees); (ii) mediascapes (lines between the "real" and the fictional landscapes are blurred through the media); (iii) technoscapes (configurations of technology); (iv) finance-scapes (financial flows have decoupled themselves from other land-scapes); and (v) ideoscapes (ideas of freedom, welfare, rights, and so on are spreading in the world). The principal idea behind this classification is that different aspects of globalization have different rhythms and different distributions. Sometimes there are contradictions between different aspects of globalization; the same phenomenon is both legitimized and questioned in the world polity. For instance, the model of the Western European nation-state is spreading but at the same time it is questioned and undermined by economic actions.

Globalization is a process that has at least two distinct dimensions: scope and intensity. Along these dimensions, globalization is a "highly uneven" process (McGrew, 1992; Hirst and Thompson, 1996). Scope means the "coverage"; it does not (yet) cover all geographical areas of the globe or all domains of life. In the sectors directly involved in globalization processes, the intensity is very high in the industrialized information societies using the most sophisticated technology.

Bergesen (1991) argues that a world system does not emerge from actions performed by nation states or national societies; instead, the world system was there from the very beginning and nation states and international companies constitute parts of the system and had and have to adapt to its characteristics. In world system theory, the globe is a system and different actors have to adapt to this fact. In globalization theories, processes are approaching a global reach or are already global but there is not necessarily any system. Internationalization refers to interactions between some nation-states or some companies. Table 1.2 summarizes types of theories and their structural and cultural-ideological aspects.

GLOBALIZATION, AN OVERVIEW

The Second World War was followed by two decades of rapid economic growth and differentiation worldwide, especially between the North[3] and the South but also within each category of countries. In the South, countries that after the Second World War had been comparatively well off, economically and educationally, continued their growth, while others stagnated. With the oil shock and the economic recession in the 1970s, growth rates declined for most countries.

Globalization takes place in a world that is predominantly capitalistic, and in Sklair's (1995:47) words "the aim of the global capitalist system is total inclusion of all classes. . . ." Attempts are made to "persuade people to consume". More countries than ever before are affected directly by these influences. Countries situated "outside" of the most intensive flows of goods, capital, and information are also indirectly influenced; their position in the world system is affected and their frame of action (even internally) is conditioned by these global changes. A symbolic and communicative contraction or compression of the globe takes place; the new media techniques and means of communication allow rapid and direct contact between individuals all over the world. This in turn provokes a relativization of cultures but also revitalization of local cultures. There are contradictory processes and a "dialectic of continuities and discontinuities" (Mittelman, 1996b:231). The concepts of *state, nation, humanity, modernity* and *the individual* are spread

TABLE 1.2 WORLD SYSTEM, GLOBALIZATION AND INTERNATIONALIZATION FROM DIFFERENT PERSPECTIVES

	Structurally	Ideologically, culturally
World system	Structuralist world systems theory: capitalist structures encompassing the whole world. A system of global economic structures.	World polity: a cultural construction that has worldwide influence: "culturalists" and institutionalists.
Globali-zation	Ever-extending capitalist structures or relationships.	Emerging global culture and globalization of cultures and ideologies.
Inter-nationa-lization	Supranational bodies and transnational companies that cover a number of countries.	Cultural diffusion and assimilation among and within countries.

ing globally (Robertson, 1991) and at the same time, some of these concepts (for instance, some of those related to human rights) are undermined and questioned through the spread of the neoliberal thoughts (Camp, 1997; McGinn, 1997). Technological innovations are causing change not only in the content of trade, but also the organization of work places, leisure-time activities, the role of finance capital, among other things (Freeman and Soete, 1994:43).

Individual and national reference points are relativized in the face of general and supranational ones and even individuals' experiences and social relationships are affected (Robertson, 1992; Waters 1995). Formerly, individuals could trust the immediate and experienced past and present; today, that which was once taken-for-granted is no longer certain. Societies, units within societies and individuals experience constraints "to produce their own unique accounts of their places in world history. Religion is obviously playing a crucial role in this—outside most of Europe. At the same time, however, religion appears to have become simply a life style option in quite a few areas of the world . . ." (Robertson, 1991:289–290). Hann (1997) perceives religion to play an important role also in east Europe in the formation of nationalism.

Economically, there is a growing global interdependency between nations, companies, organizations, individuals, and so on. Some companies tend to create chains or links across national borders (Henderson, 1996). High technology activities, growth and richness are concentrated in a geographical zone (East and Southeast Asia, Western Europe and the United States). Enormous economic differences between the areas in the South existed prior to the Second World War. After the war, there were three decades of almost worldwide, rapid economic growth, but the continuing disparities did not attract the attention of researchers, politicians and donors since continued economic growth for every country was taken for granted.

Table 1.3 shows some of the extreme differences in the national economies in the world. During the 1980s, many developing countries became marginalized in the world economy (Cheru, 1996; Ghai, 1997). The poorest countries have, according to Castells (1993:37), moved from a structural position of exploitation in the world system to a structural position of irrelevance, and Cardoso (1993:156) argues that some countries in the South have either to enter "the democratic-technological-scientific race . . . or become unimportant, unexploited, and unexploitable. . . . "

In what came to be labelled the Third World, differences and inequalities that existed after the Second World War became greater. Several authors argue that we now have to acknowledge "four worlds": (i) winners in the new international division of labor; (ii) potential winners (Brazil, Mexico); (iii) large continental economies (India, China); and (iv) clear losers that could be called the Fourth World. Most of Africa, countries not producing oil in the Middle East, and most of Latin America belong to the Fourth World (Cardoso, 1993; Carnoy & Castells, 1995; Cheru, 1996). Cox (1996) argues that globalization creates contradictions along a "three-part hierarchy in social structure":

TABLE 1.3 GNP PER CAPITA IN SELECTED COUNTRIES, 1977, 1993, AND 1995

GNP per capita	Low Income Countries			Middle Income Countries			High Income Countries		
	Tanzania	Niger	All	Colombia	Korea	All	Germany	Japan	All
1977	190	160	170	720	820	1,110	8.160	5,670	6,980
1993	90	270	380	1,400	7,660	2,480	23,560	31,490	23,090
1995	120	220	290	1,910	2,490	2,390	27,510	39,640	24,930

Based on data from World Bank 1979-81, 1986, 1995, 1998.

(i) a top layer of people who are integrated into the global economy exists in most countries but principally in the North; (ii) a category of people serving those directly involved in global affairs (also principally in the North); and (iii) those who are excluded from the global economy (in many geographical areas but principally in the South). Parkins (1996:49,62) goes even further into the North-South relationships and calls it "the global apartheid", because during the period 1982-1990: " . . . there was a net transfer of resources from the Third World to the OECD countries equivalent to six Marshall plans". Similar ideas are presented by Edwards (1998) who, referring to other studies, argues that wealth is accumulating at the top, while risk is allocated to the bottom (globally and nationally).

Globalization is a complex of processes but for the sake of description they will be presented from four perspectives: the technological/economic, the political, the cultural and the educational (Cvetkovich and Kellen, 1997; Waters, 1995)[4]. These processes are challenging national economies, national states and national education systems and they imply, are accompanied by or cause a large number of contradictions: increasing economic competition as well economic marginalization, universalization of cultural aspects as well as particularization of such aspects, and so on.

Problems are increasingly of global scale (environmental problems and AIDS, for instance) and the same applies to the awareness of such problems. HIVS/AIDS are in some degree affecting global populations mostly in Africa (UNAIDS/ WHO,

1996). Several environmental problems are also global. With more frequent travel and the increasing use of information technology, the awareness of these problems tends to be globalized as well. 75 percent of all people with AIDS, are estimated to have died from AIDS worldwide.

ECONOMIC COMPETITIVENESS OR MARGINALIZATION

Competition and marginalization take place in a capitalist world. Economic globalization is more than international exchange of goods and services, interaction of separate domestic economies and extensive reach of capital. It is, according to some researchers, a unified global economy. More than half of the world's goods and services are now produced according to strategies which involve planning, design, production and marketing on a global scale (Bretherton, 1996a). The transfer of finance capital is very rapid and may force governments in smaller countries to change their economic policy. Flows of finance capital are now more important than flows of goods and services (Cable, 1995) and the value of finance transactions is now fifty times greater than that of the flow of goods (Bretherton, 1996a). Flows of finance capital have become rather independent from investments and payment of imports.

Initially, the Foreign Direct Investments (FDIs) were a means by which to gain "traditional" comparative advantages such as access to markets and/or cheap labor, but they became more and more a measure to find and use appropriate human capital to be used in global competition (Hansson, 1990). Multinational companies in the North increased their investments in the North (Waters 1995:71). That is, most of the investments take place in already industrialized countries (Mulhearn, 1996:188).

FDIs are made by Europe, Japan and the United States in high wage sectors within these three entities and to some extent in low wage, labor intensive sectors in the Newly Industrialized Countries (NICs). These investments were and still are met with ambiguity from the governments of the host countries. Governments welcome capital and an enlarged potential for the acquisition of know-how and provision of employments but they have used and still use some type of control in order to protect the companies owned by nationals (Brander, 1995). The state, especially in France, continues to play an important role in this context, since many (MNCs) are partially or completely state-owned (Carnoy, 1993:91).

The largest multinational companies, MNCs are concentrated in a few sectors, and they have grown more rapidly than world trade (as a whole), but most multinationals are still tied to the competitiveness of their "home" economy (Carnoy, 1993). Their number has increased, and they have become bigger.

Globalization has resulted in increasing gaps between the "North" and the "South" but also in a differentiation within the "South" (Castells, 1993). In Africa, Arab countries, Asia and Latin America, a reinforcement of existing economic differences is taking place (Cheru, 1996; Cox, 1996). Countries having comparatively high economic and educational indicators after the Second World War continue their economic growth, while the situation for countries with the lowest indicators is deteriorating. Among the former category we find the NICs. They have been able to compete with the "old" countries and to gain industry product shares on the world market. The Arab countries experienced growth in their industrial sector until the 1980s due to the increase in oil prices. Then with the relative stagnation of oil prices, their economic growth followed suit. The Japanese advantage over European and American competitiveness was not due only to lower labor costs only but also to the way of organizing production (Cohen, 1993:107–108).

After independence, "economic nationalism" became a trend among the countries in the South. They had the desire to avoid dependence on capitalist economies in the North and, therefore, established import-substituting industries in order to become self-sufficient in certain branches. These industries were protected through a series of measures, most commonly custom tariffs on import of commodities produced by the import-substituting industries. With the global technological development, their exports have become old-fashioned, and some of the raw materials are no longer necessary in the metropoles, since substitutes have become common. All this has resulted in the marginalization of several countries in the South. For instance, Africa's share of non-oil primary exports fell from seven percent in 1970 to four percent in the middle of the 1980s (Mannin, 1996:241).

With the structural adjustment programs and global liberalizations, many countries were forced to open up their economies and to increase their export so as to be able to pay their international debts. However, the terms of trade for their export items deteriorated and made many countries in the South suffer still more; the value of import tended to be higher than that of export, and government revenues lower than government expenditures (Parkins, 1996). Terms of trade for the poorest countries declined by thrity percent between 1971 and 1982 and by three percent between 1987 and 1990 (Hoerner, 1995:105). Countries in this category are below the baseline from which they would be able to attain "economic take-off", and to compete in the world market. Instead, they are struggling for economic, political and cultural survival (Goontilake, 1994; M'Bokolo, 1994; Reimers and Tiburcio, 1993; Stavenhagen, 1994; UNDP, 1990, 1991, 1995; Weissman, 1990). In this context, Cardoso (1993:158) criticizes the term "Global village" which he perceives to be an empty expression.

The NICs were better off (economically, technologically and educationally) than other "Third World countries" already before the Second World War. They opted for a policy stimulating export and competition and they established very early export-oriented industries that were selectively and strategically supported by their governments and relied upon comparatively cheap labor. The expansion of their industries coincided with economic liberalization in the industrialized countries, a fact that gave them access to large markets. Their share in world output increased from 0.9 percent in 1967 to 2.1 percent in 1986, while that of the United States and Western Europe decreased from 52.1 to 44.3 percent (Carnoy, 1993:25).

When the recession came, many countries reacted with import reduction and even with protectionism. The decisions made by the oil-producing countries to increase the oil prices coincided with the fact that conservative/neo-liberal governments came into power in Germany, the United Kingdom and the United States, along with the implementation of a neo-liberal policies in their home countries. The result was that export also decreased, due to lower demand (Mosley, Harrigan and Toye, 1991; SIDA, 1994).

Firms in traditional industrial branches in Europe could not cope with competition. This applies to the textile and ship-building industries in Sweden and to import-substituting industries in the South, for example, when these countries were forced to open up their economies. Japan and Southeast Asia increased their production at a rate almost double those of Europe and the US. Employment grew most in Southeast Asia and the United States. The growth of production in Japan and Southeast Asia was due to an enlarged labor force as well as increased productivity. In Europe, on the other hand, the increased volume of production occurred without a corresponding increase in employmees. Most economies went through a process of restructuring.

In the high technology (principally IT) sectors, Japan had a considerable surplus in its trade with the other economic zones during the 1980s. Manufacturing and high technology are the areas in which competition between the countries is strongest (Carnoy and Castells, 1995; Carnoy, 1993; Hansson, 1990). In Europe, for instance, employment increased in high wage sectors involved in trade with other OECD countries, while employment decreased in medium and low wage sectors involved in trade with the rest of the world. The trade balance in high tech sectors was negative for EU countries during the 1980s; that is, the value of import of IT items exceeded the value of export. The opposite occurred in Japan (Freeman and Soete, 1994). New employment opportunities had previously been created in the public sector. This process continued until the middle of the 1980s in some of the North European countries (Therborn, 1989).

In all, the NICs profited from the wave of economic liberalizations and were able to conquer shares in the "old" sectors by using comparatively cheap labor. Japan also took advantage through its higher productivity. In the "newer" sectors, Japan made conquests due to its higher productivity based on application of technological innovations.

Due to the economic recession, many countries faced severe problems and had to accept SAPs. This applies in particular to the world's poorest countries. With the SAPs, economies were liberalized, large portions of state ownership were privatized and cuts were made in public expenditures, also in educational budgets. The implementation was expected to contribute to economic growth, elimination of deficit in balance of payment, and change the economy from an import-substituting one to a exported-oriented one (Streeten, 1987). It was taken for granted that economic growth would "trickle down" to the poorest groups (Hamilton, 1989). However, the poorest populations came to suffer most from recession as well as the SAPs (Cornia *et al.*, 1987).

Capital accumulation has become more knowledge-based and knowledge-intensive; those countries, firms, individuals, etc. that have access to the most sophisticated knowledge and information are able to compete (Gill, 1996). Competition and competitiveness are linked to the ability to create comparative advantages and may be seen from four levels: nation, sector, company and individual. The volume of production and its delivery and price are dependent on an increased volume of labor, more effective use of existing labor or both. Industrialized countries (except Japan) based their production on Fordist organization of work. This is characterized by a hierarchical structure and mass production embedded in Taylorist philosophy, according to which workers are more productive if they are satisfied with their conditions but also surveilled and supervised. Technological innovations were integrated into this framework. During the 1980s and 1990s, considerable restructuring of firms and economies took place around the world.

Some Asian countries were able to export goods (labor-intensive manufacturing) because they could take advantage of and use cheap labor when the world wide liberalization of trade started (Mulhearn, 1996). However, the nature of competition between states has fundamentally changed (Strange, 1995). Competition, presented by politicians as a national issue and perceived so by the societal interests, has, according to Cable (1995) become a struggle not primarily between nations but between companies. The intensified, global competition based on rapid technical and organizational change has resulted and continue to result in dramatic changes in industrial structure as well as in management structures (Pettersson, 1990).

The production factors or human capital *per se* no longer determine comparative advantages and competitiveness but rather the interrelationships between (i) the organization and management of work and production; (ii) development of human knowledge and skills; (iii) the conditions for and the ability to apply technological innovations (Adler, 1992); and (iv) flexible production (Ciborra and Schneider, 1992). It is possible to combine new technologies with Taylorism in a Neo-Fordist framework (Edwards, 1998), but technological innovations can not be optimally applied, if the company does not change its organization and if the appropriate human knowledge and skills are not available in the company (Adler, 1992). The organization is now changing or has to change from Fordism to Toyotism, the latter being characterized by, among other things, just-in-time delivery and functionally flexible workers (Waters, 1995).

In order to be competitive, firms have to use the latest technological innovations, but, more importantly, they have to restructure production units, so that the organization facilitates the maximum advantage of this technology and employs those who can use it or train their employees to be able to use it. An effective use of automation requires a new work content, a new work organization and a new type of training for employees (Adler, 1992). The growing automation leads to competition, but it is also a means in this competition.

There are different views on the national and international effects of globalization processes—one suggesting that globalization increases the overall need for improved learning and another one arguing that processes of skilling and de-skilling result from globalization and competition.

A German study concludes that production increasingly requires "polyvalent" and "multi-skilled" employees that can "guarantee maximum utilization of costly machinery" (Kern and Schumann, 1992:114,124). This new category of employees has theoretical knowledge and is able to "contextualize" this knowledge to the specific requirements of the branch or the company in which they work. They are also able to solve problems emerging from the use of the new technology and to communicate effectively with other employees. One of the conclusions of the German study is that more complex and more differentiated production results in an increasing demand for higher skills (Kern & Schumann, 1992:124). Also, data from the United Kingdom shows that the unskilled portion of the labor force decreased between the 1930s and the 1970s (Brown *et al*, 1997).

The opposite trend, that is an increasing number of jobs that require low skills, has also been shown to exist. During the 1970s, studies showed that automation and mass production, among other things, required less skill in an increasing portion of the labor force. This process was predicted to continue (Bravermann, 1974; Kern and Schumann, 1992). Although not due to globalization processes, the service sector has grown since the 1970s. Many of the jobs in this sector do not require any high skills. Esping-Andersen (1993) analyzes the changes that have taken place in various sectors in four OECD countries. There were large variations between the countries. In Germany and the United Kingdom, the number of jobs in the service economy increased less than in Norway and Sweden (see table 1.4).

Esping-Andersen (1994) predicts that growth in employment in the post- industrial society will depend on three sectors: business service, personal services and social service. The first mentioned will require highly qualified employees, but it will also engage many self-employed. The other two categories will be mixed with a relatively high percentage of unskilled labor. Social services is the sector in which a large proportion of women are employed.

Arnold (1996) argues that a post-Fordist mode of production requiring advanced skills is emerging, but also a category of less skilled workers. He describes post-Fordism as an ideal type in which multi-skilled teams are involved in the most globalized section of the economy. But there are also many tasks that do not require any higher skills. Arnold mentions the workers who are in charge of the electronic surveillance and control devices. Furthermore, the teams of highly qualified workers are served by a large number of persons who do not need as many skills: "the actual work in producing those goods is performed by a dispersed army of marginalised and exploited out-workers, casual workers or contract workers . . . " (p. 228).

In addition to the categories of jobs requiring low skills, the rate of unemployment should be mentioned. Since the end of the 1970s, OECD countries have had 3-15 per cent of their labour force unemployed and the percentages are still higher in the South. In all, globalization results in the requirement for a minority of highly skilled labor, a majority with continuously renewed skills and a portion of unqualified labour.

However, with globalization, management jobs involving routine production decrease in the North, due partially to automation, but also because production involving routine jobs is being moved to the South. On the other hand, in-person services are "sheltered from the direct effects of globalization" but also excluded from the possibility to take advantage of them. Competition between countries is strongest in the areas of manufacturing and high technology (Carnoy and Castells, 1995; Carnoy, 1993; Hansson, 1990); that is, "customized" goods and services in micro-electronics, telecommunications, biotechnology, financial services, consultancy, advertising, marketing, and the media (Reich, 1997:174). What Reich (1997) calls the symbolic analysts are the ones who are most involved in a global labour market and who gain most from globalization. They work primarily with symbols (communication, computer programs, texts, and so on).

The two principal views may be seen as ideal typical and are summarized in table 1.5. They have different implications for education.

TABLE 1.4 CHANGES IN THE PROPORTION OF UNSKILLED LABOR IN FOUR OECD COUNTRIES

	Germany	United Kingdom	Norway	Sweden
Fordist Occupations				
1960s	16.1	25.7	26.3	21.6
1980s	16.5	14.5	15.9	12.4
Postindustrial Occupations				
1960s	8.7	9.5	7.9	9.5
1980s	4.5	10.5	15.9	16.9
All unskilled				
1960s	24.8	35.2	34.2	31.1
1980s	21.0	25.0	27.4	29.3

Based on Esping-Andersen (1993).

TABLE 1.5 TWO DIFFERENT VIEWS ON THE EFFECTS OF GLOBALIZATION ON
EMPLOYMENT AND SKILL DEVELOPMENT

Global Competition Results in an Overall Demand for Higher Skills	Global Competition Results in Skilling, Deskilling and Reskilling
Global competition leads to techno-economic shifts. Such a shift results in the short term to unemployment but in the long term to a higher standard of living and higher employment.	Globalization is different from previous changes that were managed by national economies.
Gobal competition leads to an increasing demand for higher skills in the whole population.	Global competition leads to an increasing demand for high skills in a limited category of employees but also to deskilling and unemployment.
Lifelong learning for all.	Recurrent education for some.

Based on: Adler, 1992; Arnold (1996); Brown, 1999; Brown & Lauder (1996); Cox, 1996; Edwards, 1998; Esping-Andersen (1993); Freeman & Soete (1994); Gill, 1996; Reich (1997).

Structural Adjustment Programs

With the decolonization, countries in the North started to provide the South with economic support. The donor countries differ considerably in their volume of support (as percentage of GNP) and countries supported (geographically, politically, and economically). For instance, some give priority to the social sectors in the poorest countries while others give priority to economic and technological growth in middle income countries. The oil exporting countries emerged as important donors, when their revenues increased from the middle of the 1970s. Later, with the relative decline in oil income, these countries decreased their support. Some examples are given in Table 1.6. While Denmark has always had a tradition of high spending and continues to provide generous support, Belgium and the United States are decreasing the amount spent on development assistance. The latter has, during the whole period, had the lowest percentage of official development assistance. The Arab countries, exemplified by the United Arab Emirates, increased their economic assistance tremendously during the oil- boom and then had to adapt to the conditions of their deteriorating position in the world. Total aid decreased during the latter half of the 1980s and aid was redirected from Africa to Asia and East Europe (Hoerner, 1995).

Despite aid and due to declining terms of trade and increasing public expenditures, among other things, the economic recession was followed by financial crisis. The SAPs were implemented mainly in the South and in the former Communist countries. States that had invested much in welfare and public ownership had to restructure and cut more than other states.

There are many reasons for the high degree of state intervention and the large percentage of the GNP used for public expenditure in the South, especially Africa. Some of them were: (i) a very weak middle class or class of capitalists who were able to make the investments necessary for take-off in the process of economic growth; (ii) equity objectives; and (iii) ideological rationales, that is striving for economic independence from foreign investors and owners, (Bienen and Waterbury, 1989; Hamilton, 1989; Streeten, 1987; de Walle, 1989). Countries varied in their policies and priorities; some gave priority to education at the expense of other sectors. Economies were liberalized, large portions of state ownership were privatized and cuts were made in public expenditures.

TABLE 1.6 OFFICIAL DEVELOPMENT ASSISTANCE FROM SOME COUNTRIES AS PERCENTAGE OF GNP

	1960	1965	1970	1975	1980	1985	1990	1993
Belgium	.88	.60	.46	.59	.50	.85	.46	.39
Denmark	.09	.13	.38	.58	.74	.80	.94	1.03
United States	.53	.49	.31	.26	.28	.24	.21	.15
UAE	..	..	..	11.79	3.82	..	2.64	.66

Sources: World Bank, 1977, 1979, 1981, 1986, 1991-1995. UAE: the United Arab Emirates.

Behind the SAPs, we find a neo-liberal agenda: (i) the economic policy based on the assumptions of neo-classical microeconomic theory and rational choice theory; and (ii) the view that the state is an obstacle to maximal or at least optimal use of resources (Callager, 1993; Colclough, 1990; Gallagher, 1993, Mosley, Harrigan and Toye, 1990).

NATION STATE BETWEEN THE GLOBAL AND THE LOCAL

Some countries have been able to conquer space in the global context while others have been "pushed" more or less into positions of marginalization. That is, the position of a country in the global context implies parameters according to which internal politicians and economic actors have to function.

Economic and technological globalization is challenging the nation-state in different ways. Countries differ in relation to the processes of globalization due to their size, economic and technological level, economic position in world markets, cultural composition, relationships between the state, economy and civil sphere, and so on. Also, states react differently in relation to globalization processes. According to Mittelman (1996b:238 ff), the state in industrialized countries is using four different strategies in relation to globalization processes: (i) hyper-nationalism and fundamentalism; (ii) state-driven globalization; (iii) corporate responses; and (iv) contest of the processes of globalization. The first includes encapsulation and defence, while the second is more or less the opposite. The state takes on the challenges and makes efforts to participate in the competition. In the third case, the state does the same but in cooperation with the dominating and organized, internal interests (See also Ottone, 1996). The fourth strategy includes an active contest of the globalization forces. Similar views are presented by Offe (1996, 1997).

Cox (1996:28) defines three different types of societies: (i) a hyper-liberal Anglo-American form; (ii) a social market central and northern European form; and (iii) an East Asian form with several variants. Gill (1996:221) presents a similar typology although it is more detailed and includes four different types of societies: (i) the social market model such as Germany's; (ii) Jacques Delor´s European social democratic model; (iii) the compensatory state mercantilism of Japan; and (iv) the Anglo-American laissez-faire. These two classifications overlap to a large extent.

Brown (1999) refers to different studies and finds three strategies in relation to globalization. Progressive competitiveness implies that training and skilling are made general components of economic and welfare policies. Shared austerity includes general budget cuts and manipulation of both wages and the size of the labour force. The third strategy (internationalization of Keynesianism), consists of efforts to "shift expansionary policies from the national to the international level" (p. 9).

Thus, states have used and are using different strategies in relation to the economic challenges from the processes of globalization. As to the countries in the North, Brown and Lauder (1996) make a division into two principal "ideal typical policies" in which the role of the state differs. These policies have different implications for education, especially adult education and vocational training have different roles in the two strategies.

The first type, neo-Fordist strategy, is based on classical economic theories, maintenance of structures and productivity increase in the traditional industries. Mass production of standardized products and the help of cheap labour is one important ingredient in this strategy. This strategy was or is used by states called hyper-liberal by Cox (1996) and Anglo-American laissez-faire by Gill (1996), i.e. the conservative government in the United Kingdom up to the elections in 1997 and by the United States until the beginning of the 1990s. The idea is to participate in the global competition through productivity gains and measures to reduce social costs. Only a small category of specialist employees in strategic positions are trained.

The second strategy, the post-Fordist, is focussed on restructuring of the economy and companies for flexible production in high technology branches. Cooperation between the state, employers and trade unions and improvement of skills are all essential in this strategy. It is important to raise the educational level and skills of the whole population. This seems to be an approach used in the other countries. The state plays an active role in initiating life-long learning and vocational training. This has characterized the economic and educational policies in France and Germany, for instance. (These two strategies correspond to some extent to the views on the effects of globalization presented in table 1.5).

In relation to social and welfare policies, Esping-Andersen (1994:167–168) argues that what he calls the Fordist welfare strategy was based on the assumptions that: (i) the family had one breadwinner; (ii) citizens' life-cycles were orderly, standardized and predictable; and (iii) the political economy would assure permanent employment. Globalization processes are now undermining these assumptions; the welfare state is threatened in three areas: (i) the resources for welfare issues came to be insufficient; (ii) the state had become less able to adapt to local needs within the nation; and (iii) the importance of political parties was waning in the public opinion (Rocard, 1994). Governments, at least in the smaller nations, were obliged to dismantle parts of the welfare system.

In some countries, the interest organizations had a corporatist relationship with one another and with the state. This resulted in a tendency for elite-mass division to emerge. The top level leaders of the organizations and the state formed elites. The reinforcement of the links between the national elites and international actors creates tensions between the state entities at the central level and those at lower levels.

Globalization causes restructuring in the relationships between nation-states and companies, national as well as international ones, but also within countries between the central state and organizations, social movements, and so on (Waters, 1995). Restructuring in the relationships between nations and companies is taking place in two-way process: national elites detach themselves from internal groups and become more linked to international bodies (Ibid.). In several countries, therefore, the corporatist relationships or alliances were threatened by the globalization forces and neoliberal politics. The resources for public spending decreased, and the discontent with the state performance is said to have resulted in less legitimacy (Habermas, 1976).

Globalization has prompted the forging of stronger links between state apparatuses and between them and the actors in the international economy at the same time as it has activated popular demands for direct and participatory democracy. Decisions made by international actors sometimes undermine the decision made by bodies to which powers have been delegated from the national state to lower level entities within the country (Schmidt, 1995:93). In addition, decision-making has moved from the nation state to civil forces and market forces within each nation as well as to international bodies (Cable, 1995; Mannin, 1995; Schmidt, 1995).

The reinforcement of the links between the national elites and international players creates tensions between the state entities at the central level and those at lower levels. Players in the central state sometimes have to take rapid decisions without consulting people within their country (Strange, 1995). International pressure on the nation-state to change its legal system to correspond to the requirements of the global market forces affects many laws (and even constitutions) and not only those applying to the economic domain. Additionally, the pressure on nation-states to respect human rights has become stronger, while the economic globalization may imply a pressure in another direction (Bretherton, 1996b). It also appears that new alliances or corporatist relationships, at least in the domain of adult education and lifelong education, are emerging in countries that attempt the post-Fordist strategy.

The combined effects of the above is interference with the goals and progress of decentralization and, consequently, with participation internally in each country. These processes seem to result in declining trust for the national states but Held (1995) and Harding & Phillips (1986) argue that the extent to which people have confidence in state institutions has always differed according to socioeconomic class, at least in the UK.

Moreover, the number of NGOs and intergovernmental organizations have grown considerably (Mannin, 1996). This means that many more international and non-governmental actors affect policy-making and implementation than ever before. Despite their non-governmental status, the NGOs generally use the established channels in their contact with the state bodies. However, according to McGinn (1997), NGOs are in many places in the South forming new elites that function as de facto decision-makers or expertise in educational matters.

Since the 1960s, new types of movements emerged and they have created demands that impact lifestyles, values, ecology, and so on (Flacks, 1995). In this process, the concept of "civil society" has also re-surfaced and may function as an ideological and theoretical tool in the critics of the state (Bangura, 1992; Beckman, 1992).

A contradictory process of integration from above (extension of the European Union, for instance) and disintegration from below (demands for the creation of new states as in the former Soviet Union and former Yugoslavia) has tended to emerge. The lack of correspondence between cultural and political lines become stronger, and this has implications for the states.[5] Political leaders in areas formerly belonging to the Soviet Union and Yugoslavia have mobilized the populations along ethnic lines, and this has, according to Offe (1996) sometimes been done for tactical reasons. It has been a means for the leaders to increase their own power. In the new state of Bosnia-Herzegovina in former Yugoslavia, different school systems have been built under the umbrella of one and the same new national state (Kolouh- Westin, 1999).

On the other hand, some states have accepted the "cultural channelling" of political bodies. Indigenous populations in some countries have a self-government system based upon their ethnic positions. This is the case in Canada and the United States, for instance (see, for instance, Okuma, 1996).

The centralized socialist states had to restructure society, the state and education more than others. In the South, structural adjustments, wars or destabilizing policies, general global pressure for human rights, and pressure from international agencies concerning democracy (political freedom and freedom of organization, for instance) made many governments hold multi-party elections at the end of the 1980s and during the first half of the 1990s (Bangura, 1992; Bretherton, 1996b; Saine 1995). For these countries, structural adjustment of the economy has more than in other countries implied also "political" restructuring (Herbst, 1990).

Generally, states have, on the one hand, to adapt to the globalization processes (including cultural, political and technological standardization and homogenization) that are taking place, and on the other hand, they have to respond to particular local demands that are being more articulated than before. How all factors, internal/local as well as external/global, combine in a country is to a large extent conditioned by its political culture and economic structure (Almond & Verba, 1965; Harding & Phillips, 1986; Inglehart, 1990; Mazawi, 1998). The political culture does not change easily. Inglehart argues, for instance, that important elements of the pre- communist cultures survived the Communist regime in East European countries and the same applies to countries in Central Asia.

The predictions made by researchers and others concerning the future of the nation-state and, consequently, the implications for the national education system, differ substantially. Following Panitch´s (1996) argument, it seems that the nature of the predictions depend on the view researchers had of the state before globalization processes started to accelerate in the 1970s. Two misinterpretations emerged from the 1960s to the 1980s. The first is that the state was able to and did control capital, and the second is that the state and capital must be seen as two independent spheres rather than as parts of a totality.

Some of the predictions may be formulated in the following way: (i) The nation-state has "lost" sovereignty to regional and global institutions and to markets but has also acquired new areas of control in order to promote "national competitiveness" (Waters, 1995). Even for large states and strong governments, economic globalization makes it extremely difficult to exert control over financial and production structures organized across national boundaries (Hirst & Thompson, 1996; Vogler, 1996). (ii) The state is restructuring itself. State formation is still taking place in several areas of the world, while the most advanced states are in a process of re-formation (Cheru, 1996; Dale, 1997). (iii) The state will continue to be crucial for the overall capital-accumulation process and most multinational companies are still linked to their home-base and its Research and Development policy and formation of human skills. The nation state will also have an important role in the well-being of its citizens (Carnoy, 1993). The state will have to keep a balance between the need to attract foreign capital and accept the cultural standardization that the market economy and economic liberalizations imply, on the one hand, and to deal with national cultural identity and sub-cultural identities, on the other hand (Strange, 1995). European countries and countries in the South have made attempts, at least until mid-1990s, to solve the problem of mass unemployment with traditional investments. However, in order to attain full employment in Europe, Freeman & Soete (1994) suggest the continuation of free trade. In addition to this, they include a combination of public and private investment, and an important role for political bodies in the supervision of the market forces, in increasing the skills in the population and guaranteeing a good education.

Cultural Convergence and Divergence

The globe is predominantly capitalist and in such a system there are markets as well as oligopolistic sections and informal sectors of national economies and the global economy (Amin, 1997; Hoerner, 1995). In the capitalist systems, the driving forces as well as the profound changes are situated in the economic, material and organizational spheres of life. It is a capitalism that has advanced to a higher stage than the "industrial/commodity" stage. However, many of the forces found to work on the individual during the previous stages are important in the higher stage too. Capitalism requires a moral based on pre-capitalist values of trust, honesty, fair-dealing, promise-keeping, and so on, but at the same time it assumes that individuals actions are based on self-interest and that their actions are guided by instrumental rationality. Capitalism implies that economic imperatives dominate over all others[6]; there is a universal commodification of life and a polarization of wealth and income and recent technological trends have reinforced this process (Giddens, 1994). Commodification of political and social relationships are deepening (Mittelman, 1996a) and pricing is extended to more and more services and activities (Saul, 1997).

Still other "life models" stem from the economic imperatives.Technical rationality and competition are just two examples. Rationalization results in ". . .depersonalization of social relationships . . . and the extension of technically rational control over both natural and social processes . . . " (Waters, 1995:5). Communication and interaction between people as well as leisure time activities are increasingly being individualized and 'technified' (Waters, 1995). All the processes mentioned result in an increasing individualization which takes two different forms: one that creates individualism based on egoism, competition, market principles, and "rational choice philosophy" and another that one that creates individualism linked to altruism, autonomy, and reflexivity (Giddens, 1994; Held, 1995). The belief in social and economic planning and in collective efforts to solve common problems has been undermined by these processes, (Habermas, 1971; Offe, 1997) but also by the collapse of the Soviet Union (Escudero, 1994).

The direct influence from the macro-processes at the global level on the individual level is a new phenomenon that has drawn the attention of post-modernists, among others. Mass media and information technology make this intrusion from the global to the private possible. The individual's proper contexts of social experience are being transformed (Giddens (1994), and existing forms of authority as democratic values are undermined (Mannin, 1996; McGinn (1997). Via information technology, people communicate directly with one another around the globe. For instance, there are cyber-cafeterias in many cities not only in the North but also in the South.

The collective consciousness among people living in the some area is dispersed or undermined. As Saul (1997:47) says, "commerce has no memory . . . no particular attachment to any particular society". Thus, societies, units within societies and individuals experience constraints "to produce their own unique accounts of their places in world history . . . " (Robertson, 1991:289–290).

At the collective level, "ethnicitization" is also taking place in many areas of the world. Ethnicity does not always follow political lines and the frontiers established politically. This is evident not only in Africa, Asia and Latin America but also in east and central Europe. De-territorialization of ethnicity, nationality and cultures is taking place, since immigration has increased (Coulby, 1997; Offe, 1996, 1997). Formerly, identity was formed according to "essential" features such as class, gender and race. Today, the element of constructing identities from subjective values and preferences has become more important, according to Benhabib (1998).

In the South, many areas had not been permeated by the monetary economy and market forces in the beginning of the 1960s. State pressure immediately after independence for the formation of national identities and, after the economic liberalizations, the economic influence, have resulted in processes ranging from cultural elimination via cultural homogenization to revitalization of local cultures (M´Bokolo, 1994; Stavenhagen, 1994).[7]

Generally, complex and sometimes contradictory processes occur culturally. Differentiation along the following dimensions is taking place: (i) post-materia- list/idealism vs. consumerist values; (ii) cultural universalization and standardization vs. particularization and revitalization of local cultures; (iii) fundamentalism vs. ecumenicism; and (iv) sacralization vs. secularization.[8]

With the spread of the market model, modern technology and the monetarized exchange of goods, services and ideas, a standardized and consumer culture is spreading (Ahmed, 1992; Appadurai, 1991; Bauman, 1991). One of the features of this culture is the focus on consumption not only of food items but also of messages and symbols (Featherstone, 1991a; Lash, 1990). In some areas in the North, consumption has become the overriding framework that redirects people's attention away from issues related to power, justice and political participation (Hogan, 1992). Post-materialism, on the other hand, focuses on life styles and the importance of values as opposite to technical rationality. Life styles concern the right to live one's life according to individual values and priorities and still be accepted as a full citizen and eligible for all civil and political rights (Giddens, 1994; Held, 1995).

The tendency to hold post-materialist values varies, at least between the European countries and within them, according to level of education, socioeconomic position and age. Post-materialist values seem to be well represented among younger and well-educated individuals (Harding & Phillips, 1986; Inglehart, 1990).

The spread of global cultural features has had different outcomes, ranging from revitalization of local cultures, or particularization, via hybridization (Pieterse, 1995) to the elimination of local cultures (Goonatilake, 1994; M'Bokolo, 1994; Stavenhagen, 1994). Some aspects of local cultures are challenged and questioned through this diffusion of a "universal culture" (Mayer & Roth, 1995; Waters, 1995). According to Giddens (1994:23,24), "Traditions have to explain themselves, to become open to interpretation and discourse . . . Fundamentalism canalise in all domains of social life where tradition becomes something which has to be decided upon rater than just taken for granted . . . " Hoerner (1995) employs the concept "the informal" which is not only the informal sector of the economy but also a culture of mutual solidarity and of survival. This might imply revival of previously important visions, values and beliefs.

Globalization brings secular cultures as well as sacred cultures. Islam, for instance, is spreading globally (Ahmed, 1992; Beeley, 1992). Featherstone (1991a:145) argues that "attraction of belief systems (are) declining," while Robertson (1991) and Turner

(1991) point to the fact that mysticism and fundamentalism have increased due to the challenges implied in cultural encounters.

Since the economic globalization is capitalist and market-oriented, it does not have gender neutral effects (Blakemore, 1999). All over the world, in capitalist as well as socialist countries, gender inequalities exist (Chen, 1999; Choi, 1999; Wong, 1999; Stromquist, 1995, 1998). These inequalities are in some cases undermined by globalization processes (Tripp, 1994) but are in most cases reinforced. Also, the discourse and research on globalization tends to be silent in relation to gender issues (Blakemore, 1999).

CONTRADICTORY DEMANDS ON EDUCATION

After 1960, most of the countries in the South have had an enormous educational expansion without a corresponding growth in their economies or in job opportunities (see table 1.7). Educational arrangements expanded and, consequently, the educational expenditures. The cost per pupil increased dramatically in many countries. This fact, among other things, prompted Coombs (1968, 1985) to warn the world about the imminent educational crisis.

Until the 1980s, essential characteristics of the educational system and the likelihood that certain educational changes will be implemented in the countries in the North could be explained or understood predominantly in terms of forces within each country. Internal, national conditions that at least permitted a certain type of educational change had to be present if these changes were to be decided upon and/or implemented (Dahllöf, 1984; Marklund, 1984).

TABLE 1.7 RATE OF ADULT LITERACY AND GROSS ENROLLMENT RATES IN PRIMARY AND SECONDARY EDUCATION, PER ECONOMIC CATEGORY OF COUNTRIES

	Low income		Middle Income		Industr. Countries	
	1960	1992	1960	1992	1960	1992
Literacy Rate	29	39	51	83	..	100
Gross Enrollment in Primary Education						
All	51	74	79	104	114	103
Girls	36	66	74	..	106	103
Gross Enrollment in Secondary Education						
	14	42	16	54*	58	..

Based on data from World Bank 1979, 1981 and 1995. * Upper–middle income countries.

Education and education systems are embedded in or affected by a large number of flows, national as well as global. In addition to the general globalization processes, there is the world model (signalling education for all, quality education, efficiency, effectiveness, school-based management, privatization and lifelong learning, among other things) that is propagated by the international agencies (Lockheed, Verspoor et al 1991; Meyer et al 1997; OECD, 1998; Ottone, 1996; World Bank, 1989).

The world model consists of "tacit understandings", explicit recommendations, and so on. It informs policy-makers and researchers and states what educational policies are opportune, desirable and appropriate. From the end of the 1980s (the time for decay of the Soviet Union), it has the principal components shown in Table 1.8. Its influence on different educational policies and systems is direct as well a indirect through, for instance, borrowing, learning (from others), and imposition (Dale, 1999). Changes of educational organization, administration and delivery and regulation as well as the curriculum and classroom processes according in the direction of what the world model recommends is termed systemic reform. It is supposed to change the whole system.

TABLE 1.8 THE WORLD MODEL FOR EDUCATION

Items	Characteristics
View of education	Education good for all. Consensus perspective. Education contributes to development, economic growth, democracy, rational human beings. Lifelong education socialization has become education and learning that is monitored by the state.
Educational system	Seven to nine years, compulsory. At least three years of secondary education preferable.
Curriculum	A national core curriculum; other parts flexible and adapted to local conditions. Education for global competitiveness, education for equality, education for empowerment, democracy, human rights and citizenship, education and sexual education.
Financing	Basic subsidies from the central state but major share from local and medium levels. Private financing of education.
Organization	National skeleton, national framework. Decentralized bodies for making of decisions within this framework. Local participation community participation.
Regulation, control	Surveillance and retroactive assessment by the state; choice exerted by parents and pupils.
Goals	Effectiveness and efficiency rational production of multi-skilled people but at the same time instilling morals.

As to the lifelong leaning, the following should be mentioned. Learning throughout life has been a research theme from different perspectives: socialization, development psychology, and andragogy. Socialization in these perspectives is "the genesis and change of human personality over the entire lifespan from birth to death and for all socio-cultural conditions upon which this is dependent . . . " (Brezinha, 1994:4) or "a continuing, lifelong process" that takes place in the context of the family, school, peer group, occupational setting, and radical resocialization settings (Sturman, 1994:5588).

Thus, lifelong learning is nothing new. Such learning has to a large extent been civil and private as opposed to economically driven, official or public). In the the mid-1990s, recurrent *education*, permanent education/*éducation permanente*, lifelong education were replaced by "lifelong learning" on the agenda of certain international agencies. There was a marked shift in the discourse and the language of the lifelong learning discourse seems to appeal both to market forces and new movements and postmodernists. According to OECD (1998:7–9), "lifelong *learning*," is:

"more than recurrent education for adults . . . encompasses all purposeful learning activity undertaken with the aim of improving knowledge, skills, and competence . . . Whether education should pay more attention to meeting labour market needs or to preparing individuals for citizenship . . . These principles have an important bearing on the structure of learning provision, on its content, on resource provision and on roles and responsibilities within the education system."

Apart from the world model, globalization in itself contains a large number of contradictions and these are either affecting national education systems directly or mediated through the national state and the national economy. The state, and particularly the education system, is to a large extent under the cross-pressure between local cultures and their demands (localization of the content and local language, for instance) on the one hand, and the globalization and internationalizing aspects (more foreign languages, for instance), on the other hand (Arnason, 1991; Ginsburg *et al.*, 1990).

The national and local needs, demands and requirements may be listed in the following way: (i) unitarian vs. diversified; (ii) religious-moral vs. secular; (iii) local vs. national; (iv) local vs. international; (v) national vs. international; (vi) principally formation of human capital and merits vs. broad personality development; (vii) specific skills and knowledge vs. general knowledge and learning how to learn; (viii) individual good vs. common good; and (ix) competition vs. solidarity; (x) focus on tests and performance vs. more holistic considerations; (xi) competition and elitism vs. equality and democracy; (xii) native languages vs. international languages (Benhabib, 1998; Camp, 1997; Cha, Wong & Meyer, 1988; Cummings, Gopinathan & Tomoda, 1988; McGinn, 1997; Taylor, 1994). Thus, education is under the pressure of a global processes and a "world model" (Meyer et al, 1997), on the one hand, and national and local forces, on the other hand.

In the North, there is a combination of state withdrawal from interfering with the means and instruments of educational achievement, on the one hand, and stricter control, monitoring, assessment and distanced surveillance of this same achievement, on the other hand. In the South, the economic crisis and the adjustment policies put education under pressure, directly or indirectly, for four main types of pressure: (i) cuts in public-sector budgets which reduced the resources available for financing education an training; (ii) declining level and changing distribution of employment, which affected work opportunities; (iii) declines in level of household incomes; and (iv) changes in company incomes and tax outlays which affected training expenditures (Graham-Brown, 1991; Reimers & Tiburcio, 1993; Samoff & Taskforce, 1994; Woodhall, 1994).

Some of the flows and influences are summarized in Table 1.9. There is consensus concerning the value of education; both the political left and right agree that education is the key to future prosperity. Education has become "high politics", more than before. However, there are conflicts over education's funding, control and organisation (Brown et al., 1997a:7). Compulsory education has everywhere been prolonged and involves a larger percentage of the world´s populations than ever before.

Globalization tends to standardize and homogenize cultures. This fact together with, the spread of high and other technologies puts pressure on the educational system to produce de-contextualized knowledge. Highly globalized economies require that students in school learn certain basics but they also have to become creative, innovative, and flexible to find new solutions to new problems (Adler, 1992). On the other hand, in strongly multicultural countries, national ethnic groups place a demand on nation-states for contextualized knowledge, and so on.

TABLE 1.9 GLOBAL AND NATIONAL FLOWS AND INFLUENCES

Flows and influences from	Flows to national				
	economy	state	culture	techno-system	education
Economy					
globally	Competition, search for human capital	Requirements of rationalization and commodification. Infrastructure. Transfer of metaphors.	Universalization. Commodification. Standardization of preferences. Modular man.	?	Flexibility. Modular man. Multi-skilled human capital. Creativity. Selection.
nationally	xxxxxxxxx	-"- Relaxation	"National" pattern of preferences. Particularization.	New discoveries. R & D.	"National" human capital. Selection and sorting vs. "raise all"
Polity/state					
globally	?	De-territorialization. Inter-governmental-ization.	Universalization. Modular man. Super-ficialization. Secular-ization.	?	Global identity. Competitiveness.
nationally	Surplus. Employ-ment.	xxxxxxxxxxxxx	National identity. National loyalty. National legitimation.	National application. National discoveries.	National identity. National loyalty. National legitimacy. Competitiveness.
Culture					
globally	Differentia-tion of production.	Lifestyle issues. Participation. Cross-national demands.Informa-lization.	Individualization. Post-materialism. Consume-rism. Standardization. Superficialization. Universalization.	Availability.	Universalization. Secularization. Standardization.
nationally	-"-	Class and locality issues as well as life style issues. Participation. Diversification.	xxxxxxxxxxxx	Adaptability, availability, applicability.	Particularization. Sacralization. Diversification. Social capital. Morals and values education.
Technology					
globally	De-territorial-ization.	Relaxation. Decreased cross-border control.	De-contextualization. Consumption of symbols. Creation of images. Rationalization. De-territorialization.	De-territorial-ization.	De-contextual-ization. Creativity. Flexibility. Standardization.
nationally	Rationalization. Automation. IT.	Increased surveillance.	Rationalization.	xxxxxxxxx	-"-
Education					
nationally	Qualification. Competence formation.	Competence formation. Legitimation	Secularization. Individualization. Rationalization.	Basic techno-logical skills.	xxxxxxxxxxxx

At the school level, post-Fordist philosophy plays out in different ways. First, the structure of the educational system and the way of organizing schools is expected to become more similar to the way private companies are organized and managed, from Fordist to post-Fordist (Whitty, 1996, 1997). Secondly, according to Arnold (1996), the introduction of IT "filters" other activities in the schools. That is, interaction and learning are more and more guided by IT equipment. A third feature is the absence of educational discourse and the dominance of an economic- technocratic discourse on education (see, for instance, Ball, 1990; Samoff, 1993). Fourth, representations and symbols as opposed to directly experienced persons and objects become an increasing portion of the everyday life of young people in the North (Lash, 1990).

What finally results from the adoption of the world model is due to national and local cultures and economic situation. A research review made by McGinn (1997) shows that the globalization has not had any significant effects as far as delivery and content of education is concerned. He formulates some hypotheses concerning the de-linking of the schools from society and the relative autonomy of education and schools. Thus, policies are globalized but the degree of implementation of these policies varies and so does the outcome of what is implemented.

SOME CONCLUSIONS

Although not implying considerable elements of innovation *per se*, educational restructuring came to be seen not as a reform among a series of reforms but as something different and more than a reform. The reasons may be that (i) it was dressed in the discourse and metaphors of the economic market place; (ii) many governments, independent of political ideology, responded in a similar way to the economic imperatives and the crisis syndrome; and (iii) it became partially linked to the economic recession and competition (Beare & Boyd, 1993; Caldwell, 1993). The degree of coupling between the state/society and the education system may vary from one country to another and from time to time. It may be hypothesized that increasing drive for competitiveness results in a stronger coupling of certain aspects while the coupling has become weaker in other aspects. There also seems to be a qualitative shift in the coupling; formerly, control of the education system was first and foremost proactive in many countries (detailed rules and regulations state was should and should not be done), today it is retroactive (it takes place at distance and *ex post facto*). The latter type of control has, however, similarities with the *surveillance* as analyzed by Foucault (Neocleous, 1996).

National states and international agencies are now making attempts to institutionalize and control or at least monitor and assess the learning experiences or socialization of individuals during their lifetime. This is one of the new functions the central state has assumed due to the global competition. This control is done through appeals to rational self-relgulation and sophisticated *surveillance* (OECD, 1997, 1998b). The network of educational initative and control is globalizing. Interventions in remote areas in many countries now take place in the name of Education For All and Lifelong Learning (Jimenez & Sawada, 1999; Miressa & Muskin, 1999; Orazem, 1999; Ottone, 1996).[9]

NOTES

[1]   Bretherton (1996a:3) sees globalization as "a new, distinct phase in world politics . . . " Critics of the globalization concept argue that large geographical areas and populations are not

involved in the processes meant to be involved in globalization. However, it is evident that the frame of action of all nation-states and economies is conditioned by what takes place around them. Another category of researchers argue that what now is taking place does not differ from what previously occurred in the world economy (Hirst and Thompson, 1996). Additionally, Brown (1999) argues that globalization "has also become a discourse (which describes globalization) . . . as an irresistable and irreversible process beyond the scope of human agency to resist. . . . "

[2] A system consists of a whole of "any pattern whose elements are related in a sufficiently regular way to justify attention . . . " (Kuhn, 1974). Internationalization and globalization do not necessarily require that this characterizes the world (yet).

[3] In this book, "North" refers to economically the rich countries (principally OECD countries) and the "South" to economically poor countries.

[4] Some researchers argue that technological innovations now influence other spheres of life as much as they influence the economic sphere. If this is correct, "technological globalization" should be viewed from its own perspective (See, for instance, Lash, 1990).

[5] Two examples are the Russians in Europe and Central Asia and the Fulanis and Mandingas in West and Central Africa. for instance, Russians constituted a majority in Soviet Union but nowadays, Russians constitute important minorities in a large number of independent countries (Brubaker, 1995; Coulby, 1996). Fulanis and Mandingas form majorities or important minorities and many countries from Mali in the north to Cameroon in the south of Sub-Saharan Africa.

[6] Saul (1997) looks upon the changes in the world from a more philosophical point of departure and argues that a corporatist pattern of thought characterizes the policies of most countries of the world today; all efforts are subordinated to the overall drive for global competitiveness.

[7] Cvetkovich & Kellner (1997) use the terms "transforming" and "erasing" cultures. Examples exist in, for instance, former Africa, Asia, and the former Soviet Union. In Canada, the protests from the French speaking population in Quebec forced the federal government and some province governments give concessions to this population that other minorities or Anglophones do not have (Lawton, 1993; Lawton et al. 1997).

[8] Some of the contradictory statements are probably due to the fact that the authors do not always distinguish between North/rich and South/poor countries in the world; and they do not always make a distinction between various analytical levels, from the national down to the individual level or from the level of culture to individual attitudes and values. Moreover, cultures contain different priorities and different levels of relevance (Spiro, 1987)—from a superficial level of indifference to values deeply rooted in the culture. The contradictions are also due to the fact that some cultural features are diverging (Harding & Phillips, 1986; Held, 1995). It means that one class or stratum of people in a country may be consumerist and materialist, while another class or stratum is post-materialist.

[9] Education may be said to consist of teaching and learning. From the perspective of socialization theory, learning takes place in many different, principally informal, situations not deliberately or purposively organized for education. The "Recurrent Education Perspective" was changed to a "Lifelong Learning Perspective" and efforts are now made to measure and assess learning.

REFERENCES CITED

Adler, P.S. (1992). "Introduction." In P. S. Adler (ed.). *Technology and the Future of Work.* New York: Oxford University Press.

Ahmed, A.S. (1992). *Postmodernism and Islam. Predicament and Promise.* London: Routledge

Almond, G. A. and S. Verba (1965). *The Civic Culture*. Boston: Little, Brown & Co.

Amin, S. (1994). "L´ideologie et la pensée sociale: l´intelligensia et la crise du développement." *Bulletin du Codesria*, Vol. 3.

Appadurai, A. (1991). "Disjuncture and Difference in the Global Economy". In M. Featherstone (ed.) *Global Culture. Nationalism, Globalization and Modernity*. London: Sage Publications.

Arnold, M. (1996). "The High-Tech Post-Fordist School." *Interchange*, vol. 27 , nos 3/4.

Ball, S. (1990). *Politics and Policy Making in Education. Explorations in Policy Sociology*. London: Routledge.

Bangura, Y. (1992). "Authoritarian Rule and Democracy in Africa. A Theoretical Discourse." In P. Gibbon, Y. Bangura and A. Ofstad (eds). *Authoritarianism, Democracy and Adjustment. The Politics of Economic Reform in Africa*. Uppsala: The Scandinavian Institute of African Studies.

Bauman, Z. (1991). "Modernity and Ambivalence." In M. Featherstone (ed.). *Global Culture. Nationalism, Globalization and Modernity*. London: Sage Publications.

Beare, H. & W. L. Boyd, W.L. (1993). "Introduction." In H. Beare & W. L. Boyd (eds.). *Restructuring Schools. An International Perspective on the Movement to Transform the Control and Performance of School*. London: Falmer.

Beeley, B. (1992). Islam as a Global Political Force. In A. G. McGrew and P. G. Lewis (eds.). *Global Politics*. Oxford: Polity Press.

Beckman, B. (1992). "Empowerment or Repression? The World Bank and the Politics of African Adjustment." In P.Gibbon, Y. Bangura and A. Ofstad (eds). *Authoritarianism, Democracy and Adjustment. The Politics of Economic Reform in Africa*. (Uppsala: The Scandinavian Institute of African Studies.

Benhabib, S. (1998). "Democracy and Identity. In Search of the Civic Polity." *Philosophy & Social Criticism*, vol. 23 nos 2/3.

Bergesen, A. (1991). "Turning World System Theory on its Head." In M. Featherstone (ed.) *Global Culture, Nationalism, Globalization and Modernity*. London: Sage Publications.

Bienen, H. and J. Waterbury (1989). "The Political Economy of Privatization in Developing Countries." *World Development*, vol. 17, no. 5.

Blakemore, J. (1999). "Localization/globalization and the midwife state: strategic dilemmas for state feminism in education?" *Journal of Education Policy*, Vol. 14, no. 1.

Boli, J. (1989). *New Citizens for a New Society. The Institutional Origins of Mass Schooling in Sweden*. New York: Pergamon.

Boli, J.and F. O. Ramirez (1992). "Compulsory Schooling in the Western Cultural Context." In R. F. Arnove, P.G. Altbach and G. P. Kelly (eds). *Emergent Issues in Education. Comparative Perspectives*. New York: SUNY Press.

Boli, J. and G. M. Thomas (1997). "World Culture in the World Polity: A Century of International Non-governmental Organizations." *American Sociological Review*, Vol. 2.

Brander, J.A. (1995). "Rationales for Strategic Trade and Industrial Policy." In P. R. Krugman (ed) *Strategic Trade Policy and the New International Economics*pp. Cambridge, Mass.: The MIT Press.

Braverman, H. (1974). *Labor and Monopoly Capital*. New York: Monthly Review Press.

Bretherton, C. (1996a). "Introduction: Global Politics in the 1990s." In C. Bretherton and C. Ponton (eds.). *Global Politics. An Introduction*. Oxford: Blackwell Publishers.

Bretherton, C. (1996b). "Universal Human Rights: Bringing People into Global Politics? " In C. Bretherton and C. Ponton (eds.). *Global Politics. An Introduction.* Oxford: Blackwell Publishers.

Brezinha, B. (1994). *Socialization and Education. Essays in Conceptual Criticism,* translated by James Stuart Brice. Westport, Conn.: Greenwood Press.

Brown, T. (1999). "Challenging globalization as discourse and phenomenon." *International Journal of Lifelong Education,* vol. 18, no. 1.

Brown, P. and H. Lauder (1996). "Education, Globalization and Economic Development". *Journal of Education Policy,* vol. 11.

Brown, P., A. H. Halsey, H. Lauder and A, Stuart Wells (1997). "The Transformation of Education and Society: An Introduction." A. H. Halsey, H. Lauder, P. Brown, and A. Stuart Wells (eds). *Education. Culture, Economy, Society.* Oxford: Oxford University Press.

Brubaker, R. (1995). National Minorities, Nationalizing States and External National Homelands in the New Europe. *Daedalus,* vol. 124, no. 2.

Cable, V. (1995). The Diminished Nation-State: A Study in the Loss of Economic Power. *Daedalus,* vol. 124, no. 2.

Caldwell, B.J. (1993). "Paradox and Uncertainty in the Governance of Education." In H. Beare & W. L. Boyd (eds.). *Restructuring Schools. An International Perspective on the Movement to Transform the Control and Performance of School.* London: The Falmer Press.

Callaghy, T. M. (1987). "The State as Lame Leviathan: The Patrimonial Administrative State and Africa." In Z. Ergas (ed.). *The African State in Transition.* London: Macmillan Press

Camp, V. (1997). "Education for Democracy." *Prospects,* vol. XXVII, no. 4.

Cardoso, F.H. (1993). "North-South Relations in the Present Context: A New Dependency?" In M. Carnoy, M. Castells, S. S. Cohen and F.H. Cardoso *The New Global Economy in the Information Age.* University Park, Penn.: The Pennsylvania State University

Carnoy, M. (1993). "Multinationals in changing World Economy: Whither the Nation-State?" In M. Carnoy, M. Castells, S. S. Cohen and F.H. Cardoso *The New Global Economy in the Information Age.* University Park, Penn.: The Pennsylvania State University

Carnoy, M. & M Castells (1995). *Sustainable Flexibility. A Prospective Study on Work, Family and Society in the information Age.* Berkely and Stanford: Berkely and Stanford Universities.

Carnoy, M., M Castells, S.S. Cohen and F. H. Cardoso (1993). "Introduction." In M. Carnoy, M. Castells, S. S. Cohen and F.H. Cardoso *The New Global Economy in the Information Age.* University Park, Penn.: The Pennsylvania State University.

Castells, M. (1993). "The Informational Economy and the New International Division of Labor." In M. Carnoy, M. Castells, S. S. Cohen and F.H. Cardoso *The New Global Economy in the Information Age.* University Park, Penn.: The Pennsylvania State University.

Cha, Y-K., S-Y. Wong and J. Meyer (1988). "Values Education in the Curriculum: Some Comparative Empircial Data." In W.K. Cummings, S. Gopinathan, S. & Y. Tomoda, (ed.). *The Revival of Values Education in Asia and the West.* Oxford: Pergamon Press.

Chen, P. (1999). "Signal Theory in Gendered Fields of Study, Division of Labor and Wage Differentials in Taiwan." *Paper presented at the annual conference of the Comparative and International Education Society* in Toronto, Canada, April 14-18.

Cheru, F. (1996). "New Social Movements: Democratic Struggles and Human Rights in Africa." In J. H. Mittelman. (ed.). *Globalization: Critical Reflections.* London: Bouldner.

Educational Restructuring

Choi, S.A. (1999). "Educational Attainment and Occupational Status of Women in South Korea." *Paper presented at the annual conference of the Comparative and International Education Society* in Toronto, Canada. April 14-18.

Ciborra, C.U. and L.S, Schneider (1992). "Transforming the Routines and Contexts of Management, Work and Technology." In P. S. Adler (ed.). *Technology and the Future of Work.* New York: Oxford University Press.

Cohen, S.S. (1993). "Geo-Economics: Lessons from America's Mistakes" In M. Carnoy, M. Castells, S. S. Cohen and F.H. Cardoso *The New Global Economy in the Information Age.* University Park, Penn.: The Pennsylvania State University.

Colclough, C. (1990). "Structuralism versus Neo-Liberalism: An Introduction". In C. Colclough and J. Manor (ed.). *States or Markets? Neo-Liberalism and the Development Policy Debate.* Oxford: Clanderon Press.

Collot, A., G. Didier and B. Loueslati (1993). La société interculturelle: projets et débats: Introduction. In A. Collot, G. Didier and B. Loueslati (eds.). *La pluralité culturelle dans les systèmes éducatifs européens.* Lorraine: Centre régional de documentation pedagogique.

Coombs, P. (1968). *The World Crisis in Education: A Systems Analysis.* London: Oxford University Press.

Coombs, P. (1985). *The World Crisis in Education. The View from the Eighties.* Oxford: Oxford University Press.

Cornia, G.A., R. Jollby and F. Stewart, F. (eds.). (1987). *Adjustment With a Human Face.* Oxford: Clanderon Press

Coulby, D. (1997). "European Curricula, Xenophopia and Warfare." *Comparative Education,* vol. 33, no. 1.

Cox, R. (1996). "A Perspective on Globalization". In J. H. Mittelman. (ed.). *Globalization: Critical Reflections.* Boulder: Lynne Rienner Publishers.

Cummings, W.K., G. Gopinathan and Y. Tomoda (1988). " The Revival of Values Education. In W.K. Cummings, S. Gopinathan & Y. Tomoda (eds.). *The Revival of Values Education in Asia and the West.* Oxford: Pergamon Press.

Cvetkovich, A. and D. Kellner (1997). "Introduction: Thinking Global and Local". In A. Cvetkovich and D. Kellner (eds). *Articulating the Global and the Local.* Oxford: Westview Press

Dahllöf, U. (1984). "Contextual Problems of Educational Reforms: A Swedish Perspective." In T. Husén and M. Kogan (eds.). *Educational Research and Policy. How Do They Relate?* Oxford: Pergamon.

Dale, R. (1999). "Specifying globalization effects on national policy: a focus on the mechanisms." *Journal of Education Policy,* vol. 14, no. 1.

Edwards, R. (1998). "Flexibility, reflexivity and reflection in the contemporary workplace." In *International Journal of Lifelong Education,* vol. 17, no. 6.

Escudero, M. (1994). "Reinventing Politics." In D. Miliband (ed.). *Reinventing the Left.* Cambridge: Polity Press.

Esping-Andersen, G. (1993). Trends in Contemporary Class Structuration: A Six-nation Comparison. In G. Esping-Andersen et al (eds.). *Changing Classes. Stratification and Mobility in Post- Industrial Societies.* London: Sage Publications.

Esping-Andersen, G. (1994). "Equality and Work in the Post-industrial Life-cycle." In D. Miliband (ed.). *Reinventing the Left.* Cambridge: Polity Press.

Featherstone, M. (1991). "Global Culture: "An Introduction." In M. Featherstone (ed.). *Global Culture. Nationalism, Globalization and Modernity.* London: Sage Publications.

Flacks, R. (1995). "Think Globally, Act Politically: Some Notes toward New Movement Strategy." In M. Darnovsky, B. Epstein and R. Flacks (eds.). *Cultural Politics and Social Movements.* Philadelphia: Temple University Press.

Freeman, C. and Soete, L. (1994). *Work for all or Mass Unemployment.* London: Pinter.

Gallagher, M. (1993). "A Public Choice Theory of Budgets: Implications for Education in Less Developed Countries." *Comparative Education Review*, vol. 37, no. 2.

Ghai, D. (1997). *Economic Globalization, Institutional Change, and Human Security.* Geneva: United Nations Research Institute for Social Development.

Giddens, A. (1994). "Brave New World: The New Context of Politics." In D. Miliband (ed.). *Reinventing the Left.* Cambridge: Polity Press.

Gill, S. (1996). "Globalization, Democratization and the Politics of Indifference." In J. H. Mittelman. (ed.). *Globalization: Critical Reflections.* Boulder: Lynne Rienner Publishers.

Ginsburg, M.B., S. Cooper, R. Raghu and H. Zegarra (1990). "National and World-System Explana tions of Educational Reform." In *Comparative Education Review*, vol. 34, no. 4.

Goontilake, S. (1994). "The Futures of Asian Cultures: betwen Localization and Globalization." In *Unesco: The Futures of Cultures.* Paris: UNESCO.

Graham-Brown, S. (1991). *Education in the Developing World. Conflict and Crisis.* London: Longman.

Habermas, J. (1971). *Toward a Rational Society.* London: Heineman.

Habermas, J. (1976). *Legitimation Crisis.* London: Heineman.

Hamilton, C. (1989). "The Irrelevance of Economic Liberalization." *World Development*, vol. 17, no. 19.

Hann, C. (1997). "The Nation-state, Religions and Uncivil Society: Two Perspectives." *Daedalus*, vol. 126, no. 2.

Hansson, G. (1990). "Den internationaliserade ekonomins problem och möjligheter." (The problems and possibilities of the internationalized economy). In G. Hansson and L-G. Stenelo (eds.). *Makt och internationalisering.* (Power and Internationalization). Stockholm: Carlsons.

Harding, S.and D. Phillips (1986). *Contrasting Values in Western Europe. Unity, Diversity and Change.* London: The Macmillan Press Ltd.

Held, D. (1995). *Political Theory and the Modern State.* Oxford: Polity Press.

Henderson, J. (1996). "Globalisation and Forms of Capitalism: Conceptualisations and the Search for Synergies." *Competition and Change*, vol. 1, no. 4.

Herbst, K. (1990). "The Structural Adjustment of Politics in Africa." *World Development*, vol. 18, no. 7).

Hirst, P. and G. Thompson (1996). *Globalization in Question.* Oxford: Polity Press.

Hoerner, J-M. (1995). *Le tiers-monde. Entre la survie et l´ informel.* Paris: Harmattan.

Hogan, D. (1992). "' . . . the silent compulsions of economic relations': Markets and Demand for Education. " In *Educational Policy*, vol. 6, no. 2.

Inglehart, R. (1990). *Culture Shifts in Advanced Industrial Society.* Princeton: Princeton University Press.

Jimenez, E. and Sawada; P. (1999). "School-Based Management Reforms: Lessons from Evalua-tions." *Paper presented at the annual conference of the Comparative and International Education Society, in Toronto, Canada,* April 14-18.

Kern, H.and M. Schumann (1992). "New Concepts of Production and the Emergence of the Sys-tems Controller." In P. S. Adler (ed.). *Technology and the Future of Work.* New York: Oxford University Press.

Kolouh-Westin, L. (1999). "The Tripartite State, Ethnic Construction and Divided Education. The Case of Bosnia and Herzegovina." In H. Daun & L. Benincasa (eds). *State and Market, Civil Society and Education.*(Unpublished manuscript) Stockholm: Institute of International Education.

Kuhn, A. (1974). *The logic of social systems.* San Fransisco: Jossey-Bass.

Lash, S. (1990). *Sociology of Postmodernism.* London: Routledge.

Lawton, S.B. (1993). "A Decade of Educational Reform in Canada: Encounters with the Octo-pus, the Elephant, and the Five Dragons." In H. Beare & W. L. Boyd (eds.). *Restruc-turing Schools. An International Perspective on the Movement to Transform the Control and Performance of School.* London: Falmer Press.

Lawton, S., T. Liket, R. Reed and F. van Wieringen (1997). "Restructuring Schooling to Date: An Assessment." In S. Lawton, R. Reed and F. van Wieringen (eds). *Restructuring Public Schooling: Europe, Canada, America.* Munster: Waxmann.

Lockheed, M.E., A. Verspoor *et al.,* (1991). *Improving Education in Developing Countries.* Oxford: Oxford University Press.

Mannin, M. (1996). "Global Issues and the Challenge to Democractic Politics." In C. Brether-ton and C. Ponton (eds.). *Global Politics. An Introduction.* Oxford: Blackwell Publish-ers.

Marklund, S. (1984). "Effects of Educational Research on Educational Policy-making: The Case of Sweden." In T. Husén and M. Kogan (eds.). *Educational Research and Policy. How Do They Relate?* Oxford: Pergamon.

Mayer, R. and R. Roth, R. (1995). "New Social Movements and the Transformation to Post-Fordist Society." In M. Darnovsky, B. Epstein and R. Flacks (eds.). *Cultural Politics and Social Movements.* Philadelphia: Temple University Press.

Mazawi, A.E. (1998). "Contested Regimes, Civic Dissent, and the Political Socialization of Chil-dren and Adolescents," in O. Ichilov (ed.). *Citizenship and Citizenship Education in a Changing World.* London: The Woburn Press, 1998.

M'Bokolo, E. (1994). "African cultures and the crisis of contemporary Africa." In *Unesco: The Futures of Cultures.* Paris: UNESCO.

McGinn, N.F. (1997). "The Impact of Globalization on National Education Systems." *Prospects,* Vol. XXVIII, no. 1.

McGrew, A. G. (1992). "Conceptualizing Global Politics." In A. G. McGrew and P. G. Lewis (eds.). *Global Politics.* Oxford: Polity Press.

Meyer, J. W., J. Boli, G. M. Thomas and F. O. Ramirez (1997). World Society and Nation-State. *American Journal of Sociology,* vol. 103, no. 1.

Miressa, A and J. Muskin (1999). "Community Participation as a Strategy to Improve School Quality, Access and Demand." *Paper presented at the annual conference of the Com-parative and International Education Society, in Toronto, Canada,* April 14-18.

Mittelman, J. H. (1996a). "The Dynamics of Globalization." In J. H. Mittelman. (ed.). *Global-ization: Critical Reflections*. Boulder: Lynne Rienner Publishers.

Mittelman, J.H. (1996b). "How Does Globalization Really Work?" In J. H. Mittelman. (ed.). Globalization: Critical Reflections. Boulder: Lynne Rienner Publishers.

Mosley, P., J. Harrigan and J. Toye (1991). *Aid and Power. The World Bank & Policy-based Lend-ing. Vol. 1*. London: Routledge.

Mulhearn, C. (1996). "Change and Development in the Global Economy." In C. Bretherton and C. Ponton (eds.). *Global Politics. An Introduction*. Oxford: Blackwell Publishers.

Neocleous, M. (1996). *Administering Civil Society. Towards a Theory of State Power*. London: Macmillam.

OECD (1997). *Education at Glance, 1997*. Paris: OECD.

OECD (1998) *Education Policy Analysis*. Paris: OECD.

Offe, C. (1996). *Modernity and the State. East, West*. Cambridge, Mass.: The MIT Press.

Offe, C. (1997). *Varieties of Transition. The East European and East German Experience*. Cam-bridge, Mass.: The MIT Press.

Okuma, M. K. (1996). Aboriginal Education as a Decolonizing Method: The Nisga'a Experience. Unpublished MA Thesis. Prince George: The University of Northern British Colum-bia.

Orazem, P. (1999). "School-Based Management Reforms: Lessons from Evaluations." *Paper pre-sented at the annual conference of the Comparative and International Education Soci-ety, in Toronto, Canada*, April 14-18.

Ottone, E. (1996). "Globalization and Educational Change: Modernism and Citizenship." *Prospects*, vol. XXVI, no. 2.

Panitch, L. (1996). "Rethinking the Role of the State. In J. H. Mittelman. (ed.). *Globalization: Critical Reflections*. Boulder: Lynne Rienner.

Parkins, C. (1996). "North-South Relations and Globalization after the Cold War." In C. Brether-ton and C. Ponton (eds.). *Global Politics. An Introduction*. Oxford: Blackwell Publish-ers.

Pettersson, L. (1990). "Den svenska ekonomins internationalisering. "(The internationalization of the Swedish Economy). In G. Hansson and L.-G. Stenelo (eds.). *Makt och interna-tionalisering*. (Power and Internationalization). Stockholm: Carlsons.

Pieterse, J. N. (1995). "Globalization as Hybridization." In M.Featherstone, S. Lash and R. Robertson (eds.). *Global Modernities*. London: Sage Publications.

Reich, R.B. (1997). "Why the Rich Are Getting Richer and the Poor, Poorer. From The Work of Nations: A Blueprint for the Future, London: Simon & Schuster". Reprinted in A. H. Halsey, H. Lauder, P. Brown, and A. Stuart Wells (eds). *Education. Culture, Economy, Society*. Oxford: Oxford University Press

Reimers, F. and L. Tiburcio (1993). *Education, Adjustment and Reconstruction: Options for Change*. Paris: UNESCO.

Robertson, R. (1991). Mapping the Global Condition: Globalization as the Central Concept. In M. Featherstone, (ed.) *Global Culture. Nationalism, Globalization and Modernity*. Lon-don: Sage Publications.

Robertson, R. (1992). *Globalization. Social Theory and Global Culture*. London: Sage Publica-tions.

Rocard, M. (1994). "Social Solidarity in a Mixed Economy." In D. Miliband (ed.). *Reinventing the Left.*Cambridge: Polity Press.

Saine, A. S .M. (1995). "Democracy in Africa: Constraints and Prospects." In K. Mengisteab and I. Logan (eds.). *Beyond Economic Liberalization in Africa: Structural Adjustment and the Alternatives.* London: Zed Books.

Samoff, J. (1993). "The Reconstruction of Schooling in Africa." *Comparative Education Review,* vol. 37, no. 2.

Samoff, J.and Taskforce (1994). "Crisis and Adjustment: Understanding National Responses." In Samoff, J. (ed.). *Coping With Crisis. Austery, Adjustment and Human Resources.* London: Cassell/UNESCO.

Saul, J. R. (1997). *The Unconscious Civilization.* Harmondsworth: Penguin.

Schmidt, V.A. (1995). "The New World Order, Incorporated: The Rise of Business and the Decline of the Nation-State." *Daedalus,* vol 124, no. 2.

SIDA (1994). *State, Market & Aid. Redefined Roles.* Stockholm: Sida.

Sklair, L. (1995). *Sociology and the Global System.* Second edition. New Jersey: Prentice Hall/Harvester Wheatsheaf.

Spiro, M.E. (1987). "Social Systems, Personality and Functional Analysis." In B. Kilborn and L. L. Langness (eds). *Culture and Human Nature. Theoretical Papers of Melford O. Spiro.* Chicago: Chicago University Press.

Stavenhagen, R. (1994). "Cultural struggles and development in Latin America." In *Unesco: The Futures of Cultures.* Paris: UNESCO.

Strange, S. (1995). "The Defective State." *Daedalus,* vol. 124, no. 2.

Streeten, P. (1987). "Structural Adjustment: A Survery of the Issus and Options." *World Development,* vol 15, no. 12.

Stromquist, N. P. (1995). "Romancing the State: Gender and Power in Education." *Comparative Education Review,* vol. 39, no. 4.

Stromquist, N. P. (1998). "Institutionalization of Gender and Its Impact on Educational Policy." *Comparative Education,* vol. 42, no. 1.

Sturman, A.(1994). "Socialization", in T. Husén and N. Postlethwaite, N. (eds.). *International Encyclopedia of Education.* Oxford: Pergamon Press.

Taylor, M. (1994). *Values Education in Europe: a Comparative Overview of a Survey of 26 Countries in 1983.* Paris: Nfer/UNESCO.

Tripp, A. M. (1994). "Rethinking Civil Society: Gender Implications in Contemporary Tanzania." In J. W. Harberson, D. Rothchild and N. Chazan (eds).*Civil Society and the State in Africa.* London: Boulder.

Turner, B.S. (1991). "Politics and culture in Islamic Globalism." In R. Robertson and W. R. GDarret (eds). *Religion and Global Order.* New York: Paragon House Publishers.

UNAIDS/WHO (1996). The HIV/AIDS Situation in mid-1996, Global and Regional Highlights. Fact Sheet 1 July 1996. Geneva: UNAIDS and WHO.

UNDP (1990). *Human Development Report 1990.* New York: Oxford University Press.

UNDP (1991). *Human Development Report 1991.* New York: Oxford University Press.

UNDP (1995). *Human Development Report 1995.* New York: Oxford University Press.

van de Walle, N. (1989). Privatizaton in Developing Countries: A Review of the Issues. In *World Development,* vol. 17, no. 3.

Waters, M. (1995). *Globalization.* London: Routledge.

Weissman, S.R. (1990). "Structural Adjustment in Africa: Insights from the Experiences of Ghana and Senegal." *World Development,* vol. 18, no. 12.

Whitty, G. (1996). "Creating Quasi-Markets in Education: A Review of Recent Research on Parental Choice and School Autonomy in Three Countries." *Oxford Studies of Comparative Education,* vol. 6 , no. 1.

Whitty, G. (1997). "Marketization, the State and the Re-formation of the Teaching Profession." In A. H. Halsey, H. Lauder, P. Brown, and A. Stuart Wells (eds). *Education. Culture, Economy, Society.* Oxford: Oxford University Press.

Wilson, R.A. (1997). "Human Rights, Culture and Context: An Introduction." In R. A. Wilson (ed.). *Human Rights, Culture and Context. Anthropological Perspectives.* London: Pluto Press.

Wong, M.S. (1999). " Gender Equity in China." *Paper presented at the annual conference of the Comparative and International Education Society,* in Toronto, Canada. April 14–18

Woodhall, M. (1994). "The Context of Economic Austerity and Structural Adjustment". In J. Samoff (ed.). *Coping With Crisis. Austery, Adjustment and Human Resources.* London: Cassell/UNESCO.

World Bank (1977). *World Development Report 1977.* Washington, D.C.: World Bank.

World Bank (1979). *World Development Report 1979.* Washington, D.C.: World Bank.

World Bank (1980). *World Development Report 1980.* Washington, D.C.: World Bank.

World Bank (1981). *World Development Report 1981.* Washington, D.C.: World Bank.

World Bank (1986). *World Development Report 1986.* Washington, D.C.: World Bank.

World Bank (1989). Sub-Saharan Africa. From Crisis to Sustainable Growth. Washington, D.C.: World Bank.

World Bank (1991). *World Development Report 1991.* Washington, D.C.: World Bank.

World Bank (1992). *World Development Report 1992.* Washington, D.C.: World Bank.

World Bank (1993). *World Development Report 1993.* Washington, D.C.: World Bank.

World Bank (1994). *World Development Report 1994.* Washington, D.C.: World Bank.

World Bank (1995). *World Development Report 1995.* Washington, D.C.: World Bank.

World Bank (1997). *World Development Report 1997.* Washington, D.C.: World Bank.

World Bank (1998). *World Development Report 1998.* Washington, D.C.: World Bank.

CHAPTER 2

Shifts in Nation-State, Social Theory and Educational Research

Holger Daun

Introduction

The *national* dimension of the state, educational systems and research paradigms have, since the beginning of the 1980s, been questioned or even rejected by some alternative movements and post-modernist researchers. Until the 1980s, the nation-state was taken by politicians, economic actors and scientists as the basis for politics and economic policies as well as being the primary unit for social analysis and educational policies. Globalization processes and ideological shifts then came to challenge this view. This chapter describes the sweeping changes in the state, education and theories on these two units following the second World War. After the war, most countries in the world experienced a rapid economic growth, a reinforcement and an extension of the nation state and an expansion of primary and secondary education. There was also an increasing use of social (including educational) science in the formulation, implementation and evaluation of policies. Some of the theories contributed more than others to the restructuring of education that started in the 1980s.

The Nation-State and National Education Systems

There was in many countries a general desire among politicians, scientists and others to eliminate or at least neutralize such economic, political and cultural conditions that led first to the economic crisis during the 1930s and then to the war itself. A welfare system had to be constructed and in several countries only a strong national state was perceived to be able to guarantee that this project could be accomplished. Implicitly, eligibility to welfare from the state often required cultural conformity. Research and education were seen as decisive instruments in achieving this. Education was seen as an instrument for human development, as an investment for future production and citizenship competencies or both. The role given to welfare, education and scientific development varied from one country to another (Johnson, 1987; O'Connel, 1989; Therborn, 1989). The state and education expanded rapidly and in the North, secondary education became almost universal. The increasing complexity of society and a growing number of functions and tasks to be performed nationally, contributed to the reinforcement and centralization of the state. Both the world wars and the application of the Keynesian economic policies also were instrumental in bringing about a strong state. Economic, educational, and other types of policy had the national state, the nation and the individual as their points of reference and social (including educational) theories used the nation and its socioeconomic classes and individuals as their units of analysis.

When nation-states had been established, centralization started to take place. Not only state bodies but also companies and organizations went through this process. Thus, seen from a historical perspective, certain tasks and functions that originally were handled by the local communities were centralized and are now decentralized again. On the other hand, there are issues or functions that did not exist, when state apparatuses grew. They are the result of innovations and inventions implemented by the state and have never belonged to the civil sphere and the local communities (Cohen & Spillane, 1992; Svensson, 1981; Swanson, 1993).

The Keynesian approach applied in the political economy from the 1930s, was based on three principles: (i) the nation-state and a national economy; (ii) the organization of capital into large and stable firms that dominated industry; and (iii) the existence of a more or less determinate working class (Dow, 1993). All of these features are eroding due to the globalization processes.

Criticism of the state has always existed, and the modern state has been criticized from different fronts: liberals, marxists and anarchists (Curtis, 1981). The effect of globalization forces, the growth of the state apparatuses, the bureaucratization of society, and the fact that development in the South did not take place in a way hoped for contributed to an increasing criticism of the state in the 1970s. Various groups came to join in the attack on the state: neo-liberals who wanted to minimize the state and let the market forces regulate relationships between people, reformist socialists who argued for maintenance of the state but in a decentralized form and communitarians who wanted to base democracy and decision-making at the local level (Boyd, 1992; Chubb & Moe, 1988; Crowley, 1987; Curtis, 1981; Dougherthy & Sostre, 1992; Etzioni, 1995; Hunter, 1995; Johnston, 1990).

NATIONAL AND INTERNATIONAL EDUCATIONAL THEORIES

Social theories, including theories on education, were and are embedded in modern Northern thought. Taken for granted as units of analysis and policy-making are, crudely speaking, the nation, nation-state, national economy, national culture and the individual. National society and the individual (as a social and cultural being) develop through a long-term evolutionary process. Scientific thought differed as to the nature of society, the individual, and so on, but shared ideas were those of progress and increasing rationality (Smart 1993). Modern social theories are either consensus or conflict oriented (Cuff & Payne, 1979).

Consensus, Functionalism and the Rational Individual

Consensus and macro-oriented theories have at least the following features in common: (i) consensus orientation, that is society is held together and survives due to shared values; (ii) functionalism, that is the political system, the education system, and other institutional arrangements in society fulfill functions that are vital to the society and the individual; (iii) an evolutionary and modernization perspective in that all societies are perceived to follow the same path of development as that of the industrialized societies in the North, that societal change occurs gradually, and that individuals become more rational; (iv) focus on equilibrium, which means that societies tend to maintain a dynamic balance between different powers and interests; and (vi) the subjectivity of the individual, apart from the manifestations of rational preferences in the market, is not relevant for theoretical analysis.

Theories in this category are to a large extent compatible with or complement one another. Behaviorist theories and exchange theories in psychology and social psychology, for instance, are compatible with modernization and functionalist theories, rational choice theory and human capital theory (Bandura & Walters, 1972; Blau, 1964; Crowley, 1987; Curry & Wade, 1968; Homans, 1961; Inkeles, 1968; Parsons, 1964). Individuals are seen as rational and self-seeking in that they make attempts to gain rewards for as little effort as possible or to increase rewards through the same amount of effort.

Analyses of the state and education were born and developed in the North. Principally, the state was seen as (i) a pluralist arena for negotiation and maintenance of equilibrium between different groups in society or (ii) as an instrument for the ruling class in the capitalist society or an arena of class struggle. Some of the most common theories were:(a) functionalist/modernization analysis of education in developing countries (Coleman, 1960; Murray Thomas 1983, Parsons 1964); (b) the reproduction and correspondence analysis of education in the capitalist society (Bourdieu & Passeron 1977; Carnoy & Levin 1986, for instance); and (c) institutionalist approaches (Boli & Ramirez, 1992; Meyer et al 1997; Ramirez, 1992).

In the *functionalist theories*, structures and institutions, for instance, are assumed to fulfill functions that are vital to the maintenance of society (Nagel, 1961), such as: (i) adaptation; (ii) goal attainment; (iii) integration; and (iv) pattern maintenance (Parsons, 1964). Increasing structural differentiation and cultural secularization require a change from recruitment on the basis of ascription to recruitment on the basis of achievement. In order to function, modern society needs mass education and recruitment of individuals to societal roles, based on achievement and merit. That is, achievement leads to attainment of well rewarded positions. Intelligence and efforts are remunerated by merit (Brown, Halsey, Lauder & Stuart Wells (1997a, 1997b). Apart from this, education also creates common values, that is consensus, and contributes to social mobility.

Modernization means increasing individual rationality (Inkeles, 1968), mass participation in policis and education and that ascription is replaced by achievement. Education is the most important instrument for: (i) allocating the most talented to the most important positions in society; (ii) matching of educational opportunity to competence;

and (iii) making achievement (and not ascription) the basis of social inequality (Goldthorpe, 1996: 663) . Intelligence, whether it be inherited or acquired, plus one's own efforts equals merit. Inequalities are due to differences in intelligence, achievement or both. School education is seen as functional in that it provides the pupils with the competencies required, if they also make the efforts themselves. Society and school are meritocratic and it means that people are allocated to societal positions according to their merits (education credentials).

According to the *human capital theory*, formulated in the 1960s, education should be seen as a productive investment rather than consumption. Individuals invest in education because it is profitable. Such investments accumulate and raise national as well as personal income levels. For instance, Psacharopoulos & Woodhall (1987) have shown that (i) returns to primary education are highest among all educational levels; (ii) private returns are in excess of social return, especially at the university level; (iii) all rates of return to investment in education are above the ten percent common yardsticks of opportunity cost of capital; and (iv) the returns to education in less developed countires are higher relative to corresponding returns in more advanced countries (Woodhall, 1997).

The concept of meritocracy is based on the assumptions that merits derived from education lead to efficiency, justice, assimilation and democracy. Human capital theory takes a rather stable economy and labor market for granted. All these assumptions are also being questioned, as the concept itself is problematic and relative (Brown, Halsey, Lauder & Stuart Wells, 1997a). The merits derived from education vary with particular periods, conjunctures, and economic sectors. With globalization, uncertainty concerning labor market returns has increased and according to Brown & Lauder (1996), meritocracy might be regarded as a necessary myth.

Critics argue that social class still has a lot of influence on the type of schooling children receive and their level of academic achievement. Race, not only in the United States but also in other countries, can determine the type and quality of schooling offered children. It is not evident what proportions in the formation of intelligence that can be explained by social and economic conditions and inheritance, but it is clear that they play an important role. What pupils learn in school is conditioned by their class background. That is, the human capital acquired is not determined merely by schooling. Also, feminists see the concept of human capital as ahistorical and gender-blind. It does not differentiate between individuals even though gender makes a difference in schooling and human capital formation (Blakemore 1992; Parpart, 1988).

Globalization causes considerable change in national economies and national labor markets. Consequently, it has become more difficult than before for the human capital acquired in education to be appropriate in the labor market (Blakemore, 1992). At the micro level there is now a great deal of uncertainty as to the actual labor market requirements for technical skills, both on the part of the employee and the employer. Therefore, "employability" is probably the only requirement that can be fulfilled. The rapid changes of labor market requirements have perhaps contributed to the drive for lifelong education or lifelong learning.

Levin & Kelley (1994) argue that at the macro level, human capital theory assumes an essentially structural-functionalist view of the education-society relationship. It presumes a direct, linear and positive correlation between education and individual productivity, and between education and national economic productivity. In contrast to these basic assumptions, however, in reality such relationships are found only in certain conditions. To compensate for this weakness, human capital theory is now increasingly combined with studies of the formation of social capital (Coleman, 1988; Gopalan, 1997; Knack & Keefer, 1997; Schuller & Field, 1998).

Rational choice theory and *public choice theory* have their basis in classical economic theory. Individuals are self-seeking and attempt to maximize their own utility. When they calculate means and ends in terms of utility, they have to take certain "externalities" into account and the marginal utility of further efforts. When applied to the state and its policies, this analysis is often called public choice theory. Politicians and bureaucrats are assumed to act out of self-interest (to stay in power) and they have to calculate the support from voters, for instance, and gains they can make by distributing welfare strategically (Gallagher, 1993). Also, from the rational choice perspective, individual voting and interest group activity may be seen as a function of the gains expected from the political process (see, for instance, Downs, 1957). In their own interest, the holders of state office must also maintain and support the accumulation of capital because their position is dependent on the state revenues (Macpherson (1981).

This theory has been applied also in the education sector. Those who control the public provision of education or provide education make choices on the basis of (a) their own interpretation of public interests, and (b) their own self-interest (Brown, D.J. 1990; Gallagher 1993). Rational choice theory also assumes that teachers, school leaders and educational administrators pursue their own interests. It means, for instance, that teachers will not implement reforms if it means more work without corresponding personal benefits (Grace, 1997). Public choice theory has to a large extent stimulated educational restructuring, since this type of reform was expected to neutralize the vested interest and rational choice behavior of educational administrators[1] (Brown, Halsey, Lauder & Stuart Wells (1997a). Brown, Halsey, Lauder & Stuart Wells (1997c) make several remarks in relation to public choice theory. Periodic crises are endemic to the capitalist system. During such periods the labor market is in flux and, consequently, it is hard to see how this theory is able to explain or predict what is rational for the individual.

Teachers are assumed to be reluctant to expend extra effort to change their classroom methods for the better, without the prospect of immediate economic rewards. This assumption ignores not only the possibility of genuine motivation and genuine altruism but also the possibility that teachers are motivated by professional ideals. Another criticism applies also to human capital theory and certain groups of post-modernists. It is the failure to see the exercise of power in society as linked to the state, education and economy. They perceive social divisions and conflicts in society to concern not structures and macro power relations but merely individual actions based on preferences.

From a practical point of view, *empiricism*, that is the purely empirical research, does not belong to the category described here since it is not explicitly or deliberately linked to theories but its epistemological foundation is similar to that of the other approaches[2]. These studies have in common the following features: (i) they do not make any explicit reference to theories or theoretical concepts; (ii) they have to a large extent been in the service of the welfare state in that they either aimed at finding solutions to social problems or have resulted from commissioned research. Studies of this type have, however, contributed heavily to educational discourse and policy. Research on school efficiency and school effectiveness preceded the restructuring movement and lent some of its findings and ideas to this movement. Most of this research was purely empirical (Jansen, 1995).

The consensus analyses of the state may be called autonomist, since the state is seen as autonomous in relation to groups, classes and other collectivities. Since the beginning of the 1980s, the autonomist vision of societal and educational development has had a renaissance, although it has taken another form than before. The argument is, in short, that individuals are rational enough to make their own choices. When all individuals chose rationally, the whole society optimizes its resources and develops into a higher stage (Crowley,1987). Structural adjustment, educational restructuring and the introduction of multiparty systems in Eastern Europe and in many countries in the South are some indications of this vision. However, the aim of the changes is not more autonomy for the state, but rather to marginalise it and make it more dependent on national as well as global market and civil forces. Decentralization, introduction of choice and application of market forces in the educational domain are important ingredients in the struggle for more freedom.

All consensus approaches have been criticized for the remarkable neglect of power conditions, nationally as well as internationally. Neither are gender inequalities taken into account in this type of analysis (Kabeer & Humphrey, 1990).

Conflict, Collective Forces, and Critical Theory

Neo-marxist theories are the most important among the conflict-oriented theories. Neo-marxist theories differ from one another in two important dimensions: (i) the conceptualization of the relationships between economic, political, social and cultural instances (to what extent the latter are affected by the first mentioned); and (ii) scope of analysis (from the national to the global). As to the first dimension, economic instances, such as mode of production and class formation, are seen to either determine or condition the other instance; education, for instance, is an instrument for economic interests (Althusser, 1972). Thus, there are two strands in neo-Marxist theory: the deterministic (capital logic school, for instance) where state, ideologies, education, and so on, are determined by economic structures and class conflicts; and the relative autonomy approach, according to which these entities have relative autonomy. It means that they may appear as causes of social change and may also have feedback effects on the economy or are interacting with economic structures and forces (Held, 1994; Offe & Ronge, 1981). When the education system has relative autonomy it may function in ways that, at least for certain periods, contradict economic interests (Dale, 1989, 1997).

Returning to dimension (i), the scope of neo-marxist theory can be national, international (like imperialist theories and dependency theory) (Frank, 1969), or global (that is, one variant of world systems theory) (Sklair, 1995; Wallerstein, 1991). Internationally, the state in the periphery may be dominated and exploited by the state and capitalist class in a metropole (Baran & Sweezy, 1966; Frank, 1969; Shaw, 1985). In later analyses of the state, focus is directed upon (a) its position in the world system; (b) its degree of incorporation into this system; and (c) its internal class division (Higgot, 1986; Shaw, 1985, 1988). The African states, for instance, have a weak position in the world system, and their degree of incorporation into the world economy varies. Most of them are peripheral (Shaw, 1985).

In Offe's (1984, 1996, 1997) analysis, the state in capitalist society has relative autonomy. In his earlier writings he views society as consisting of three spheres or sub-systems: (a) the economic sub-system, (b) a political-coercive and administrative sub-system and (c) a normative or legitimation subsystem, that is the locus of socialization and the sphere where conflict and consensus processes occur (Offe, 1984). In a later work, Offe (1996) defines four societal spheres: material production, cultural reproduction, political participation and bureaucratic domination. The political-coercive and administrative system has been replaced by two spheres: political participation and bureaucratic domination. Politics thus may be seen to have shifted from coercion and administration to participation and domination through bureaucratic control.

The fundamental function of the state is to stabilize and protect the primacy of the principle of exchange relationships. Offe identifies three forms of intervention: (i) regulation; (ii) manipulation of fiscal resources; and (iii) the use of information and persuasion (Dale, 1997, 1999). The capitalist state is no longer characterized as an *instrument* of the interest of capital, an interest which is neither homogeneous nor generally understood (Offe, 1984: 51). Rather than being allied with capital, the state guarantees a set of relationships necessary for the maintenance of the present system of production. Due to corporatist arrangements and the need to maintain a high level of production, the state does not defend the interests of any particular class or group but the common interests of all members of society. However, it tends to favor certain key groups that are strategic in production.

The state has to provide the cultural motivation (the willingness) for the labor power to be willing to enter the supply side of the labor market. This is done through socialization, mainly schooling. Offe argues that the Western capitalist state is, due to its expanded functions, itself the source of its crisis: the state is now increasingly taking on the function of creating the conditions under which values can regain their function as commodities (Offe & Ronge, 1981:78).

Dale (1989) specifies the relationships between capitalist society, the state as a whole and the education system as one of the state apparatuses. Bodies that are publicly financed are state apparatuses in his definition. The relationship between different apparatuses may vary but all of them have to contribute to the solution of certain core problems, if they are to survive: (i) support to the capital accumulation process, (ii) guarantee a context for continued expansion of capital accumulation, and (iii) legitimize the capitalist mode of production including the state's own part in it (Dale 1989:29). Apart from these functions (or within their framework) the state is more or less autonomous in relation to the national society. It is, however, dependent on the amount of surplus value that is generated in the economy, and, therefore, the three core problems have to be solved in one way or another.

Bourdieu (1990) and Bourdieu & Passeron (1977) as well as Bowles & Gintis (1976) argue that education reproduces the class structure of capitalist society, although their emphases are somewhat different. The former emphasize the cultural aspect, while the latter emphasize the production skills and acquisition of class affiliated characteristics. Three different types of capital are produced and reproduced: economic capital, cultural capital and social capital (Bourdieu, 1990). Cultural capital is acquired with the values and cognitive patterns that children internalize from home and and other instances apart from school. They come to school provided with this capital (Bourdieu, 1993; Bourdieu & Passeron, 1977). In later studies, cultural capital has been seen to accompany social capital (Bourdieu, 1990; Brown, 1995; Lareau, 1987). Cultural and social capital are used in schools so as to reproduce socioeconomic structures. In the medium and long term, the cultural capital that the pupils bring to the school is not only reproduced but also converted into economic capital.

Some researchers who do not use conflict theory assert that education systems have adapted or been adapted to the economic characteristics and requirements of society. Goodman (1995), for instance, found that the school life has been functioning in this manner from the pre-industrial period and through the various phases of industrialism. Arnold (1996) argues in his analysis of post-Fordist production that an important feature among employers today is that they see a need for pupils who are trained in information technology and for schools and classroom processes that are organized along the same lines in the most advanced high-tech units in the sphere of production

Critics have argued that it is difficult to find a direct correspondence between educational processes and production processes. The educational system has a wide spectrum of activities and products than just what a limited sector of the economy requires (Dale, 1989). Reproduction theory does not make very evident what the schools do with pupils so as to reproduce societal structures. However, Apple (1980), Aronowitz & Giroux (1993) and others have developed resistance theory and demonstrate more specifically how the schools work in society and what is going on in the schools. Pupils' cultures correspond more or less with the culture of the school. For children with a culture different from that of the school, the fact that pupils act according to their home culture is perceived by teachers, school principals, educational administrators and others as resistance. It is through their resistance to the school knowledge and the ways it is distributed in the schools that pupils contribute to their own 'inferior' level of achievement in the school. For instance, lower class children and children of minorities tend to resist. The processes of sorting do not necessarily take place in relation to class characteristics; children of minorities may also make resistance to the school knowledge and the ways it is presented in the schools.

Another variety of the marxist theory was developed in Italy by Antonio Gramsci, an Italian marxist, during the 1920s. The concept of civil society, one of central importance in Gramsci's (1971, 1981) work more or less disappeared from the research agenda and later experienced a renaissance during the 1980s. In addition, the role Gramsci assigned to ideas (cultures and ideologies) makes him the first important proponent of the relative autonomy category of Marxism. Along with civil society, central concepts in Gramsci's analysis are state society, economy, civil society and hegemony. State society has a certain degree of autonomy in relation to the economic society. The same applies to civil society, which is a sphere that includes more than people's lives as producers, consumers and citizens. There are three sets of social relations of which civil society relations are made up of relations not dealing with production and the coercive relations of the state (Codd, Gordon & Harker, 1990). The class of capitalists may be able to establish ideological hegemony, which means that their world view is internalized by all members of society and becomes taken for granted. However, there is some space for beliefs and actions which are not determined by the dominating class. Hegemony tends to create counter-hegemony, which, for the sake of simplicity, may be seen as an alternative world view (including a vision of another type of society).

The *corporatist approaches* have elements of both the autonomist and instrumentalist theories and they have been used principally for studies of the welfare construction. Corporatism refers to a view of society "as consisting of diverese elements, unified into one body, forming one corpus . . ." (Held, 1995:64). The corporates have a "shared interest in the collective existence and cooperation expressed through the strategic exercise of power by a strong central state" (ibid, p.67). According to the corporatist analysis, the state makes efforts to incorporate the interests (such as those of employers' associations, trade unions or established churches) into the policy-making process, or at least to secure their loyalty to the decisions to be made. This is often made in the name of the national interest (Therborn, 1989; Waters, 1995). The corporatist arrangements tend to create alliances between the leaders of the big organizations and leading politicians. These top leaders tend to form an elite that is divorced from the popular masses of organization members or non-members.

It may be inferred from corporatist theory that educational changes of the restructuring type are less likely in strongly corporatist states than in other countries, because those groups, that were involved in the design of the educational system, also have a vested interest in its maintenance (Dale, 1989; Rust & Blakemore, 1990). That is, educational reforms were the result of compromises between the most articulate interests in the state

Critical Theory is another category of comprehensive theories. Its ultimate aim is not only understanding but also human emancipation (Habermas, 1971). Habermas, one of the proponents of critical theory, makes a principal distinction between the system and the life world in the capitalist society. The former consists of sub-systems (the economy and the political system, for instance) and it is characterised by purposefulness (technical rationality), while in the life world relations are personal, emotional and value-oriented. Due to features inherent in the system and its relationship to the lifeworld different types of crisis emerge. Four types of crisis are identified: system crisis (i) problem of economic surplus and accumulation; (ii) over-rationalization and identity crisis (iii) legitimation crisis, and (iv) motivation crisis. The economic system is constantly threatened by the risk of not producing and accumulating enough surplus. Legitimacy derives from the life-world. When people feel that they do not get what they deserve and when politics does not deal with value issues, people lose confidence in the system. Motivation (peoples' willingness to participate as citizens and producers) is created in the socio-cultural system (civil society and the family) but "used" in the economic and political systems. The role of education is to provide, for instance, motivation and legitimacy for the system.

The life world, on the other hand, is reproduced through the communicative act. Interaction is communicative action, which is governed by consensual norms that

define reciprocal expectations about behavior. The economy is dominated by the pur-
poseful-rational action, and this type of rationality enters into many other areas. Pur-
poseful-rational action also impregnates more and more the life-worlds, where values
and norms originally were predominant and guided action. Capitalist development
leads to an ever greater penetration of bureaucratic and administrative rationality into
more and more areas of life (Habermas, 1987). Since the life worlds are increasingly
rationalized, the ability to base action in a communicative platform becomes increasingly difficult. Habermas refers to this as the colonization of the life-world by the system (Norager, 1985:190ff.).

Different views on education emerge in Habermas' works. Education, like military
service, is an example of state intervention in the private sphere. Habermas mentions
education together with coercive means as both are means for influencing the voting
behavior of the people.

The School and the Subjective Individual

A third category of theories dealing with micro-macro and structure-agent are the phe-
nomenologist and interactionist approaches and the so called the New Sociology of
Education. Many studies of education during the 1960s and 1970s dealt with the relationship beween pupils' home background and their achievement in school. Functionalist and related theories, structuralist theories and empiricism shared this lack of
attention to the factors and processes in the classroom. In the end of the 1960s, anthropological and ethnographical methods and techniques started to be employed in school
and classroom research (Hargreaves, 1972; Woods, 1983). A group of British
researchers started in the end of the 1960s to analyze the relationships between societal factors, the curriculum, knowledge and classroom processes. The approach came
to be called the "New Sociology of Education" (see, for instance, Bernstein, 1977 and
Young, 1971). They saw knowledge as socially constructed and the curriculum as an
arbitrary selection of knowledge to be distributed in schools. What happens in the
classrooms is due to many factors, some of which are the frame factors (political, cultural, legal, and so on, regulations and control), teacher interpretation of the curriculum and the socioeconomic background of the pupils(Hargreaves, 1972; Woods, 1983).
The language is an important issue in classroom studies since it is linked to class affiliation of the pupils.

One group of theories in this category deal with the individual in his or her nearest
environment and their overall aim so to understand individuals´ behaviour and what
makes them construct the (micro) world in the way they do (Hargreaves, 1972). Inter-
actionists and ethnomethodologist have studied processes such as labelling and
stigmatization. Goffman´s (1961, 1963) analyses of "total institutions" and the
labelling theory is relevant in relation to the de-instutionalization that has taken and is
taking place in the educational domain. Institutions that are able to control most
aspects of a person's life are total institutions (hospitals and jails are two examples)
and, therefore, oppression, labelling and stigmatization takes place. Those who have
power in personal relationships or institutions are able to label others and treat them
according to the label. Therefore, ethnomethodologists suggested de-hospitalization

(de-institutionalization) of the patients. These concepts are relevant to education and educational research. In this context, mention can be made of Illich's (1971) arguments concerning de-schooling (abolition of schooling in its current form). Children should have the opportunity to learn without necessarily being taught by professionals in educational institutions such as schools.

Finally, mention should be made of Paulo Freire who became known worldwide in the 1970s and strongly influenced the debate on schooling and pedagogy. He is not easily placed in one scientific category. Freire (1972) worked with literacy program in Brazil in the 1960s. Individuals reproduce social structures by participating in them and by fulfilling their roles but could be active agents and transformers of their own realities if they become conscious of these structures and their own role in them. Pedagogy can, according to Freire, make the participants conscious of their situation in society and empower them so as to make them be able to liberate themselves not only from exploitation and oppression but also the "culture of silence"[3].

Although ideological and scientific perspectives on society differed in regard to the nature of society and factors that held society together, the nation, the nation-state, the national economy, socioeconomic classes and/or the individual were, until the end of the 1970s, taken for granted concepts and units in policy-making and research.

From the National to the Global, From Modernity to Post-modernity?

Internationalization and globalization, disappointment with the development in the Third World, the collapse of the Soviet Union, increasing economic competition and the emergence of the post-materialist philosophy, all contributed to a reorientation in social science. Indirectly or directly, two completely different types of researchers (neo-liberals and Marxist), contributed to the criticism of the (capitalist) state. The oil shock in the 1970s affected not only economies but also the collective consciousness in the North; a crisis perception emerged and there was a collective loss of self-confidence (Kumar, 1995). In addition, globalization, economic recession, the impact of mass media and the development of IT paved the way for post-modernist theorization. While human capital theory, rational/public choice theory and organizational theory have provided the theoretical foundations for educational restructuring and de-institutionalist theories contributed to legitimate shrinking of the state and large-scale bodies, neo-Marxist and some branches of post-modernist analysis have served the criticism of restructuring.

Kumar (1995) argues that the concept of information society fits well in the liberal, progressivist tradition of western thought. Some of the characteristics of this society and the changes in the world since the 1970s may be summarized in the following way.

  * The Cold War between the East and the West has been replaced by the United States hegemony and a large number of local tensions and conflicts as well as conflicts in which the United States is in struggling for Northern ideals against Islamic ideals. Economically, there is competition between the United States, Europe, and East Asia, and ideologically primarily between the United States and the Arab countries (Ahmed, 1992).

* Technology seems to have acquired a new function; it is no longer linked merely to production nor to consumption as they are traditionally defined (Kumar, 1995);

* National economic policies have been undermined and the economic nationalism abolished. The national unit as a base for economic activities and application of economic policies which are adapted to the global conditions, especially among smaller countries (Brown, Halsey, Lauder & Stuart Wells, 1997a);

* Democratization around that world in that liberal, representative form of democracy was implemented in many places and the discourse on human rights became a global concern (Bretherton, 1996b; Wilson, 1997)). Civil society and local participation are key features in policy and scientific discourse.

* Globalization and shrinking of the public sector threaten the middle class and make if feel insecure and uncertain (Brown, 1990, 1995).

* A contradictory process of, on the one hand, a decline of the family and its role in the socialization of children, increasing female participation in and increasing gender competition on the labor market (Carnoy & Castells 1995) and, on the other hand, an increasing role of the family in determining type of education for the children (Ball, Bowe & Gewirtz, 1995; Brown, 1990).

* The emergence of three driving forces, rationales or ideals: (a) the state/command/equality; (b) the market/technical rationality/efficiency/egoism; and (c) network/civil society/community (Barber, 1996; Dale, 1997; Daun, 1998; Thomas, 1994).

* Transformation or trivialization of key concepts: differences in power and class inequalities have become a matter of equity; class is being trivialized "to the point where it becomes parental attitude"; values have become an issue of preferences; cultures and lifestyles tend to become a matter of tastes and preferences; equality has become equity; work tasks are becoming skills (Brown, Halsey, Lauder & Stuart Wells, 1997c; Lauder, 1991) and socialization and recurrent education became "lifelong learning" (OECD, 1998b);

* Cultural issues have become an important theme in educational discourse and policies (Stuart Wells, 1996; West, 1990);

* A renewed optimism concerning education; it is seen as the key to progress. Education is perceived to be able to create greater efficacy and greater freedom. The World Conference in Jomtien in Thailand in 1990 became the event that finally and globally confirmed non-governmental organizations as legitimate receivers of aid and implementers of educational policies. This conference may also be said to have legitimized the liberal view of civil society according to which the market principles and economic agents are acceptable in the area of development assistance and aid.

All these features have changed the conditions for political and other ideologies, social sciences and education.

World Polity and National Adaptations

The institutionalist theory uses a world system approach (see Chapter One), utilizing the world polity as one of his key concepts conceptualizes the world polity as a "broad cultural order" that is highly institutionalized and functions as a model for all national societies. The world model prescribes the way of organizing societies (type of state, type of economy, type of education system, and so on) and how the relationships between different elements in society (human rights, citizenship, and so on) should be formed.

The national polity (or the social collectivity) is the largest social unit of a society and it constitutes the "political, economic and social system that makes the individual's activity possible, meaningful and rewarding" (Boli 1989:42). At the other end of the spectrum is the smallest unit, the individual, who had to be constructed during the nation-building period when the state was also constructed. As a new entity, the individual has to play specified and determined roles in relation to the polity. These roles are defined in terms of citizenship, which is membership in the polity, surrounded by a large number of rules and regulations that define how individuals and new units should be related to the polity. When the "old" states were constructed, childhood was also invented. Children had previously been seen as incomplete adults but now they started to be perceived more or less as *tabula rasa*. Schooling was the most important instrument in this construction of the individual (Boli, 1989; Fuller, 1991). By participating in the state initiated project of modernization, the individual contributes to the processes of individualization and atomization (Boli 1989, Boli & Ramirez 1992).

Today, the world polity, initially established in the northern industrialized countries, imposes on all countries an ideal societal model. Consequently, the institutions of the industrialized countries are taken for granted as models for organizing national societies everywhere in the world. The world polity legitimizes and justifies these institutions (Meyer et al., 1997). Despite the scarcity of resources, peripheral states endeavor to replicate the institutions developed in the metropole. This is made in the name of "institution building" and "capacity building". Fuller (1991) has the institutionalist approach as his point of departure when he analyzes primary education in Africa (exemplified by his observations from Malawi). He takes these views to their extreme and argues that primary education in Africa to a large extent functions as *rite de passage* to modernity.

New Movements, Civil Society and Communitarians

By definition, popular movements emerge from the grassroots. Collective efforts and actions that become permanent and institutionalized tend to take the form of organizations. Movements, on the other hand, are more flexible, less organized and institutionalized (Smelser, 1967).

The movements that emerged outside established institutions and organizations from the end of the 1960s have taken different forms: struggle for human rights and cultural pluralism, civil society, and human rights, creation of communities and adherence to post-modernist philosophy (Wilson, 1997). They are to some extent overlapping. Social analysis as well as policy-making also started to take the "civil" as their point of departure (Hall, 1986). This applies to both modernist and post-modernist analyses.

The New Social Movements

In the 1960s, movements started that did not accept the bases, goals and means of the established organizations; these had been formed according to class, religious, or other patterns. Many of the new movements (NMs) do not opt to create formal organizations with a broad, administrative structures, membership and membership fees, and so on. Individuals who have something in common tend to, tend to join the same movements. The NMs differ from the "old" movements in (i) social basis; (ii) goals; (iii) issues they promote; and (iv) organization and mode of operation. The NMs are often led by segments of the new middle classes and the well-off part of the working class but it is widely recognized that they do not have a class basis and challenge the primacy of the labour movement as a framework for progress (Darnovsky, Epstein & Flacks, 1995). The old movements often started as local movements, later merging into movements or organizations that were national in scope. The NMs are not always national but local or international or both (Etzioni, 1995; Offe, 1996). Many of the NMs came to follow a strategy including (a) internationalization, (b) community empowerment, and (c) participatory democracy. They established communities and demanded direct and/or participatory democracy. Participation in the new movements is not bound to ties of kinship or economic relations but is a non-utilitarian arrangement (Sturgeon, 1995: 38-39).

Many NMs focus on the rights of individuals. They tend not to make claims related to national citizenship, professional categories or market interests, though they may sometimes have ethnic "boundaries" (Etzioni, 1995; Offe, 1996) and they came to function as a platform for formation of identities that are not defined primarily in ethnic, national or citizenship terms, also in the South (Schuurman, 1993b). The right to choose one´s lifestyle (feminist, gay, ecologist, and so on) emerged as an important theme (Darnovsky, Epstein & Flacks, 1995: xiii). Most of the NMs accept society and do not struggle for revolutionary change. The fact that they are not interested in gaining power within the state makes them problematic and challenging for the existing institutions such as educational institutions. They do not have to be strategic and tactical in order to maximize support and can, therefore, raise deeply divisive issues and generate conflicts (Piven & Cloward, 1995).

Politics for them is about the capacity to participate and about life choices and oppotunities (Held, 1994, 1995). This refers to the potential to share the resources that are generated in a society. Participation requires autonomy and this is not only freedom from coercion, and is far from egoistically pursued material welfare, happiness, and so on. Instead, autonomy implies reciprocal responsibility, interdependence, and active trust (Giddens, 1994).

Cultural politics and cultural struggle are important themes for the NMs. The relationship between class, race, gender and democracy are highlighted, and the cultural struggle is, according to Brown, Halsey, Lauder & Stuart Wells (1997a:18), a "struggle over power to name . . . to create the ´official´ version of history and events". They find a gap in research on race and education and this gap is due to the distinction between (a) structure and culture, (b) macro and micro and (c) historical variation versus essentialism (McCarthy, 1990). Only theoretical frameworks that include both aspects will be able to represent cultural and racial issues in their totality.

Another matter is the relationship between culture and poverty. It is often assumed that "cultural deprivation" (low class or minority culture) leads to economic poverty. The argument from these movements is that equality and similarity have to be distinguished from each other. Equality has to do with material conditions and power, while similarity is a cultural (life style) phenomenon. Cultural difference should not automatically imply inequality, and equality should not automatically require similarity (Collot, Didier & Loueslati, 1993; Held, 1995; Meehan, 1994; Wilson, 1991).

McLaren (1997) is critical of the assumption made by some post-modernists and neo-Liberals that multiculturalism is simply a matter of attitudes and temperament and "textual disagreement and discourse wars". Mohanty (1997) criticizes the discourse of "harmony in diversity" and argues that differences are based on hierarchies. Her own studies in mixed schools show, for instance, how black pupils in the United States are expected to live up to and adapt to the white framework that stipulates how communication in schools should take place.

The critics of the new movements argue that activists of these movements ignore the questions of power and conflict which are important features of the capitalist society. The activists criticize "statism" but also take it for granted; they do not question the state and capitalism as such but see both as a necessary foundation for freedom and welfare *per se*. However, they do reject their extreme forms, such as a high degree of state centralization and alliances between lobbying pressure groups and the state. They fear elitism and tend to see the Keynesian approach as suppression of difference, individual rights and freedom. On the other hand, the state is seen as the only guarantor against the complete takeover by capitalist and market forces (Etzioni, 1995; Hunter, 1995). The NMs reject the idea of the "melting pot" in American minority policies since it implies homogenization of cultures. Instead, they argue for a "rainbow society" in which each culture has its place and its members are eligible to all the rights existing in society (Hunter, 1995).

Also, with the idealism on which a large portion of the new movement and communitarian activities are based, there is a lot of *ad hoc*-ism. The activities are maintained only as long as the stakeholders are directly involved.

Civil Society

Before the emergence of the modern western state, the kinship network, the local community and the neighborhood or village exerted a strong control over the individual's life. In several countries, both the community and the church dominated many spheres of the individual's life. With population growth, urbanization and industrialization, the influence of the church on private life decreased. At the same time other locally based forms of identity and loci of loyalty were weakened. This created space for civil society (CS). Segments of the population protested against the dominating religion, established own free churches and demanded civil and political rights.

The Western state was constructed before and during the period of industrialization. Popular movements, organized from the class basis, principally became interest organizations, while value oriented organizations emerged from the cultural-religious movements. The movements came to occupy some of the "space" between the individual, the economy and the state. The emerging working class did not have access to the state and the workers did not have any civil or political rights. They formed popular movements that demanded such access that substituted for the care they no longer received from the family.

Processes of civil society formation were taking place in Eastern Europe as well, until they were frozen with the installation of the Communist regimes: all civil initiatives were demolished or put under the control of the state and party. This meant that, after the breakdown of the Communist system, civil society as it is generally defined was very weak in these countries and had to be reconstructed (Misztal, 1995).

The type of popular movements and interest organizations that for a long time had existed in the North, and they were exported by the colonial powers to the South. In many countries in the South, the state established by the colonial powers continued to exist after independence. At the same time, the individual continued to be controlled by the kinship network, on the one hand, and by the state, on the other. The state made efforts to get more control, and some states attempted to attain a hegemonic position from which they would be able to secure complete control over the individual's life. The new independent governments established after the colonial period tended to view popular movements and organizations with suspicion (Krugman, 1995). Tripp (1994:163) even argues that (in Tanzania) "after independence, the state gradually harassed, coopted, absorbed or eliminated autonomous organizations . . . ".

Later it became evident that in most countries in the South the state was not able to stimulate economic growth nor to improve the welfare of the masses. From the end of the 1980s, and in the wake of the liberalizations, people in the South came to protest and organize in ways different from before. A large number of governments collapsed during the early 1990s. Most of them had implemented structural adjustment programs that severely hit the urban populations. Since the masses did not have access to the state and could articulate their interests through political parties, organizations, and so on, people demonstrated in the streets.

These processes have resulted in the creation of thousands of voluntary organizations which in most definitions of CS constitute its core (Saine, 1995). The processes described led researchers to study the CS in the South (Africa, the Islamic world, China, and Latin America) and East Europe (Mardin, 1995; Misztal, 1995; Rothchild & Lawson, 1994; Wesolowski, 1995). CS became an important issue not only in academic discourse but also in practical policies related to development issues (Azarya, 1994; Bratton, 1994). Attention was directed toward the rules regulating the relationships between the state and society and the extent to which grassroot initiatives were possible to take, in order to achieve collective but not necessarily national development goals.

There is no commonly agreed definition of CS (Ahrne, 1996; Harbeson, 1994:6). The definitions differ as to whether the economy or "total institutions", such as the family and the clan, are included or not and different definitions have different implications for educational analysis. The perspectives on CS may grouped as follows:

Civil society as that which, together with the state, constitutes the national society. That is, the economy and the market belong to CS (Harbeson, 1994). Gellner (1994) perceives CS to be "a realm apart from the political . . . Civil society is based on the separation of the polity from economic and social life . . . i.e., the residual left when the state is subtracted . . . " (212). Held (1995) also sees CS as that which is not the state and for him it is "the realm of privately owned and voluntarily run . . . activities and political interaction which are organized by private and voluntary arrangements between individuals and groups outside the direct control of the state . . . " (p. 162).

These views may be called liberal since they also include the economy and the market. Individuals and associations compete with one another pursuing their private interests in various activities, and the state guarantees the conditions for these activities to take place. The market is the organizing principle of CS. The basic social units are the individual and the associations that the individuals form, which may be communities, friendship networks, spontaneous groups and movements (Ahrne, 1996). Individuals and associations are part of CS to the extent that they seek to take part in the activities by which society works out the "rules of the game" (Harbeson, 1994).

Green (1993) finds that competitive markets are necessary but insufficient condition for freedom. There are collective needs that cannot be satisfied by the operations of the market and the administrative system. The welfare state limits the space of CS by suppressing not only the incentive system for competitive markets but also "outlets for idealism, service and achievement" (4). Instead of being an institution for individuals, the state uses individuals as instruments. Green rejects economic rationality as a guiding principle for behaviour and interaction and argues that it can not substitute morals. Common institutions are necessary not least for the support of moral values. In this context, the family is a crucial institution since it is the most important body for transmitting moral values.

In the second perspective, the segment of society situated between the state and the family and interacts with the state is CS (Azarya, 1994). It is a relational rather than locational concept. Azarya excludes many associations and groups from CS: those that are private, those that are holistic or totalistic and attempt to substitute or capture the state and exert ultimate control over the individual. Such a definition of CS excludes any type of fundamentalist movement. (These delimitations are not explicitly mentioned in the first mentioned perspective). In this view, too, the market is included in CS.

A third view posits society consists of three spheres: the state, the market and CS. CS is thus more restricted; it is situated between the state and the economy (Krugman, 1995; Pérez-Díaz, 1995). Barber (1996) adheres to this view: "Civil society or civic space occupies the middle ground between government and the private sector. It is the space that we occupy when we are engaged neither in government . . . nor in commerce" (271). It is public without being coercive and it is voluntary without being privatized. It includes what is public or of common concern.

The neo-Marxist view of CS also belongs to this category; CS is seen as a mediator between the state and the economy. It influences the policies of the state, economic policies included, but at the same time it is essential in the capitalist process because it is the locus of the reproduction of the labor force.

Most of the definitions of CS assume (a) non-totalistic associations, (b) individual autonomy, and (c) a particular type of interaction between the state and the society over which it rules. The first point means that CS associations do not and cannot claim total control over or adherence/support from the individual, who chooses to become a member and remains on a voluntary basis. Membership in totalistic collectives, such as families and clans, instead, is ascribed and total. Therefore, such collectives are excluded from the established visions of CS. The second condition, individual autonomy, is taken for granted in the North, but it is not always fulfilled in the countryside in the South (Reisman, 1990; Shweder & Bourne, 1984). Thirdly, the relationships that came to be established in the North between associations or organizations and the state are the ones seen as necessary for CS to emerge. These three features developed in pluralistic and liberal democracies in the North (Beckman, 1992).

The concept of CS is undifferentiated because it is based on the idea of the individual. The individual has no gender, no age, or any other concrete characteristics. In this respect, the CS view of society is similar to that of the neo-Liberals. Tripp (1994) criticizes this view for treating CS as undifferentiated (in relation to class and gender) and for neglecting the effects of gender division of work in the family. The civil society perspective has also been critized for being naîve, romantic and consensus-oriented. Bangura & Gibbon (1991:21), for instance, argue that "Everything in civil society is not democratic. The romantic attribution of essentially democratic and egalitarian properties to both the informal sector and (especially) civil society tends to further downplay the ambivalence of many of the characteristics of the latter in Africa. Life in an African village is, according to Éla (1990:133) "not only a life of solidarity within the framework of age classes, lineages, families, and gender"; it is also characterized by contradictions and conflicts. Also, Harbeson (1994) warns that the liberal view may reduce CS to what is the market.

Communitarianism

The basic communitarian idea is that the individual in the North once belonged by birth to his/her community. Each community formed an organic whole, implying control and pressure to conform but also support networks (Barber, 1996). Such conditions of life are now lost and have been substituted by a direct "contract" between the individual and the state (Etzioni, 1995; McCarthy *et al.*, 1981).

A community, in the traditional sense of the word, is the people within a given geographical area and within a nation. Each person identifies with the group within this area. A nation is a community to the extent that national identity and national citizenship are a high priority (Miller, 1989). However, in some of the more recent versions of communitarianism, the criterion of a common geographical location is not important. Instead, people around the world might have something else in common and form communities on the basis of this (Offe, 1996).

Traditional communities differ from voluntary associations, since they are the ones where people were born, or are related by religion or family, and are totalisic. They give meaning to life exactly because they are not chosen and they can be physically and psychologically coercive. Before the second World War, communitarians in the United

States, for instance, wanted to reconstruct the traditional communities.[4] More recent communitarians want to construct at least the spirit of the old communities. Etzioni (1995:254) argues that "The basic communitarian quest for balances between individuals and groups, rights and responsibilities, and among the institutions of the state, market and civil society is a constant, ongoing enterprise."

According to communitarians, people who have something in common form communities. What they have in common may vary from "everything" to a particular issue (Offe, 1996). Wesolowski (1995) discusses the following types of ties between people: associative ties, communal ties, and communitarian ties. Associative ties, typical of Western societies, are freely joined and freely left. Groups based on these ties pursue interests and goals defined by their members. Groups built around communal ties are of a different nature because "the individual is born with them . . . Individuals are integrated into the group by a set of symbols, values and beliefs that produce a high degree of loyalty and devotion to the group" (Wesolowski, 1995: 111). Such ties do not easily allow for outsiders to become members. Communitarian ties combine characteristics of both associative and communal bonds. There, freedom of access to the group is coupled with acceptance of some fundamental values.

Something of a vacuum has emerged between the individual and the state. The holistic dimension of life that individuals experienced in traditional communities has been replaced by individualism and even atomism (Etzioni, 1995; McCarthy *et al.*, 1981). Certainly, it is important to have in mind that this is a Euro-centric view, and these conditions do not apply everywhere. Still today, in many places in the South, the community is more important than the individual (Mannin, 1996; Shweder & Bourne, 1984) Large scale arrangements and solutions create anonymity and alienation. What is needed, instead, is solidarity and a feeling of belonging. Individuals have learned to demand liberties and rights, forgetting their responsibilities in relation to others.

Waters (1995) distinguishes between two categories of communitarians: (a) the New Right (conservative), that is searching for an organic and integrated association between people who have many features in common; and (b) the New Left (the radical communitarians), according to which communities based on some common interests or common lifestyles form a basis for identity formation and democratic participation. The New Right stresses individual autonomy and the right to consume. They have a minimalist approach to the role of the state. The New Left emphasizes the empowerment of minorities, and the importance of environmental issues (Waters, 1995). They are critical of the neo-Liberal concept of freedom as something neutral and independent of social and cultural context. They see the common good as resulting from shared activities and transmitted values from which the individual derives his or her freedom and choice possibilities.[5] Freedom is linked to responsibilities and preferences are acquired in a context (Haldane, 1996; Kukathas, 1996).

The communitarians share with the neo-Liberals criticism of the bureaucratization that has accompanied the growth of the welfare state; it has become a threat to democracy. The intermediation of parties and parliaments, formally existing to serve the will of the people, actually obscure the effects of excercising democratic from individuals within that democracy. (Offe, 1996).

From an analytical point of view, the concept of social capital may be seen as central to the idea of community (Miller, 1989). Social capital as defined by Bourdieu (1990) and Coleman (1988) is essentially to have a network of mutual obligations, expectations, information, rewards and sanctions. Social capital may also be seen as a part of kinship and family. Schools that have a coherent "philosophy" or "ethos" and frequent interaction with the parents produce social capital. For instance, a study by Coleman (1988) conducted in the United States, found that the dropout rate was significantly lower in religious schools (regardless of type of religion) than in other private schools or public schools. He interpreted this as an indication of differences in coherence of the school and home environment.

However, "community" and "local community" have been used rather uncritically for implementation of educational policies in the South. It is not always clear what a local community includes and what characteristics it has (Bray 1998; Durston & Nashire 1998; Rawlings, 1999; Rowley, 1999; Tikly 1998).

Feminist Theories

Feminism as a movement has a long tradition, but with the increase of female participation in education and the labor market, it expanded and was radicalized. Weiner (1994) classifies the following types of feminist theory: liberal, marxist, radical, psychoanalytic, socialist, existentialist and postmodern. They differ in their view on the relationships between class, race, gender and patriarchy. With the influence from the new movements the issues of culture and identity contributed to a further differentiation, resulting in: Christian feminism, humanist feminism, Muslim feminism, eco-feminism, and so on.

In feminist theory, gender inequalities are not a matter of biology (as assumed by conservatives and some neo-Liberals), preferences or tastes (as assumed in neo-Liberal theories) nor of class divisions alone (as assumed in neo-Marxist theories), but rather the result of the reproduction of the institutionalized patriarchy (Connel, 1993; Weiner, 1994; West, 1990). This patriarchy impregnates all spheres of society, including the state (Stromquist, 1995, 1998).

The cultural politics of the new movements came to include criticism of "the mainstream (or *male*stream)" (Blakemore, 1992), the white and male European and North American syndrome. The feminist movement acts in three areas against this syndrome: intellectually (how to think about representational practices in terms of history, culture and society), existentially (how they live) and politically.

Connel (1993) has studied masculinity and argues that masculinity has to be seen in its institutional context: state, workplace, labor market, and family and that cultural forms cannot be abstracted from sexuality. Gender inequalities existed historically and they do not not cease with the shift from modernity to postmodernity. Many feminists had rejected the theoretical frameworks established principally by male researchers already before the emergence of post-modernism (Stromquist, 1995). For instance, they rejected the view that development takes place in an evolutionary and linear fashion. Therefore, according to Giroux (1997:119), "post-modern feminism rejects the opposition between modernism and post-modernism in favor of a broader theoretical attempt to situate both discourses critically within a feminist political project . . . "

Feminist critiques of two dominant theoretical frameworks—human capital theory and neo-Marxist theory—may be summarized in the following way. Human capital theory argues that it is inefficient and irrational not to consider female labor just because it is female, but at the same time this theory assumes that individuals are equal actors and that "women's lower economic rewards are a consequence of individual 'choice' not to invest in longer periods of training" (Blakemore, 1992:226). It ignores the sexual division of labor, and obligations and responsibilities within, as well as outside, the markets.

Labor markets, especially those affected directly by globalization, have an increasing need for social competence that women possess, but according to Blakemore (1992:235), their qualities have "now been 'co-opted' for managerialist ends." That is, female social competence is used as an instrument in the struggle for competitiveness and profit maximization. Neo-Marxist theory is criticized for not giving sufficient attention to the male reproduction of cultural capital and patriachical structures.

According to Giroux (1997), both types of theories are also criticized by feminists for the fact that they do not take into account that education systems are still run according to the Fordist model, with its hierarchies and discrimination along gender dimensions. A reformulation of the "knowledge-as-accumulated-capital" model is required. Education should instead link to history and be based on the subjective construction of knowledge (Mohanty, 1997). Since inequalities (according to class, gender, race, and so on) continue to be reproduced in schools, some feminists argue for single-sex schools.

During the 1970s and first half of the 1980s, literacy programs for women were often based on marxist feminism, especially in Latin America; women should be empowered to emancipate themselves from the male-dominated capitalist system. However, many of the literacy programs changed in the mid-1980s and took on a utilitarian dimension; literacy should make women more productive and competent as citizens (Hee Pedersen, 1988, 1997).

Post-modernity and Postmodernism

Whether or not the technologically and economically most advanced societies have left the capitalist-industrialist stage and entered a stage of "late capitalism", "post-industrialism" or, even another type of society (a post-modern society) distinct from the capitalist society (Bell, 1978; Giddens, 1994; Smart, 1993). According to Habermas (1987), we are still in a modern society and modernity has itself a counter-discourse that rejects the characteristics of modernity. The problem is not reason in itself but the dominance of a one-sided reason—the technical rationality. Lash (1990) views post-industrialism as a property of the capitalist society and post-modernism as a cultural phenomenon. In Robertson's (1991) view, post-modernism is "an intellectual standpoint in response to a globalization process which relativizes the West . . ." (p. 289). It is a reaction against the rationalization of life and established constructions such as political parties, ideologies, scientific paradigms, and so on. Brown, et al (1997a:13) see post-modernism as "a loosely textured set of theories" according to which great emphasis is placed on "significance of images, signs and language in the constitution of the self and society."

If, on the other hand, the technologically advanced societies have entered into a new and different phase of development, as some post-modernists argue, society is a post-modern society and post-modernity is the conditions and characteristics of this society. Post-modernism is the philosophical/theoretical/ideological way of perceiving and analyzing this type of society (Best, 1994; Kenway, 1997; Kumar, 1995). Smart (1993) employs the term post-modernity on conditions or characteristics of contemporary society and reserves the term post-modernism for the social, aesthetic, scientific, and so on, perspectives that reject the scientific paradigms that had been constructed up to the 1970s.

It is a fragmented, pluralist, and highly individualistic information society in which the local is linked to the global. Mass media, mass communication, signs and symbols play an important role in everyday life of individuals (Kumar, 1995). Globalization processes and increasing individualization and secularization have dissolved the old order and created uncertainty and anxiety; therefore, past time solutions and large scale arrangements cannot be trusted any longer (Smart 1993). Differentiation has taken place not only structurally and functionally in society but also in knowledge and science: differentiation between the aesthetic realm, the theoretical realm and the moral-political realm, and between and within scientific disciplines (Habermas, 1971; Lash, 1990).

Generally, post-modernism is a break with Enlightenment's universalism and meta-narratives, generalizations and rationality, its totalizing methodologies and its humanistic theories that anchor knowledge in a rational consciousness (Best, 1994:27). There are, then, different post-modernist approaches. In his early works, Focault (1970:342-343) argues that "it is not man, the 'knowing subject' who should be the ground of the human sciences; what needs to be studied are the discursive practices of the human sciences that constitute and construct man". According to the deconstructionist branch, language, discourse, power and subjectivity go together, and, therefore, it is sufficient to analyze discourse. On the other hand, there are post-modernists who emphasize the subjective agent in the context of "structured" hierarchies conditioned by race and class.

Some of the differences between modernism and modern life, on the one hand, and post-modernism and post-modern life, on the other hand, may be summarized in the following way.

Object of experience/perception consists of symbols and representations

Most social theories today attribute an important role to media and mass communication (Kumar, 1995). In individuals' everyday lives, images and commerce are omnipresent (Kenway 1995:138). According to Baudrillard, culture no longer reflects the signifieds but the signifier; that is, culture does not mirror direct experience but rather symbols which do not have localized meanings (Blake et al, 1998; Doyal &

Gough, 1991). Reality is "hyper-real"; a reality which is to an increasing extent "represented" by mass media and IT; it is "a world of simulation." In hyper-reality it is no longer possible to distinguish the imaginary from the real, the signifier from the signified, the true from the false. The world of simulation is a world of *simulacra*, of images (Dickens & Fontana, 1994).

Deconstruction of meta-narratives

The relationships between science, politics and art that are said to have existed before the Renaissance are re-established. De-differentiation is merging of features differentiated through the process of modernization, and according to Lash (1990), post-modernism implies de-differentiation of the three realms mentioned above (the aesthetic realm is colonizing the other realms). It means, for instance, that social analysis does not have to follow the rules and criteria for truthfulness, and verifiability, and so on, that were established in the research community from the Enlightenment forward (Norager, 1985). Existing theories and ideologies are seen not to correspond to the perceptions and values of individuals but are "meta-narratives" or "grand narratives", that is constructions intended for control of the individuals. Post-modernism, thus, rejects totalities or 'meta-narratives' (scientific paradigms and disciplines, political ideologies, capitalism, colonialism, and patriarchy). Feminist post-modernists add "white, male, metropolitan knowledge" to the list of meta-narratives (Blake et al, 1998; Kenway, 1995).

The process of deconstruction of meta-narratives is accompanied by a new interest in differences, particularities, localities, local traditions, and so on. Kumar (1995) finds a common denominator among the post-modernists in the focus on fragmentation and pluralism, and the absence of any centralizing or 'totalizing' force . . . Science functions for control and oppression and in this context McLaren (1997:522) makes the comment that "some of the most painful lessons provided by post-modern criticism have been that a teleological and totalizing view of scientific progress is anipathetic to liberation. . . . "

The irrational and the rational

Rationalization, a concept criticized by post-modernists, goes back to Weber. According to him, technical rationality accompanies the capitalist development and is gaining position (Gerth & Mills, 1974). The spread and penetration of technical rationality has been further analyzed by Habermas (1971) who argues that the purposeful (technical) rationality is invading every space of the individual's life. Post-modernists reject the rationalization of society as well as Habermas's idea that we can create a 'communicative rational' consensus through a dialogue and in this way achieve human emancipation. Post-modernism is, according to Ashley (1994) "a catastrophic *reversal* of Weber's thesis of rationalization." In the post-modernist view, the "over-rationalized" capitalist societies face the challenge of peoples' desires and meanings, which do not derive from or follow this technological rationality and scientific postulates. The capitalist and bureaucratic society is, thus, irrational and distorts the rationality that emanates from genuine human needs. Lash (1990) argues that in the beginning of the twentieth century, the irrational came primarily from the Freudian primary processes (the unconscious and that which mainly belongs to the Id): "A half century later, the problematization of the real comes not from the depths of the id but from a society whose very surface, whose very empirical reality, is largely made up of images or representations (p. 13)."

Power and language

In Foucault's (1981) view, knowledge is linked to power, and truth is, more or less, what we define it to be: "truth is to be understood as a system of ordered procedures for the production, regulation, distribution, inculcation and operation of statements" (131). Foucault's approach allows for studying the exercise of power at the molecular level (Best, 1994).

In the light of globalization processes, the national society and the nation-state are questioned as appropriate not only as a unit of analysis in social science but also as a principle for the organization of individuals' lives and activities (Sklair, 1995). The state is questioned as a social and political phenomenon but also an object for theorization.

Post-colonialism is sometimes seen as a variety of post-modernist thought among people of color in their struggle for power to name, to represent common sense, to create the 'official' version of history and events.

Post-modernisms

There are different perspectives within the post-modernist philosophy and analysis (Blake et al 1998:59). Kumar (1995) distinguishes between: (i) deconstructionism; and (ii) post-structuralism. The first focuses on symbols and discourse, is supportive of market governance, and is consumer-oriented and highly individualist. Politics is textual and discursive. This category of post-modernism can "lead post-modern theorists towards a radical individualism, not easily distinguishable from the individualism of contemporary radical right" (Kumar 1995:104). Blake et al (1998), Jenkins (1995) and Schuurmann (1993b) consider this to be nihilism. The post-structuralists, on the other hand, tend to perceive hierarchies (classes, power, patriarchy, and so on) and individuals' lives as conditioned by these.

As far as education is concerned, some post-modernists and adherents to the new social movements argue that there are crucial links between security of cultural identity, self-esteem and educational performance. Children will feel more secure and achieve better if their culture is recognized in school and if it is the point of departure for teaching, evaluation of performance, and so on. Only critical and individualized pedagogy can achieve this (Giroux, 1997). Education can not and should not be the rationalization of man.

Post-modernism has been criticized principally for neglecting 'hard' social and economic structures and class differences and for giving too much importance (in their analysis) to either the individual agent or discourse. One of the critics, Apple (1993:599), argues that "the fact that class does not explain all does not excuse to deny its power." Also, the fact that people do not construct their identities solely or principally on the basis of class affiliation does not mean that their life conditions are not affected by this affiliation. Neither does it mean that social classes have disappeared. The extreme relativism in postmodernism ("there is no truth", "knowledge is private", "there is no self", "there is no trust", and so on) has also been criticized by Blake et al (1998), for instance. They find it difficult to suggest any type of education under such circumstances.

TABLE 2.1 TWO PRINCIPAL TYPES OF POST-MODERNISM

Postmodernism 1:	Postmodernism 2
Self constructed in discourse.	There are no such things as self and consciousness.
Tends to foster radical-democratic and decentralized worker resistance.	Fosters subjects that are positioned in xed places and social hiearchies based on cultural objects.
Community governance, de-commo ed market.	Market governance.
Use value.	Promotes values of consumer capitalism inside the working class. Consumption of goods as sign values.
Vision: reconstruction of community.	Vision along the individual line.
Emphasizes distinction and hierarchy within a fragmented social order	Positively celebrates difference and heterogeneity
Post-structuralism (from neo-Marxism). Positions, hierarchies, subjects, cultures.	Deconstructionism (from French philosophers): Discourse. The subject does not exist any longer.
Resistance post-modernity: Sometimes also called critical postmodernism or radical critique-al theory.	Limited in its ability to transform oppressive social and political regimes of power.

Based on: Ashley (1994); Best (1994); Blake et al 1998; Jenkins (1995); Kautz, 1996; Kukathas, 1996; Kumar (1997); Lash (1990); McLaren (1997); Schuurmann (1993b); Tennant, 1998; Whitty (1996, 1997).

Finally, some feminists are critical of the fact that the post-modernist analyses and discourse have been monopolized by males and they wonder "why men have found 'the new gospel of postmodernism to be so significantly compelling at this current historical moment'" (McLahren, 1997:523).

Development Theory

Development theory and development policy were, until the first half of the 1980s, characterized by large scale models and projects respectively. They also tended to be state-centered. According to neo-Liberals and some post-modernists, the state had proved not to be able to be the motor of development. Neo-Marxists, one the other hand, argue that international capital had become global so that all players, in North as well as in the South are dominated or at least conditioned by the drive for profit and competition.

Large scale Keynesian and Leninist theories and policy paradigms have been criticized by "Southern" researchers (See, for instance, Escobar, 1997, and Rahnema, 1997), for their cultural insensitivity and linear view of development. Such approaches have been replaced by small-scale theories and policies inspired by neo-Liberalism, communitarianism and post-modernism. *Civil society, diversity, small-scale, NGOs, agents, empowerment, participation* and *entrepreneurs* became key concepts in development discourse and policy (UNDP 1990, 1991, 1995, 1998).

In an overview of the conceptualizations of development, Schuurmann (1993a) classifies development theories into three principal categories: neo-Marxist theories (dependency theory, modes of production theory, and world systems theory); neoliberal theories (classical micro economic theories); and postmodernism (neo-conservative communitarianism, progressive communitarianism and nihilism). He divides postmodernism into three branches. The two first correspond to the distinction between two types of communitarianism made previously in this chapter. The third, he finds, is a branch that is very much associated with the German philosopher Nietzsche.

Educational Research and Knowledge Production

During the "national" period of the industrial societies a great deal of empirical research was in the service of the welfare state. Yet the boundaries between and the functions of the policy province and research province were clear. Practically all research took place at universities, and basic research, for instance, had a distinct role. Now the position of research has changed. The increasing participation in post-compulsory education has resulted in a spread of scientific principles. Knowledge production increasingly takes place outside the universities (Gibbons et al 1994). According to Etzkowitz & Leydesdorff, 1998:203: ". . . The university and the firm are each assuming tasks that were once largely the province of the other. The boundaries between public and private, science and technology, university and industry are in flux . . ."

The New Knowledge Production, as it is designated by Gibbons *et al* (1994), has the several interrelated characteristics, a few of which can be mentioned. Firstly, it is cross-disciplinary; the relevance and validity of scientific knowledge is determined not only by scientific criteria but also by utility, marketability and reflexivity. Knowledge production becomes part of a larger process in which discovery, application and use are closely integrated (passim.). As a consequence, the "tradition of university-based research is threatened by the encroachment of industry and the profit-making mentality and values" (p. 76).

This phenomenon applies in particular to technology and natural science but similar processes are taking place in social (and educational) science. In the same way, the major international agencies (OECD, Unesco, the World Bank, for instance), like many NGOs, have established their own research bodies or hire researchers to work on problems defined by the policy-makers.

One category of researchers argues that policy-making and practice can and should be more based in and on empirical research findings (See, for instance, Wang, Haertel & Walberg, 1993), while another category is critical to this position (Kerdeman & Phillips, 1993). Additionally, there are diverse views when it comes to research methodologies in comparative education. However, studies more frequently than before combine large scale statistical analysis and small scale, case studies (See, for instance, Mitter, 1997).

Conclusions

Particular conceptions of the state and/or civil society influence the perception of education's role in society, especially in relation to the type of educational restructuring that has taken place during the past two decades. In a world of accelerating globalization, national societies are being transformed and educational systems adapt or are deliberately adapted to these changes. A large number of countries have changed their education systems in a similar way. Certain issues have been handed over by the state to economic and civil actors, while at the same time, state control and regulation have increased. Seen in this context, the modes of organizing educational systems seem to converge. Concepts, such as *public vs. private, the common good, the public good* and the *private good*, become problematic.

What is not public, that is belonging to the state sphere, may belong to the market but also to the civil sphere. The market and the civil sphere are driven by completely different ideals and incentives; the former by individual utility and egoism, the latter may be driven by struggle for autonomy and altruism. Secondly, the "common" does not necessarily apply to the geographical area corresponding to a nation-state; it may apply to a local, particularistic and sectarian group but also to a worldwide movement.

Educational restructuring may from the perspectives mentioned be seen as a response to the drive for global competitiveness but also to communitarian and post-modernist demands for local decision-making and autonomy. Educational theories are going through a process of differentiation, convergence and widening of the scope. Differentiation means that different theories and methods are used for different objects of research, while convergence is an increasing consensus—at least at the practical level—as to research methodology. Large scale and quantitatively oriented studies are combined with small scale case studies. Case studies and qualitative methods are probably employed more than ever before. The scope of educational studies more and more seem to include global or, at least, international aspects.

In development approaches and policy implementation there is more of pluralism than before. On the other hand, civil actors such as NGOs, are more and more rationalized; their actions and implementations are increasingly evaluated in terms of effectiveness and effiency and according to technical rationality.

Notes

[1] For instance, if parents have the opportunity to follow their self-interst, economic and technical efficiency will increase and there will be an equilibrium between supply and dermand.

[2] Research that is merely empirically oriented tends to produce what Merton (1968) calls 'empirical generalizations'.They have been given assorted names and include different aspects of research themes. 'Abstracted empiricism' is the term used by Mills (1967), while others use the term 'methodological indvidualism' (Nagel, 1961:535) or 'methodological empiricism' (Karabel & Halsey, 1977).

[3] Other ideas also questioning the institutionalized and structured schooling were presented by Maslow (1971) and Rogers (1969).

[4] This is to reverse the transition from mechanic to organic solidarity as analyzed by Durkheim (1978) or a return from *Gesellschaft* to *Gemeinshaft* as defined by Toennies (Collins & Makowsky, 1972). Robertson (1992) interprets the efforts of some of the new movements as a struggle for global mechanical solidarity/*Gemeinschaft*.

[5] The "common" does not necessarily apply to the national unit.

REFERENCES CITED

Ahmed, A.S. (1992). *Postmodernism and Islam. Predicament and Promise.* London: Routledge

Ahrne, G. (1996). "Civil society and Civil Organizations." *Organization,* vol 3, no 1.

Althusser, L. (1972). "Ideology and Ideological State Apparatuses." In R. Cosin (ed.) *Education: Structure and Society.* Harmondsworth: Penguin.

Apple, M. (1980). *Education and Power.* London: Routledge and Kegan Paul.

Apple, M. (1993). "What Postmodernists Forget: Cultural Capital and Official Knowledge." *Curriculum Studies,* Vol 1, reprinted in A. H. Halsey, H. Lauder, P. Brown, and A. Stuart Wells (eds). *Education. Culture, Economy, Society.* Oxford: Oxford University Press.

Arnold, M. (1996). "The High-Tech Post-Fordist School." *Interchange,* vol 27 , nos 3/4.

Aronowitz, S. & H.A. Giroux (1993). *Education Still Under Siege. 2nd Education.* London: Bergin & Garvey.

Ashley, D. (1994). "Postmodernism and Anti-foundationalism." In A. Dickens and A. Fontana (eds.). *Postmodernism and Social Inquiry.* London: UCC press.

Azarya, V. (1994). "Civil Society and Disengagement in Africa." In J. W. Harberson, D. Rothchild and N. Chazan (eds.). *Civil Society and the State in Africa.* London: Boulder

Ball, S. J., R. Bowe and S. Gewirtz (1995). "Circuits of Schooling: A Sociological Exploration of Parental Choice of School in Social-Class Contexts." *The Sociological Review,* vol 43.

Bandura, A. and R. H. Walters (1971). *Social Learning and Personality Development.* New York: Holt, Rinehart & Winston.

Bangura, Y. and P. Gibbon (1992). "Adjustment, Authoritarianism and Democracy: An Introduction to some Conceptual and Empirical Issues." In P. Gibbon, Y. Bangura and A. Ofstad (eds). *Authoritarianism, Democracy and Adjustment. The Politics of Economic Reform in Africa.* Uppsala: The Scandinavian Institute of African Studies

Baran, P. and P. M. Sweezy (1966). *Monopoly Capital.* New York: Monthly Review Press

Barber, B.R. (1996). "An American Civic Forum: Civil Society Between Market Individuals and the Political Community." In R. F. Paul and F.D. Miller, Jr. (eds). *The Communitarian Challenge to Liberalism.* New York: Cambridge University Press

Beckman, B. (1992). "Empowerment or Repression? The World Bank and the Politics of African Adjustment." In P.Gibbon, Y. Bangura and A. Ofstad (eds). *Authoritarianism, Democracy and Adjustment. The Politics of Economic Reform in Africa.* (Uppsala: The Scandinavian Institute of African Studies

Bell, D. (1978). *The Cultural Contradiction of Capitalism.* New York: Basic Books.

Bernstein, B. (1977). "Class and Pedagogies: Visible and Invisible." J. Karabel and A. H. Halsey (eds). *Power and Ideology in Education.* New York: Oxford University Press

Best, S. (1994). "Foucault, Postmodernism and Social Theory." In A. Dickens and A. Fontana, (eds). *Postmodernism and Social Inquiry.* London: UCC press.

Blake, M., P. Sneyers and P. Standich. *Thinking Again. Education After Postmodernism.* London: Bergin & Garvey.

Blakemore, J. (1992). "The Gendering of Skill and Vocationalism in Twentieth-Century Australian Education." *Journal of Education Policy*, vol 7.

Blau, P. (1964). *Exchange and Power in Social Life.* New York: Wiley.

Boli, J. (1989). *New Citizens for a New Society. The Institutional Origins of Mass Schooling in Sweden.* New York: Pergamon.

Boli, J. and F. O. Ramirez (1992). "Compulsory Schooling in the Western Cultural Context." In R. F. Arnove, P.G. Altbach and G. P. Kelly (eds). *Emergent Issues in Education. Comparative Perspectives.* New York: SUNY Press.

Bourdieu, P. (1990). *The Logic of Practice.* Stanford: Stanford University Press.

Bourdieu, P. and J-C. Passeron (1977). *Reproduction in Education and Society.* London: Sage Publications.

Bowles, S. and H. Gintis (1976). *Schooling in Capitalist America: Educational Reform and the Contradictions of Economic Life.* New York: Basic Books.

Boyd, W. L. (1992). "The Power of Paradigms: Reconceptualizing Educational Policy and Management." In *Educational Administration Quarterly*, vol 28 no 4.

Bratton, M. (1994). "Civil Society and Political Transitions in Africa." In J. W. Harbeson, D. Rothchild and N. Chazan (eds).*Civil Society and the State in Africa.* London: Boulder.

Bray, M. (1998). "Financing Education in Developing Asia: Patterns, Trends, and Policy Implications." *Paper presened at the World Congress of the Comparative Education Societies in Cape Town, South Africa,* July 12-17, 1998.

Bretherton, C. (1996). "Universal Human Rights: Bringing People into Global Politics? A In C. Bretherton and C. Ponton (eds.). *Global Politics. An Introduction.* Oxford: Blackwell Publishers.

Brown, P. (1990). "The 'Third Wave': Education and the Ideology of Parentocracy." *British Journal of Sociology of Education*, vol 11.

Brown, P. (1995). "Cultural Capital and Social Exclusion: Some Observations on Recent Trends in Education, Employment and the Labour Market." In *Work, Employment and Society*, vol 9.

Brown, P. and H. Lauder (1996). "Education, Globalization and Economic Development". *Journal of Education Policy*, vol. 11.

Brown, P., A. H. Halsey, H. Lauder and A, Stuart Wells (1997a). "The Transformation of Education and Society: An Introduction." In A. H. Halsey, H. Lauder, P. Brown, and A. Stuart Wells (eds). *Education. Culture, Economy, Society.* Oxford: Oxford University Press.

Brown, P., A. H. Halsey, H. Lauder and A, Stuart Wells (1997b). "Introduction to Part VI: Meritocracy and Social Exclusion." In A. H. Halsey, H. Lauder, P. Brown, and A. Stuart Wells (eds). *Education. Culture, Economy, Society.* Oxford: Oxford University Press.

Brown, P., A. H. Halsey, H. Lauder and A, Stuart Wells (1997c). "Politics, Markets and School Effectiveness." In A. H. Halsey, H. Lauder, P. Brown, and A. Stuart Wells (eds). *Education. Culture, Economy, Society.* Oxford: Oxford University Press.

Carnoy, M. & M Castells (1995). *Sustainable Flexibility. A Prospective Study on Work, Family and Society in the information Age.* Berkeley and Stanford: Berkeley and Stanford Universities.

Carnoy, M. and H. Levin (1986). *Schooling and Work in the Democratic State.* Stanford: Stanford University Press.

Chubb, J.E. and T.M. Moe (1988). "Politics, Markets and the Organization of Schools." In *American Political Science Review,* vol 82, no 4.

Codd, J., K. Gordon and R. Harker (1990). "Education and the Role of the State: Devolution and Control Post-Picot." In H. Lauder and C. Wylie (eds.). *Towards Successful Schooling.* London: Falmer Press

Cohen, D. and J.P. Spillane (1992). "Policy and Practice: The Relation Between Governance and Instruction." In *Review of Research in Education,* vol 18.

Coleman, J.S. (1960). "The Politics of Sub-Saharan Africa." In G. A. Almond and J. S., Coleman (eds.). *The Politics of the Developing Areas.* Princeton: Princeton University Press

Coleman, J.S. (1988). "Social Capital in the Creation of Human Capital." In *American Journal of Sociology,* Vol 94, Supplement.

Collins, R.and M. Makowsky (1972). *The Discovery of Society.* New York: Random House.

Collot, A., G. Didier and B. Loueslati (1993). "La société interculturelle: projets et débats: Introduction." In A. Collot, G. Didier and B. Loueslati (eds.). *La pluralité culturelle dans les systèmes éducatifs européens.* Lorraine: Centre régional de documentation pedagogique.

Connel, R.W. (1993). "The Big Picture: Masculinities in Recent World History." In *Theory and Society,* vol 22.

Crowley, B.L. (1987). *The Self, the Individual and the Community. Liberalism in the Political Through of F.A. Hayek and Sidney and Beatrice Webb.* Oxford: Clanderon Press.

Cuff, E.C. and G. C. F.& Payne (1979). *Perspectives in Sociology.* London: George Allen & Unwin.

Curry, R.L. and L. L. Wade (1968). *A Theory of Political Exchange. Economic Reasoning in Political Analysis.* Englewood Cliffs, N.J.: Prentice Hall.

Curtis, M. (ed.). (1981). *The Great Political Theories. Vol 2.* New York: Avon Books.

Dale, R. (1989). *The State and Education Policy.* Milton Keynes: Open University Press.

Dale, R. (1997). "The State and the Governance of Education: An Analysis of the Restructuring of the State-Education Relationship". In A. H. Halsey, H. Lauder, P. Brown, and A. Stuart Wells (eds). *Education. Culture, Economy, Society.* Oxford: Oxford University Press.

Dale, R. (1999). "Specifying globalization effects on national policy: a focus on the mechanisms." *Journal of Education Policy,* vol 14, no 1.

Darnovsky, M. B. Epstein and R. Flacks (1995). "Introduction." In M. Darnovsky, B. Epstein and R. Flacks (eds.). *Cultural Politics and Social Movements.* Philadelphia: Temple University Press.

Daun, H. (1998). "Conceptual Framework: National Society and the Globe." In H. Daun and L. Benincasa (eds.). *Restructuring Education in Europe. Four Country Studies.* Report No 109. Stockholm: Stockholm University, Institute of International Education.

Dickens, D.R. and A. Fontana (1994). "Postmodernism in the Social Sciences." In A. Dickens and A. Fontana (eds.). *Postmodernism and Social Inquiry.* London: UCL Press.

Dougherthy, K.J. and L. Sostre (1992). "Minerva and the Market: The Sources of the Movement for School Choice." *Educational Policy,* vol 6, no 2.

Dow, G. (1993). "What Do We Know About Social Democracy." In *Economic and Industrial Democracy*, vol 14.

Downs, A. (1957). *An Economic Theory of Democracy.* New York: Harper & Row.

Doyal, L and I. Gough. (1991). *A Theory of Human Need.* London: The MacMillam Press Ltd.

Durkheim, E. (1978). *Sociologins metodregler.* (Swedish Translation of Rules of Sociological Methods). Gothenburg: Korpen.

Durston, S. and N. Nashire (1998). "Community Participation in Education: Policies, Practices and Real Lives." *Paper presened at the World congress of the Comparative Education Societies in Cape Town*, July 12-17, 1998.

Éla, J.-M. (1990). *Quand l'État pénètre en brousse. Les ripostes paysannes à la crise.* Paris: Karthala.

Escobar, A. et al. (1997). "The Making and Unmaking of the Third World Through Development." In M. Rahnema (with V. Bawree) (eds). *The Post-Development Reader.* London: Zed Books.

Esteva G. and M. S. Prakash (1997). From Global Thinking to Local Thinking. In M. Rahnema (with V. Bawree) (eds). *The Post-Development Reader.* London: Zed Books.

Etzioni, A. (1995). *The Spirit of community. Rights, Responsibilities and the Communitarian Agenda.* London: Fontana Press.

Etzkowitz, H. and L. Leydesdorff (1998). "The Endless Transition: A "Triple Helix" of University-Industry-Government Relations" *Minerva, A Review of Science, Learning and Policy*, vol 36.

Focault, M. (1970). *The Order of Things: An Archeology of the Human Sciences.* London: Tavistock.

Focault, M. (1981). *Power/Knowledge: Selected Interviews and Other Writings: 1972-1977.* (Ed. C. Gordon). Brighton: Harvester.

Frank, A.G. (1969). *Capitalism and Underdevelopment in Latin America.* New York: MR.

Freire, P. (1972). *Pedagogy of the Oppressed.* Harmondsworth: Penguin.

Fuller, B. (1991). *Growing Up Modern. The Western State Builds Third World Schools.* London: Routledge.

Gallagher, M. (1993). "A Public Choice Theory of Budgets: Implications for Education in Less Developed Countries." *Comparative Education Review*, vol 37, no 2.

Gellner, E. (1994). *Conditions of Liberty. Civil Society and Its Rivals.* London: Harnish Hamilton.

Gerth, H.H. and C. W. Mills (eds.). (1970). *From Max Weber. Essays in Sociology.* London: Routledge & Kegan Paul Ltd.

Gibbons, M, C. Limoges, H. Nowotny, S. Schwatzman, P. Scott and M. Trow (1994). *The New Production of Knowledge.* London: Sage Publications.

Giddens, A. (1994). "Brave New World: The New Context of Politics." In D. Miliband (ed.). *Reinventing the Left.* Cambridge: Polity Press

Giroux, H. (1997). "Crossing the Boundaries of Educational Discourse: Modernism, Postmodernism and Feminism in the Age of Postmodernism." In A. H. Halsey, H. Lauder, P. Brown, and A. Stuart Wells (eds). *Education. Culture, Economy, Society.* Oxford: Oxford University Press

Goffman, E. (1961). *Asylums.* Garden City, N.Y.: Doubleday Anchor Books.

Goffman, E. (1963). *Stigma: Notes on the Management of Spoiled Identity.* Englewood Cliffs, N.J.: Prentice Hall

Goldthorpe, J. H. (1996). "Problems of Meritocracy." In R. Eriksson and J. O. Jonsson (eds). *Can Education Be Equalized? The Swedish Case in Comparative Perspective.* London: Westview Press.

Goodman, J. (1995). "Change Without Difference: School Restructuring in Historical Perspective." *Harvard Educational Review*, vol no 1.

Gopalan, P. (1997). "The Trust Factor in Participation and Social Education." *The Annals of the American Academy of Political and Social Science*, Nov.

Grace, G. (1997). "Politics, Markets, and Democratic Schools: On The Transformation of School Leadership." In A. H. Halsey, H. Lauder, P. Brown, and A. Stuart Wells (eds). *Education. Culture, Economy, Society.* Oxford: Oxford University Press.

Gramsci, A. (1971). *Selections from Prison Notebooks.* New York: International Publishers.

Gramsci, A. (1981). "The Prison Notebooks." In M. Curtis (ed.), *The Great Political Theories. Vol. 2.* New York: Avon Books.

Green, D.G. (1993). *Reinventing Civil Society. The Rediscovery of Welfare Without Politics.* London: IEA Health and Welfare Unit.

Habermas, J. (1971). *Toward a Rational Society.* London: Heineman.

Habermas, J. (1978). *Knowledge and Human Interests.* London: Heineman.

Habermas, J. (1987). *The Theory of Communicative Action. Vol. 2. Lifeworld and System: A Critique of Functionalist Reason* (Trans. T. McCarthy). Cambridge: Polity Press.

Haldane, J. (1996). "The Individual, the State and the Common Good." In R. F. Paul and F.D. Miller, Jr. (eds). *The Communitarian Challenge to Liberalism.* New York: Cambridge University Press.

Hall, J.A. (1995). "In Search of Civil Society." In J.A. Hall (ed.). *Civil Society. Theory, History, Comparison.* Cambridge: Polity Press

Harbeson, J.W. (1994). "Civil Society and Political Renaissance in Africa." In J. W. Harberson, D. Rothchild and N. Chazan (eds). *Civil Society and the State in Africa.* London: Boulder.

Hargreaves, D.H. (1972). *Interpersonal Relations and Education.* London: Routledge & Kegan Paul.

Hee Pedersen, C. (1997). *Recordando o futuro.* Lima: Escuela para desarollo.

Held, D. (1994). "Inequalities of Power, Problems of Democracy." In D. Miliband (ed.). *Reinventing the Left.* Cambridge: Polity Press.

Held, D. (1995). *Political Theory and the Modern State.* Oxford: Polity Press.

Higgot, R. (1986). "Africa and the New International Division of Labour." In J. Ravenhill (ed.). *Africa in Economic Crisis.* London: Macmillam.

Homans, G. (1961). *Social Behavior: Its Elementary Forms.* New York:

Hunter, (1995). "Rethinking Revolution in the Light of the New Social Movements." In M. Darnovsky, B. Epstein and R. Flacks (eds.). *Cultural Politics and Social Movements.* Philadelphia: Temple University Press.

Illich, I.D. (1971). *Deschooling Society.* Harmondsworth: Penguin Books.

Inkeles, A. (1968). "Society, Social Structure, and Child Socialization". In J. Clausen (ed.). *Socialization and Society.* Boston: Little, Brown & Co.

Jansen, J. D. (1995). "Effective Schools?" In *Comparative Education,* vol 31, no 2.

Jenkins, R. (1995). *Rethinking History.* London: Routledge.

Johnson, N (1987). *The Welfare State in Transition.* Brighton: Wheatsheaf Books

Johnston, B.J. (1990). "Considerations on School Restructuring." *Journal of Educational Policy,* vol. 4, no. 3.

Kabeer, N. and J. Humphrey (1991). "Neo-Liberalism, Gender and the Limits of the Market." In C. Colclough and J. Manor (eds.). *States or Markets? Neo-Liberalism and the Development Policy Debate.* Oxford: Clanderon Press.

Karabel, J. and A.H. Halsey (eds.) (1977). *Power and Ideology in Education.* New York: Oxford University Press.

Kenway, J. (1995). "Having a Postmodernist Turn or Postmodernist Angst: A Disorder Experienced by an Author Who is Not Yet Dead or Even Close to It." In R, Smith and P. Wexter (eds). *After Postmodernism: Educational Policies and Identity.* London: Falmer Press.

Kerdeman, D. and D. C. Phillips (1993). "Empiricism and the Knowledge Base of Educational Practice." *Review of Educational Research,* vol 63, no 3.

Knack, S. and Keefer, P. (1997). "Does social capital have an economic payoff? A cross country investigation." *Quarterley Journal of Economics,* vol 112.

Krugman, H. (1995)."Overcoming Africa's crisis: adjusting structural adjustment towards sustainable development in Africa." In K. Mengisteab and I. Logan (eds.). *Beyond Econmomic Liberalization in Africa: Structural Adjustment and Alternatives.* London: Zed Books

Kukathas, C. (1996). "Liberalism, Communitarianism and Political Community." In R. F. Paul and F.D. Miller, Jr. (eds). *The Communitarian Challenge to Liberalism.* New York: Cambridge University Press.

Kumar, K. (1995). "Post-Industrial to Post-Modern Society: New Theories of the Contemporary World." London: Blackwell, pp 1-4, 121-137, 172-178, 201 reprinted in A. H. Halsey, H. Lauder, P. Brown, and A. Stuart Wells (eds). *Education. Culture, Economy, Society.* Oxford: Oxford University Press.

Lareau, A. (1987). "Social-Class Differences in Family-School Relationship: The Importance of Cultural Capital." *Sociology of Education,* vol 60.

Lash, S. (1990). *Sociology of Postmodernism.* London: Routledge.

Levin, H.M. and C. Kelley (1994). "Can Education Do It Alone?" *Economics of Education Review,* vol 13, no 2.

Macpherson, C.B. (1981). "Do We Need a Theory of the State?" In R. Dale, G. Esland, R.Ferguson and M. Macdonald (eds.). *Education and the State. Vol I. Schooling and the National Interest.* London: Falmer Press.

Mannin, M. (1996). "Global Issues and the Challenge to Democractic Politics." In C. Bretherton and C. Ponton (eds.). *Global Politics. An Introduction.* Oxford: Blackwell Publishers

Mardin, S. (1995). "Civil Society and Islam". In J. A. Hall (ed.). *Civil Society. Theory, History, Comparison.* Cambridge: Polity Press.

Maslow, A. (1971). *The Further Reaches of Human Nature.* New York: Viking Press.

McCarthy. C. (1990). *Race and Curriculum: Social Inequality and the Theories and Politics of Difference in Contemporary Research on Schooling.* New York: Falmer Press.

McCarthy, R., D. Oppewal, W. Peterson, and G. Spykman (1981). *Society, State & Schools. A Case for Structural and Confessional Pluralism.* Michigan: William B. Edwards Publishing Co.

McLaren, P. (1997). "Multiculturalism and the Postmodern Critique: Toward a Pedagogy of Resistance and Transformation." (Reprinted from H.A. Giroux & P, McLaren (eds). *Between Borders: Pedagogy and Politics of Cultural Studies.* In A. H. Halsey, H. Lauder, P. Brown, and A. Stuart Wells (eds). *Education. Culture, Economy, Society.* Oxford: Oxford University Press.

Meehan, E. (1994). "Equality, Difference and Democracy." In D. Miliband (ed.). *Reinventing the Left.* Cambridge: Polity Press.

Merton, R. (1967). *Social Theory and Social Structure.* 2nd edition. New York: The Free Press.

Meyer, J. W., J. Boli, G. M. Thomas and F. O. Ramirez (1997). World Society and Nation-State. *American Journal of Sociology*, vol 103, no 1.

Miller, D. (1989). *Market, State and Community.* Oxford: Clanderon Press.

Mills, C.W. (1967). *Power, Politics & People* (ed. Irving Louis Horowitz, London: Oxford University Press.

Mitter, W. (1997). "Challenges for Comparative Education: Between Retrospect and Expectation." *International Review of Education,* vol 43, nos 5-6.

Mohanty, C. T. (1997). "On Race and Voice: Challenges for Liberal Education in the 1990s" (in *Cultural Critique*). Reprinted in A. H. Halsey, H. Lauder, P. Brown, and A. Stuart Wells (eds). *Education. Culture, Economy, Society.* Oxford: Oxford University..

Murray Thomas, R. (1983). "The Symbiotic Linking of Politics and Education." In R. Murray Thomas. (ed). *Politics and Education. Cases From Eleven Nations.* Oxford: Pergamon Press.

Nagel, E. (1961). *The Structure of Science.* New York: Harcourt Brace & World, Inc.

Norager, T. (1985). *System og livsverden.* (System and lifeworlds). Åhus: ANIS.

O'Connel, P.J. (1989). "National Variation in the fortunes of labor: a pooled and cross-sectional analysis of the impact of economic crisis in the advanced capitalist nations." In T. Janoski and A. M. Hicks (eds.). *The Comparative Political Economy of the Welfare State.* Oxford: Oxford University Press.

OECD (1998). *Education Policy Analysis.* Paris: OECD.

Offe, C. (1984). *Contradictions of the Welfare State.* Cambridge, Mass.: The MIT Press.

Offe, C. (1996). *Modernity and the State. East, West.* Cambridge, Mass.: The MIT Press.

Offe, C. (1997). *Varieties of Transition. The East European and East German Experience.* Cambridge, Mass.: The MIT Press.

Offe, C. and V. Ronge (1981). "Theses on the Theory of the State." In R. Dale, G. Esland, R. Ferguson and M. MacDonald (eds). *Education and the State. Vol 1. Schooling and the National Interest.* London: Falmer Press.

Parsons, T. (1964). *The Social System.* Glencoe, Ill.: The Free Press.

Perez-Diaz, V. (1995). "The Possibility of Civil Society: Traditions, Character and Challenges." In J. A. Hall (ed.).*Civil Society. Theory, History, Comparison.*Cambridge: Polity Press

Piven, F.F. and R. A. Cloward (1995). "Movements and Dissensus Politics." In M. Darnovsky, B. Epstein and R. Flacks (eds.). *Cultural Politics and Social Movements.* Philadelphia: Temple University Press.

Psacharopolous, G.and M. Woodahll (1986). *Education for Development. An Analysis of Investment Choices.* Oxford: Oxford University Press.

Rawlings, L. (1999). "School-Based Management Reforms: Lessons from Evaluations." *Paper presented at the annual conference of the Comparative and International Education Society, April 1-18, in Toronto, Canada.*

Reisman, P. (1990). "The Formation of Personality in Fulani Ethno-psychology." In M. Jackson and I. Karp (eds.). *Personhood and Agency. The Experience of Self and Other in African Cultures.* Uppsala: Acta Universitatis Uppsaliensis.

Robertson, R. (1991). Mapping the Global Condition: Globalization as the Central Concept. In M. Featherstone, (ed.) *Global Culture. Nationalism, Globalization and Modernity*. London: Sage Publications.

Robertson, R. (1992). *Globalization. Social Theory and Global Culture.* London: Sage Publications.

Rogers, C. (1969). *Freedom to Learn.* Columbus, Ohio: Charles E. Merrill Publishing Company.

Rothchhild, D. & L. Lawson (1994). "The Interactions Between State and Civil Society in Africa." In J. W. Harberson, D. Rothchild and N. Chazan (eds).*Civil Society and the State in Africa.* London: Boulder.

Rowley, D. (1999). "Social Capital and Education Reform: The Top-Down and Sideways Angles of a Bottom-Up Approach to Improving School Quality and Access in Ethiopia." *Paper presented at the annual conference of the Comparative and International Education Society, April 1- 18, in Toronto, Canada.*

Rust, V.D. and K. Blakemore (1990). "Educational Reforms in Norway and in England and Wales." *Comparative Education Review,* vol 34, no 4.

Schuller, R. and J. Field. (1998). "Social Capital, human capital and the learning society." *International Journal of Lifelong Education*, vol 17, no 4.

Schuurmann, F. J. (1993a). "Development Theory in the 1990s." In F. J. Schuurmann (ed.). *Beyond the Impasse. New Directions in Development Theory.* London: Zed Books.

Schuurmann, F. J. (1993b). "Modernity, Post-Modernity and the New Social Movements." In F. J. Schuurmann (ed.). *Beyond the Impasse. New Directions in Development Theory.* London: Zed Books.

Shaw, T. (1985). *Towards a Political Economy for Africa.* London: Macmillan.

Shaw, T. (1988). "International Constraints, Contradictions and Capitalism." In D.Rotchild and N. Chazan (eds.) *The Precarious Balance: State and Society in Africa.* London: Westview Press.

Shweder, R.A. and E. J. Bourne (1984). "Does the concept of the person vary cross-culturally?" R. A. Shweder and R.A. LeVine (eds). *Culture theory. Essays on Mind, Self and Emotion*. Cambridge: Cambridge University Press.

Sklair, L. (1995). *Sociology and the Global System*. Second edition. New Jersey: Prentice Hall/Harvester Wheatsheaf.

Smart, B. (1993). *Postmodernity*. London: Routledge.

Smelser, N.J. (1967). *Theory of Collective Behavior*. London: Routledge & Kegan Paul.

Stromquist, N. P. (1995). "Romancing the State: Gender and Power in Education." *Comparative Education Review*, vol 39, no 4 .

Stromquist, N. P. (1998). "Institutionalization of Gender and Its Impact on Educational Policy." *Comparative Education,*vol 42, no 1.

Stuart Wells, A. (1996). "African-American Students' View of School Choice." In B. R. Fuller, R. Elmore and G. Arfield (eds). *Who Chooses? Who Loses? Culture, Institution and the Unequal Effects of School Choice*. New York: Teacher College Press.

Sturgeon, N. (1995). "Theorizing Movements: Direct Action and Direct Theory in Cultural Politics and Social Movements." In M. Darnovsky, M. Epstein and R. Flacks (eds.). *Cultural Politics and Social Movements*. Philadelphia: Temple University Press.

Svensson, R. (1981). *Offentlig socialisation*. (Public Socialization). Lund: Liber.

Swanson, A. D. (1993). "A Framework for Allocating Authority in a System of Schools." In H. Beare & W. L. Boyd (eds.). *Restructuring Schools. An International Perspective on the Movement to Transform the Control and Performance of School*. London: Falmer Press.

Therborn, G. (1989). "'Pillarization' and 'Popular Movements.' Two Variants of Welfare State Capitalism: the Netherlands and Sweden." F. G. Castles (ed.). *The Comparative History of Public Policy*. pp. 192-241. Cambridge: Polity Press.

Thomas, H. (1994). "Markets, Collectivities and Management." In *Oxford Review of Education*, vol 20, no 1.

Tikly, L. (1998). "Redefining Community Involvement in the Finance and Governance of Education in Developing Countries: A New Role for Local Government?" *Paper presented at the World congress of the Comparative Education Societies in Cape Town, July 12-17*, 1998.

Tripp, A. M. (1994). "Rethinking Civil Society: Gender Implications in Contemporary Tanzania." In J. W. Harberson, D. Rothchild and N. Chazan (eds).*Civil Society and the State in Africa*. London: Boulder.

UNDP (1990). *Human Development Report 1990*. New York: Oxford University Press.

UNDP (1991). *Human Development Report 1991*. New York: Oxford University Press.

UNDP (1995). *Human Development Report 1995*. New York: Oxford University Press.

UNDP (1998). *Human Development Report 1998*. New York: Oxford University Press .

Wallerstein, I. (1991). "Culture as the Ideological Battleground of the Modern World- System." In M. Featherstone (ed.). *Global Culture. Nationalism, Globalization and Modernity*. London: Sage Publications.

Wang, M.C., G.D. Haertel and H.J. Walberg (1993). Toward a knowledge base for school learning. *Review of Educational Research*, vol. 63, no. 3.

Waters, M. (1995). *Globalization*. London: Routledge.

Weiner, G. (1994). *Feminisms in Education: An Introduction*. Buckingham: Open University Press.

Wesolowski, W. (1995). "The Nature of Social Ties and the Future of Postcommunist Society: Poland After Solidarity." In J. A. Hall (ed.). *Civil Society. Theory, History, Comparison.* Cambridge: Polity Press.

West, C. (1990). "The New Cultural Politics of Difference. In *October,* Summer, vol. 53.

Willis, P. (1977). *Learning to Labour.* Farnborough: Saxon House.

Wilson, R.A. (1997). "Human Rights, Culture and Context: An Introduction." In R. A. Wilson (ed.). *Human Rights, Culture and Context. Anthropological Perspectives.* London: Pluto Press.

Wilson, W.J. (1991). "Studying Inner-City Social Dislocations: The Challenge of Public Agenda Research." *American Sociological Review*, vol 56.

Wong, M.S. (1999). "Gender Equity in China." *Paper presented at the annual conference of the Comparative and International Education Society, April 1-18, in Toronto, Canada.*

Woodhall, M. (1997). "Public versus private education: Changing perceptions of boundaries and roles." *Paper presented at the Oxford Conference, Oxford University, UK,* September 1997.

Woods, P. (1983). *Sociology and the School: An Interactionist Viewpoint.* London: Routledge & Kegan Paul.

Young, M.F.D. (1972). "An Approach to the Study of Curriculum as Socially Approved Knowledge." In M. F. D. Young (ed.). *Knowledge and Control. New Directions for the Sociology of Education.* London: Collier-MacMillam Publishers.

CHAPTER 3

Conceptualization and Results of Educational Restructuring

HOLGER DAUN

INTRODUCTION

Educational policies have become increasingly uniform worldwide since the beginning of the 1980s. However, the extent to which they have been implemented and the results of their implementation vary considerably due to economic, political and cultural differences between countries. The restructuring reforms are, more than previous reforms, dependent on the response from people at the local level, that is, school directors, teachers, and parents.

In the countries where these reforms have been implemented, beginning in the 1980s, the response from the parents and students has been rather weak. On the other hand, a few parents can change the character of the schooling for a majority of children when they choose another school (Lauder, 1991). Educational restructuring came to be seen as more comprehensive and far-reaching than merely an additional species of reform, as a panacea for solving educational problems.

The concepts used in political discourse on and research analysis of decentralization/centralization, freedom of choice, privatization, and systemic reform are discussed in this chapter. The main patterns of research findings on the resturcuting of these measures will also be discussed. The findings suggest that nearly two decades of restructuring around the world have not improved student achievement.

BACKGROUND

Historically, children's education was a a matter for the family, the kinship group, and/or the local community. In several countries, education became a task for religious institutions, and during the nineteenth century, the state made education a public responsibility. Education was until then private in the sense that it did not belong to the state; it was decentralized and national curricula were very rare (Boli, 1989; Mallison, 1980). After the Second World War, economies were restructured in at least three ways: a transition from agricultural to industrial production and from industry to provision of service; from the 1950s to the 1980s, state ownership and regulation of economies increased, followed privatization, deregulation, and market pressures in the public sector; and companies and their subsidiaries were reorganized to become more efficient and competitive (Carnoy, 1993b; Hamilton, 1989). In the southern part of the world, educational restructuring has in many cases been a corollary to the SAPs (Graham-Brown, 1991). The educational policies that have been formulated in a large number of countries since the 1970s may be divided into: (i) conventional, piece meal changes;[1] (ii) single or combined restructuring measures; and (iii) systemic shift, which includes all restructuring measures plus other measures such as such as curriculum change, teacher professionalization, introduction of teaching based on constructionist psychology, and so on. (Murphy, 1991).

In the educational debate and research on restructuring, a common denominator is found in three principal types of change: *decentralization/centralization,* introduction or reinforcement of *choice, privatization,* or *systemic reform.*[2] Systemic reforms have all the ingredients mentioned, i.e. decentralization/centralization, choice, privatization, and a series of measures pertaining to the inner workings of the school and the classroom and student learning. (see table 3.1).

TABLE 3.1 STRATEGIES OF EDUCATIONAL CHANGE IN RESPONSE TO CHANGING SOCIETAL CONDITIONS

PIECE-MEAL OR CONVENTIONAL MEASURES	RESTRUCTURING	
	CHANGE IN GOVERNANCE, MANAGEMENT AND/OR OWNERSHIP	SYSTEMIC SHIFT (STRUCTURES AS WELL AS SCHOOL ORGANIZATION)
Budget cuts; increased efficiency (e.g. more students per teacher), quality improvement (e.g. teacher competence); more languages of instruction (curriculum flexibility).	Decentralization, including shift of finance; centralization of curriculum, assessment and evaluation; reinforced opportunity for choice; reinforced opportunity to establish independent schools; higher probability for formalized, institutionalized and surveilled lifelong learning. From proactive regulation to retroactive surveillance.	Restructuring measures and change *within* schools (e.g. way of organizing teaching, curricula, and pedagogy; teacher professionalization, change in grade division); performance-orientation; assessments. From pro-active regulation to retro-active surveillance.

On a general level, the policies with regard to these measures have been similar in most countries. However, there are considerable differences in the details. Systems that were intended to arise from restructuring sometimes existed in some form or were established historically, in many countries (even those that ended up restructuring their systems). Old ideas were presented in a new context and in a language different from that used before. However, three patterns emerged among countries: (i) the measures were dressed in the discourse and metaphors of the market; (ii) many governments, independent of political ideology, responded to the formulation of educational policies in a similar way to economic imperatives; and (iii) restructuring became somewhat linked to worldwide economic recession and competition (Beare and Boyd, 1993; Caldwell, 1993).

Educational changes have taken place in most of the countries in the world, but all are not characterized by restructuring. For instance, some Arab and Asian countries had not changed their systems in this way until 1996–1997, (Green, 1997b; Lee and Bray, 1997; Morsi, 1990). The countries that did restructure may have had the following motives: economic decline; decreasing legitimacy of public institutions; cultural changes; high educational costs; and declining performance of the educational system. In many cases these issues are intertwined.

The idea of decentralization has three main sources: the free market philosophy, the political-participatory philosophy and organization theory (de-institutionalization) (see Chapter 2). In the political participatory thought of the new movements, participation in organizational and political life is seen not only as instrumental but also as a value in itself (Etzioni, 1995; Held, 1995; Piven and Cloward, 1995). From a de-institutionalist perspective, institutions are repressive and, therefore, decentralization may be seen as a step in the direction of de-institutionalization (Goffman, 1963; Illich, 1971; Lewis, 1993).

CONCEPTS AND DEFINITIONS

The language of economics first entered into the educational domain with the advent of manpower planning and human capital theory. It was taken for granted in educational discourse and policies and this language became "part of a general ideology of progress." Economic thought and language thereby penetrated the educational domain (Cibulka, 1990; Hallinan, 1994; Johnston, 1990; Martin and Burke, 1990; Raywid, 1985). The term restructuring itself has been borrowed from economics. In education and educational research, there is no commonly agreed–upon definition and, therefore, researchers and politicians give different meanings to the term (Brown et al, 1997). This is partly due to the fact that the term has become an important instrument in political discourse and that various groups of people, neo-Liberals, communitarians, and so on, have adhered to the "restructuring movement" (Ball, 1990; Elmore, 1990; Henig, 1993; James, 1991; Papagiannis, Easton and Owens, 1992; Raywid, 1985).

All of the restructuring measures imply an essential change in strategic educational variables such as governance, decision-making, resource generation or resource allocation, and value orientation (Guthrie and Koppich, 1993; Papagiannis, Easton and

Owens, 1992). However, this primarily concerns structures and less attention is given to cultures, attitudes and classroom processes (Hargreaves, 1994; Marshall, 1993).

Cibulka (1990) uses "restructuring" in a very broad sense but focuses on choice. He utilizes 'parameters of restructuring' from which he derives *core restructuring strategies* and *ancillary restructuring strategies*. He finds four core strategies: teacher professionalization, school empowerment, high-order thinking skills, and dropout prevention. In the ancillary group of strategies he includes performance incentives, deregulation, and accountability reporting. A still broader view on what pertains to educational restructuring has been presented by Murphy (1991). He argues for the need for restructuring and includes almost all types of changes/improvements in the concept; from the application of constructivist psychological theory and progressivist pedagogy to organizational and structural variables of a sociological nature. His definition includes what might be called systemic reform.

In relation to educational changes implemented in the context of structural adjustment programs, ILO (1996:6–12) makes a distinction between between *competitiveness-driven reforms*, *finance-driven reforms*, and *equity-driven reforms*. The competitiveness-driven reforms are implemented in order to improve a country's competitiveness on the world market. Decentralization, centralization, improved management of educational resources and improved teacher recruitment and training are considered to belong to this first category. Finance-driven reforms consist of privatization, shifting public funding from higher to lower levels of education, and the reduction of costs per student. Equity-driven reforms are often targeted towards groups that are neglected or are more affected by the consequences of structural adjustment programs.

In the policy and research discourse, "restructuring" is used instead of "reform" but is restructuring something other than reform? According to Guthrie and Koppich (1993), a reform implies a shift in decisions, resoucres, regulations, and/or values; in the latter case, a shift in the priority given to the principal values of equality, efficiency and liberty. The term implies that *structures* are changed. Structures are relatively permanent and persistent features of societies and organizations. If restructuring is a type of change that affects the educational structures, it is what Fullan (1991) refers to as second-order changes; they affect *"the fundamental ways in which organizations are put together."*

DECENTRALIZATION AND CENTRALIZATION

From What Level to What Level?

Once nation-states had been established in the North, centralization started to take place in most countries. This tendency was then reinforced by the modernization project and the transfer from an agricultural to an industrial society, the application of Keynesian policies, and so on. In many countries, not only state bodies but also companies and organizations went through this process of centralization. Certain items and functions that are now being decentralized were originally handled by the local communities, but came to be centralized at the nation-state level. Others are the result of innovations and inventions implemented by the state, which have never belonged to the civil society or the local communities (Cohen and Spillane, 1992; Svensson, 1981).

In the 1960s, ideas about decentralization came from various factions, and policies of decentralization of the public sector were created in some countries during the 1970s, that is, before the restructuring movement. By that time decentralization was seen as a political affair and, in some countries, it was perceived as a tool for regionalization policies, that is a measure to improve the conditions in populated areas. Decentralization of welfare bodies to local units was decided upon in the 1970s in France, Germany, Italy, the United States, the Nordic countries and some countries in the South (Hall, 1986; Hanson, 1990,1995; Johnson, 1987). In Tanzania, for instance, it arose from the politics of self-reliance.

In education, decentralization started in large scale in the 1980s and it has become the most commonly implemented restructuring policy. Decentralization was to many a panacea (Morris, 1990). Its popularity, according to Slater (1993:176), is associated with educational finance, efficiency, accountability, effectiveness and redistribution of political power. Centralization of certain aspects has been implemented in a few countries that had a federative or other type of decentralized political structure, i.e. Australia, Canada, the United Kingdom and the United States. Re-centralization has been a measure in relation to problematic schools that were not able to manage when decentralization was implemented in, for instance the US (Walberg, 1998).

There is some conceptual confusion about various types of decentralization, and since countries differ in size and administrative structure, comparisons are not easily made (Winkler, 1993). In some cases, different terms are used across countries for the same type of decentralization and vice versa. Hansson (1995) makes a distinction between political decentralization and administrative decentralization. The former is the transfer of "political power for decision-making to citizens or their elected representatives," while the latter is "the transfer of responsibility for planning, management and the raising and allocation of resources from the central government and its agencies to field units of government" (Hansson, 1995:101). Three types of administrative decentralization are defined: (i) devolution, or the transfer of authority to autonomous units that can act independently; (ii) delegation, or the transfer of decision-making authority from higher to lower hierarchical levels; and (iii) de-concentration, or the transfer of work (but not power) from higher to lower organizational levels. Winkler (1993) defines deconcentration as delegation of decision-making and decentralization as decision-making for the local electorate, while Maro (1990:673) sees deconcentration as "delegation of administrative authority or powers within the government structure" and devolution as "transfer of political powers and functions from central government to local institutions at the district or lower levels." The type of decentralization is important since it determines whether or not a measure can be rapidly and effectively re-centralized. Delegation, for instance, is easily reverted to a higher position in the hierarchy, whereas devolution is not easily reversed.

Some principal questions have to be considered in studies of decentralization/ centralization: *What* level should have *how much influence, of what kind,* and *over which factors* (Elmore, 1993:51)? *When* and for what *purpose?* (Brown, 1990:31; Slater, 1993:183). These questions may be grouped as follows: (a) levels and kinds; (b) period of time; and (c) purpose. Some examples of levels of decentralization, logically and empirically, are given in table 3.2. In both New Zealand and Sweden, for instance, decentralization took place from the national level down to the school level. In Sweden, the regional boards that had functioned as the antennas of the state were abolished and decision-making was decentralized to the municipalities and the schools and in New Zealand the regional boards were abolished.

TABLE 3.2 BASELINES AND LEVELS OF DECENTRALIZATION AND CENTRALIZATION

Level to which decentralization/ centralizatrion is taken	Level from which decentralization/centralization starts			
	Central/national/ federal	Regional/ state/*Länder*	Municipality/ District	School
		Centralization		
Central/national	-	Canada	Australia, UK	
Region/state/ *Länder*	Brazil, Colombia, France, Finland, Mozambique, Spain	-		
Municipality/ district	Czech Rep. United Kingdom Sweden Tanzania	Sweden	-	Cases in the US and Latin America
School	Colombia Sweden New Zealand	Australia Germany Sweden	Denmark Finland Sweden, United Kingdom, some states in United States	-

In most of the literature and reports on decentralization, it is not clear which type of decentralization is being implemented. This applies also to reports published by Ministries of Education. As regards decentralization to the school level, Odden (1994:106) observes that "Research within education of school-based management, however, produces only vague hints of how decentralized management is effectively structured" and Elmore (1993) argues that it is not clear to whom management and decision-making authority was decentralized. On the whole, however, it seems that the most common approach in industrialized countries has been to delegate fiscal responsibility from central or regional level down to district or school level. School leaders are given more autonomy and more freedom to take initiative (Codd, Gordon and Harker, 1990). Decentralization down to the school level is generally termed: *site-based management* (SBM), *shared decision-making* (SDM) or *school-based decision-making* (SBDM) (Papagiannis, Easton and Owens, 1992). However, the content of these three types differ considerably. During the 1970s, many countries also introduced school-based curriculum development (SBCD). For Levacic (1995:3), SBM implies increasing school autonomy, especially in relation to budget control, combined with local participation involving teachers, students, parents and/or other community members. Michigan Charter schools are a good example of both one component in a choice program and a type of school autonomy. Such schools "operate independently under charter granted by a variety of public agencies . . . " and they are funded by public authorities on the same basis as public schools (Arsen et al 2000:11).

Countries vary considerably as to the details of the content and form of decentralization that has been adopted (delegation, deconcentration, and so on) (Barro, 1996; OECD, 1995a). (see table 3.3). Some examples are: New Zealand decentralized decisions on local adaptation of the content and examination work from the central level to the school level (see 3:b in table 3.3). In Mozambique, a degree of decentralization in the form of delegation and deconcentration has been implemented in the 1990s; the regional bodies took over teacher recruitment, school construction and financial and managerial audits from the Ministry of Education (1:d-g). When Spain was transformed into a democratic state in the 1970s, many items were decentralized from the central level to the regional, district, or school levels. Examination and evaluation were moved to the regional level, and among a number of items, municipalities came to be responsible for teacher recruitment. In Sweden, for instance, curriculum decentralization from the central to the school level (see 3:a) partially occurred. Evaluation was moved in part from the regional to school or district level (5:b), while recruitment of teachers was decentralized from the municipality or district level to the school level (6:d).

The standard arguments for decentralization have been that those factors with "the best information about a particular subject should have the discretion to make decisions about the subject" (Hannaway, 1993), but like previous reforms, decentralization and other restructuring measures are, paradoxically, initiated from above (Brown et al 1997a).

From the latter perspective, decentralization is assumed to lead to more flexibility, more accountability and higher productivity (Brown, 1990:40), to greater efficiency (Levacic, 1995:50) and to a feeling among the voters that service becomes more efficiently performed. Decentralization is also expected to improve the professional performance of the service, and to generate and mobilize more and new resources from the local level (Dale, 1989; Papagiannis, Easton and Owens, 1992; Weiler, 1989).

From a critical point of view, decentralization may be seen as an attempt by states to increase their legitimacy, to neutralize or "atomize" conflicts in society and to mobilize more resources from civil society (McGinn and Pereira, 1992; Offe, 1984, 1997;

Table 3.3 Some Levels and Items of Decentralization

Items	From central level to		From regional level to		From district level to	
	Regional level	District level	School level	District level	School level	School level
Curriculum	1:a	2:a	3:a	4:a	5:a	6:a
Examination, evaluation	1:b	2:b	3:b	4:b	5:b	6:b
Teacher competence	1:c	2:c	3:c	4:c	5:c	6:c
Teacher recruitment	1:d	2:d	3:d	4:d	5:d	6:d
Expenditures	1:e	2:e	3:e	4:e	5:e	6:e
School construction	1:f	2:f	3:f	4:f	5:f	6:f
Financial and managerial audits	1:g	2:g	3:g	4:g	5:g	6:g

Weiler, 1989). Slater (1993) argues that centralization, decentralization and restructuring are "terms intended for the explicit purpose of obscuring the presence of power." Weiler (1989, 1993) maintains that centralization and decentralization have to be perceived within the context of the state exercizing power and control and as a means to handle conflicts, to increase the legitimacy of the state and to mobilize resources from the local level. He classifies decentralization into three types. The first of these, the 'redistributive model', implies that power is distributed downward from the highest level of the hierarchy. In addition to having multiple advantages, this model has a value in itself. The second type is the 'effectiveness model', which deals with financial aspects of decentralization, taking for granted that it is cost efficient. Finally, the fact that many societies are composed of different ethnic and linguistic groups means that different "learning cultures" are likely to exist. In the third type of decentralization, curricula and the content of education are adapted to these local and varying conditions, in order to make education more efficient. For instance, learning becomes more efficient if the language of instruction is the native language of the students.

RESULTS OF DECENTRALIZATION

Various political and administrative levels are involved and some countries have decentralized from the federal or central state level to the provincial level. This has not been found to be radical enough to change the school processes (Hannaway, 1993; Hanson, 1990, 1995; dos Santos Filho, 1993; Winkler, 1993).

Schools and districts start from very different baselines. There are indications that existing inequalities tend to increase with the implementation of decentralization measures (dos Santos Filho, 1993; Hanson, 1990; Levacic, 1995). In Colombia, where decentralization was optional, poor areas or schools were reluctant to join the reform since they had to begin from a relatively weak position lacking facilities such as appropriate school-buildings, and so on (Hanson, 1990). In Chicago, schools differed initially and came to differ even more with decentralization. The schools situated in poor areas or those with a large proportion of children with learning difficulties were not able to attract high achieving students but instead lost students and were re-centralized, and so on, decision-making power was given back by the city government (Walberg, 1998).

Most often when decentralization at the school level occurs, schools are given the authority to decide upon personnel, budget, local adaptation of certain parts of the curriculum, and so on. Wylie (1995) has followed the decentralization process in New Zealand since its inception in 1987. The problems of school-based management are school leadership, lack of external support, and relations with central government. Two of the conclusions she draws are that SBD by itself does not solve the problem of economic inequality, and that educational issues become more politicized. Wylie recommends that rules, regulations and decision-making authority be clearly defined before decentralization is implemented in order to not create confusion and tensions.

Research makes it possible for us to construct a picture of what happens during the first phase of decentralization, which may last two or more years. New functions and roles emerge, and individuals at lower levels receive more tasks and duties. Despite the increased workload at the bottom levels the staff is not always increased at this level or diminished at higher levels (Levacic, 1995; Wylie, 1995). School directors and teachers become more active and interact more often, not only with one another but also with other local institutions and authorities. Confusion and conflicts emerge from the uncertainty over decision-making competence (Hannaway, 1993; Möller, 1995; Papagiannis, Easton and Owens, 1992). For instance, administrators at higher levels come into conflict with administrators and teachers at lower levels in the system; politically elected representatives of local bodies and authorities are pitted against school councils representing teachers and parents (Caldwell, 1993; Elmore, 1993). Conflicts tend to emerge when bodies higher in the administration use their veto to obstruct decisions taken at lower levels (Papagiannis, Easton and Owens, 1992; Odden and Wohlstetter, 1993).

Elmore (1993) argues, on the basis of a review of school-based management in the United States, that there is ambiguity in decentralization processes with regard to responsibility and authority. Similar phenomena have been observed in Sweden (Skolverket, 1997b, 1999a). The principal sources of conflict, confusion and misunderstanding are (i) the unclear definition of who decides what and (ii) the interpretation of the new rules.

In a four-year study of eleven school districts in the United States, Canada, and Australia, Odden and Wohlstetter (1993) followed the implementation of SBM. They found that SBM requires a re-designing of the whole school organization that goes far beyond a change in school governance, and they argue that "for SBM to work, people at the school site must have 'real' authority over budget, personnel and curriculum" (2). In order to attain this, the following is necessary: "professional development, information about student performance, parents and continuity satisfaction and a reward system" (Ibid).

Decentralized management works best, according to Odden (1994), when four resources are developed in the decentralizing units: information about goals and objectives, knowledge, and power to make decisions and rewards. Decentralization down to the school level has many implications for school finance. Authority over the budget has to be moved from more central levels so that schools become the key organizational unit, and each school needs to develop a comprehensive information system.

Decision-making and policy-making take place within the context of organizational structures. Structures differ in degree of formalization, complexity, and centralization/ decentralization and these features affect the interaction and the influence various groups have in schools. Levacic (1995) and Slater (1993:176) have found that the nature of the structures is seldom taken into account when decentralization is suggested. Brown (1993: 228) draws the conclusion that "decentralization of decision-making appears to work effectively when it is part of an organization that is already functioning well . . . " Smaller case studies in Sweden support this conclusion (Daun, 2000; Daun and Slenning, 1998; Möller, 1995).

There is a complex of instances, structures and roles implied in decentralization programs: local communities—boards or councils—schools—school principals—teachers—students—parents. The relationships between them vary from one program to another and according to actors' own interpretations of the roles (dos Santos Filho, 1993; Hanson, 1990; Skolverket, 1997c, 1998a). In many countries, there are elected municipality or district boards, like the Local Educational Authorities in England. They have the authority over several schools. Municipalities and districts may differ a great deal not only economically, politically, culturally, and so on, but there are also differences in the way their boards interpret and practice decentralization processes and choice schemas (Daun, 2000; Levacic, 1995). In England and Wales, school-based management gives considerable powers of the governing body but in Australia, Canada and the US, school councils are advisory (Levacic, 1995:77).

Kogan *et al* (1984) define four different types of bodies at schools: (i) the accountable governing body; (ii) the advisory governing body; (iii) the supportive governing body; and (iv) the mediating governing body. They have different functions and give teachers and parents, for instance, different roles in relation to the schools.

The real influence that local factors can have on educational policies depends on the type of governing. Should the school have a council, board or committee? These three types of mechanisms for parental involvement assign parents varying influence. According to Beare (1993), these combinations have various implications for parental roles in the school, but in most of the decentralization efforts, these questions were not addressed or clarified prior to implementation.

The discourse on decentralization is also related to the demands among certain politicians and researchers for strong leadership. For other researchers, however, there is a contradiction between school autonomy (which should imply initiatives from teachers and parents) and strong leadership (Grace, 1997; Hargreaves, 1994). In this context, mention can be made of Levacic´s (1995:108) argument, based on an in-depth study of eleven schools in England, that local management has brought about "significant changes in the roles of the key personnel in schools . . . The role most affected . . . has been that of the headteachers." The latter enjoy considerably more power than before the reforms.

From a review of research on choice and decentralization in New Zealand, the United Kingdom and the United States, Whitty (1996) draws the conclusion that since the reforms, school principals are more satisfied and teachers involve themselves more in decision-making even as their stress levels increases. Although opinion differs among teachers, head teachers in the same schools claim that local management increased involvement and improved overall job satisfaction. Similar results have been reported from Sweden (Falkner, 1997; Francia, 2000) and England (Levacic, 1995).

Teachers are involved or affected in varies degrees. In England, according to Levacic (1995), they have been directly affected only when budget cuts have required staff cuts. Generally, in combination with choice or arrangements for parental involvement in school, teachers may have to face the pressure from parents to improve school and more specifically teaching and their work load increases. Should they be compensated for this extra work or should their teaching load be proportionately decreased? This seems to be an issue when SBD is introduced (Whitty, 1997). Hannaway (1993) found that the teachers became more controlled through decentralization. She argues that teachers in public systems were not over-regulated before decentralization but ignored; that is, teacher autonomy already existed in many schools in the US before the wave of decentralization. Nobody gave them feedback: good work was not appreciated and bad work was not criticized. Decentralization measures thus multiplied external demands on the teachers (principally from parents), while at the same time amount of support was increased.

As far as improvement or reinforcement of local participation (parental involvement, for instance, in educational decision-making are concerned, SBM or SBD seem to be the most controversial types. Parental involvement may vary from sporadic school visits by parents to a situation in which parents form the majority in a school council with decision-making power. Lareau (1987) states, however, that parental involvement has not been a high priority of research and thus few generalizations can be made. Fine (1993) concludes that parents have ideological power but material power is held by the central administration and the financial élites. Lareau (1987) found that the following factors condition parents' participation: parents' educational capabilities; their view of appropriate division of labour between the teachers and themselves; the information they had about their children's lives at school; and time available and economic resources in the families, while in Dale's (1997) view parents are, at least in the United Kingdom, left with the technical aspects of management.

To what extent are students involved and do the classroom processes and learning change due to decentralization? Regardless of the school of thought, the basic assumption behind decentralization is that if school leaders, teachers and parents are given more autonomy, students' levels of academic achievement will improve (Chubb and Moe, 1990; Papagiannis, Easton and Owens, 1992). Having pointed this out, however, the effects of decentralization on student performance are seldom investigated. Beare (1993) argues that the driving forces behind the creation of school councils have been more political than pedagogical. Thus, pedagogical theory has not informed the policy of decentralization. Hannaway (1994) concludes from a review of available research that school-based management alone has little effect on student achievement. Elmore (1993) maintains that research in the US has not exmined the relationship between structural reform and the classroom itself. He describes the ideal school that should result from restructuring. It now has school-based management, but a large number of other changes have been implemented at the school level as well. In studies there is no clear evidence that offers new directions.

Cohen and Spillane (1992) argue that a relationship between the type of governance/management and classroom processes is often implicitly assumed to exist, and that decentralization, therefore, indirectly improves student learning. However, they doubt that change in governance automatically results in changes in classroom instruction and that the context of decentralization is specific to each country. A review of the research by Levacic (1995:165) concluded that there is no support for the assumption that there exists any relationship between decentralization and the quality of teaching.

Wehlage, Smith and Lipman (1992) evaluated a five-year project in four American cities. Although one of the primary objectives was to enhance student achievement, this did not occur, principally because the teachers did not take the opportunity they were given to alter their teaching methods. Interaction and exchange of messages had increased within schools but also between schools and other public authorities. Success resulted more from teachers' basic perception of teaching and learning than from SBDM. Changing classroom practice is not a problem for school-based management but primarily for motivation among teachers to be innovative (Cohen, 1995; Odden and Clune, 1995; Peterson, McCarthy and Elmore, 1996). Morris (1990) ventures a guess that decentralization could perhaps change the teaching-learning processes in highly centralized systems such as those in the Scandinavian countries. Autonomous schools make more decisions but there is no measurable effect on achievement has been observed (Jimenez and Sawada, 1999; Rawlings, 1999). Levacic (1995: 151, argues that "There was no hard evidence that the chosen way of using resources (due to SBM) was more effective or efficient in terms of students' learning than alternatives which had not been considered or had been considered and rejected."

In his review of research on the effects of globalization on the school system, McGinn (1997) finds that decentralization has been globalized as a policy. However, he also concludes that this type of restructuring has not changed classroom processes very much, nor what the students learn. He discusses four different hypotheses: schools are already decentralized; important decisions are not decentralized; teachers are guardians of quality and continue to work in the way they always have done; and even when decentralization is actually implemented there is often inertia in the schools and classrooms.

The costs of decentralization have not been studied systematically. There are indications that they actually increase, at least during the first phases of decentralization (Möller, 1995; OECD, 1994). Related to costs of decentralization are efficiency gains, which are one of the goals of the restructuring process. In her study in England, Levacic (1995) found that such gains were made in the areas of utilities and property services. Greater effectiveness was due more to the flexible use of funds (resulting from SBM) than to "improved decision-making" (p. 165). Delegated budgeting allows schools to use economic resources in a more flexible way. SBM has been successful in England—in implementing the administrative and organizational changes that are required to implement the policies. Green (1997) compared student achievement in highly centralized and highly decentralized education systems. However, the number of variables not controlled for undermines any other conclusion than that decentralized systems do not seem to produce better rresults than centralized systems.

Overall, the role of the central and regional governments for decentralized education systems, is critical to ensure minimum spending and equity, protect minority interests, provide comparative information on school finance and performance, and to stimulate and disseminate innovation to reduce costs and improve performance (See, for instance, Hanson, 1990, 1995; Henig, 1993).

CHOICE

What Options for Whom?

Choice is not a new phenomenon in education; in some places, it has always existed, due to the fact that the state never implemented regulations that would to any large extent limit parents' freedom to choose education for their children. However, with the restructuring movement, choice was linked to the language of the market and to market principles. According to Henig (1993), the movement for choice is driven by political theory and not by educational theory, and Cibulka (1990:44) argues that choice is appealing because the surrounding discourse has been able to blur the distinctions between the political Left and Right.

Many arguments for or against choice have been presented. They may be arranged from a philosophical level to more practical/technical concerns and they may be summarized as follows: (i) freedom of choice is a human right; (ii) choice in education is an essential element in the preservation of freedom in a democratic society (Mason, 1989:289); (iii) parents and students have different educational preferences and should therefore have the option to choose; and (iv) when there is only one system (state monopoly), there is no incentive to improve (Hallinan, 1994; Levin, 1994). Public schools are not able to respond to all preferences (Levin, 1994). The principal arguments against choice are that (i) the most privileged and informed parents have knowledge about the possibilities and know what to choose; and (ii) choice results in segregation and reinforcement of inequalities. Glenn (1990/1991) argues that the choice system can improve individual schools, but that it is questionable whether or not a global improvement takes place.

As with decentralization, a myriad of labels and terms to denote choice arrangements exists (Bastian, 1990:178). It is, however, possible to distinguish two principal choice approaches, one *public choice-oriented* and one *market choice-oriented*. In the former, parents are allowed to choose within the public sector. Choice is seen as a democratic right and is not necessarily combined with vouchers. In the market-oriented choice, the public and the private sectors are implied, schools compete in the market place for students, and a certain amount of money is allocated per student (Chubb and Moe 1990; Hallinan, 1994; Levin, 1991; Papagiannis, Easton and Owens, 1992; West 1986). Some countries, such as Denmark, the Netherlands and US, have a long tradition of choice based on value patterns and not necessarily on the drive for academic achievement (Doyle, 1989).

France, the Netherlands, and Spain officially recognize as fundamental the right of those who operate a private school to determine its distinctive character. For instance, Muslim and Hindu schools have been provided subsidies in the Netherlands since the end of the 1980s and the early 1990s, and in Sweden since the beginning of the 1990s, and the United Kingdom since1997. As to other varieties, parents are able to choose schools according to language of instruction in, for instance, Belgium, Canada, New Zealand, Switzerland, Wales and Kyrgyzstan (Glenn, 1994; Kanaev, 2000; Wylie, 1995). In countries where the conditions for private schools are favourable, a parallel system—generally, religious—exists. A comparatively large proportion of the schools belong to the private sector (See table 3.5).

Choice programs vary in several key variables, such as degree of regulation, degree of redistribution, teacher competence, level of support and scope. Regulation concerns various aspects, but mention can be made of the extent to which schools have to use a certain quota in relation to the socio-economic, ethnic, and so on, composition of the district in which the school is situated (Boyd, 1991; Martin and Burke, 1990; Raywid, 1985). The scope may vary from one public school to public as well as private schools in a whole country. Choice arrangements can be organized within a school, in which certain sections or teachers of the school are rather autonomous and can apply a particular profile, pedagogy or methodology. Such schools-within-schools exist in the United States; some magnet schools are of this type. Students within the catchment area may then choose between the section with the ordinary pedagogy or the profiled section.

Choice policies differ also in other features, such as: financing, attendance, staffing and content (Elmore, 1990). Financing may be handled through school fees or vouchers, for instance. In the latter case, state subsidies are distributed on a per student basis. Attendance may differ according to the type of students that are recruited, and the content may differ considerably if the schools do not have to follow a national curriculum. Attendance may also vary according to content offered by the schools and parent preferences for pedagogical profiles, language of instruction, and so on.

Table 3.4 presents a simplified picture of choice arrangements. It is based on three variables: sector, scope and regulation. All three are a matter of degree but here they have been dichotomized. First, it should be mentioned that, theoretically, it is possible that there is no freedom of choice. This was the case in former Soviet Union. General-ly, children were not allowed to enroll in any school other than the one they had been assigned to.

The patterns that emerge are theoretically possible and what takes place in practice is due mainly to the costs involved for parents and whether certificates or diplomas from the alternative schools are valid or not in the education system at large. At one extreme, choice applies to one public school only and is strictly regulated (combina-tion 1 in table 3.4). At the other extreme, choice applies to a whole country, to all types of schools and is not circumvented by strong government control and regulation (com-bination 16 in table 3.4). This combination gives the maximum freedom for schools as well as parents. Parents may choose any school anywhere, provided that the school is authorized by the state, and no regulations are made with regard to the ethnic and/or socio-economic composition of the students. In theory, this combination has been in use in Sweden since 1992. In reality, of course, only a few parents can afford to send their children to schools situated far away from the home. When changes within schools (division of grades, teaching style, and so on.) are added to combination 16, this may be called systemic reform (Cibulka, 1990; Elmore, 1990; Henig, 1993; Odden and Wohlstetter, 1993; OECD, 1994). More specifically, the least regulated is open enrollment in some states in the US (Elmore, 1993) and Australia (Angus, 2000), called de-zoning as in New Zealand (Lauder, 2000). Open enrollment means that schools are not obliged to give priority to children living in the area where the schools is situated.

Combination 2 means that choice may be made between public schools within a school district. This combination exists in the United States and other countries. Com-bination 6 includes private schools as well and has traditionally existed in many coun-tries.With combination 14, parents can choose between various types of schools in one school district and choice is not regulated. In practice, this has applied in Sweden since 1992. Combination 3 means that choice can be made between public schools in various school districts (within the same county or municipality) and that choice is reg-ulated. Some type of quota system is used. This exists in the United States and some other countries.

Choice may be seen both from the perspective of supply and demand. Of principal interest in relation to supply are access and diversity. According to OECD (1994:36), supply has until 1993 not to any large extent been diversified in the countries that introduced or reinforced it in the 1980s. In order for choice to function optimally, edu-cation practioners should be empowered to organize and manage schools and to be autonomous enough to respond to preferences. In relation to demand, information, pref-erences and access are important. Parents and students should be empowered to choose among schools or among programs within schools.

According the public choice approach, the supply may be diversified in that the schools create their own profiles, but they do not necessarily compete for students. Rather they respond to different preferences. Parents may choose according to broad-er concerns such as the well-being and personality formation of the child, and so on, but three principal categories of preferences tend to be (a) pedagogical, (b) linguis-

TABLE 3.4 THEORETICALLY POSSIBLE COMBINATIONS OF CATCHMENT AREAS, REGULATION AND SECTOR

Regu-lation	Sector	Area of recruitment of students (scope)			
		Within the school	Within school district	Across school districts	Within the whole state, province or nation
Strong regulation	Public only	1	2	3	4
	Public as well as private	5	6	7	8
Weak or no regulation	Public only	9	10	11	12
	Public as well as private	13	14	15	16

tic/cultural/religious and (c) achievement (Barrington, 1994; Glenn, 1994; Henig, 1993; OECD, 1994; Wylie, 1995). Policies supporting choice on the basis of pedagogy are found in the Netherlands, Sweden, Poland, Czech Republic, and Russia, among other countries. In the United States, for instance, parents are allowed to choose to have their children educated at home (Cizek, 1990). In case (c) above, schools are chosen that have a reputation for producing high educational performance as measured by grades or on tests.

In the market approach, schools compete for students and they receive an amount of money per student from the state. According to Arsen et al (2000:6), "policies that utilize market mechanisms often feature decentralization of administrative responsibility, use of private contracting for public services, elimination or "streaming" of regulation, reliance on incentives rather than mandates, introduction of competitive pressures in the delivery of public services." Most market choice schemes in education are based upon establishing funding that will use public support to enable market choice. The two most common approaches are tuition, tax credits, and educational vouchers. The thinking behind the voucher system is that in improving education for the individual the benefits will extend to society as a whole. Voucher plans differ in at least the following dimensions finance (e.g. how large, for what); educational alternatives; regulation (curriculum content, personnel, admissions standards); information (knowledge about alternatives that exist); and scope (e.g. the geographical area to which they are applicable).

If we also consider the possibility for parents to establish schools on their own initiative, the picture becomes more complicated, since, in this case, neither the market nor the public choice approaches are applicable. Using an enlarged concept of education and taking a broader view, we find that in islamized countries, parents can choose between Western type of education and Islamic education

Does Choice Enhance Student Achievement?

Cookson Jr. (1992), Henig (1993), and Whitty (1996, 1997) all maintain that the literature on choice in education is either empirically weak or ideological; Witte (1992) argues that the experiences from real choice in the United States are limited. Papagiannis, Easton and Owens (1992) point to the fact that no longitudinal studies have been conducted on educational restructuring. Whitty (1996) finds that research on choice has the following characteristics: the gender perspective is absent; popular schools do not expand but become more selective; academic achievement is the only indicator to measure success (for example, in the US no improvement has been noted); and choice increases segregation. The first and the second characteristics are evident from research reviews (Daun, 1993; Levacic, 1995) and some studies support the fourth (Lauder, 2000; OECD, 1994; Waslander and Thrupp, 1995).

That which is most problematic in the context of choice arrangements is information to parents (see, for instance, Chira, 1992; Olsson, 1992). Moore and Davenport (1990) conducted a study on the effects of choice arrangements and the establishment of magnet schools in four American cities. They argue that most families did not understand the process of choice. Poorly educated and low-income parents and parents who have another mother tongue than the official or main language(s) of the country may be difficult to reach with information, and these problems have resulted in unexpected costs in several choice arrangements. Some remedies to the information problem have been found, as there are cases in the United States where particular units were established for this purpose.

In a different study, Bauch (1989) reports on the basis of five studies of Catholic high schools in the United States that poor parents are able to make informed choices. He found that the division between well-informed and poorly-informed parents did not follow socio-economic or race criteria, but degree of motivation. He criticizes classical sociology for presuming that poor parents are culturally 'deprived', uninformed, and unmotivated. Conran (1989–1990) analyzes the results presented by Moore and Davenport (1990) and argues that the conditions for the satisfactory functioning of choice, whether or not they are external, were not fulfilled in the case of their case schools. He (1989–1990) concludes, however, that choice in itself is not enough and that research has not focussed on the difficult question of whether choice improves children´s motivation and achievement or whether it simply serves to concentrate highly motivated achievers in certain schools.

Glenn (1990–1991) and Coons and Sugarman (1990–1991) are of the opinion that choice arrangements in schooling can not follow pure market principles, but strong efforts have to be made to provide information to the users and to take other measures targeted towards low-income and low- educated parents.

As to the costs of choice arrangements, OECD (1994:41–42) reports that choice can make education more expensive. However, it is difficult to verify to what extent this is true since in many cases, budget cuts are made at the same time as choice is introduced (Hewton, 1986; Levacic, 1995; Möller, 1995). Various studies have covered aspects of restructuring related to choice mechanisms. For instance, Raywid (1985) forwards that, on the basis of a research review focussing on elementary schools,t "schools of choice" are less expensive than public schools. Martin and Burke (1990) report from Cambridge, Massachusetts, where open and regulated enrollment is practiced, that transport costs have increased considerably. As Walberg (1989) points to the fact that more than half of the choice systems that have been reviewed by Raywid have less than 100 students. None of the two researchers, however, mention anything explicit about how this affects costs. According to Edwards and Whitty (1992) and Maddaus (1986), proponents of choice argue for subsidized transport of students, inasmuch as transport possibilities should not determine whether and to what extent parents choose. The authors also call for further research on costs in relation to choice arrangements.

Practically all countries have policies including a component dealing with equity, though studies show that this goal is not automatically attainable with decentralization and choice programs (Schneider, 1989). In addition, measures or mechanisms to prevent inequalities from increasing are expensive. This may affect the costs of choice arrangements (Henig, 1993).

As to parental attitudes towards school choice, opinion polls have shown that a majority of parents would rather have the option to choose school for their children but in reality they themselves exploit this possibility to a rather small extent. In some place in the United States, for instance, the existence of vouchers and tax reductions does not appear to motivate many parents to change schools, as is evidenced by their not exercizing the choice option. In the industrialized countries where choice was introduced since the beginning of the 1980s, 2–15 percent of parents took the advantage of this option. Most parents, however, do not behave as the market models predict. For them, it seems to be more important to find a solution that satisfies much more aspects or other aspects than the focus on academic achievement. They choose holistically and academic achievement in the narrow sense is not always a priority. Parents with a secure economic and social situation choose where to live, and this choice also includes school. If choice is implemented, given the area of residence, they choose schools according to the program they offer. Parents with low education and low income, on the other hand, do not use the choice possibility to the same extent. When they do, they tend to choose a school in the area where they live (Maddaus, 1986). For other parents, distance to the school, for instance, is an important factor.

At the very least, the following factors influence parents' choice of school for their children: whole situation, academic quality of the school; school program; the distance between their home, the school and their workplace; the teachers; their children could get more help and support in the school; school size and atmosphere; openness to parental influence; possibility for children to stay on before and after the school day, religious profile of the school; and previous attendance among family members (See, for instance, Adler, Petch and Tweedie, 1989; Chira, 1992; Edwards and Whitty, 1992; Maddaus, 1986; Martin and Burke, 1990; Olson, 1992; Skolverket, 1996; Walford, 1992).

When the possibility to choose school is introduced, choice is conditioned by the quality of the local community. The reputation of the geographical area in which the school is situated plays an important role for parental choice (Stuart Wells, 1997; Söderqvist, 1999). Where there is social and cultural homogeneity and cohesion, parents opt for the local school. In Sweden, it has been found that choice is more common in heterogeneous communities than in homogeneous communities, because in the former, parents with longer education and parents from the Nordic countries prefer to have their children enrolled in another school district where children of a similar background are more frequent (Skolverket, 1996). In other cases, the choice of school is more important than the neighbourhood; parents opt for a school even if it is situated outside the local community (Edwards and Whitty, 1992).

Ball, Bow and Gewirtz (1995) found that in the United Kingsom, that common choice is influenced by class culture, networks of reciprocal obligations, and the capacity for children to travel some distance. Parents and the students use different strategies according to patterns of motivation and identification. Middle class parents had a broader and more long-term view concerning their children's future than working class parents. Stuart Wells (1996) followed African-American students and parents when choice was introduced in an area in the United States. She found that "three overlapping and intertwined factors affected school choice: degree of parental involvement; students' acceptance or rejection of the achievement ideology; and students' and parents' racial attitudes. Parents who did not involve themselves in the schooling of their children left the choice to them and the children tended to choose the school which they already attended. However, students differed in achievement ideology. Those who were for achievement performed well regardless of school and they opted for "any high status school." Parents and their children could be achievement oriented and still opt for the nearest school if they felt that there would be racial discrimination in other schools or if they felt that, according to the school cultures, achievement was not legitimate for their race.

Brown (1990) found that middle class parents in the United States use choice strategically. Since meritocracy does not function so as to guarantee middle class children access to good jobs upon completion of schooling, middle class parents choose schools with the best reputation, for their children. As such, rather than his or her own ability and effort at school, a child's education is increasingly dependent upon the wealth and wishes of the parents, rather than the ability and efforts of the students. Brown calls this phenomenon *parentocracy*. In the Moore and Davenport (1990) study mentioned above, choice arrangements made, according to the authors, the schools function as new "sorting machines." They conclude, among other things, that schools engaged in selective recruitment of students; had unclear and questionable admission standards and that there was a consistent bias toward choosing the most motivated students, and there was limited evidence of program effectiveness.

In general, the proponents of choice voice concern as to the slow rate at which diversification of supply has taken place; schools have been very slow in responding to the challenges emerging from the introduction of choice (Nathan 1989). When choice has been introduced, school directors and teachers tend to react in the following ways: (1) no considerable change takes place in the some schools and these schools lose students to other schools; (2) as in the first case but efforts are made by the schools to innovate and attract students and they succeed in getting more students; and (3) in schools situated in well-off areas, and schools already functioning well or having a good reputation, school leaders and teachers continue in much the same manner as before and are able to maintain their students or attract more students. In such cases when leaders and teachers have risen to meet the challenge, they become more content with their work, more active, and cooperate more than before (Martin and Burke, 1990). If the school is reorganized on the initiative of the school director and/or the teachers, the reorganization is based on a shared view of educational matters or such a view emerges from the development work (Glenn, 1990–1991; Raywid, 1992).

Diversification of the supply may take place when previously established schools reform themselves or are divided into more school units (magnet schools or schools-within-schools). The latter has taken place in the United Kingdom and the United States. Newly established schools tend to become alternative schools in that they form a new pedagogical profile or use alternative teaching methods. Waslander and Thrupp (1995) found that the most frequently chosen schools in New Zealand selected their students on the basis of social class, and that schools reacted differently to the decision to abolish catchment areas: overt responses in terms of marketing; non-response; political responses which seek to change the rules or terms on which schools compete; networked responses which involve collusion and cooperation. A basic assumption in the choice discourse is that good schools expand, and bad schools are ultimately forced to close down. However, schools with a good reputation do not see any reason to change or increase the number of student places, while schools with a bad reputation either do not react at all or come into crisis (Edwards and Whitty, 1992). Schools that are in high demand do not expand but become, on the contrary, more selective. This has also been observed in Sweden (Daun, 2000; Daun and Slenning, 1998). In terms of the least popular schools, as was reported for one municipality featured in a Swedish case study, some of the schools very heavily in debt ever since the introduction of the choice system in the beginning of the 1990s, but these schools had not been closed down (Söderqvist, 1999). If they had been closed, there would not have been places enough for all the students in the municipality.

Adler, Petch and Tweedie (1989) investigated the criteria that were applied in the admission of students. The most common criteria was "catchment area." That is, students from the area where the school is situated were admitted first. If there still were places left, various and often very unclear criteria were used for selection of the students who had applied. These researchers argue that it is difficult to establish whether or not schools have been able to respond to parental desires, preferences and demands, since these are often such that schools cannot respond to them.

Raywid (1985) suggests that magnet schools seem to represent all characteristics that are supportive of a good education. She presents nine points concerning choice applied to whole districts, and among these points mentioned can be made of clarity in school programs and plans of action, and controlled admission of students so that the socio-economic and ethnic composition of the school population in each school corresponds to that of the district in which the schools are situated.

In a later article, Raywid (1990) argues that public schools involved in choice systems differ a great deal and, therefore, it is difficult to generalize as to their successes and defeats. One point, however, does stand out: it is most often concluded that successful schools are small and very cohesive. This fact prompts Raywid to draw the conclusion that the school climate or the school ethos is the key to success. Schools that are characterized by cohesion among the teachers, clearly defined goals for education, and enthusiasm among the staff are more successful than others. She argues that the school structure and organization are not decisive. This conclusion is not compatible with Chubb and Moe's (1990) thesis, according to which the institutional structure of the school determines whether it will be successful or not; public schools are hindered by the bureaucratic organization of which they are part.

With the introduction of choice, processes of selection and self-selection begin and flows of students emerge between the schools. During the past fifteen years, the following has been noted with regard to the biggest cities in the United States: white middle class children move to schools, often private, in suburban areas; and white and high achieving students from minority groups leave their schools and enroll in magnet schools. Once open but regulated choice was introduced in Cambridge, Massachusetts, white students moved to schools with a small portion of children from minority groups (Martin and Burke, 1990). The same is observed in other countries as well. In Sweden, for instance, there are indications that highly educated parents are more likely than others to choose schools in which students' background closely corresponds with their own children's, while immigrant parents with low education are more likely than others to choose schools established by immigrants (Skolverket, 1996, 1997a). Thus in several cases what emerges is an influx of students to school districts having on average, a higher family income and a lower percentage of immigrants emerge (for Michigan, see Arsen et al 2000; for Sweden, Daun, 2000, and for New Zealand, Lauder, 2000).

Schools that have lost students are situated in areas with low status and poor reputations in regard to school population composition, discipline and/or achievement. Consequently, inequality between schools increases since schools with a declining number of students lose economic resources. Lauder (1991) argues that the quality of education is affected also in schools that lose even a small number of students. That is, a minority is able to determine the educational quality for the majority.

According to Astin (1992), the most serious result of freedom of choice will be that the public sector will become even more stratified. Coleman (1992) argues that within the public system, there are no incentives to improve education because the students (consumers, clients) come to the school in any case, as they are obliged to do so; and there is already a high degree of stratification among schools within the public sector and it is linked to the socioeconomic status and ethnicity of the parents. Choice in the public sector will also stratify the schools but the ranking will be according to student achievement, a point which Coleman argues is positive.

Researchers have reported on changes in school populations following the introduction of choice reforms. In New Zealand socioeconomic segregation was present long before the abolition of catchment areas, but subsequent to the reforms, schools became stratified along ethnic lines (Waslander and Thrupp, 1995). Walford (1992) reports, that choice in the UK has increased the degree of integration for children who have been able to and wished to choose schools located near their homes. In other cases, segregation has increased for the students left in the schools that were not chosen.

Overall improvement of student achievement has not been shown in any study, neither in a school district nor in a larger geographical area. In case schools (mainly magnet schools) improvements have been registered, but these results are questioned on the grounds that relevant variables have not been controlled for, principally the level of student motivation and achievement before the choice was made. Conran (1989–1990) states that valid results of the effects of choice on student achievement are rare, and that in the United States they are principally from smaller studies. One example is magnet schools in a district; such schools started in the beginning of the 1970s during the drive for desegregation.

Martin and Burke (1990) agree but at the same time they suggest that the results should be interpreted carefully, since student level of motivation and knowledge, at the time they enroll in the magnet schools, has never been measured. According to Elmore (1990), there is little evidence that greater choice for consumers and providers of education will, by itself, dramatically change the performance of schools. In an overview of the effects of choice on student achievement, Hallinan (1994) states that in the United Kingdom no improvement in student results has been verified. According to OECD (1994:33–34) it is difficult to verify whether or not choice arrangements result in better quality of education, since many variables are not controlled for. Elmore (1990:40) also argues that no positive influence on student achievement has been found, and furthermore that: " . . . one effect of introducing choice may simply be to increase competitiveness without increasing quality. . . ." In addition to student achievement and school performance, there is to date no convincing evidence that choice arrangements improve the teaching-learning processes in the classrooms. In Michigan, for instance, no innovations due to choice and implementation of charter schools have been observed in the classrooms (Arsen *et al* 2000).

Concerning the impact of choice, Papagiannis, Easton and Owens (1992:35) argue that only comprehensive and long term research can provide the information necessary for judging the effects of the choice arrangements decided upon and implemented since the end of the 1970s. Thus, reliable conclusions cannot yet be drawn. For the time being, we may summarize this section by quoting two researchers studying educational restructuring and choice systems. The first, Cibulka (1990:58) states: "In short, choice proposals, like other restructuring plans, often beg the question of what purpose they serve. The perfect choice proposal—responsiveness, productive, cost-efficient, and equitable—has yet to be designed. . . . " Bastian (1990:181) maintains that: "What we do know is that if choice is genuinely pursued as a way to serve quality, equality and diversity in schooling, then it cannot be separated from a comprehensive agenda for school improvement and it cannot be divorced from the resource question. . . . "

On a final point, it has been argued that comprehensive schools facilitate democratic training of children and that the selection that takes place when choice has been introduced undermines the possibility for such training. Advocates of market approaches underestimate the potential importance of the common experience that students from various backgrounds have when mixed in public schools while they overestimate the benefits produced in private schools (Levin, 1994).

PRIVATE EDUCATION

There is an increasing role for private schools in many places in the world (See, for instance, Angus, 2000; Kitaev, 1999 and World Bank, 1986, 1991, 1998). Just to mention one example, enrollment in private schools has increased from 22 to 30 percent between 1975 and 1999 in Australia (Angus, 2000: 5).

Profit-driven or Altruistic?

Private schools are not a new phenomenon. In most places, schools were established by religious or local communities, before a central state had been well established. That is, all education was private in the sense that it was neither controlled nor subsidized by the state. The degree of state intervention came to vary considerably between countries, but the state came to subsidize most schools (James, 1991). The key variables in the relationship between the state and private education are (i) the method of financial support; (ii) the level of financial support; and (iii) the degree of independence vs. control/regulation. These variables seem to a large extent to determine the proportion of primary school students enrolled in private schools.

There are large variations between the countries, as shown in table 3.5. Most recognized private schools in the world receive subsidies from the state, a fact that makes researchers debate whether it is meaningful or not to divide schools into private and public school, since most of the schools labelled private are heavily dependent on public subsidies.

The term "private" is a simplification, since practically no recognized schools function without direct or indirect subsidies. Moreover, a school is called private, regardless of which non-government entity runs it; a school may be established and governed by a group of parents who run it for idealistic and altruistic reasons, but also by a company that organizes it as a for-profit enterprise. Public funds can go to private schools or to students (vouchers) in such schools (Durston, 1993). In Singapore, parents receive a certain annual subsidy for education of their children to be used at the school of their choice (Yeoh, 1994).

Private schools vary from small units owned by a group of parents, a group of teachers or an altruistic organization to big schools owned by profit-making companies. In addition to this, the differences between the schools within each sector are sometimes larger than the differences between the sectors. Generally, the greater the control private schools accept, the larger subsidies they receive. This results in a comparatively large private sector that is similar to the public sector. Education in the Netherlands is one example (James, 1989).

Countries differ in the amount and the manner in which they subsidize and regulate schools in the private sector. Another way to actively support private schools is to stimulate parents to enroll their children in private schools. This is done by giving them some economic support to realize their choice possibilities. In the United States, two of the most common measures are to distribute vouchers or to provide tax reduction for school fees paid by low-income parents, who have their children enrolled in private schools. In the first case, parents are given a voucher, whose value is equal to the average cost of a student in the public system.

TABLE 3.5 VARIATION IN PRIVATE ENROLLMENT AMONG PRIMARY SCHOOL STUDENTS

Africa	Asia and Oceania	Europe	North America	South America
Lesotho 100	Fiji 90–100	Ireland 100	USA 10	Most countries
Zimbabwe 80–90	Hong Kong 90–100	Netherlands 69–70		15–25
Swaziland 80	Australia 20–30	Belgium 50–60		Chile 20
Cameroon 40–50	Singapore 25–30	Spain 30–40		Uruguay 16
Gabon 30–40	Indonesia 20	France 15		

Source: Unesco, 1995.

In some countries, full funding requires integration into the public system (England and New Zealand), while gradual arrangements exist in Australia, France, the Netherlands, Spain and Senegal, among other countries (Durston, 1989; Mason, 1989). Some odd arrangements also exist; in Ontario in Canada, for instance, Catholic schools receive public support, while no other private schools do. Some countries have various degrees of subsidies/regulation. In France, for instance, schools may choose the degree of state regulation and are funded in relation to the degree accepted (France, 1990, 1992; Monchablon, 1994; Teese, 1989).

In one category, countries permitted private schools but they were given very small subsidies or no subsidies at all so that they never came to be a realistic alternative for the large majority of parents. Examples are the Northern European countries (except Denmark), Japan, and some countries in the South (James, 1991). In another category, private schools were given more generous subsidies, but still only a minority of parents came to enroll their children. This was the situation in, for instance, some European countries, New Zealand, and countries in the South (Senegal, for instance). In a third category, private schools were given very large subsidies very early and came to dominate the educational scene (Durston, 1989; Mason, 1989). Examples are Belgium, Cameroon, Fiji, Ireland, Lesotho, the Netherlands, Swaziland and Zimbabwe (James, 1991).

James (1991) has made an overview of private education in a large number of countries. Two of her principal hypotheses are supported, namely that the high percentage of the general student population that opts for private rather than public schooling is due to excess demand (this applies in particular to secondary schools in the South) or to differentiated demand (this applies to primary and secondary education in the North). In the first case, local communities or NGOs establish their own schools (Harambee schools in Kenya is one example) as a way to meet the demand. In the latter case, the demand is more differentiated than the supply in the public sector; parents establish or choose schools according to their values or ethnic, linguistic or pedagogical preferences, since public schools are not able to respond to their demands.

The contemporary idea of private schools originates from at least three sources or traditions: (i) schools which traditionally belonged to civil society and continued to do so; (ii) those established as a response to pleas from cultural movements for more freedom; and (iii) institutions which were to satisfy the neo-liberal drive for efficiency, productivity and formation of human capital for the labor market. The first two ideas are important in communitarianism and in the arguments of the new movements.

Bray (1996) identifies four major models of privatization of education: transfer of ownership of public schools (which is very rare); a shift in sectoral balance without re-designing existing institutions; increased government funding and support for private schools; and increased private financing and/or control of government schools. For Africa, Kitaev (1999:45-47) makes the following classification of private schools: community schools; religious schools; spontaneous schools; for profit schools, and schools for expatriates. (Some schools can, of course, fall into two or more of these categories).

Thus, privatization is not necessarily driven by market forces nor does it necessarily follow market principles and practices. However, the linkage between privatization and market forces is new in the educational discourse. According to pure market principles, schools should be managed like companies, and they should offer education that students (consumers) demand. Moreover, choice should, from the market perspective, apply to all types of schools. In a more modified form, freedom of choice applies to public schools only; private schools are given such small subsidies that they have to charge large school fees and are, consequently, not able to compete for the students.

Different combinations of ownership, governance, management, degree of subsidization, type of control and type of students may serve as a basis for the classification of private schools. Boyd and Cibulka (1989:13) define two categories of schools according to the demands that parents make on education for their children: (i) religious and ethnic schools with a special moral or philosophical standpoint; and (ii) schools to which greater prestige is attached. Cookson Jr. (1991b) finds fifteen different categories of private schools and Raywid (1985) distinguishes 35 different types of schools (including public schools) in the United States. Rodhe (1988) establishes a similar typology with the purpose of the schools as a point of departure. She argues that schools may be established to function as a substitute for public education (they teach something which is not taught in the public schools); as status raising or status maintaining organizations for those who participate (ethnic, cultural or other minorities); and schools that offer an alternative pedagogy. Anderson (1990:15–16) also categorizes private schools according to the functions that they have for the users, and she finds six such functions: elite schools, which are selective and have large school fees; schools that maintain a sub-culture (a religious profile, for instance), reform or alternative schools, such as Montessori, community schools that recruit students within a particular geographical area; profit-oriented schools, that are organized by private companies for the sake of making profit, and charity schools that cater primarily to underprivileged children.

Although only three variables (amount of state subsidies, degree of state control and certification) are used in table 3.6, it should become clear that the picture of private school arrangements becomes very complex.

TABLE 3.6 THE STATE AND VARIOUS TYPES OF PRIVATE PRIMARY EDUCATION

State subsidies	State control	Certificate or competence*	Examples
1. No	The state does not tolerate private schools.	No	All private schools or at least religious schools in central socialist states before 1990.
2. No	The state tolerates and does not intervene.	No	Koranic schools in Sub-Saharan Africa. Home education in some states in the US.
3. Varies	Varies	Not unconditionally	Denominational schools in the US. Independent Catholic schools in France.
4. Some	Some	Yes	French Catholic schools with the lowest degree of integration into the public system. Franco-Arabic schools in West Africa.
5. Large	Some	Yes	Private primary schools in the Nordic countries.
6. Large	Strong	Yes	Private primary schools in the Netherlands. Primary schools with the highest degree of integration in France.
7. Large	Weak	Yes	Catholic schools in Australia.

* Certificate or competence formally valid for continued education or the formal labour market,

It is also worth mentioning that Australia is the only OECD country in which private schools are subsidized unconditionally (Angus, 2000: 17).

In a wider perspective, we find that in the South, Muslim education is a common alternative in many Asian and African countries including Afghanistan, Indonesia, Senegal and Mozambique. This is the case for Koranic schools or other Islamic schools in Asia, Arab countries and Africa (Baadi, 1994; Carter, 1988; Embalo et al. 1993; Massialas and Jarrar, 1991). In countries such as Saudi Arabia, Senegal, Sri Lanka and Mali, schools under Muslim governance and management may receive subsidies if they teach according to the national curriculum in certain core subjects (Belloncle, 1984; Brenner, 1993; BREDA, 1995). There are also mixed schools, several of which are recognized, such as Franco-Arabic schools in Mali, Senegal, Sudan and some other countries (Unesco, 1993). These schools provide access to general secondary education in the public system. After the Jomtien conference on education in Thailand in 1990, certain types of Muslim schools have come to be established in Sub-Saharan Africa, for instance, by internationally-established NGOs and with the support not only from Middle Eastern countries but also from Unicef (Aporpor, 1993; BREDA, 1995; Hoa, 19 93; Hueto, 1993).

Are Private Schools Better than Public Schools?

Efforts have been made to compare private and public schools in order to find out which of them is most efficient and effective. For several reasons, such comparisons are difficult to make and research has reached "opposite conclusions" (Woodhall, 1997:2). Marks and Lee (1994) summarize some of the findings concerning differences between private and public schools with regard to student achievement in a selection of countries. In Australia, students in private schools score slightly better than do their peers in public schools. Angus (2000), however, remarks that the studies in question were not conducted in a systematic manner. In the United Kingdom, a larger percentage of students in private schools than in public schools pass the A level. In Kenya, there is no considerable difference between public and private secondary schools in the percentage of students attaining the O level in examinations. The levels mentioned are the highest levels. Riddell (1993) reports findings from comparisons between public and private secondary schools in the Dominican Republic, Kenya, the Philippines, Thailand and Zimbabwe. With the exception of Kenya, private schools had higher levels of performance than public schools, but this difference was, in most cases, found to be explained by peer group effect. Riddell concludes: "What one can say with certainty is that there is no overwhelming conclusion regarding the advantages of private schools over public schools . . . "(p. 384) In Sweden, private schools have, on average, a higher level of achievement than public schools, but the range is significantly larger among the former than among the latter (Skolverket, 1999b).

There are different views on the reasons for this difference between the two sectors. Those who are sceptical to the suggestion that private governance makes schools more able to stimulate students' learning tend to find explanations to the differences in terms of parents' and students' cultural capital and degree of school motivation. Some portion of the private schools are elite schools, in which better off parents enroll their children.

The argument is that there are differences between the students when they enroll in private and public schools respectively. Those students who opt for private elite schools have higher motivation and more cultural capital when they enroll. It is more common that privileged parents actively choose elite schools for their children. This is consistent in all countries where private education is an option (Anderson, 1990; Boyd and Cibulka, 1989; Cookson Jr, 1989; Fowler, 1992; James, 1991). How big these differences are is seldom, if ever, investigated, and, therefore, comparisons between the sectors are not very meaningful (Edwards and Whitty, 1992:106; Smart and Dudley 1989).

As far as students' performance in the United States, Witte (1992:217) states: "What is the effect of private schools on student achievement? The simple answer is very little." He argues that, when all relevant variables are considered, the difference between the two sectors is of no pratical political importance. Also, it is a generally accepted argument that differences within each sector are very large. Schools in the private sector vary from small, religious charity schools with low student achievement to large elite institutions with high student achievement (Anderson, 1990; Fowler, 1992; Garin, 1992).

Conran (1989/1990) refers to the results from the Coleman *et al.*, (1982) and Chubb and Moe (1988) studies. She admits that the differences are evident. She concludes that we know what characteristics good schools have; the question is then what we can do to make all schools good. Choice and privatization alone do not create good schools.

Coleman's et al (1982) comparative study of public and private education in US high schools made a strong contribution to the renewed debate. The study shows that students have greater acquisition of knowledge, as measured on tests in Catholic high schools than in public high schools. This holds even when socioeconomic background and other relevant variables are controlled. These results were brought into the political discourse by two political scientists, Chubb and Moe (1988, 1990). They are two of the most prominent proponents of market solutions in the educational domain. Many of the political and scientific arguments on the role of private schools, not only within the United States but also around the world, were taken from this study (Henig, 1993; Marks and Lee, 1994; Telhaug, 1990). Chubb and Moe (1988) re-analyzed the data and argued that the bureaucratic organization of the schools was the most important obstacle to the improvement of student achievement in public schools. They even stated that representative democracy, as it is presently practised, creates bureaucratic inertia that prevents schools from improving (Chubb and Moe, 1988, 1990). Both the Coleman study and Chubb and Moe's (1988) re-analysis have been criticized for the fact that certain variables were not controlled for and that the difference between the sectors is negligible from a policy point of view, even if the difference is statistically significant. For New Zealand, Lauder (2000) argues that when intake variables are taken into account, there are no considerable differences between the two types of schools.

Private schools are generally smaller units, and often there is stronger cohesion among the staff as regards pedagogical and methodological issues (see, for instance, Cookson Jr, 1991c; Skolverket, 1997a:15). It is, according to some researchers, these particular features that contribute to the differences in student achievement in public and private schoold (Raywid 1990, Witte 1992). Schneider (1989) argues that private schools establish high academic standards, enforce disciplinary policies and involve parents in school decision-making.

Until the mid-1990s, there was no comprehensive voucher system anywhere in the world. It is not possible to ascertain how common the experiments with vouchers and/or tax reduction are in the United States, but the first experiment was made in the 1970s. Although enrollment in private schools was subsidized, parents chose—to a large extent—to enroll them in the school in their home area (Witte, 1992). In the United Kingdom, the assisted places scheme was introduced in 1980. Low income parents get financial support to enroll their children in private schools. Walford (1992) states that a rather large portion of the students receiving such assistance are children whose parents are middle class and have lost some of their privileges, due to the economic recession and the budget cuts that were made during the 1980s. The few studies conducted in schools that receive "voucher" students show that no improvement in student achievement has taken place (Chira, 1992).

In most countries, the cost per student is lower in the private sector than in the public sector. In Australia in 1992, per-student costs for Catholic schools were seven percent lower than that recorded for public schools (Angus, 2000:5). Walberg (1989) finds that in the United States, the cost per student for public schools is 3.8 times higher than that for Catholic schools and 2.9 times higher for private schools that receive state subsidies; this is partly due to the fact that public school teachers are paid higher salaries (Krashinsky, 1986). Levin (1991) and Fowler (1992), among others, argue that private schools have hidden revenues and expenditures. In some cases they can use publicly financed infra-structures and equipment, for instance. Denominational schools in the US, for instance, should not be subsidized, but indirectly they get more than one fourth of their economic support from public funds in the form of infrastructure, access to public pedagogical materials and tests, and so on (Cookson Jr. 1991a:187). On the other hand, the state does not control denominational schools. It means that fundamentalist Christian schools are free to teach anti-democratic beliefs, for instance (Peshkin, 1988).

In the Netherlands, it is comparatively easy for a group of parents and teachers to start a private school. The result is that many schools are underused, which means that overall the cost per student tends to be higher. During the past years, however, cuts have been made in Dutch educational budgets (James, 1989; World Bank, 1991-1995). Levin (1991) compares public and private utility of choice across the sectors. Even with market choice, the public sector has to intervene and finance some aspects; the government has to establish criteria for the distribution of vouchers and to be prepared to intervene when the market mechanisms fail. He argues that the voucher system requires finance, regulation and information. Henig (1993) has found that choice and private schools function better in districts in the US where there is a political tradition of positive interaction between the public authorities and the population.

At the micro level, private schools cost less per student than public schools, and they produce higher levels of knowledge. However, some portion of the costs in private schools are not known (gifts, public provision of infrastructure, the duty of public school to take care of "expensive" students, and so on). At the macro level, both types of choice systems require more expensive arrangements, if they are to function well.

The spread of the market model of choice requires more expansion and more centralization of the public sector than does choice within the public sector because the necessary coordination and control become more difficult.

Apart from the formal education system and institutionalized parental and communitarian contributions in nature and cash to the schools (Graham-Brown, 1991; Kitaev, 1999), there are also some other forms of private efforts: (i) education organized by NGOs, such as BRAC in Bangladesh or other arrangements in Bolivia, Ecuador, Peru and Venezuela, for instance (Behrstecher and Carr-Hill, 1990; Dave *et al.*, 1990; Reimers and Tiburcio, 1993); (ii) parallell non-recognized *juku* in Japan and Muslim schools not only in Muslim areas but also in the North (McLean, 1985); (iii) idealistic work done by parents not only in private but increasingly also in public schools when decentralization has taken place (Daun, 1998; Graham-Brown, 1991; Samoff, 1990).

Systemic Reform

Restructuring is about changing the structure. However, many studies show the importance of individuals' definitions of reality and their cultures in the reception of education (McCarthy, 1990 West, 1990). Hargreaves (1994) analyzes different dimensions in education and educational change. One of them is "structure vs. culture" and in this context he writes: "the cultural view. . . . sees existing practice as heavily determined by deeply rooted beliefs, practices and working relationships among teachers and students . . . " (350), that is, something more than organizational and structural change is involved.

After a period of decentralization, some educationists in the United States came to the conclusion that SBM or other types of decentralization are not enough if the teaching-learning processes in the classroom are to improve. Therefore, it was argued, the internal processes, primarily classroom processes, had to be improved. Implementation of systemic reform started in the United States (Clune, 1993; Cohen, 1994, 1995; Odden and Clune, 1995) and is now suggested or implemented in many places in the world (see, for instance, DeStefano, Hartwell and Tjetjen, 1995). That is, single measures of restructuring are not sufficient but the whole register of reforms have to be implemented.

There are certain relationships between the three types of restructuring. Choice can apply effectively only if (i) public schools are autonomous enough to change what they have to offer (i.e. decentralization and SBD or SBM); and (ii) private schools are stimulated through higher subsidies and less regulation. According to Odden (1994) it includes the following components:

> . . . ambitious student outcomes and expectations that all students will perform at high levels on thinking and problem-solving skills, high quality curriculum standards, new forms of performance assessment, strongly linked to curriculum standards, definition of teacher expertise to teach this curriculum, restructured management and governance including site-based implementation" (pp. 104-105).

Systemic reform combines the three restructuring measures described above and other measures especially related to school and classroom processes and students' learning.

The purpose of table 3.7 is to show the structural combinations that are possible. Although each measure is dichotomized, as many as twelve combinations emerge. In reality, decentralization and privatization are continuous, a fact that makes many more combinations possible. In combination (1), decentralization, full scale choice schemes and reinforcement of private arrangements are implemented. This constellation can be called systemic reform if it is combined with measures concerning the processes internal to the schools such as teacher professionalization, teaching methods, application of modern learning theories, and so on. It is also possible that no restructuring measures are taken but other (piece-meal) changes might be implemented (combination 12).

All types of restructuring considered here are highly sensitive in that (i) they involve basic values and basic organizational patterns; and (ii) smaller changes in certain key variables (such as type and degree of regulation and subsidies to private schools) may have large scale consequences. They also differ from other types of reforms in that decisions taken in the political body have to be implemented by people at the grass-roots level. Teachers and school leaders have to handle decentralization. Choice and the opportunity for private initiatives are implemented to the extent that parents and teachers use these opportunities. That is, the scope of implementation is due to individuals' responses and initiatives.

TABLE 3.7 COMBINATIONS OF THE MOST COMMON RESTRUCTURING MEASURES

Subsidies	Decentralization: Yes			Decentralization: No		
	Choice			Choice		
	Private as well as public	Public only	Not at all	Private as well as public	Public only	Not at all
Large	1	2	3	7	8	9
Small or none	4	5	6	10	11	12

CONCLUSIONS

There is a myriad of forces behind the argument for educational restructuring: from anarchist and de-institutionalist demands for human emancipation and broad personality development of children to neo-liberal arguments based on the ideas of efficiency, technical rationality and formation of human capital. The type of schools aimed at through restructuring measures is only to a small extent something new; decentralized systems, private schools and choice possibilities have always existed in several countries. What *is* new is the "marketization" of the process, the economic terminology, the scale of the changes, and the globalization of restructuring policies. Full use of market forces occurs only if choice is possible across the public and private sectors and is some type of voucher system is used; that is, money accompanies the students. For the schools, each student represents a unit valued in monetary terms. Marketization can most probably take place only in a capitalist society, but a considerable "space" in such a society is not subject to market forces or principles. Capitalism is something more than markets (Rocard, 1994) and privatization is not necessarily marketization.

Decentralization, freedom of choice and privatization have been introduced or reinforced as means (i) to save costs; (ii) to improve student achievement in schools; and (iii) to increase accountability. All three of these measures have been preceded by intensive discourse, but with little preparation and involvement of educational researchers. And all three are real reforms whatever kind of established definition is used. Although all the conditions for reforms, as mentioned by Guthrie and Koppich (1993) among others, have not always been present these reforms have taken place. This indicates that a shift in educational policy-making has occurred.

Raywid (1985, 1990) has found that successful schools are small, and have a homogeneous culture/ideology, an explicit ethos, and strong links to the local community, among other things. This links to Coleman's (1988) analysis of social capital and his argument for networks and social relationships of the type suggested by the communitarians.

The results of restructuring measures have not been studied in a comprehensive and systematic way. Comparisons between countries with different degrees of decentralization and different arrangements for choice and private are not easily conducted since many factors undermines the comparability (See, for instance, Green, 1997). Longitudinal studies of countries that have introduced choice do not exist. However, there exist a larger number of small studies and they tend not to give any unambiguous results. A summary of the findings from such studies is made in table 3.8.

A striking feature not only in the restructuring discourse but also in its practical policy is the absence of considerations of power and power relations. Individuals are treated as if they have identical power and resources to choose, establish schools, and so on. The only instance in which inequality is considred is when the question of information on choice possibilities are discussed. Parents have different access to and possession of information concerning alternatives. Behind this difference we may find differences in power, although this is never made explicit. The critics of restructuring have power relations in mind although it is not always made explicit (See, for instance, Hogan, 1992).

Educational restructuring may be seen as a response of the nation-state to (i) changes of the state and its financial situation and management capability (i.e. a means to increase state legitimacy); (ii) global competition and formation of human capital; (iii) communitarian and post-modernist demands; and (iv) a blurring of ideologies, cultures, and so on.

TABLE 3.8 SUMMARY OF SOME OF THE IMPACT OF RESTRUCTURING MEASURES

	Decentralization	Choice	Privatization
School, classroom	More interaction and activities within schools and between schools and other bodies. No effect on classroom processes.	Well functioning schools respond to the challenge, other schools stagnate. Sorting and segregation between schools.	Differences between public and private sectors. More small schools in private sector. Coherence and school ethos in private sector.
Parental involvement	Arrangements for parental involvement differ considerably. Parents with cultural and/or human capital tend to be more involved.	Already highly involved parents become more involved.	Parents more involved, especially if they are among the founders of the school.
Costs	No systematic studies. Indications that costs increase, at least during the first phase. Shift of costs to private agents.	No systematic studies. Indications that costs increase due to the need to informing parents.	Lower per student costs in private sector. However, large differences within this sector: from low costs/low quality to elite fee-charging schools.
Student achievement	No systematic studies. No effect on student achievement.	Higher level of average achievement in chosen schools. However, no control of achievement and motivation levels before choice. No findings from systematic and controlled studies.	Higher in private sector. However, no control of level of motivation and cognitive ability among students before choice. No findings from systematic and controlled studies.

NOTES

[1]   There are more varieties of conventional type than those listed in table 3.1.

[2]   Each of the four types of change vary substantially in their details. They may be analyzed against the background of the following questions: Who owns what and how in the educational domain (ownership)? Who governs what and how (governance/regime)? Who controls what and how (regulation and control)? Who pays what, how and how much (finance)? Who teaches what, how and to whom (school units, curricula, teaching methods)? Who gets what education where, how and for how much? Where there existed a national curriculum, local adaptations came to be

allowed, and countries without a national curriculum, implemented such a one. The same happened to decentralization and centralization.

REFERENCES CITED

Adler, M., A. Petch and J. Tweedie (1989). *Parental Choice and Educational Policy.* Edinburgh: Edinburg University Press.

al-Baadi, H.M. (1994). "Saudi Arabia: System of Education." In T. Thusén and N. Postlethwaite (eds.). *International Encyclopedia of Education.* Oxford: Pergamon.

Anderson, D. S. (1990). "The Unstable Public–Private School System in Australia." Paper presented at NBEET First National Conference, November 1990.

Angus, M. (2000). "Choice of Schooling and the Future of Public Education in Australia." *Paper presented at the International Conference on Choice in Education, Michigan State University,* March 15-17, Lansing, USA.

Aporpor, S. (1993). "Experiencias das escolas comunitárias da cidade de Bissau." In *Coloquio Internacional sobre Experiencias Alternativas no Ensino de Base.* Bissau: UNICEF/Ministry of Education.

Arsen, D. L., D. Plank and G. Sykes (2000). *School Choice in Michigan: The Rules Matter.* Lansing: Michigan State University.

Astin, A. W. (1992). "Educational 'choice': Its Appeal May Be Illusory." *Sociology of Education,* vol. 65, no. 4.

Ball, S. (1990). *Politics and Policy Making in Education. Explorations in Policy Sociology.* London: Routledge.

Ball, S. J., R. Bowe and S. Gewirtz (1995). "Circuits of Schooling: A Sociological Exploration of Parental Choice of School in Social Class Contexts." *The Sociological Review*, 43: 52–78.

Barrington, J. E. (1994). "New Zealand: System of Education." In T. Thusén and N. Postlethwaite (eds.). *International Encyclopedia of Education.* Oxford: Pergamon.

Barro, S. M. (1996). "How Countries Pay for Schools. An International Comparison of System for Financing Primary and Secondary Education." Paper prepared for the Center of the Consortium for Policy Research in Education (CPRE), University of Wisconsin.

Bastian, A. (1990). "School Choice: Unwrapping the Package." In W. L. Boyd and H. L. Walberg (eds.). *Choice in Education. Potential and Problems.* Berkeley: McCutchan Publishing Corp.

Bauch, A. (1989). "Can Poor Parents Make Wise Educational Choices?" In W. L. Boyd and J. G. Cibulka (eds.). *Private Schools and Public Policy. International Perspectives.* London: Falmer Press.

Beare, H. (1993). "Different Ways of Viewing School–site Councils: Whose Paradigm Is in Use Here?" In H. Beare and W. L. Boyd (eds.). *Restructuring Schools. An International Perspective on the Movement to Transform the Control and Performance of Schools.* London: Falmer Press.

Beare, H. and W. L. Boyd (1993). "Introduction." In H. Beare & W. L. Boyd (eds.). *Restructuring Schools. An International Perspective on the Movement to Transform the Control and Performance of School.* London: Falmer Press.

Behrstecher, D. and R. Carr-Hill (1990). *Primary Education and Economic Recession in Devloping World Since 1980.* Unesco: WCEA, Jomtien.

Belloncle, G. (1984). *La question éducative en Afrique noire.* Paris: Karthala.

Boli, J. (1989). *New Citizens for a New Society. The Institutional Origins of Mass Schooling in Sweden.* New York: Pergamon.

Boyd, W. L (1991). "Choice plans for public schools in the U.S.A.: issues and answers." *Local Government Policy Making,* vol 18 , no 1.

Bray, M. (1985). "Education and Decentralization is Less Developed Countries: a comment on general trends, issues and problems with particular reference to Papua New Guinea." *Comparative Education,* vol 21 , no 2.

Bray, M. (1996). *Privatization of secondary education: Issues and policy implications.* Paris: UNESCO.

Bray, M. and W.O. Lee (1997). "Education and Political Transitions in Asia: Diversity and Commonality." In W.O. Lee and M. Bray (eds.). *Education and Political Transition: Perspectives and Dimensions in East Asia.* Honkong: The University of Hong Kong.

Breda (1995). *Education de base et éducation coranique au Sénégal.* BREDA Series no 10. Dakar: UNESCO.

Brenner, L. (1993). "La culture arabo-islamique au Mali." In R. Otayek (ed.). *Le radicalisme islamique au Sud du Sahara.* Paris: Karthala.

Brown C. (1993). "Employee Involvement in Industrial Decision-Making: Lessons for Public Schools." In J. Hannaway and M. Carnoy (eds.). *Decentralization and School Improvement. Can We Fulfill the Promise?* San Fransisco: Jossey-Bass Publishers.

Brown, D.J. (1990). *Decentralization and School-based Management.* London: The Falmer Press

Brown, P. (1990). "The 'Third Wave': Education and the Ideology of Parentocracy." *British Journal of Sociology of Education,* vol 11.

Brown, P., A. H. Halsey, H. Lauder and A, Stuart Wells (1997). "The Transformation of Education and Society: An Introduction." In A. H. Halsey, H. Lauder, P. Brown, and A. Stuart Wells (eds). *Education. Culture, Economy, Society.* Oxford: Oxford University Press.

Caldwell, B. J. (1993). "Paradox and Uncertainty in the Governance of Education." In H. Beare & W. L. Boyd (eds.). *Restructuring Schools. An International Perspective on the Movement to Transform the Control and Performance of Schools.* London: Falmer Press.

Carnoy, M. (1993). "School Improvement: Is Privatization the Answer?" In J. Hannaway and M. Carnoy (eds.). *Decentralization and School Improvement. Can We Fulfill the Promise?* San Fransisco: Jossey-Bass Publishers.

Carter, L. (1988). *Assessment of Current Activities and Priorities in Primary Education and Teacher Training for Aghans.* Peshawar: UNESCO.

Chira, S. (1992). "Research Questions Effectiveness of Most School-Choice Programs." *New York Times,* 26 October 1992.

Chubb, J. E. and T. M. Moe (1988). "Politics, Markets and the Organization of Schools." *American Political Science Review,* vol 82, no 4.

———. (1990). *Politics, Markets and America's Schools.* Washington: The Brookings Institution.

Cibulka, J. G. (1990). "Choice and the Restructuring of American Education." In W. L. Boyd and H. L. Walberg (eds.). *Choice in Education. Potential and Problems.* Berkeley: McCutchan Publishing Corp.

Cibulka, J.G. and W.L. Boyd .(1989). "Introduction: Private Schools and Public Policy." In W. L. Boyd and J. G. Cibulka (eds.). *Private Schools and Public Policy. International Perspectives.* London: Falmer Press.

Cizek, G. J. (1990). "Home Education Alternatives vs. Accountability." *Journal of Educational Policy,* vol 4 , no 2.

Clune, W. (1993). "The Best Path to Systemic Educational Policy: Standardized/centralized or Differentiated/decentralized?" *Consortium for Policy Research in Education (CPRE).* Wisconsin: University of Wisconsin Press.

Codd, J., K. Gordon and R. Harker (1990). "Education and the Role of the State: Devolution and Control Post-Picot." In H. Lauder and C. Wylie (eds.). *Towards Successful Schooling.* London: Falmer Press

Cohen, D. K. (1994). "Evaluating Systemic Reform. Issues and Strategies in Evaluating Systemic Reform." Paper Presented for the US Department of Education. Washington: US Department of Education.

Cohen, D. K. (1995). "What Is the system in Systemic Reform?" *Educational Researcher,* vol 24, no 9.

Cohen, D. and J. P. Spillane (1992). "Policy and Practice: The Relation Between Governance and Instruction." *Review of Research in Education,* vol 18.

Coleman, J. S. (1988). "Social Capital in the Creation of Human Capital." *American Journal of Sociology,* vol 94, Supplement.

Coleman, J. (1992). "Some Points on Choice in Education. *Sociology of Education,* vol 65, no 4.

Coleman, J.S., T. Hoffer and S. Gilmore (1982). *High School Achievement.* New York: Basic Books.

Conran, P. (1989/90). *Issue Analysis: Public Schools of Choice.* ASCD.

Cookson Jr.,P.W. (1989). "United States of America: Contours of continuity and controversy in private schools." In G. Walford (ed.). *Private Schools in Ten Countries. Policy and Practice.* London: Routledge

———. (1991a). "A Review. Politics, Markets and America's Schools." *Teachers College Records,* vol 93 , no 1.

———. (1991b). "Private Schooling and Equity. Dilemmas of Choice." *Education and Urban Society,* vol 23, February 1991.

———. (1991c). "Degrees of Imperfection: A Note from a Political Polyanna." *Teachers College Records,* vol. 93, no. 1.

———. (1992). "Introduction to The Choice Controversy: Current Debates and Research" *Educational Policy,* vol 6 , no 2.

———. (1993). "A Review. Politics, Markets and America's Schools." *Teachers College Records,* vol 93 , no 1.

Coons, J. J. and S. D. Sugarman. (1990/91). "The Private School Option in Systems of Educational Choice." *Educational Leadership,* December 90/January 91

Dale, R. (1997). "The State and the Governance of Education: An Analysis of the Restructuring of the State-Education Relationship." In A. H. Halsey, H. Lauder, P. Brown, and A. Stuart Wells (eds). *Education. Culture, Economy, Society.* Oxford: Oxford University Press.

Daun, H. (1993). "*Omstrukturering av skolsystemen. Decentralisering, valfrihet och privatisering. En internationell utblick.*" ("Restructuring School Systems. Decentralization, freedom of choide and privatization. An International Research Review). National Agency for Education/Institute of International Education, Stockholm.

———. (1998). "Comprehensive Schooling in the Intersection of Market, State and Civil Forces: Two Swedish Case Studies." In A. TJELDVOLL (ed.). *Education and the Scandinavian Welfare State in the Year 2000. Equality, Policy and Reform.* New York: Garland Publishing.

———. (2000). "Market Forces and Decentralization in Sweden - a Threat to Comprehensiveness and Equity and an Impetus for School Development?" *Paper presented at the International Conference on Choice in Education, Michigan State University in Lansing, USA,* March.

Daun, H. and K. Slenning (1998). "Equity and Introduction of Choice in Education. Case Study Results from Sweden." Paper presened at the World Congress of the Comparative Education Societies in Cape Town, South Africa, July 12–17, 1998.

Dave, R.H., A.M. Ranaeweera and P.J. Sutton (1990). *Meeting the Basic Learning Needs of Out-of- school Children: Non-formal Approaches.* Unesco: WCEA, Jomtien.

DeStefano, J., A. Hartwell and K. Tiedjen (1995). *Basic Education in Africa. USAIDs Approach to Sustainable Reform in the LDCs.* Washington: USAID.

Dos Santos Filho, C.J. (1993). "The Recent Process of Decentralization and Democratic Management of Education in Brazil." *International Review of Education,* vol 39, no 5.

Dougherthy, K.J. & L. Sostre (1992). "Minerva and the Market: The Sources of the Movement for School Choice." *Journal of Educational Policy,* vol 6 , no 2.

Doyle, D. P. (1989). "Family Choice in Education: the Case of Denmark,Holland and Australia." In W. L. Boyd and J. G. Cibulka (eds.). *Private Schools and Public Policy. International Perspectives.* London: Falmer Press.

Durston, B.H. (1989). "Issues in Public Funding and Governance." In W. L. Boyd and J. G. Cibulka (eds.). *Private Schools and Public Policy. International Perspectives.* London: Falmer Press.

Edwards, T. and G. Whitty (1992). "Parental Choice and Educational Reform in Britain and the United States." *British Journal of Educational Studies,* vol XXXX , no 2.

Elmore, R. F. (1990). "Options for choice In Public Education." In W.L. Boyd and H.L. Walberg (eds.). *Choice in Education. Potential and Problems.* Berkeley: McCutchan Publishing Corp.

————. (1993). "School Decentralization: Who Gains? Who Loses." In J. Hannawy and M. Carnoy (eds.). *Decentralization and School Improvement. Can We Fulfill the Promise?* San Fransisco: Jossey-Bass Publishers.

————. (1995). "Structural Reform and Educational Practice. *Educational Researcher,* vol 24, no 9.

Embalo, T., *et al.,* (1993). "Experiencias das escolas madrassas na Guiné-Bissau." In *Coloquio Internacional sobre Experiencias Alternativas no Ensino de Base.* Bissau: Unicef/Ministry of Education.

Etzioni, A. (1995). *The Spirit of Community: Rights, Responsibilities and the Communitarian Agenda.* London: Fontana Press.

Falkner, K. (1997). *Lärare och skolans omstrukturering: Ett möte mellan utbildningspolitiska intentioner och grundskollärares perspektiv på förändring i den svenska skolan.* (Teachers and school restructuring, An encounter between education policy intentions and teachers' perspective on change in the Swedish School). Uppsala: Uppsala University.

Fine (1993). "(Ap)parent Involvement: Reflections on Parents, Power and Urban Public Schools." *Teachers College Record,* vol 94.

Finn, C. (1990). "Why We Need Choice." In W.L. Boyd and H.L. Walberg (eds.). *Choice in Education. Potential and Problems.* Berkeley: McCutchan Publishing Corp.

Fowler, F. C. (1991). "One Approach to a Pluralist Dilemma: Private School Aid Policy in France, 1959-1985. Summery of Dissertation." Paper Presented at a Symposium on Division A at the Annual Meeting of the American Educational Research Association, April 3, 1991.

Fowler, F. C. (1992). "American Theory and French Practice: A Theoretical Rationale for Regulating School Choice." *Educational Administration Quarterly,* vol 28 , no 4.

France (1990). *Education por tous: Politiques et stratégies rénovées pour les années 1990.* Paris: Ministère de l'Éducation nationale de la Jeunesse et des sports.

————. (1992). *Rapport de la France.* 43ème session de la conference internationale de l'éducation. Paris: Ministère de l'éducation nationale et de la culture.

Francia, G. (2000). *Policy som text och som praktik. En analys av likvärdighetsbegreppet i 1990-talets utbildningsreform för det obligatoriska skolväsendet.* (Policy as text and as practice. An analysis of the equivalency concept in the 1990s´ reform of comprehensive education). Stockholm: Pedagogiska institutionen, Stockholms universitet.

Fullan, M. G. (1991). *The New Meaning of Educational Change.* New York: Cassell.

Garin, C.. (1992). "La gauche incertaine face aux ghettos scolaires. *Le Monde,* 12 November, 1992.

Glenn, C. L. (1989). "Parent Choice and American Values." In J. Nathan (eds.). *Public Schools by Choice. Expanding Opportunities for Students and Teachers.* St. Paul, Minnesota: Institute for Learning and Teaching.

————. (1990/91). "Will Boston Be the Proof of the Choice Pudding?" *Educational Leadership,* December 1990/January 1991.

————. (1994). "School Choice and Privatization." In T. Husén and N. Postlethwaite (eds.). *International Encyclopedia of Education.* Oxford: Pergamon.

Goffman, E. (1963). *Stigma: Notes on the Management of Spoiled Identity.* Englewood Cliffs, N.J.: Prentice Hall.

Goodman, J. (1995). "Change Without Difference: School Restructuring in Historical Perspective." *Harvard Educational Review,* vol 1.

Grace, G. (1997). "Politics, Markets, and Democratic Schools: On The Transformation of School Leadership." In A. H. Halsey, H. Lauder, P. Brown, and A. Stuart Wells (eds). *Education. Culture, Economy, Society.* Oxford: Oxford University Press.

Graham-Brown, S. (1991). *Education in the Developing World. Conflict and Crisis.* London: Longman.

Green, A. (1997). "Educational Achievement in Centralized and Decentralized Systems." In A. H. Halsey, H. Lauder, P. Brown, and A. Stuart Wells (eds). *Education. Culture, Economy, Society.* Oxford: Oxford University Press.

Groth, A.J. (1987). "Third World Marxism-Leninism: the case of education." *Comparative Education,* 23 , no 3.

Guthrie, J.W. and J. E. Koppich. (1993). "Ready, A.I.M., Reform: Building a Model of Education Reform and 'High Politics'." In H. Beare and W.L. Boyd (eds.). *Restructuring Schools. An International Perspective on the Movement to Transform the Control and Performance of School.* London: Falmer Press.

Hall, A. (1986). "Education, Schooling and Participation." In J. Midgley (ed.). *Community Participation, Social Development and the State.* London: Methuen.

Hallinan, M. T. (1994). "Foundations of School Choice." In T. Husén and N. Postlethwaite (eds.). *International Encyclopedia of Education.* Oxford: Pergamon.

Hannaway, J. (1993). "Decentralization in Two School Districts: Challenging the Standard Paradigm." In J. Hannaway and M. Carnoy (eds.). *Decentralization and School Improvement. Can We Fulfill the Promise?* San Francisco: Jossey-Bass Publishers.

Hanson, E. M. (1990). "School-based Management and Educational Reform in the United States and Spain." *Comparative Education Review,* vol 34 , no 4.

————. (1995). "Democratizaion and Decentralization in Colombian Education." *Comparative Education Review,* vol 39 , no 1

Hargreaves, A. (1994). "Restructuring Restructuring: Postmodernity and the Prospects for Educational Change." *Education Policy,* vol 9.

Held, D. (1995). *Political Theory and the Modern State.* Oxford: Polity Press.

Henig, J. R. (1993). *Rethinking School Choice. Limits of the Market Metaphor.* New Jersey: Princeton University Press.

Hewton, E. (1986). *Education in Recession. Crisis in County Hall and Classroom.* London: Allen & Unwin.

Hoa, P. T. (1993). "Instituto Islámico do Senegal." In *Coloquio Internacional sobre Experiencias Alternativas no Ensino de Base.* Bissau: Ministry of Education and Unicef.

Hueto, C. (1993). "Experiencia de Burkina Faso." In *Coloquio Internacional sobre Experiencias Alternativas no Ensino de Base.* Bissau: Ministry of Education and Unicef.

Illich, I. D. (1971). *Deschooling Society.* Harmondsworth: Penguin Books.

ILO (1996). *Impact of Structural Adjustment on the Employment and Training of Teachers.* Geneva: ILO, Sectoral Activities Programme.

James, E. (1989). "Benefits and Costs of Private and Public Services: Lessons from Dutch Educational System." *Comparative Education Review,* vol 28 , no 4.

———. (1991). "Public Policies Toward Private Education: An International Comparison." *International Journal of Educational Research,* vol 15 , no 5.

Jimenez, E. and P. Sawada (1999). "School-Based Management Reforms: Lessons from Evaluations." Paper presented at the annual conference of the Comparative and International Education Society, April 1-18, in Toronto, Canada.

Johnson, N (1987). *The Welfare State in Transition.* Brighton: Wheatsheaf Books.

Johnston, B. J. (1990). "Considerations on School Restructuring." *Journal of Educational Policy.* vol 4, no 3.

Kitaev, I. (1999). *Privat education in sub-Saharan Africa: a re-examination of theories and concepts related to its development and finance.* Paris: UNESCO.

Krashinsky, M. (1986). "Why Educational Vouchers May Be Bad Economics." *Teacher College Records,* vol 88 , no 2.

Lareau, A. (1987). "Social-Class Differences in Family-School Relationship: The Importance of Cultural Capital." *Sociology of Education,* vol 60.

Lauder, H. (1991). "Education, Democracy and the Economy." *British Journal of Sociology of Education,* vol 12.

———. (2000). "School Choice and Educational Change: New Zealand, A Case Study." Paper presented at the International Conference on Choice in Education, Michigan State University, March. 15-17, in Lansing, USA.

Lauglo, J. (1995). "Forms of Decentralization and Their Implications for Education." *Comparative Education,* vol 31 , no 1.

Levacic, R. (1995). *Local Management of Schools. Analysis and Practice.* Buckingham: Open University Press.

Levin, H.M. (1991). "The Economics of Educational Choice." *Economics of Education Review,* vol 10 , no 2.

———. (1994). "Foundations of School Choice." In T. Husén and N. Postlethwaite (eds.). *International Encyclopedia of Education.* Oxford: Pergamon.

Lewis, D.A. (1993). "Deinstitutionalization and School Decentralization: Making the Same Mistake Twice.."In J. Hannaway and M. Carnoy (eds.). *Decentralization and School Improvement. Can We Fulfill the Promise?* San Fransisco: Jossey-Bass Publishers.

Maddaus, J. (1986). "Parental Choice of School: What Parents Think and Do." *Teacher College Records,* vol 93 , no 1.

Mallison, V. (1980). *The Western Idea in Education.* Oxford: Pergamon Press.

Marks, H.M. and V.E. Lee (1994). "Public vs. Private Schools: Research Controversies" In T. Husén and N. Postlethwaite (eds.). *International Encyclopedia of Education.* Oxford: Pergamon Press.

Maro, P. S. (1990). "The Impact of Decentralization on Spatial Equity and Rural Development in Tanzania." *World Development,* vol 18 , no 5.

Marshall, S. (1993). "Managing the culture: the key to effective change. *School Organization,* 13, no 3.

Martin, M. and D. Burke (1990). "What's Best for Children in the Schools-of-choice movement." *Educational Policy,* vol 4 , no 2.

Mason, P. (1989). "Elitism and Patterns of Independent Education." In W. L. Boyd and J. G. Cibulka (eds.). *Private Schools and Public Policy. International Perspectives.* London: Falmer Press.

Massialas, B. G. and S. A. Jarrar (1991). *Arab Education in Transition. A Source Book.* London: Garland Publishing.

McCarthy, C. (1990). *Race and Curriculum: Social Inequality and the Theories and Politics of Difference in Contemporary Research on Schooling.* New York: Falmer Press.

McGinn, N.F. (1997). "The Impact of Globalization on National Education Systems." *Prospects,* Vol XXVIII, no 1.

McGinn, N. and L. Pereira (1992). "Why States Change the Governance of Education: An Historical Comparison of Brazil and the United States." *Comparative Education Review,* vol 28 , no 2.

McLean, M. (1985). "Private Supplementary Schools and the Ethnic Challenge to State Education in Britain." In C. Brock and W. Tulasiewicz (eds.). *Cultural Identity & Educational Policy.* Pp. London: Croom Helm.

Miressa, A and J. Muskin. (1999). "Community Participation as a Strategy to Improve School Quality, Access and Demand." Paper presented at the Comparative and International Education Societies in Toronto, Canada, April 14-18, 1999.

Möller, M. (1995). *Educational Management and Conditions for Competence.* Unpublished Masters thesis. Stockholm: Stockholm University, Institute of International Education.

Monchablon A. (1994). "Education system: France." In T. Husén and N. Postlethwaite (eds.). *International Encyclopedia of Education.* Oxford: Pergamon.

Moore, D.R. and S. Davenport. (1990). "School Choice: The New Improved Sorting Machine." In W.L. Boyd and H.L. Walberg (eds.). *Choice in Education. Potential and Problems.* Berkeley: McCutchan Publishing.

Morris, P. (1990). "Bureaucracy, Professionalism and School–Centered Innovation Strategies." *International Review of Education,* vol 36 , no 1.

Morsi, M.M. (1991). *Education in the Arab Gulf States.* Qatar: University of Qatar.

Murphy, J. (1991). *Restructuring Schooling: Capturing and Assessing the Phenomenon.* New York: Teacher's College Press.

Nathan J. (1989). Introduction to *Public Schools by Choice. Expanding Opportunities for Students and Teachers.* St. Paul, Minnesota: Institute for Learning and Teaching.

Odden, A. (1994). "Decentralized Management and School Finance." *Theory into Practice,* vol 33, no 2.

Odden, A. and W. Clune (1995). "Improving Educational Productivity and School Finance." *Educational Researcher,* vol 24, no 9.

Odden, A. and P. Wohlstetter (1993). "Strategies for Making School-Based Management Work." New Brunswick: Consortium for Policy Research (CPRE).

OECD (1994). *School: A Matter of Choice.* Paris. OECD.

OCED (1995). *Decision-making in 14 OECD Education Systems.* Paris: OECD/CERI.

Olsson, L. (1992). "Claims for Choice Exceed Evidence, Carnegie Reports." *Education Week,* Vol XII, no 8.

Papagiannis, G. J., P. A. Easton and J. T. Owens (1992). *The School Restructuring Movement in the U.S.A.: An Analysis of Major Issues and Policy Implications.* Paris: UNESCO.

Peshkin, A. (1988). "Fundamentalist Christian Schools: Should They Be Regulated." *Journal of Educational Policy,* vol 3 , no 1.

Piven, F. F. and R. A. Cloward (1995). "Movements and Dissensus Politics." In M. Darnovsky, B. Epstein and R. Flacks (eds.). *Cultural Politics and Social Movements.* Philadelphia: Temple University Press.

Peterson, P. L., S. J. McCarthy and R. F. Elmore (1996. *Learning from School Restructuring. Consortium for Policy Research in Education.* Lansing: Michigan State University and Harvard University.

Psacharopolous, J. (1992). "The Privatization of Education in Europe. " *Comparative Education Review,* vol 36 , no 1.

Rawlings, L. (1999). "School-Based Management Reforms: Lessons from Evaluations." Paper presented at the annual conference of the Comparative and International Education Society, April 14-18, in Toronto, Canada.

Raywid, M. A. (1985). "Family Choice Arrangements in Public Schools: A Review of Literature." *Review Review of Educational Research*, vol 55 , no 4.

———. (1990). "Successful Schools of Choice: Cottage Industry Benefits in Large Systems." *Journal of Educational Policy*, vol 4 , no 2.

———. (1992). "Choice Orientations, Discussions and Prospects." *Journal of Educational Policy*, vol 6 , no 2.

Riddel, A. R. (1993). "The Evidence on Public/private Educational Trade-off in Developing Countries " *International Journal of Educational Development*, vol 13 , no 4.

Rodhe, B. (1988). "Skilda lärohus II. Offentlig skola och fristående undervisning i internationellt perspektiv." (Separate school houses. Public School and Independent Teaching in an International Perspective). In *Utbildningshistoria 1988* (Educational history 1988). Stockholm: Föreningen för svensk undervisningshistoria.

Samoff, J. (1990). "The Politics of Privatization in Tanzania." *International Journal of Educational Development*, vol 10, no 1.

Schneider, B. L. (1989). "Schooling for Poor and Minority Children: An Equity Perspective." In W. L. Boyd and J. G. Cibulka (eds.). *Private Schools and Public Policy. International Perspectives.* London: Falmer Press.

Skolverket (1996). *Att välja skola - effekter av valmöjligheter i grundskolan.* (Choosing school - effects of choice in comprehensive education). Stockholm: National Agency for Education.

———. (1997a). *Barn mellan arv och framtid. Konfessionella, etniska och språkligt inriktade skolor i ett segregationsperspektiv* (Children between Inheritance and future. Confessionally, ethnically and linguistically oriented schools in a segregation perspective). Dnr 97:810. Stockholm: National Agency for Education.

———. (1997b). *Resultat från en kunskapsmätning 1995.* Rapport nr 139. (Results from a Test of Knowledge 1995. Report Nu 139). Stockholm: National Agency for Education.

———. (1999a). *Nationella kvalitetsgranskningen 1998.* (The National Quality Assessment 1998). Stockholm: National Agency for Education.

———. (1999b). *Barnomsorg och skola i siffror, 1999. Del 1: Betyg och utbildningsresultat.* (Child Care and School in Figures, 1999. Part 1: Marks and Educational Relsults). Stockholm: National Agency for Education.

Slater, R. O. (1993). "On Centralization, Decentralization and School Restructuring: A Sociological Perspective." In H. Beare and W.L. Boyd (eds.). *Restructuring Schools. An International Perspective on the Movement to Transform the Control and Performance of Schools.* London: Falmer Press.

Smart, D. and J. Dudley (1989). "Australia: Private Schools and Public Policy." In G. Walford (ed.). *Private Schools in Ten Countries. Policy and Practice.* London: Routledge.

Söderqvist, B. (1999). *Market Forces in Lower Secondary Education. A Case From a Swedish Municipality.* M.A. Thesis. Stockholm: Institute of International Education.

Stuart-Wells, A. (1996). "African-American Students' View of School Choice." In FULLER, B., R. ELMORE & G. ARFIELD (eds). *Who Chooses? Who Loses? Culture, Institution and the Unequal Effects of School Choice.* New York: Teacher College Press.

Svensson, R. (1981). *Offentlig socialisation.* (Public Socialization). Lund: Liber.

Teese, R. (1989). "France: Catholic Schools, Class Security, and the Public Sector." In G. Walford (ed.). *Private Schools in Ten Countries. Policy and Practice.* London: Routledge.

Telhaug, A. O. (1990). *Den nye utdanningspolitiske retorikken.* (The New Rethoric of Educational Policies). Oslo: Universitetsforlag.

UNESCO (1993). *Regional seminar of experts on Quoranic schools and their Role in the Univesalization and Renewal of Basic Education.* Paris: UNESCO.

UNESCO (1995). *World Education Report 1995.* Paris: UNESCO.

Walberg, H. J. (1989). "Educational Productivity and Choice." In J. Nathan (eds.). *Public Schools by Choice. Expanding Opportunities for Students and Teachers.* St. Paul, Minnesota: The Institute for Learning and Teaching.

Walberg, H. J. (1998).

Walford, G. (1992). "Educational Choice and Equity in Great Britain." *Journal of Educational Policy,* vol 6 , no 2.

————. (2000). Paper presented at the International Conference on Choice in Education, Michigan State University in Lansing, USA, March.

Waslander, S. and M. Thrupp (1995). "Choice, Competition. and Segregation: An Empirical Analysis of a New Zealand School Market, 1990–1993." *Journal of Educational Policy,* vol 10:1–26.

Wehlage, G., G. Smith and P. Lipman (1992). "Restructuring Urban Schools: The New Futures Experience." *American Educational Research Journal,* vol 29 , no 1.

Weiler, H. N. (1989). "Education and Power: The Politics of Educational Decentralization in Comparative Perspective." *Educational Policy,* vol 3 , no 1.

Weiler, H. N. (1993). "Control Versus Legitimation: The Politics of Ambivalence." .In J. Hannaway and M. Carnoy (eds.). *Decentralization and School Improvement. Can We Fulfill the Promise?* San Fransisco: Jossey-Bass Publishers.

West, E. G. (1986). "An Economic Rationale for Public Schools: The Search Continues." *Teacher College Records,* vol 88 , no 2.

West, C. (1990). "The New Cultural Politics of Difference." *October,* Summer, No 53.

Whitty, G. (1996). "Creating Quasi-Markets in Education: A Review of Recent Research on Parental Choice and School Autonomy in Three Countries." *Oxford Studies in Comparative Education,* vol 8 , no 1.

————. (1997). "Marketization, the State and the Re-formation of the Teaching Profession." In A. H. Halsey, H. Lauder, P. Brown, and A. Stuart Wells (eds). *Education. Culture, Economy, Society.* Oxford: Oxford University Press.

Winkler, D. R. (1993). "Fiscal Decentralization and Accountability in Education: Experiences in Four Countries." In J. Hannaway and M. Carnoy (eds.). *Decentralization and School Improvement. Can We Fulfill the Promise?* San Fransisco: Jossey-Bass Publishers.

Witte, J. F. (1992). "Public Subsidies for Private Schools: What We Know and How to Proceed." In *Journal of Educational Policy,* vol 6 , no 2.

Woodhall, M. (1997). "Public versus private education: Changing perceptions of boundaries and roles." Paper presented at the Oxford Conference, Oxford University, UK,Sept ember 1997.

World Bank (1981). *World Development Report 1981.* Washington, D.C.: World Bank.

World Bank (1986). *World Development Report 1986.* Washington, D.C.: World Bank.

World Bank (1991). *World Development Report 1991.* Washington, D.C.: World Bank.

World Bank (1992). *World Development Report 1992.* Washington, D.C.: World Bank.

World Bank (1993). *World Development Report 1993.* Washington, D.C.: World Bank.

World Bank (1994). *World Development Report 1994.* Washington, D.C.: World Bank.

World Bank (1995). *World Development Report 1995.* Washington, D.C.: World Bank.

World Bank (1998). *World Development Report 1998.* Washington, D.C.: World Bank.

Wylie, C. (1995). "School-site Management—Some Lessons from New Zealand." Paper given at the annual AERA meeting, San Francisco, United States, 18–21 April, 1995.

Yeoh, O. C. (1994). "Singapore: System of Education." In T. Husén and N. Postlethwaite (eds.). *International Encyclopedia of Education.* Oxford: Pergamon.

Part II

Standardized Policies in a World of Diversity

CHAPTER 4

Education for Competitiveness and Diversity in the Richest Countries

HOLGER DAUN

INTRODUCTION

Some of the richest countries in the world, that is the United Kingdom and the United States, were important contributors to the world model for educational policy. Their responses to the educational restructuring movement were identical in some aspects, while they differed in others. With the exception of Japan, most of the OECD countries have adopted the policy of restructuring, which means that educational policies are converging. Centralized systems had to be decentralized, while decentralized systems had to have some components, for example, curricula and assessment, centralized. At the same time, there is evidence of divergence in that profiles of schools within countries are becoming more diverse, with local adaptation of curricula and changes in the language of instruction.

The policies of restructuring seem to be conditioned less than before by existing national social, cultural, economic educational characteristics, such as degree of centralization-decentralization, educational costs, and academic achievement. The policies have to be seen also in the light of the global drive for competitiveness and the multi-cultural and local demands for diversity. However, despite a large number of similarities among the OECD countries in regard to policy formulations, their educational systems vary considerably in certain respects (Daun, 1998; OECD, 1994, 1995). In other words, state policies have become more homogeneous than before while there are differences as to their degree of implementation and, still more, in their outcomes (Barro, 1996; OECD, 1994).

This chapter describes some of the principal features of educational changes in the OECD countries and relates them, first to the internal characteristics of each country and then to some indicators of these countries' position in the global economy.

General Background

The OECD countries started from very different educational baselines; the war had affected them differently and their education systems had few similarities. Until the mid-1980s, it was argued that the educational systems were so deeply rooted in their national and local contexts that it would be difficult to establish common features in the schools of certain EU countries (Husén & Kogan, 1984; Mauriel 1993). Internal factors that traditionally have or may be assumed to have conditioned the educational system in Western countries are (i) degree of cultural homogeneity- heterogeneity; (ii) the relationship between the church and state; (iii) type of state; (iv) type of welfare system; and (v) political party constellations. In comparatively homogeneous countries, the state came to implement a uniform public education system (Austria, Finland, France, Norway and Sweden). There are some exceptions; Denmark is culturally homogeneous but has, for historical reasons, a relatively large private sector and developed choice arrangements. New Zealand and Spain are not homogeneous but have a unified system, mainly because minorities (Maori, Basques, and Catalonians, respectively) were neither considered in state policies nor able to make their voices heard before the 1970s. A more recent factor that affects the degree of cultural homogeneity is immigration. After the second World War, the countries differed in their immigration policies, resulting, for instance, in a relatively low percentage of immigrants in Finland and a high percentage in Canada, the Netherlands and the United States (OECD, 1995). The immigrants differ from country to country in their organizational capacity and in their ability to articulate their educational interests to the state. At the end of the 1970s, immigrants in the European countries had not become numerous enough nor had they become organized enough to articulate their educational needs to the state.

In most European countries, the church established schools centuries ago and in most countries this right has been maintained. The role of the church in educational matters derives from the relationship between the church and the state. In Protestant countries, the church became subordinate to the state and Protestantism became the state religion, while religion became a school subject. Later, the influence of the church was undermined and the secular state came to dominate educational policies. In some countries (France, Italy and Spain) the Catholic church has been able to exert influence over the state's educational policy, at least when it comes to the regulation of and subsidies to private schools (Altrichter & Posch, 1994; Fowler, 1991a). In France, for instance, there was a struggle in the 1980s between the state and the Catholic church over the level of subsidies and control (Fowler, 1991b). Countries in which the church was subordinated to the state tended not to have strong choice possibilities (with Denmark as a notable exception).

Degree of state corporatism is another factor that is likely to have conditioned educational policies.[1] Before the wave of restructuring policies, the church had an important corporate role in Austria and Ireland. In other countries, secular interests, such as labor movements, teacher unions, employers, and so forth, were involved in corporatist relationships and were heavily represented in the formulation of policies, decision-making and implementation of educational policies.

In the Netherlands, there are at least three distinct pillars, and some researchers mention four: the Catholic, the Calvinist, the socialist and according to some, the liberal pillar. Therborn (1989:202) defines the pillars sociologically as "a set of closed, tightly interlocking organizations held together by a common cultural orientation." It could be expected that the higher the degree of corporatism, the higher the educational costs per pupil in primary and lower secondary school and the lower the number of pupils per teacher. However, a high degree of corporatism was not an obstacle to educational restructuring in any OECD country. Rather, the corporatist relationships themselves were weakened by the liberalizations of external trade and globalization processes (Daun, 1997, 1998a). Some countries, such as Germany and Sweden, seem to have developed a new type of corporatism in the face of globalization forces and the struggle for competitiveness.

Restructuring is assumed by politicians and researchers to improve educational quality and, consequently, pupil performance. In the Anglophone countries, restructuring was, at least until the beginning of the 1990s, combined with a neo-Fordist strategy, while Germany and Sweden, for instance, have combined educational restructuring with a post-Fordist strategy (see Chapter 1).

Welfare systems among these countries vary. They can take the form of a public monopoly or a task divided between the public sphere and the voluntary organizations and/or commercial interests (Badelt, 1988; James, 1988; Kramer, 1988). In the first case, the state finances and provides welfare. When voluntary organizations are in charge of the provision, the state tends to provide economic resources. There was, until the end of the 1980s, to some extent a correspondence between type of welfare system and educational policy; countries with a broad coverage and state provision of welfare tended more than others to have a comprehensive educational system.

Political party constellations also vary between countries. Whether the size of a country's public sector, welfare system and policies correspond or not with the relative power of the political parties, trade unions and religious movements has been the object of research. However, party constellations do not make any difference in policies concerning educational restructuring (Caldwell, 1993; Durston, 1993). Rather, it seems that Social Democratic governments have been the initiators of educational restructuring, sometimes in opposition to their "corporates" (e.g. Australia, the United Kingdom, Canada, New Zealand, Norway and Sweden). On the other hand, educational budgets tend to be higher and comprehensive schooling tends to be more common in countries with a history of dominance by the political Left.

There are, by tradition, large differences between countries in the characteristics of their education systems, such as in educational costs, degree of centralization, and academic performance. Educational costs, measured as a percentage of the GNP, and the level of government expenditures or cost per pupil, are tightly connected variables that affect of restructuring. Educational costs in the end of the 1990s were considerably higher in Canada, Denmark, the Netherlands, Norway, Finland, and Sweden than in the other OECD countries[2]. In Denmark, there is even an increase in the cost per pupil from the 1980s to the mid-1990s, despite a period of economic recession (Conrad 1998).

In Canada, Finland, Norway and Sweden, the populations are highly dispersed and schools are found even in sparsely populated areas, factors which account for some proportion of the costs[3]. The Nordic countries are ambitious in providing all children with a school within a reasonable distance from home. They also have a policy of integrating children with learning or other difficulties in "ordinary" schools. All high-spending countries restructured considerably, as did some low-cost countries such as New Zealand and the United Kingdom. Denmark is also an exception: its education system had very early the features that are expected to be attained through restructuring. A comparatively high level of performance did not prevent some countries from restructuring, while previous degree of decentralization/centralization meant different potentials for changes in the level for decision-making. Some of the most centralized countries (Finland, New Zealand, Norway and Sweden) have decentralized to a large extent, while Greece, Italy, Japan and Portugal did not at all before the mid-1990s. France did so less than was possible based upon its baseline.

Several countries conduct regular national assessments of academic performance and participate in the IEA comparisons, while others do not. The level of academic performance varies considerably between the countries. Finland and Japan, for instance, had the highest or among the highest scores at the beginning of the 1970s as well as ten and twenty years later, while England and the United States scored among the lowest (Keeves, 1992; OECD, 1995). Generally, there is no clear relationship between academic performance and restructuring. In the case of the United Kingdom and the United States, such a relationship exists, however, Finland, New Zealand and Sweden carried out the maximum degree of restructuring even though pupils in these countries have always performed well in national assessments (Daun, 1997, 1998).

The whole cultural-linguistic issue has emerged during a period in which other forces, such as economic scarcity and competition, are also at work. In Europe, the EU's ambition to create a European dimension in education is also relevant in this context (Collot, Didier & Loueslati, 1993; EU 1994; Gordiani, 1993). Apart from international migration, revitalization of long-term minority and indigenous cultures have taken place in, for instance, Canada, Spain and the United Kingdom. The changes mentioned put various and sometimes contradictory demands on the education systems: (a) cultural affiliation versus class affiliation; (b) local culture and local identity versus national or even regional culture and identity; (c) assimilation versus integration; and (d) learning the mother tongue as an affair for the family or for the school. Multicultural measures, such as the introduction of more than one language of instruction and local adaptations of the curricula, have been taken by some countries. The general emphasis put on values or moral education during the past decade may be interpreted as a response the cultural challenges (Taylor, 1994).

COMPETITIVENESS AND EDUCATIONAL CHANGE

We have seen that internal factors, such as state-church relationships, degree of corporatism, and so on, that traditionally have conditioned educational reform, apparently did not have a significant influence on more recent policies in education. Instead, we look at educational changes in the context of each country´s relative position in the world economy. We cannot assume that there is a direct relationship between growth rates and the tendency to restructure the education system. Rather, long-term decline or deterioration in the rate of GNP per capita growth should be seen as a context in which educational changes take place. Changes in GNP per capita are summarized in table 4.1.

TABLE 4.1 GNP PER CAPITA, IN US DOLLARS (EACH COUNTRY 1973=100)

	1973	1977	1984	1989	1993
Austria	3510	174	260	492	402
Australia	4350	169	270	330	396
Belgium	4560	166	189	356	475
Canada	5450	155	244	344	366
Denmark	5210	154	214	393	513
Finland	3600	171	299	614	536
France	4540	161	215	393	495
Germany	5320	153	209	384	443
Greece	1870	150	202	286	395
Ireland	2150	134	231	405	605
Italy	2450	140	262	617	810
Japan	3630	156	293	655	867
Netherlands	4330	165	220	361	484
Norway	4660	183	299	478	557
New Zealand	3680	119	210	328	342
Portugal	1410	134	140	301	648
Spain	1710	187	260	546	745
Sweden	5910	157	201	365	485
UK	3060	144	280	477	590
USA	6200	137	248	326	399

Sources: World Bank 1973, 1979, 1986, 1991 and 1995.

From the mid-1970s and at least until the mid-1990s, Europe lost shares on the world market, along with its competitive edge, not only to Japan and Southeast Asian countries but also to the United States. Additionally, unemployment in some European countries was higher than in other regions mentioned (European Commission, 1994). The governments and companies in New Zealand, Sweden, United States, Australia, Canada, Greece, and the Netherlands should be concerned considering their declining economic position in the world economy. The first three countries mentioned had low growth rates throughout the period, and are among those that restructured most.

The British and American economies, on the other hand, improved their economic standing from the end of the 80s. Both countries started to restructure their educational systems early and continued on the path of educational restructuring. Finland and Norway deviate most from the traditional direction of educational change; their internal conditions were not favorable for educational restructuring. Norway continued to have a stronger international position than most other OECD countries due to oil exports, while Finland experienced a setback during the last years of the 1980s and the first half of the 1990s. Both countries implemented full restructuring measures later than, for instance, New Zealand, Sweden, the United Kingdom and the United States. Internally, all the Nordic countries except Denmark have factors such as a strong labor movement that traditionally have not favored changes of the restructuring type. Considering the traditional patterns of educational reform, we might expect that countries having low rates of economic growth throughout the period or having deteriorating growth rates would make attempts to restructure their systems accordingly.

To summarize, Denmark, Finland, New Zealand, Norway, Sweden and the United Kingdom restructured more than expected, given their particular internal conditions as previously described. All these countries except New Zealand are comparatively culturally homogeneous. And all except Denmark, the United Kingdom and the Southern European countries had comparatively high levels of educational performance. With the exception of Denmark and the United Kingdom, all had a very centralized education system. In other words, the United Kingdom, more than other countries, accumulated internal features that would make educational restructuring more probable. In the global context, New Zealand, Sweden and the United Kingdom became less competitive. This might be assumed to constitute an important context for the educational changes that were implemented. In the UK, educational restructuring started in the beginning of the 1980s when the British economy was in the last phase of a severe decline. Norway is the only country that restructured despite both internal and external conditions "unfavorable" for restructuring (Rust & Blakemore 1990). The opposite is true for Greece and Portugal.

In chapter 3, it was shown that restructuing measures, especially decentralization, are very complex. The results from three studies (Barro, 1996; EU, 1997; OECD, 1995) demonstrate that there still are considerable differences between the countries.

Education for Competitiveness and Diversity in the Richest Countries

LEVELS OF DECISION-MAKING IN VARIOUS COUNTRIES IN THE MID-1990S

What was the result, in the mid-90s, of the educational changes that had been decided upon since early 1980s? Countries in which private schools have traditionally played an important role have seen a small increase in private enrollments during the past two decades. In countries where freedom of choice was introduced during the 1980s or the beginning of the 1990s, about ten percent of parents came to use this opportunity (OECD, 1994, 1998; Skolverket, 1996b). Barro (1996) compared financing of compulsory, secondary and vocational education in these countries. He found that there were big differences between the countries as to the level from which sources came and the items that were financed from different levels.

In the review of education in the EU and EFTA countries made by the European Commission, it was found that all countries have maintained the aims and goals of compulsory education despite certain changes in some countries and a high degree of restructuring in others. The goals may be grouped into six categories: equal social opportunities; basic education for all; promoting both stability and social change; preparing children for adult life; acquiring motivation for routine learning and preparation for a changing world; and well-being or personal development of the child (EU, 1997:13).

Half of the countries have, during the past two decades, extended the duration of compulsory schooling. The highest degree of decentralization of financial issues have taken place in Finland, France, the Netherlands, Portugal, Spain and Sweden. Curriculum reforms had been implemented in eight countries.

In an OECD study in which all member countries participated (with the exception of Australia, Canada, Greece and Italy), thirty-four types of decisions in four fields were studied: the organization of instruction; the planning of education and the establishment within which it is delivered; personnel management; and resource allocation and use. The decision-making levels were divided into:school; intermediate I (municipality, district); intermediate II (regional); and central government. The three classifications for modes of decision-making were: full autonomy; in conjunction or after consultations with local bodies; and by the schools independently but within a framework set by a higher authority. In the first case, schools decide themselves, while in the second, decisions are made above the school level but the schools are consulted prior to the final decision. In the third case, the schools can make decisions but within a framework established by a higher authority. Decision-making was studied at basic, lower secondary and upper secondary levels of education.

From the findings, several noteworthy points can be made. Recruitment of staff is made at the local level in Finland and Sweden. The most extensive decentralization of administration of economic resources exists in Finland, France, the Netherlands, Spain and Sweden. Apart from this, all of these countries except the Netherlands had, until the 1990s, very centralized systems and still do in some respects.

When the private sector is comparatively large, decision-making levels tend to be similar in both public and private sectors. Some countries have a single, dominant level; in Ireland and New Zealand it is the school level, in Belgium and the United States, the local, while in Portugal the national government is dominant. Other countries have two dominant levels, such as in Denmark, Finland, Germany, Norway, Sweden, and Switzerland, where the school and local authorities have more decision-making power relative to other levels. A third category of countries have multi-level systems: Austria, France and Spain. On the basis of the school's share of the decisions made, the countries can be grouped into six different categories according to the proportion of all decisions made at school level: (a) Ireland, New Zealand (>70 percent); (b) Sweden (48 percent); (c) Austria, Denmark, Finland, Portugal (38–41 percent); (d) Germany, France, Norway (31–33 percent); (e) Belgium, Spain, United States (25–28 percent); and (f) Switzerland (10 percent).

In some countries (Germany, Sweden and the United States) the changes are coherent meaning that the decision-making structure is exactly the same for all levels of schooling. When decision-making is concentrated at the local level, there seems to be competition between the municipal board and the school. In the Nordic countries these powers are split between the schools and the local authorities (OECD 1995:42–44). The most extreme cases are Switzerland which has very little decision-making at the school level but very much at the intermediate level and New Zealand, where seventy-five percent of the decisions are made at the school level. There is also a tendency that the higher the level of education, the more decisions are taken by the schools. The way in which decisions are made differs greatly from country to country. In the case of lower secondary education the proportion of decisions taken at one level or another in complete autonomy ranges from nineteen percent (United States) to seventy percent (Norway). In all countries, except the United States and Finland, some decisions are made entirely autonomously.

It is concluded that there were two principal reasons for the reforms during the last fifteen years: (i) concern for the effectiveness and equality of education systems, and (ii) the upsurge in regional sentiment (OECD, 1995:9). Another conclusion is that "No easily identifiable (administrative/decision-making) model is common to the majority of countries and the straightforward contrast between centralized and decentralized systems is no longer valid" (Ibid.:49). Also, Barro (1996) identifies what he calls "four stabilized models of school finance" among the OECD countries: the North American model; the British model (the United Kingdom after 1988): the Continental European centralized model; and the Continental European Federal model. In other words, a great deal of convergence has taken place with regard to the dimensions of centralization–decentralization of structures but when it comes to each level's share of decision-making and the content of the decisions, there are still considerable differences between the countries.

EDUCATIONAL CHANGE IN SELECTED COUNTRIES

United Kingdom

The United Kingdom had lost its colonies and the important characteristics of a world power. Its rate of economic growth was one of the lowest among the OECD countries until the mid-1980s, and output even decreased during some years in the decade. Industry suffered greatly from competition, and no employment or export compensation was attained in budding industries, such as high technology. The balance of trade has for the most part been negative; the value of imports has been higher than that of exports. That is, the United Kingdom accumulated more negative national factors than most of the other OECD countries, if the education system is not taken into consideration.

When Thatcher came into power, she used the restructuring discourse as an instrument to bypass the established political structures and to appeal directly to the masses in order to reinforce her own position (McLean, 1985; McLean and Voskresenskaya, 1992). At the national level, there was a weak degree of corporatism; this fact would make educational change of the restructuring type more easy. However, at the local level strong corporatism existed between the Local Education Authorities (LEAs) and the teachers' unions; this could make such changes difficult. The degree of decentralization that already existed was comparatively high.

The LEAs had been established with the 1902 Education Act, and they became a means to undermine the power that the churches had over educational matters (Dunleavy, 1989). Two types of schools came to be termed "state" schools: (i) regular county schools that were established and operated by the LEAs; (ii) voluntary schools established by churches or benevolent individuals and financially supported by the LEAs (Britain, 1994). The second category included (a) voluntary schools controlled by the LEAs; (b) volunteer-supported schools; and (c) special agreements. Independent schools are not controlled by the state bodies, and they are the only ones generally referred to as "private." According to the 1944 Education Act, volunteer supported schools received fifty percent of school capital building costs from the LEAs. This percentage was increased on different occasions and in 1975 it was up to eighty-five percent. With the rise of the Conservative government after 1980, these subsidies were gradually diminished (Arthur, 1996).

Conservative educational policy caused the disagreement between themselves and the Labor Party to become manifest and open (Hewton, 1986). The conservatives and neo-liberals stated that the economic decline was at least partially due to the low standards of the educational system. Various studies in the 1970s and the first half of the 1980s showed that employers were not satisfied with what the pupils learned in the school system (Freeman & Soete, 1994:120). This contributed to the demand for radical measures to be taken in order to improve compulsory education.

Changes in the restructuring direction were announced already by the Labour Minister of Education in 1976, but it was the Conservative government that implemented this type of educational policy (Ball, 1990:23). At the local level, power alliances had emerged between teacher unions, LEAs and the Labour Party (Beare & Telford, 1994), and according to the Conservatives they were an obstacle to improvement of the education system. In 1980, parents were given the option to choose which school within the public system their children would attend. The "Assisted Places Scheme" was also introduced; underprivileged high-achieving pupils were given special support to continue in secondary schools of their choice.. The school districts reacted very differently to the introduction of choice; some implemented the system, while others were reluctant.

In 1983, some of the decision-making power was decentralized from the local education authorities to the schools, on the one hand, and centralized to the Ministry of Education, on the other hand (Walford, 1992). The 1988 Education Act instituted a national curriculum and national assessment of achievement for pupils aged 7, 11, 14, and 16 years; all secondary schools and some primary schools were to control their own budgets; choice possibilities were extended, and parents could now choose any school within the district; and government schools were given the right to "opt out" and become "grant maintained" schools (McLean, 1989; Walford 1990:128-129).

According to Wallace (1990), the central government now became involved in educational matters more than ever before. From 1990, open enrollment was in force; schools had, according to their capacity, to accept all students and money "accompanied" the pupils. The LEAs were no longer able to formulate and implement their own policies. Financial responsibility and hiring and firing of teachers had been moved from the LEAs to the schools (Thomas, 1990). Quasi-markets started to emerge (Whitty, 1996, 1997). The 1993 Education Act extended the principles of diversity, choice and institutional autonomy (Britain, 1994). One indication of the acceptance of diversity is the fact that since 1998, two Muslim schools have been approved for state subsidies (Walford, 1999).

The United Kingdom could have improved educational efficiency and somewhat relaxed the regulations for choice and privatization, but the decisions actually taken were unexpected. On the one hand, decentralization and deregulation were more extensive than could be predicted, and, on the other, centralization with the implementation of a national curriculum and national assessments was not foreseen by educational practitioners or educational researchers. On the whole, the restructuring policies did not correspond to the EU suggestions for harmonization of the education systems (Flude & Hammer, 1990) and until 1998, the United Kingdom refused to sign the EU agreements on social policy.

United States

Despite the increase in the amount of money spent on education and the implementation of various reforms during the 1960s and 1970s, public discontent with schooling was widespread. The economy was declining at least until the end of the 1980s, and the decrease in foreign investments in the United States may be mentioned as one indicator (Carnoy 1993). During the 1980s, the sensitivity of the United States economy to global trends and shocks increased as it became more multinational (Carliner, 1995:259). During the 1990s, the American economy improved considerably but a similar improvement in education was not reported.

There has always existed a clear division of functions between various levels of the educational administration. Through the decades, immigration, increasing socioeconomic stratification and external conditions provoked the federal government to intervene and invest more in education. It became important to "Americanize" various subcultures and to create national unity. With the implementation of policy for minority groups, mainly intended to improve equality, the federal government became more involved in the financing of education (Apple, 1993; Cohen & Spillane, 1992; Weiler 1989). At the end of the 1950s, it covered 4.4 percent of the education costs, and in 1980 the figure had increased to 9.2 percent (McGinn & Pereira, 1992:175; Walberg, 1989:77). The educational expenditures (as percentage of GNP) doubled during the period 1939–1970 but no corresponding increase in productivity of the economy was observed (Walberg 1989). Despite these centralizing tendencies the country's education system is regarded as one of the most decentralized in the world (McGinn & Pereira, 1992).

Under the federal network of laws there are considerable variations within and between the states, between the fifteen thousand districts and between the schools with regard to choice and privatization. Below the state level there are local educational authorities that have a relatively large amount of autonomy, since the states have delegated many of their former tasks to these authorities and the schools. No national examinations exist and schools use different tests, which do not always measure knowledge within the areas covered in the schools and it is not known to what extent they are comparable. Much of the decision-making takes place at the school level; schools decide upon educational programs, student assignment and teacher assignment, for instance. The United States is probably the country where the local traditionally has played an important role in education. In some states choice has always existed but the conditions for coice have differed.

According to a decision by the Supreme Court in the middle of the 1920s, the country did not have any state religion and therefore private, religious schools could not receive any subsidies from public authorities (Boyd, 1987; Cookson, 1992). Some amendments were made in 1965 and 1981 that make it somewhat easier for non- confessional schools to receive public subsidies. The American constitution allows parents to educate their children at home and home education is more important than in many other OECD countries (*The Economist*, 1998). Parents who opt for home education may be divided into two groups: ideologists and pedagogues (Cizek, 1990). The former do not want to send their children to an educational institution for ideological or religious reasons, while the latter chose to teach their own children for pedagogical reasons.

Approximately ten percent of all primary school pupils received their education in Catholic schools during the 1960s. At that time alternative schools were established by groups of parents (Cookson Jr., 1991). The private sector is currently dominated by the Catholic church. There are large variations between the states in this regard; seventeen percent of students in the state of Connecticut and one percent in the state of Wyoming attend private schools. These schools are small units, and half of them have less than 150 pupils (Cookson Jr., 1989). It has been estimated that the annual cost per pupil in the early 1980s was $2,016 in the public sector, $1,353 in Catholic schools, $5,000 in elite private schools, and $2,777 in private schools overall (ibid.). These figures demonstrate that there are considerable differences within the private sector.

The discourse on and the policies of restructuring included four elements: (i) school-based management; (ii) parental choice; (iii) national goals; and (iv) national assessment (McGinn & Pereira, 1992:176–177). According to Hannaway (1994), four basic school choice plans existed in the United States in the beginning of the 1990s: magnet schools, open enrollment, tuition tax credits, and voucher plans. Magnet schools had been introduced during the 1960s as a way to facilitate desegregation. Some experiments with open enrollment had also been attempted. However, it was not until the beginning of the 1980s that the introduction of decentralization, choice, tax reduction, and voucher systems became common themes in the educational debate.

A new trend in education started during the first year of the Reagan administration (Boyd, 1991). In the beginning of the 1980s, the government published "A Nation At Risk," in which the critical educational situation was described and solutions suggested. The situation was described as catastrophic and many recommendations were made for improving the system: introduction of a national core curriculum, increased demands on pupils, increased number of school hours and improved management of the schools (Johnston, 1990:221). The level of achievement among American pupils decreased in relation to previous cohorts in the 1980s and in relation to those of pupils from other industrialized countries. Private schools, primarily Catholic, had always existed but had not received any particular attention until this time of perceived crisis in public education (Cookson, 1989).

President Ronald Reagan made attempts in the beginning of the decade to pass a bill on subsidies to all types of private schools but failed (Henig, 1993). This proposition was integrated into a large package of reforms that apparently would improve the situation of the most underprivileged pupils; vouchers would be given to the poorest pupils, for instance. This package also failed (Dougherthy & Sostre 1992). President George Bush then made attempts to implement voucher plans that were said to improve the situation for underprivileged children but would also include religious schools (Henig, 1993:91–92).

In the beginning of the 1990s, for instance, twenty-nine states discussed the introduction of choice within the public sector, and fifteen others had already introduced it (Martin & Burke, 1990; Raywid, 1990). In most cases it is possible to choose between public schools within the same school district. However, in some states the pupils may choose across districts, and in Minnesota and Colorado, open enrollment statewide was introduced. In some districts, parents can deduct private school fees (Cohen & Spillane, 1992; Cookson Jr., 1989).

The combination of rapidly expanding federal policy initiatives of educational restructuring, such as choice arrangements, on the one hand, and the fragmented and diversified governance at the state and local levels, on the other hand, creates tensions and contradictions (Cohen & Spillane, 1992). Despite school-based management, some decisions are still made at the state and district levels.

There is a tendency in the United States to look to school education for solutions to social problems, and to link economic performance to educational quality (Hogan, 1992; Stern, 1992). However, there are researchers who question the crisis syndrome. They argue that education has not deteriorated to that extent. Henig (1993), for instance, maintains that studies of pupil achievement do not show any clear evidence of a crisis. Therefore, he interprets the use of the crisis terminology as a strategy for attaining certain political goals. Papagiannis, Easton & Owens (1992:55), argue in their review of research on educational restructuring in the United States: "consideration of the larger political economic framework of restructuring can lead one to question whether the announced crisis in American education, the one that has provided much of the impetus for school restructuring, is entirely real . . . " Indirectly, they state that there are other (political) reasons for the emergence of the crisis perspective and that restructuring measures were seen as the most appropriate steps to be taken. The school, they argue, has to be considered in a context of economic decline and budget cuts in education. The internal problems of the United States economy have, until mid-1990s, to be interpreted in relation to changes in the world economy. From the 1970s, the United States also started to lose terrain on the world market, while Germany and Japan, for example, became stronger.

Parental response to more than ten years of struggle for freedom of choice in education has until now been weak. The choice possibilities have been exploited by only a small percentage of the parents who had this option (Chira, 1992; Olsson, 1992).

A new wave of systemic reforms were initiated in the early 1990s. From a systems perspective it was argued that changes in governance and regime were not enough; changes internal to the schools have to be accomplished in order to affect the processes of teaching and learning in the classrooms. According to Clune (1993), systemic reform assumes that the curriculum and teacher competence should be improved and pupils should be able to attain higher order learning—apart from the introduction of

SBD and SBM. During the past years, the number of charter schools has increased. Such schools are most frequent in districts with low performance and a larger percentage of African-Americans (Arsen et al., 2000). Charter Schools also play an increasing role in some states, such as Arizona, California, and Michigan (Arsen et al., 2000). According to ECS (2000:2), two trends have dominated educational reform for the past fifteen years: (i) push to establish high standards and use them to improve performance and strengthen accountability, and (ii) push to decentralize decision-making to the school level.

Canada

There are indications that the federal government feels pressure from two directions to take more overall initiatives in education; on the one hand, the internal multicultural diversity and demands, especially from the French-speaking population, and, on the other hand, the increasing global competition (Lawton, 1993). A council of ministers of education was established at the federal level in the 1960s to coordinate educational activities in the country but every province has its own system (Fullan, 1991).

Canada had a high rate of GDP growth per capita during the 1960s and 1970s and then the economy slowed down. The percentage of public expenditures and of GNP spent on education has through the decades been among the highest in the OECD countries (World Bank, 1979, 1986, 1995). During the past decade, attention has been focused on the declining position of the country in the global economy; the trade agreements during the past decade have made Canada more open to the United States economy. Furthermore, domestic issues relating to the culturally heterogeneous citizenry and the more recent influx of immigrants have created pressure for educational diversity. During the last years of the 1980s and the first half of the 1990s, Canada probably had the highest rate of immigration in the world. Annually, more than 200,000 individuals immigrated into the country (Lawton, 1997).

In religious and linguistic composition, the differences between the provinces are very great. More than sixty-one percent of the population is Anglophone, while roughly more than twenty-six percent are Francophiles (Canada, 1992). In the federation, there are ten provinces and two "territories." Provincial authorities determine the number and types of school boards (Gayfer, 1991) in approximately one thousand school districts. The school boards or school councils are elected according to type of school and type of community. This means that within a particular geographical area, there may exist one board for Catholic schools, and another for the public schools. The school council is in charge of implementation of curricula, administration and operation of schools, acquisition of financial resources, and initiation of proposals for the establishment of new schools. School councils receive grants from the provincial government but also have the authority to impose taxes on local citizens. Canada does not have a centralized educational system, since the power of the federal government in relation to educational matters is relatively limited.

There are private schools or alternative schools in all provinces. Many different religious communities are involved in education (Barro, 1996). The public subsidies to these schools vary from one state to another. In one province, seventy percent of their revenues derive from school fees and in another state one-third of the school expenditures are covered through subsidies from the province government. Despite the variety in governance and regime, most of the schools are rather similar with the exception of a minority of expensive elite schools (Bergen, 1989).

Freedom of choice is a tradition few parents have utilized, as only a small percentage of primary school pupils attend private schools (Bergen 1989). 2.3 percent in 1973, 4.7 percent in 1982, with no change in 1990 (Gayfer, 1991; Lawton, 1989:178). The percentage of primary school pupils in private schools and the level of subsidies to private schools vary considerably between the provinces (Gayfer, 1991).

As a nation, Canada has neither made national assessments nor participated in international comparisons of pupil achievement. However, four provinces took part in the last IEA study in mathematics. The results were not encouraging to the federal government, so initiatives were taken to collect statistics and information on a regular basis in order to monitor school achievement and by mid-1990s province wide testing had been introduced (Lawton, 1997). Researchers argue that Canada has not yet centralized decision-making in education to the extent that both New Zealand and the United Kingdom have; nor has it permitted as much market influence in education as the United States (Fullan, 1991; Lawton, 1993).

Japan[4]

Japan has seen two dramatic educational transformations in its modern history. The first took place after the Meiji Restoration in 1868, when education was redesigned as part of an effort to build a strong, industrialized nation-state.The second major reform was brought about by the American occupation after the second World War, when democratization became the main concern of educational reform (Schoppa, 1991). The contemporary educational system was established after the war under the supervision of the United States. The Fundamental Law of Education was passed in 1947 and this law did became not only the basis for educational reform in post-war Japan, but also reflected the universal value of liberalism (Uzawa, 1998). Together with the new constitution that was established under the occupation, this law became one of the foundations for democratic control and egalitarianism (Schoppa, 1991).Under this transformation, the education system was decentralized, the compulsory three–year junior secondary level was added, and the levels of the school system were reorganized (Haiducek, 1991:28). Compulsory education was to include six years of primary school education and three years of lower secondary schooling. The current national curriculum is very detailed and the schools are required to teach in eight core subjects, four of which are art, handicrafts, sports and music (Holmes and McLean, 1992).

In the 1950s, the ruling conservative Liberal Democratic Party began to regard the reform initiated by the Occupation powers as an imposition by foreign military authorities. A series of changes to centralize the educational system were implemented during this period. The Ministry of Education gradually took direct control of educational policy by amending regulations and weakening the local autonomy with which Japan had little experience (Horio, 1997a; Schoppa, 1991; Uzawa, 1998). Schools have, according to the constitution, the authority to make some local adaptations of the curriculum and to hire teachers. However, the former has in practice not been used to any considerable extent (Cohen & Spillane, 1992).

In the rapid economic growth of the 1960s, the business circles put pressure on the education system to be meritocratic (Horio, 1997a; Uzawa, 1998). Diversification according to merit was the overall aim of educational changes from the 1960s to the 1990s (Horio, 1997a). From the end of World War II to the beginning of the 1990s, the Japanese economy had a continuous and strong growth rate. After the oil crises of 1973–1974 and 1979–1980, Japan's rate of economic growth slowed, but not as much as that of other OECD countries (Haiducek, 1991; World Bank, 1979, 1990). The state has been active in formulating strategies for the export industry. Japan was initially competitive in traditional industries and had a tremendous growth until mid-1990s. When the NICs started to expand on the world market, Japan entered into high technology industries and became competitive. The Japanese state then gave emphasis to high technology and supported such companies to develop and expand rapidly in these areas (Carliner, 1995:148–150).

Specific educational reforms were suggested from 1969–1971 by the Central Council for Education (CCE), a permanent advisory body to the Minister of Education, which included compulsory kindergarten education, revision of the levels of the system, earlier entrance into the school system and integration of lower and upper secondary education as well as changes in higher education and reforms concerning teachers and teacher training. As soon as these proposals were published by the CCE, however, they met with great resistance from different groups. This resistance coincided with other social and financial factors such as budget constraints. As a result, no major reform took place in the 1970s (Schoppa, 1991). Japanese society has the structure of a trinity between the polity, the officialdom, and the business circles. In the process of political reforms and privatization policies in the 1970s and 1980s, the business circles gradually increased their influence over the polity and, consequently, over educational policy (Horio, 1997b). During the first decades, the interests of the business circles became more articulated and competition for places in upper secondary schools and higher education became very stiff.

In 1984, the National Council on Educational Reform (NCER) was established as an ad hoc council when Prime Minister Nakasone came into power. Some of the important themes in the proposal launched by the NCER during the three years of its work were liberalization and flexibility. Less restrictive rules for establishing private primary and lower secondary schools were encouraged as a way to increase competition in the system. School districts were to be enlarged or abolished in order to give parents and students more choices (Hayano, 1993). Flexibility referred to policies that were to end the uniformity of primary and lower secondary education. Less regulation of curriculum guidelines by the Ministry of Education, more decentralization, and significant reduction of Ministry control over the textbook screening system were recommended, among other things. These recommendations, however, were vague and did not propose that the Ministry itself give up any powers (Hayano, 1993; Jgarashi, 1988; Schoppa, 1991).

Practically all school-age pupils are enrolled in public schools at the primary level. Only one percent attended regular private schools during the 1980s and 1990s (Anderson, 1990:3; Outline, 1989; World Bank, 1993). Competition for places in secondary and higher education is very intense. For this reason, the majority of pupils also take part in *juku*, which is private, supplementary teaching, either in the form of individual lessons or regular classes in institutions (Holmes, 1989; Walberg, 1989). Almost all kindergartens are private, in addition to being subsidized by local authorities and the central state (Holmes, 1989:200). Japan still has one of the most centralized educational systems in the world. Educational costs are comparatively low, while the level of academic achievement has consistently been one of the highest in the world. However, there are hidden costs which the parents must shoulder, such as *juku* and very comprehensive uniforms.

France

The state is known for its high degree of intervention in the economy. This means that the government plans a certain level of production to be achieved in different sectors but it does not interfere in the private sector. Secondly, France has a long tradition of direct state involvement in the economy; the proportion of state ownership in the economy increased with the Socialist presidency although some privatization has taken place during the 1990s (Carliner, 1995). The state is highly involved in the high technology industry and stimulates innovations within this domain. Despite these efforts, France's position in the global economy declined during the 1980s and the beginning of the 1990s. The transfer from primary sector production to production in other sectors accelerated during the 1980s. Loss of employment in agriculture and industry was not replaced by employment in the service sector. In other words, unemployment was high during the whole period from the 1970s and onwards. Shares in traditional sectors of the world market were lost due to competition from other countries with lower labor costs. The same applies to the high technology sectors, despite the efforts of the government to invest in these sectors.

Economic and social planning had existed since the end of the second World War, and education was integral part of this project. Detailed plans were used for the provision of schools according to demographic changes such as birth rates, rates of immigration, and so on. New schools were to correspond to these plans, if they were to receive subsidies. The necessary number of places in schools are estimated for a certain period, and new places are approved only if they correspond to this estimation. Fifteen percent of all children in elementary and secondary schooling receive their education within the private sector. Most of the private schools are run by the Catholic church.

A weakening position on the world market, weak corporatist relations, increasing educational costs and increasing demands from immigrant groups suggest that measures such as extensive rather than limited or partial decentralization could have been taken, along with concerted efforts to lower educational costs. However, the educational costs continued to be comparatively high during the first years of the 1990s.

The high degree of centralization of the French education system until mid-1980s was seen by researchers as a means to guarantee educational equality economically, geographically and culturally (Caré, 1988; France, 1990, 1992). Primary and secondary schools were administered by the Ministry of Education through the twenty-eight provincial offices that were headed by directors appointed by the government. The provinces were divided into departments and were staffed with inspectors appointed by the government (France 1990, 1992).

In the end of the nineteenth century the Catholic church was separated from the state; public schools were not allowed to teach religion and the decision was also made not to subsidize private religious schools. With the installation of Charles de Gaulle as President, the laws were changed. According to the Debré Act of 1959, the following possibilities exist for private schools: (1) status quo: minimal regulation and small, specific subsidies; (ii) simple contract: the school teaches the national curriculum in core subjects and teacher salaries are subsidized; (iii) association contract: the national curriculum is followed and inspection accepted; the state pays teacher salaries and some other recurrent costs; (iv) total integration: the school is integrated into the public system but managed by the private body (Fowler, 1991a).

Schools that receive subsidies also have to accept state inspection of contracts, buildings, teacher competence, and so on. However, from the 1950s to the 1990s a series of smaller changes have been made in the educational laws, and this has resulted in reduced control of the private schools (ibid.). All schools have to follow the national curriculum to the extent that they are subsidized by the state. Due to the control and processes of secularization, Catholic schools have become more and more similar to public schools. For instance, teachers recruited by these schools are no longer required to be Catholics (Fowler, 1992; Teese, 1989). Fowler (1992) even uses the term "quasi- private" schools. Within the private sector there are some elite schools, but their profile is more traditional than that of the schools in the public sector (Teese, 1989).

When the Socialist party gained the presidency in the beginning of the 1980s, to limit the subsidies to private, religious schools, a proposal was made. It was met with such strong protest that it was withdrawn. No substantial changes were then made in relation to private schools. During the 1990s, subsidies for teacher salaries were increased and the conditions for teachers in private schools were improved (EU, 1997).

According to Fowler (1991a, 1992) the discourse on private schools differs between France and the United States in many respects. In France, equality is still an important theme, while freedom and civil rights dominate the debate in the United States. The strict regulation of private schools in France has prevented competition between public and private schools, causing them to converge. Any demands for restructuring similar to and as strong as those in the United Kingdom and the United States did not arise in France, although influential Catholic groups have questioned the strong regulation of private schools. However, in the end of the 1990s, the population in Bretagne and some other areas insisted that their languages be allowed to be used as the language of instruction in primary schools. Moreover, Muslims have for a long time demanded that they should have the right to establish schools. Although it is stated in the law that religious groups may own schools (as do French Catholocs) their demands have been rejected by the state.[5]

The education system seems to be conditioned by the power struggle between the state and the Catholic church. The state has made attempts on several occasions to achieve a monopoly over educational matters while the church has defended its position. However, it seems to be the right to establish non-public schools rather than religiosity that prompts the masses to support the Catholic church when there are conflicts (Fowler, 1991a, b, 1992).

Germany

Germany had a high level of GNP per capita and also a high growth rate until the beginning of the 1990s. Growth in output, principally due to increased productivity, was also high, and external trade has been balanced. After the first years of the 1990s, the German economy also faced problems due partly to the unification of East and West Germany. Along with the economy, education was said to need improvement (Manning, 1998). Expansion of employment opportunities in the tertiary sector did not substitute for the decrease in the secondary sector of the economy; the rate of unemployment was rather high during the whole period from the 1970s.

In analyses of the German welfare system and political economy, it is argued that (i) there is a high degree of political control of the economy; (ii) priority has always been given to inflation control at the expense of employment, especially after 1973; and (iii) in contrast to the American model, political authority is not allocated to any particular level but is shared between the federal government and Länder governments. In this way, important issues have to be accepted not only by the National Parliament but also by the Federal council (Schmidt, 1989). In combination with the striving for consensus despite large differences between the Länder and the federal government, this creates inertia in decision-making and policy implementation (Schmidt, 1989).

German education policy after the second World War can, according to Telhaug (1990), be divided into three different phases: (i) until the middle of the 1960s, no important reforms were implemented; (ii) during the next ten years the Social Democratic government made attempts to implement the comprehensive schools system; and (iii) from the end of the 1970s, no extensive reforms have been decided upon. Telhaug (1990) attributes the stability to two factors: (a) the decentralized education system; the Länder (states) have strong autonomy in relation to the federal government; and (b) the German economy was expanding until the beginning of the 1990s. A fourth period may be added: the post-unification period.

The upper primary/lower secondary level is divided into different branches, one academic and one vocationally oriented. During the 1970s, the Social Democratic federal government made attempts to introduce comprehensive education according to the North European model. These attempts met with strong protests not only from the Länder governments but also from powerful economic interests in society. The introduction of comprehensive schooling was therefore left to the Länder governments and school districts to decide. If a certain number of parents in a school district request it, the school can be made comprehensive.

East Germany had a highly centralized system with ten years of comprehensive education and no private schools. The level of achievement had been comparatively high, especially in the vocational branches. After unification, some states came to subsidize all costs in private schools, while others paid ten percent or more of the total expenditures (ibid.). Comprehensive schools tend to be more prevalent in the eastern part of the country and the variation between the states became more pronounced following unification (Manning, 1998).

The German constitutional court found in 1987 that state funding of alternative private schooling was essential to the constitutionally-guaranteed free development of individual personality (Glenn, 1994). The educational laws allow parents and others to establish private schools but the same laws also protect children from "inadequate" educational institutions. It means that private schools are regulated and inspected and subsidies are conditional. The amount of subsidies per pupil must not exceed the average cost per pupil in the public sector, but private schools are allowed to charge school fees. The amount and types of subsidies vary from one state to another (Weiss & Mattern 1989). In 1994, seven percent of the pupils attended a comprehensive school (Manning, 1998).

There are two types of private schools: substitute schools and complementary schools. The former substitute for general elementary or secondary education and they have to apply for approval from the Länder government. They have to follow the same regulations as the public schools, that is, the public curriculum, inspection and control, and so on (Mason, 1989). Complementary schools are principally vocational or professional schools and they provide types of education that are not found in the public sector. They are to a large owned by or work in cooperation with private companies and need only to register and are then neither controlled by the state nor eligible for subsidies. The portion of pupils in private schools increased from 2.8 percent in 1960 to 5.8 percent in 1986 (Weiss, 1989); most of which were Catholic (Psacharopoulos, 1992) and in the end of the 1990s the figure was almost the same.

Two types of restructuring were implemented before the unification of Germany: (i) decentralization of some issues from Länder to school level; and (ii) increased monitoring and assessment of school quality and performance from the Länder level. In addition, school inspectors were appointed in every state. Cost-cutting measures were also taken, as the number of pupils per teacher was increased.

The fact the authority was situated at the Länder (regional) level would make some degree of educational decentralization probable. On the other hand, low educational costs and some degree of corporatism, some choice possibilities, at least theoretically, and a comparatively high level of performance did not constitute a basis for change.

New Zealand

The growth in GNP per capita was one of the lowest among the industrialized countries, and economic growth was slower than the average for the OECD countries. The transition from an agricultural society to a society based on the industry and service sectors took place later than in the highly industrialized European countries and the United States. Since the 1950s, New Zealand has had a GNP per capita similar to that of some of the Eastern European countries. The export of agricultural products, mainly to the United Kingdom, constituted the largest portion of the total export. The situation changed when the United Kingdom entered the European Community in the beginning of the 1970s.

The transition in exports from primary commodities to manufactured goods was important, but the merchandise export from New Zealand was still principally based on agricultural products as late as 1993. In 1960, this share was ninety-seven percent and in 1993 it dropped to sixty-six percent, while it was nine percent in the United Kingdom in 1993, for instance (World Bank, 1979, 1981 and 1995). A comparatively large proportion of the population was, therefore, employed in agriculture until the middle of the 1970s.

Out of the 3.3 million inhabitants at the beginning of the 1990s, the Maori minority constituted fourteen percent. In the past, an assimilationist policy was practiced in relation to the Maori population and their language was banned as the language of instruction and Maori children were punished for speaking Maori at school (Middleton, 1992). Since the second World War, a large number of Asians have immigrated to New Zealand (Barrington, 1994).

The educational system consisted of seven years of comprehensive schooling in the beginning of the 1980s. The system had become centralized as a result of the Keynesian policies and general centralization tendencies. A national curriculum was established some decades ago, along with automatic promotion. Private school regulations were strict and subsidies were low. Only two percent of all primary school pupils attended private schools at the beginning of the 1980s (Anderson, 1990:3), and in 1990 the percentage had increased to three (Barrington, 1994:4106).

In the 1970s, the Maori population began to revive and restore its cultural heritage, and the cultural-linguistic movement became more articulate. English had always been the language of instruction in schools and Maori could be opted for as a second language. Segments of the Maori population had demanded a legitimate place for their language in the New Zealand society and that this language be important in education.

Politically, the state is described as non-corporatist. In the beginning of the 1970s, government expenditure as a percentage of GNP was comparatively large (larger than in Sweden and the OECD average). When the Labour party came into power in the 1980s and formed its fourth government in the history of New Zealand, it began to implement a policy that can be characterized as neo-liberal including such elements as economic restructuring, shrinking of the state apparatus, budget cuts, privatization and decentralization (Barrington, 1994; Wylie, 1995). In education, decision-making and budgets were decentralized at the school level (SBD), arrangements for the regulation of private schools were revised so that it became more favourable to establish such schools. School districts were given the right to decide upon the language of instruction (Barrington, 1994; Wylie, 1995). Some hundred schools in areas where Maori was more frequently spoken, took the opportunity to begin instruction in the language. On the other hand, education had to attain national goals and national assessments were suggested (Barrington, 1994). Among the majority of the population there was no disquiet about educational quality (Whitty, 1997).

Apart from the Maori request for cultural and linguistic recognition in education, no important interest had demanded the broad spectrum of restructuring that was rapidly implemented. It was implemented even without consulting educational researchers or some important interests within the Labour party. Responsibility for major educational decisions was devolved from the central state level to the boards of trustees of each school. These boards are composed of parents and school staff members. Bulk grants are paid for by the central level to the school boards, with the exception of teacher salaries, school transport, capital investments and long-term maintenance costs. The Labor Party lost in the 1990 elections to the National Party. The policies of educational restructuring continued, and since 1991, the boards also include business people from the local community (Whitty, 1997a).

In a comparative perspective, the educational costs had not been high, and the level of pupils' academic achievement had been among the highest. The expenditure on education as a percentage of GNP has always been lower than in many other OECD countries. It increased slowly until the middle of the 1980s, when the formation of human capital became a priority. At the beginning of the 1990s, educational expenditures constituted 5.8 percent of GDP (Barrington, 1994). That is, the dramatic educational changes could not be justified in terms of educational costs and the level of achievement. Since the population is rather dispersed, small schools in rural areas have been maintained, which explains to some extent the relatively high costs per pupil. New Zealand has participated in the IEA comparisons of pupil achievement, and it has scored among the highest countries in all these studies.

Unlike the restructuring in the United Kingdom and the United States, for instance, the New Zealand´s version "specifically included goals of social equality and cultural inclusiveness" (Middleton, 1992:301). However, Lauder (2000) and Whitty (1997) claim that inequalities have increased.

Northern European Countries: Denmark, Finland, Norway, and Sweden

Denmark, Finland, Norway and Sweden formed a special group in Europe due their educational policies (Bjorndal, 1994; Conrad, 1998; Denmark, 1997; Finland, 1990, 1992; Lauglo, 1995; SMES, 1997). They had, according to Eide (1992), a more welfarist and child-centered orientation. In the 1980s, the Nordic systems were alike in the structure of the compulsory comprehensive schooling, and they had almost identical policies in regard to integration of children with learning difficulties in ordinary schools. Denmark differed in that it had a much more decentralized structure, more choice possibilities and enrollment in private schools was higher than the other countries in this group. Finland and Sweden had national evaluations. In the mid-1990s, the four countries became yet more similar in that the previously highly centralized structures had been drastically decentralized and choice possibilities had been considerably reinforced and subsidies for private education increased in Finland, Norway and Sweden.

CONCLUSIONS

Educational reforms had, until the mid-1980s, been conditioned by internal factors such as the relationship between church and state, religious and cultural composition of the country, type of state, and so on. Once global competition became a reality, many countries were forced to be economically competitive in a global context, and the neo-Liberal discourse attained a hegemonic position. With the economic recession, the emergence of new movements and the Neo-liberal paradigm, many OECD countries restructured their educational systems to an extent that cannot be understood primarily in terms of internal, national factors. Countries (Finland, New Zealand, Norway, Sweden, the United Kingdom and the United States) in which the most far–reaching restructuring measures were taken would not, considering certain internal factors, normally be expected to implement such policies. On the other hand, all of them except Norway had lost their former positions in the global economy.

However, despite all the restructuring measures, such as choice and reinforced subsidies to private schools, the OECD countries have maintained the goals and objectives for their education systems, such as equity in access regardless of gender, place of residence and socioeconomic class. Moreover, in the details, such as levels of decision-making and arrangements for regulationl of choice arrangements, there are still many differences between the countries.

NOTES

[1] Austria, the Netherlands, Norway and Sweden are generally considered to have a high degree of corporatism, while Australia, Canada, France, New Zealand, Spain, the United States and the United Kingdom have a low degree. Denmark, Finland and Germany are situated somewhere in between these two extremes (Johnson, 1987; O'Connel, 1989).

[2] All of these countries have been defined to have a high or medium degree of state corporatism.

[3] In Sweden, for instance, the most important factor explaining variation in muncipalities' cost per pupil is the average residence distance between the inhabitants in the municipality (See Skolverket, 1996a).

[4] We want to thank Michiyo Kiwako Okuma, at the Institute of International Education, Stockholm University, for her contribution to this section.

[5] Suchs schools have been recognized and receive subsidies in, for instance, England and Sweden.

REFERENCES CITED

Altrichter, H. and P. Posch (1994). "Austria: System of Education." In T. Husén and N. Postlethwaite (eds.). *The International Encyclopedia of Education*. Oxford: Pergamon.

Anderson, D. S. (1990). "The Unstable Public-Private School System in Australia." Paper published at NBEET First National Conference, November 1990.

Apple, M. (1993). "The Politics of Official Knowledge: Does a National Curriculum Make Sense?" *Teachers College Record*, vol 95, no 2.

Arsen, D., D. Plank and G. Sykes (2000). *School Choice Policies in Michigan: The Rules Matter*. Lansing: Michigan State University.

Arthur, J. (1996). "Government Education Policy and Catholic Voluntary-Aided Schools 1979-1994." *Oxford Review of Education*, vol 2, no 4.

Badelt, C. (1988). "Government versus Private Provision of Social Services: The Case of Austria." In E. James (ed.). *The Non-Profit Sector in International Perspective. Studies in Comparative Culture and Policy*. New York: Oxford University Press.

Ball, S. (1990). *Politics and Policy Making in Education. Explorations in Policy Sociology*. London: Routledge.

Barrington, J.E. (1994). "New Zealand: System of Education." In T. Husén and N. Postlethwaite (eds.). *The International Encyclopedia of Education*. Oxford: Pergamon.

Barro, S.M. (1996). "How Countries Pay for Schools. An International Comparison of System for Financing Primary and Secondary Education." *Paper prepared for the Center of the Consortium for Policy Research in Education (CPRE)*, University of Wisconsin.

Beare, H, and A. H. Telford (1994). "School Reform and Restructuring." In T. Husén and N. Postlethwaite (eds.). *The International Encyclopedia of Education*. Oxford: Pergamon.

Bergen, J.J. (1989). "Canada: Private Schools." In G. Walford (ed.). *Private Schools in Ten Countries. Policy and Practice*. London: Routledge.

Bjorndal, I.R. (1994). "Norway: Systemof Education." In T. Husén and N. Postlethwaite (eds.). *The International Encyclopedia of Education*. Oxford: Pergamon.

Boyd, W.L. (1987). "Balancing Public and Private Schools: The Australian Experience and American Implications." *Educational Evaluation and Policy Analysis*, 9 no 3.

Boyd, W.L. (1991). "Choice plans for public schools in the USA: issues and answers." *Local Government Policy Making*, vol 18 no 1.

Britain (1994). "Education." In *Britain 1994: An official handbook*. London: Central Office of Information.

Caldwell, B.J. (1993). "Paradox and Uncertainty in the Governance of Education." In H. Beare & W. L. Boyd (eds.). *Restructuring Schools. An International Perspective on the Movement to Transform the Control and Performance of School*. London: The Falmer Press.

Canada (1992). *L'enseignement au Canada 1988-1992*. Rapport à la 43e session, Conference internationale de l'éducation, Genéve du 14 au 19 septembre 1992. Toronto: Conseil des ministres de l'education (Canada).

Caré, C. (1988). "Educational Reform in France." *International Journal of Educational Research*, vol 12, no 2.

Carliner, G. (1995). "Industrial Policies for Emerging Industries." In P.R. Krugman (ed.). *Strategic Trade Policy and the New International Economics*. Cambridge, Mass.: The MIT Press.

Carnoy, M. (1993). "Multinationals in changing World Economy: Whither the Nation-State?" In M. Carnoy, M. Castells, S. S. Cohen and F.H. Cardoso *The New Global Economy in the Information Age*. University Park, Penn.: The Pennsylvania State University.

Chira, S. (1992). "Research Questions Effectiveness of Most School-Choice Programs." *New York Times*, Oct 26, 1992.

Cizek, G.J. (1990). "Home Education Alternatives vs. Accountability." *Journal of Educational Policy*, Vol 4, No 2.

Clune, W. (1993). "The Best Path to Systemic Educational Policy: Standardized/centralized or Differentiated/decentralized?" *Consortium for Policy Research in Education (CPRE)*. Wisconsin: University of Wisconsin-Madison.

Cohen, D. and J.P. Spillane (1992). "Policy and Practice: The Relation Between Governance and Instruction." *Review of Research in Education*, vol 18.

Collot, A., G. Didier and B. Loueslati (1993). "La société interculturelle: projets et débats: Introduction." In A. Collot, G. Didier and B. Loueslati (eds.). *La pluralité culturelle dans les systèmes éducatifs européens*. Lorraine: Centre régional de documentation pedagogique.

Conrad, J. (1998). "Traditional Diversity and the New Drive for Competition." In H. Daun and L. Benincasa (eds.). *Restructuring Education in Europe. Four Country Studies*. Stockholm: Institute of International Education.

Cookson Jr, P.W. (1989). "United States of America: Contours of continuity and controversy in private schools." In G. Walford (ed.). *Private Schools in Ten Countries. Policy and Practice*. London: Routledge.

Cookson Jr., P.W. (1991). "Private Schooling and Equity. Dilemmas of Choice." *Education and Urban Society*, vol 23, Febr.

Cookson Jr, P.W. (1992). "The Choice Controversy: Current Debates and Research—Introduction." *Journal of Educational Policy*, vol 6, no 2.

Daun, H. (1997). "National Forces, Globalization and Educational Restructuring: some European response patterns." *Compare*, vol 27 no 1.

Daun, H. (1998). "Globalization, National Characteristics and Educational Restructuring in European Countries." In H. Daun and L. Benincasa (eds). *Restructuring Education in Europe. Four Country Studies*. Stockholm: Institute of International Education.

Denmark (1997). *Principles and Issues in Education, Education in Denmark.*. Copenhagen: Ministry of Education.

Dougherthy, K.J. and L. Sostre (1992). "Minerva and the Market: The Sources of the Movement for School Choice." *Journal of Educational Policy*, vol 6, no 2.

Durston, B.H. (1989). "Issues in Public Funding and Governance." In W. L. Boyd and J. G. Cibulka (eds.). *Private Schools and Public Policy. International Perspectives*. London: Falmer Press.

The Economist, June, 1998.

ECS (2000). Education Commission of the States. Governing America´s Schools: Changing the Rules. Report to the National Commission on Governing Americas Schools. Washington.

Eide, K. (1992). "The Future of European Education as Seen from the North." *Comparative Education*, vol 28 , no 1.

EU (1994). European Commission: Growth, Competitiveness, Employment. The Challenges and Ways Forward into the 21st Century. White Pare. Brussels: European Commission.

EU (1997). European Commission: Accomplishing Europe through Education and Training. Brussels: European Commission.

Finland (1990). *Developments in Education, 1988-1990, Finland*. Helsinki: Ministry of Education.

Finland (1992). *Developments in Education, 1990-1992, Finland*. Helsinki: Ministry of Education.

Flude, M. and M. Hammer (1990). "Introduction." In M. Flude and M. Hammer (eds.). *The Education Reform Act 1988. Its Origins and Implications*. London. The Falmer Press.

Fowler, F.C. (1991a). "One Approach to a Pluralist Dilemma: Private School Aid Policy in France, 1959-1985. Summary of Dissertation," *Paper Presented at a Symposium on*

Division A at the Annual Meeting of the American Educational Research Association, April 3, 1991.

Fowler, F.C. (1991b). "Challenging the Assumption that Choice is All That Freedom Means: A French Case Study." *Paper Presented at the UCEA Annual Meeting, Baltimore*, October 26, 1991.

Fowler, F.C. (1992). "American Theory and French Practice: A Theoretical Rationale for Regulating School Choice." *Educational Administration Quarterley*, vol 28 , no 4.

France (1990). *Education por tous: Politiques et stratégies rénovées pour les années 1990.* Paris: Ministère de l'Éducation nationale de la Jeunesse et des sports.

France (1992). *Rapport de la France.* 43ème session de la conference internationale de l'éducation. Paris: Ministère de l'éducation nationale et de la culture.

Freeman, C. and Soete, L. (1994). *Work for all or Mass Unemployment.* London: Pinter

Fullan, M.G. (1991). *The New Meaning of Educational Change.* New York: Cassell.

Gayfer, M. (1991). *An Overview of Canadian Education.* Fourth edition. Toronto: Canadian Education Association.

Glenn, C.L. (1994). "School Choice and Privatization." In T. Husén and N. Postlethwaite (eds.). *The International Encyclopedia of Education.* Oxford: Pergamon.

Gordiani, T.J. (1993). "Ecole, identités nationales, identité européenne." In A. Collot, G. Didier and B. Loueslati (eds.). *La pluralité culturelle dans les systèmes éducatifs européens.* Lorraine: Centre régional de documentation pedagogique.

Haiducek, N. J.(1991). *Japanese Education Made in the U.S.A.* New York: Praeger.

Hannaway, J. (1993). "Decentralization in Two School Districts: Challenging the Standard Paradigm." In J. Hannaway and M. Carnoy (eds.). *Decentralization and School Improvement. Can We Fulfill the Promise?* San Fransisco: The Jossey-Bass Publications.

Hayano, K. (1993). *The Japanese Prime Minister and Public Policy.* Pittsburgh: University of Pittsburgh Press.

Henig, J.R. (1993). *Rethinking School Choice. Limits of the Market Metaphor.* New Jersey: Princeton University Press.

Hewton, E. (1986). *Education in Recession. Crisis in County Hall and Classroom.* London.

Holmes, B. (1989). "Japan: Private education." In G. Walford (ed.). *Private Schools in Ten Countries. Policy and Practice.* London: Routledge.

Holmes, B. and M. McLean (1992). *The Curriculum. A Comparative Perspective.* London: Routledge.

Horio, T. (1997a). *Kyoiku Nyumon (The Guidance to Education).* Tokyo: Iwanami Shoten.

Horio, T. (1997b). *Gendai Syakai to Kyoiku (The Modern Society and Education).* Tokyo: Iwanami Shoten.

Igarashi, K. (1988). "Recent trends in educational reform in Japan." *International Journal of Educational Research*, vol 12 , no 2.

James, E. (1988). "The Private Nonprofit Provision of Public Services. A Comparison of Sweden and Holland." In E. James (ed.). *The Non-profit Sector in International Perspective.* New York: Oxford University Press.

Johnson, N (1987). *The Welfare State in Transition.* Brighton: Wheatsheaf Books.

Johnston, B.J. (1990). "Considerations on School Restructuring." *Journal of Educational Policy.* vol 4 , no 3.

Keeves, J.P. (1992). *Learning Science in a Changing World. Cross-national Studies of Science Achievement: 1970 to 1984.* Hague: The International Association for the Evaluation of Educational Achievement.

Kramer, R.M. (1988). "The Use of Government Funds by Voluntary Social Service Agencies in Four Welfare States." In E. James (ed.). *The Non-profit Sector in International Perspective.* New York: Oxford University Press.

Lauder, H. (2000). "School Choice and Educational Change: New Zealand, A Case Study." *Paper presented at the International Conference on School Choice Organized by the Michigan State University, M arch 15-17,* Lansing, USA.

Lauglo, J. (1995). "Populism and Education in Norway." *Comparative Education Review,* vol 39, no 3.

Lawton, S.B. (1989). "Public, Private and Separate Schools in Ontario: Developing a New Social Contract for Education?" In W. L. Boyd and J. G. Cibulka (eds.). *Private Schools and Public Policy. International Perspectives.* London: Falmer Press.

Lawton, S.B. (1993). "A Decade of Educational Reform in Canada: Encounters with the Octopus, the Elephant, and the Five Dragons." In H. Beare & W. L. Boyd (eds.). *Restructuring Schools. An International Perspective on the Movement to Transform the Control and Performance of School.* London: Falmer Press.

Lawton, S. B. (1997). "Structures and Restructuring in Canadian Education." In S.R. Lawton, Reed and F. van Wieringen, F. (eds). *Restructuring Public Schooling: Europe, Canada, America.* Munster: Waxmann.

Manning, S. (1998). "Restructuring Education in Germany." In H. Daun and L. Benincasa (eds.). *Restructuring Education in Europe. Four Country Studies.* Stockholm: Institute of International Education.

Martin, M. and D. Burke (1990). "What's Best for Children in the Schools-of-choice movement." *Journal of Educational Policy,* vol 4 , no 2.

Mason, P. (1989). "Elitism and Patterns of Independent Education." In W. L. Boyd and J. G. Cibulka (eds.). *Private Schools and Public Policy. International Perspectives.* London: The Falmers Press.

Mauriel, M. (1993). "La compréhension culturelle dans le contexte géo-stratégique de 1993." In A. Collot, G. Didier and B. Loueslati (eds.). *La pluralité culturelle dans les systèmes éducatifs européens.* Lorraine: Centre régional de documentation pedagogique.

McGinn, N. and L. Pereira (1992). "Why States Change the Governance of Education: an historical comparison of Brazil and the United States." *Comparative Education Review,* vol 28, no 2.

McLean, M. (1985). "Private Supplementary Schools and the Ethnic Challenge to State Education in Britain." In C. Brock and W. Tulasiewicz (eds.). *Cultural Identity & Educational Policy.* London: Croom Helm.

McLean, M. (1989). "Populist Centralism: The 1988 Education Reform Act in England and Wales." *Journal of Educational Policy*, vol 3 , no 3.

McLean, M. and N. Voskresenskaya (1992). "Educational Revolution from Above: Thatcher's Britain and Gobachev's Soviet Union." *Comparative Education Review*, vol 36 , no 1.

Middleton, S. (1992). "Equity, Equality, and Bilculturalism in the Restructuring of New Zealand Schools: A Life-History Approach." *Harvard Educational Review*, vol 62 , no 3.

O'Connel, P.J. (1989). "National Variation in the fortunes oflabor: a pooled and cross- sectional analysis of the impact of economic crisis in the advanced capitalist nations." In T. Janoski and A. M. Hicks (eds.). *The Comparative Political Economy of the Welfare State*. Oxford: Oxford University Press.

OECD (1994). *School: A Matter of Choice*. Paris. OECD.

OECD (1995). *Decision-making in 14 OECD Education Systems*. Paris: OECD/CERI.

OECD (1998). *Education at a Glance*. Paris: OECD.

Olsson, L. (1992). "Claims for Choice Exceed Evidence, Carnegie Reports." *Education Week*, vol XII, no 8.

Outline of Education in Japan (1989). Ministry of Education, Tokyo.

Papagiannis, G. J., P.A. Easton and J. T. Ownes (1992). *The School Restructuring Movement in the USA: an analysis of major issues and policy implications*. Paris: Unesco.

Psacharopolous, J. (1992). "The Privatization of Education in Europe." *Comparative Education Review*, vol 36 , no 1.

Raywid, M.A. (1990). "Successful Schools of Choice: Cottage Industry Benefits in Large Systems." *Journal of Educational Policy*, vol 4 , no (2): 93-105.

Rust, V.D. and K. Blakemore (1990). "Educational Reforms in Norway and in England and Wales." *Comparative Education Review*, vol 34, no 4.

Schmidt, M.G. (1989). "Learning from Catastrophes. West Germany's Public Policy." In F. G. Castles (ed.). *The Comparative History of Public Policy*. Cambridge: Polity Press.

Schoppa, L. J. (1991). *Education Reform in Japan*. London: Routledge.

Skolverket (1996a). *Varför kostar elever olika? En analys av skillnaderna i kommunernas kostnader för grundskolan.* (Why do the pupils costs vary? An analysis of the differences in the municipality costs for the comprehensive school). Stockholm: The National Agency for Education.

Skolverket (1996b). *Att välja skola - effekter av valmöjligheter i grundskolan.* (Choosing school - effects of choice in comprehensive education). Stockholm: National Agency for Education.

SMES (1997). *The Swedish Education System, August 1997*. Stockholm: The Ministry of Education and Science.

Taylor, M. (1994). *Values Education in Europe: a Comparative Overview of a Survey of 26 Countries in 1993*. Paris: Nfer/Unesco.

Teese, R. (1989). "France: Catholic schools, class security, and the public sector." In G. Walford (ed.). *Private Schools in Ten Countries. Policy and Practice*. London: Routledge.

Telhaug, A.O. (1990). *Den nye utdanningspolitiske retorikken.* (The New Rethoric of Education-al Policies). Oslo: Universitetsforlag.

Therborn, G. (1989). "'Pillarization' and 'Popular Movements. Two Variants of Welfare State Capitalism: the Netherlands and Sweden." In F. G. Castles (ed.). *The Comparative History of Public Policy.* Cambridge: Polity Press.

Uzawa, H. (1998). *Nihon no Kyoiku wo Kangaeru (Thinking of Japanese Education).* Tokyo: Iwanami Shoten.

Vuyk, E.J. (1994). "Netherlands: System of Education." In T. Husén and N. Postlethwaite (eds.). *The International Encyclopedia of Education.* Oxford: Pergamon.

Walberg, H.J. (1989). "Educational Productivity and Choice." In J. Nathan (ed..). *Public Schools by Choice. Expanding Opportunities for Parents, Students and Teachers.* St.Paul, Min-nesota: The Institute for Learning and Teaching.

Walford, G. (1990). "The 1988 Education Reform Act for England and Wales: Paths to Privati-zation." *Journal of Educational Policy,* vol 4 , no 2.

Walford, G. (1992). "Educational Choice and Equity in Great Britain." *Journal of Educational Policy,* 6 , no 2.

Walford, G. (2000). School Choice and Educational Change in England and Wales. *Paper pre-sented at the International Conference on Choice in Education, Michigan State Uni-versity,* March 15-17, Lansing, USA.

Wallace, R. (1990). "The Act and Local Authorities." In M. Flude and M. Hammer (eds.). *The Education Reform Act 1988. Its Origins and Implications.* London. The Falmer Press

Weiler, H.N. (1989). "Education and Power: The Politics of Educational Decentralization in Comparative Perspective." *Journal of Educational Policy,* vol 3 , no 1.

Weiss, M. (1989). "Financing Private Schools: The West German Case." In W. L. Boyd and J. G. Cibulka (eds.). *Private Schools and Public Policy. International Perspectives.* London: The Falmers Press.

Weiss, M. and C. Mattern (1989). "Federal Republic of Germany: The situation and development of the private school system." In G. Walford (ed.). *Private Schools in Ten Countries. Policy and Practice.* London: Routledge.

Whitty, G. (1996). "Creating Quasi-Markets in Education: A Review of Recent Research on Parental Choice and School Autonomy in Three Countries." *Oxford Studies of Com-parative Education,* vol 6 , no 1.

Whitty, G. (1997). "Marketization, the State and the Re-formation of the Teaching Profession." In A. H. Halsey, H. Lauder, P. Brown, and A. Stuart Wells (eds). *Education. Culture, Economy, Society.* Oxford: Oxford University Press.

World Bank (1973). *World Development Report 1973.* Washington, D.C.: World Bank.

World Bank (1979). *World Development Report 1979.* Washington, D.C.: World Bank.

World Bank (1981). *World Development Report 1981.* Washington, D.C.: World Bank.

World Bank (1986). *World Development Report 1986.* Washington, D.C.: World Bank.

World Bank (1990). *World Development Report 1990.* Washington, D.C.: World Bank.

World Bank (1993). *World Development Report 1993.* Washington, D.C.: World Bank.

World Bank (1995). *World Development Report 1995.* Washington, D.C.: World Bank.

Wylie, C. (1995). "School-site Management—Some Lessons from New Zealand." *Paper given at the annual AERA meeting,* San Fransico, United States, 18-21 April, 1995.

CHAPTER 5

Educational Reforms in Eastern Europe
Shifts, Innovations and Restoration

HOLGER DAUN AND DANA SAPATORU

INTRODUCTION

With the collapse of the Soviet Union, the unitarian education system in Eastern Europe was dismantled. The nature of the systems then emerging in the transition countries was conditioned by a return to and restoration of what existed before the second World War, on the one hand, and the ambition to modernize, on the other hand. All education systems were restructured along the same dimensions as those generally debated or changed in the West (privatization, choice and decentralization) but at the same time most the features of these systems were also colored by the unique history of each country.

BACKGROUND

The economic, political, and social changes that took place in Eastern Europe since the collapse of the socialist systems were conditioned by the particular characteristics of each country at that time and their interplay with the uniform political system of the communist states. The differences among countries shaped the development of the countries throughout the revolutionary events of 1989-1991 and the subsequent years. Features specific to each country were also reflected in the evolution of educational systems. The dimensions along which the countries of central and Eastern Europe differed include (not necessarily in order of importance) level of economic development, political arrangements, religious and ethnic composition, and connections to the West. Table 5.1 summarizes these differences. However, this chapter only discusses briefly the last two dimensions, while the first two are addressed separately in more detail in sections 5.2 and 5.3, respectively.

The religious composition of the East European societies and the degree to which the church exercised power in the state varied greatly across countries. Some were predominantly Greek Orthodox (such as Romania), or Russian Orthodox (such as Russia), while others were predominantly Catholic (such as Poland and Hungary). Protestants existed only in Germany, Czechoslovakia, and the Baltic states. The church played a significant role in Poland but not in any of the other countries.

The sense of "belonging" to the West was stronger in some countries (such as Czechoslovakia, Hungary, Poland, and the GDR, for instance) than in others (Offe, 1997). The first three of the countries enumerated attempted to break away from the uniform system of communist states, through social and political movements which, although rather quickly repressed by the Soviet Union, had long-lasting effects in the psyche of the population. This helped promote early reforms in the late 1980s. Among the countries which were more oriented towards the East, Romania was the only country which tried to distance itself from the regional specialization doctrine and subservience to the Soviet Union. Nonetheless, it remained a very closed and repressive society, with no opening to the West.

TABLE 5.1 RELIGIOUS, SOCIAL, ECONOMIC AND POLITICAL DIFFERENCES BETWEEN SELECTED EAST EUROPEAN COUNTRIES BEFORE 1989

Country	Religious composition	Role of Church	Economic level (GNP in Russia = 100)		Non-communist elite	Western orientation	Democracy between the Wars
			1979	1993			
Bulgaria	Greek Orthodox	Weak	90	49	Weak	Weak	No
Czech Republic	Catholic, Protestant	Weak	129	129	Strong	Strong	Yes
GDR	Catholic, Protestant	Weak	NA	NA	Weak	Strong	Short Period
Hungary	Catholic	Weak	94	143	Strong	Medium	No
Poland	Catholic	Strong	93	96	Strong	Strong	No
Romania	Eastern Orthodox	Weak	NA	49	Weak	Weak	No
Russia	Eastern Orthodox	Medium	100	100	Medium	Weak	No

Note: Russian GNP=100 for each year.

All the countries had a very rapid economic growth until the 1970s, but in the 1980s their economies started to decline. Various explanations—internal as well as external—to this stagnation and subsequent collapse have been offered. McLean and Voskresenskaya (1992) mention over-bureaucratization, the struggle for redistributing economic and political power among the middle class intellectuals, and state employees' lack of technological and economic innovation as important internal factors. The political control of the state and of the communist party over the population was enhanced by the fact that state-owned enterprises and trade unions provided many of the social benefits in society, often not only to their employees but to the local communities at large. Work places and work collectives were multi-functional, and supplied educational and other social services (day care, housing, catering, vacations etc.), and they partially substituted for the family. Also, employment was to a large extent guaranteed (Offe, 1996). Moreover, the economies were not flexible enough the meet the new needs of information and communication technology (Freeman & Soete, 1994).

Among the external factors, Freeman & Soete (1994) point to the inability to shift from a traditional industrial society to a post-industrialist one and to introduce IT-innovations. Swain (1992) notes the increasing commercial contacts between the East and the West, through which bureaucrats and leaders of state enterprises became aware of the innovations taking place in the West. The countries of the Eastern Bloc also suffered from the increasing competition from Asian countries in the world market. Their share in world merchandise trade decreased from 12.1 percent in 1963 to 10.0 and 10.8 in 1973 and 1986, respectively (Mulhearn, 1996). It is evident that the gradual weakening control of state and party over the individual and their ability to ensure welfare contributed to a decrease in the legitimacy of the state (Swain, 1992). It was this situation that prompted Gorbachev to start the campaign of *perestroika* and *glasnost*, a campaign that finally ended in the collapse of the communist block.

In all, many factors contributed to the disintegration of the political and economic systems in Eastern Europe. But the processes of liberalization and relaxation of state control started before 1989 in some countries, such as Hungary and Poland (Swain, 1992). And the differences among countries along the several dimensions discussed prompted varied responses to the collapse of the old systems, including in the educational systems of these states.

ECONOMIC RESTRUCTURING

After the second World War, the countries of Central and Eastern Europe had very different levels of economic development: Bulgaria and Romania, for instance, were agricultural societies, while Czechoslovakia had a much higher degree of industrialization. In addition, the rate of growth varied not only across countries of the region, but also within the same country over time. In the 1980s, economic growth in Bulgaria was equal to that of the average OECD countries, while the other five Eastern European countries were growing at a rate similar to that of the slowest growing Western economies. The driving forces of economic growth also varied across countries: while the main factor of economic growth was industrial expansion in Bulgaria and the Czech Republic, in Hungary the growth of the service sector predominated. Table 5.2 summarizes the rates of growth for these East European countries.

TABLE 5.2 GDP GROWTH RATES AND GNP PER CAPITA IN SELECTED EAST EURO-
PEAN COUNTRIES, SELECTED YEARS

	Average Annual Percentage GDP Growth Rates (%)				GNP per capita US dollars, 1996
	1960-1970	1970-1979	1980-1990	1990-1997	
Bulgaria	5.9	6.2	4.0	-3.5	1,190
Czech Rep.	3.1	4.8	1.7	-1.0	4,740
Hungary	3.8	5.3	1.6	-0.4	4,340
Poland	4.3	6.1	1.8	3.9	3,230
Romania	8.6	10.6	0.5	0.0	1,600
Russia	5.2	5.1	2.8	-9.0	2,410

Sources: Based on data from World Bank (1976, 1981, 1986, 1995, and 1998).

All throughout the period after the second World War and to the present, the economic development in most of the countries of Central and Eastern Europe was characterized by high foreign borrowing rates. In 1980 Hungary registered the highest foreign debt as a percentage of GNP among the countries of the region (44.8 percent). Romania was a special case, as it had repaid its foreign debt almost in its entirety by 1989. However, all the selected countries had started to borrow by 1991. In 1993, the debt was highest (119 percent of GNP) in Bulgaria and lowest (16.4 per cent) in Romania (World Bank, 1995).

The countries of central and Eastern Europe also varied with respect to the structure of their economies before 1989.[1] Nonetheless, despite the significant structural changes which occurred in recent years, these differences still persist. The rate of change of employment in the primary, secondary and tertiary sectors also differed across countries in the region. While Romania and Bulgaria had 65 and 57 percent, respectively, of their labor force employed in agriculture in 1960, the figure for the Czech Republic was only 26 percent. Furthermore, compared to the OECD countries, a large portion of the labor force was employed in agriculture, but it contributed only little to total GDP, as agricultural productivity was low (World Bank, 1980, 1992, 1995). Table 5.3 summarizes the structural changes in several Central and Eastern European countries as measured by changes in employment by sector.

Given the differences in the levels of economic development, in their structural compositions and in the priorities of the respective governments, it is no surprise that the share of public expenditure in GNP also varied across the countries of Central and Eastern Europe. Table 5.4 summarily presents public expenditure shares in selected countries in 1993.

After the collapse, the countries faced three major problems of transformation: privatization of property, liberalization of prices, and stabilization of state budgets (Offe, 1996). No capitalist class existed that actively could promote capitalist development, and therefore, marketization and privatization were not initiated and implemented from below but from above (from the central state) (Offe, 1997).

TABLE 5.3 STRUCTURAL COMPOSITION OF EMPLOYMENT IN CENTRAL AND EASTERN EUROPE

Country	Labor Force in Agriculture (% of total labor force)		Employment in Agriculture, Industry and Service, 1960-1995
	1970	1990	
Bulgaria	35	13	57 percent in agriculture in 1960. Rapid transition from agriculture to industry 1960 - mid-1970s. Then transition to service.
Czech Republic	17	11	26 percent in agriculture in 1960. From mid-1970s larger portion in service sector than any other of the East European countries compared.
Hungary	25	15	From 38 percent in agriculture in 1960. Maximum employment in industry in the middle of the 1970s. Then increased employment in the service sector; in 1990 this sector employed a larger portion than in any other of the selected countries.
Poland	39	27	A little more than one third in the service sector.
Romania	49	24	65 percent in agriculture in 1960. Less in the service sector than in any other of the countries.
Russia	19	14	Less than the Czech Republic and Hungary in industry until mid-1970s. Transfer from industry to service slower in Russia than in all other countries except Romania.

Source: Based on data from World Bank (1976, 1981, 1986, 1995, and 1998).

TABLE 5.4 PUBLIC EXPENDITURE OF GNP IN SOME EAST EUROPEAN COUNTRIES 1993

	% of GNP to central state expenditures	Compared to OECD countries	
Bulgaria	47.8 %	Less than Belgium, Netherlands, Norway, Sweden.	More than most other OECD countries.
Czech Republic	41.7 %	Less than most OECD countries.	More than Austria, Australia, Germany, New Zealand, the US.
Hungary	75.0 %	---	More than all OECD countries.
Romania	40.4 %	Less than most OECD countries.	More than Austria, Australia, Germany, New Zealand, the US.

Source: World Bank (1995). Data for Hungary derives from NIPE (1996).

While the populations in central Europe were more positive to market solutions compared to those in Eastern Europe, ambiguity towards privatization existed in some countries (Pastuovic, 1993). It seems that during the first half of the 1990s, no considerable efforts were made to create market oriented industries; most of the changes took place in the trade and services sector (Wesolowski, 1995).

Politics and the Civil Sphere

The critical question after the collapse of the communist system in Central and Eastern Europe was "What should there be instead of communism?" Apart from the desire for freedom and liberty, there were no clear or homogeneous ideas concerning the appropriate changes that society should undergo, neither among the masses nor among the new leaders; the collapse of the old system had been unanticipated and had left a relative vacuum behind it. There were no institutions for dealing with the relationships between the state and the population (Roskin, 1994). And democratic practice was scarce, as only Czechoslovakia had been a true democracy between the wars. According to Pastuovic (1993), the old strata and classes were not ready when the communist regimes collapsed and the result was diffuse populism. The Baltic states, the Czech Republic, Hungary and Poland had non-communist elites that were capable of filling the vacuum, while other countries had to rely upon former communists (Ponton, 1996). In countries such as Bulgaria and Hungary, the communists had to share power with other groups and there the transition to the new system was more peaceful (Kozma, 1992).

The various ideologies and interest groups that emerged after 1989 run the whole political spectrum. For instance, at one extreme, some groups advocate a return to the pre-war situation of strong nationalism and a revival of the institutions that existed at that time. At another extreme, some groups want to Westernize and modernize and allow pluralism (Misztal, 1995).

According to Kozma (1992), the populist and conservative groups are found among the less educated in the countryside, while other categories are well represented among the more educated groups in urban areas. In addition, Roskin (1994) argues that the conservatives are not as much for a free market and mini-state as in the West, but for a significant role for the church and the nation. These ideological categories may be hard to delineate so clearly at the individual level; however, Lowe (1997) claims that the splits exist not only at the aggregate levels but also within many individuals.

New alternatives to economic organization and growth were not present immediately after the collapse of the socialist block and, therefore, according to Misztal (1995)

> . . . autonomy and democracy did not bring to an end previous structural
> problems and strains but reinforced them . . . (273) . . . the reconstruction
> of society (civil society), economy (free market), and polity (the state of law)
> can neither be returned to component practices (citizenship rights, produc-
> tion and distribution based on market prices, equal opportunities) nor sep-
> arated from the interplay of cultural and structural factors that determine

change . . . the interaction of these three processes constitutes the social context of the life-world (312) . . .

Table 5.5 below is based on the references used and summarizes the different views of various ideological categories on the state, nation, and education. Misztal (1995) also argues that many of the inequalities existing before the collapse are maintained, since the ability to implement new policies is weak.

TABLE 5.5 IDEOLOGICAL CATEGORIES IN CENTRAL AND EAST EUROPEAN COUNTRIES

Views	Ultra-conservatives/ Populists	Moderate Conservatives	Liberals	Neo-Liberals	Social Democrats	Communists, Socialists
Politics	Minimal state, local community important	State should guarantee liberties and national autonomy	Minimal state, free market	Minimal state, free market	Modern Welfare state	Redefined state hegemony
Nation	Glorification of The past, restoration of the Golden age that existed before the Communist period	Restore the national proud and prestige	Westernize and modernize. Individual rights and freedom important	Westernize and modernize. Competition	-"-	?
International arena	Inward orientation, isolation	Inward orientation	Europeani-zation	Europea-nization	Internatio-nalism	Internatio-nalism, inter-national solidarity
Education	Individual improvement and culture heritage. Restore religion, nationalist elements. Private education.	Religion. Individual improvement. Nationalism, modernize but also maintain what is nationally unique.	Modern citizens. Modern producers	Modern producers and consumers	Common good. Modern citizens	Rational and productive individual .

The usual development of the social and political sphere in the Western nation states followed a certain path: (a) formation of consolidated nation-states; (b) civil liberties and negative freedom protecting life and property; (c) democratic political rights; and (d) positive welfare state rights. In Eastern Europe, however, after the collapse of the communist systems, this natural development did not take place. This complicates the relationship between the individual citizen and the modern state. Offe (1997) distinguishes four types of relationships that may exist between the citizen and the modern state, in general: (1) the state is a political threat to the citizen, (2) the citizen is the ultimate actor and legitimating agent of the democratic state, (3) the citizen as a client depends upon state-organized provision of material security and welfare, and (4) the citizen is a member of a cultural community, as defined by a shared language, artistic tradition and way of life.

In Central and Eastern Europe, with the dismantling of the communist system, the social provisions could have been taken over by voluntary and non-profit agents, but such agents were present only in Poland. Therefore, these provisions were immediately commodified in part or entirely (Misztal, 1995). Thus, there has been a change from a situation in which the central government appropriated most of GNP (as most economic activities and provision of welfare and education were handled by the state), to a situation in which the state has left these activities to other societal forces. The result, according to Misztal (1995), was the erosion of the state, of welfare politics, the development of sectarian politics, and an emerging denominational state. The degree to which these features are present, however, varies across countries. The countries of central and Eastern Europe differ greatly in the extent to which voluntary organizations, popular and ethnic movements exist. Immediately after 1989, there were no "parameters" according to which the new social movements could function (Offe, 1997). This fact did not impede the emergence of such movements but it conditioned their forms and functioning.

Ethnic divisions also exist in some countries, and Offe (1997) maintains that there are two principal ethnically contested issues: (a) issues of symbolic recognition and (b) issues of material distribution. The former are concerned with ethnic life styles, language and identity, while the latter question the distribution of privileges. Ethnic divisions were suppressed under the communist regimes but they have now been revived, and are used strategically by political leaders in some cases. Offe (1997) presents ten reasons why it might be rational to mobilize ethnicity, some of which are that ethnicity might be an instrument to overcome the old regime; the state power is weak; a country might have internal minorities that are majorities in neighbour states; and there is a vacuum between the state and the individual or "an associational wasteland, atomized, no organizations or interests" (p. 63ff).

While it is difficult and beyond the scope of this chapter to predict what turns the political development of the East European countries will take in the future, perhaps one conjecture is worth mentioning: according to Wesolowski (1995), two contrasting models of political systems may emerge: (i) bureaucratic authoritarianism (using old structures and nationalism) in the cases of Ukraine, Russia, Serbia, Romania), and (ii) the opposite in the cases of Czech Republic, Hungary, and Poland.

EDUCATIONAL SYSTEMS AND RESTRUCTURING

After the communist takeovers in the region in the late 1940s, the communist parties strove for hegemony and legitimacy in society, and education was an important instrument in this struggle. Given this prevalent feature, the national educational systems in Eastern Europe were formed and developed in rather similar ways.

Education had three principal aims in all the countries of central and Eastern Europe: (i) to create good socialist citizens; (ii) to make people highly productive; and (iii) to contribute to equality in society. Therefore, training in Marxist-Leninist theory and ideology became compulsory, and many hours were dedicated to teaching science in schools. Administrative and political procedures for selecting students into secondary and tertiary education were employed to ensure equality at least in access to education, and to fulfill the manpower plan for the economy, in coordination with the socialist production plans.[2] Stratification was built into the social system, however, through centralized pay scales which rewarded higher levels of education with higher wages, *ceteris paribus*. But this income stratification by education was dampened both by the "equalizing" wage policy practiced by the socialist states (in order to suppress income inequality) (Mateju & Rehakova, 1996), and by the existence of party and bureaucratic hierarchies, which added an extra dimension along which compensation was set. These reduced the returns to education, and may have contributed to the waning faith in the socialist education systems. Mateju and Rehakova (1996) found that the degree to which the population believes that income was actually determined by education was considerably lower in East European countries than in OECD countries. Interestingly, however, they also found that the thinking that education should determine income was stronger in the former group of countries.

Despite the fact that one ultimate aim of education was the construction of the communist, collectivist-oriented individual (Kozma, 1992), indoctrination went on in smoother and in more sophisticated ways in countries where the political leadership felt its position to be safe, such as in Hungary, Poland, Bulgaria, Croatia and Slovenia (Kozma, 1992). Little or no reform or changes took place in the educational systems of the countries of Eastern Europe. Hungary, after the revolt in 1956, was able to moderate its educational system more than other countries in this area, but before the collapse of the Communist order, the education system was very similar to that of the other countries.

Comprehensive and compulsory education was one of the first measures to be introduced by the new socialist regimes (Tomiak, 1992; Szebenyi, 1992). Most countries adopted an eight-year compulsory education system initially, with the exception of Romania, Bulgaria (seven years), and Czechoslovakia (nine years) (Kozma, 1992). Some countries later prolonged the length of compulsory education: the GDR, for instance, raised the compulsory educational level to ten years during the 1970s, and Romania made twelve years of schooling compulsory in 1989.[3]

All education was given in public schools and private education was banned. Given the importance placed by the socialist state on education as an instrument of creating the communist society and the states' need for control of the educational system, the socialist countries were characterized by relatively high spending on education. During the period from 1960 to the collapse of the socialist regime, Russia spent more of its GNP on education than all other countries in the region, and, until the beginning of the 1980s, more than all OECD countries with the exception of the Netherlands and Sweden (World Bank, 1977, 1981, 1986, 1993). Romania, on the other hand, devoted only a small percentage of its GNP to educational spending during the whole period. This situation persisted to a large extent after 1989 as well, as can be seen in table 5.6 below).

TABLE 5.6 TOTAL EDUCATIONAL EXPENDITURE AS PERCENTAGE OF GNP

Year/Country	1960	1980	1986	1988	1990	1991	1992
Bulgaria	2.6	5.6	4.4	6.9	6.9	NA	5.9
Czech Republic	NA	4.8	NA	5.3	5.3	NA	NA
Hungary	3.2	4.7	3.8	5.7	6.7	6.1	7.0
Poland	3.8	NA	4.5	3.6	4.9	4.9	5.6
Romania	2.9	3.3	1.8	2.1	3.1	NA	3.6
Russia	4.7	7.3	5.2	NA	7.9	NA	4.0

Source: UNESCO (1991, 1995).

With the collapse of the socialist systems, economic and political transformations were accompanied by educational restructuring. During the first chaotic years, in all countries education was not high politics (Rydl, 1998). The political leaders seemed to have a passive, permissive (rather than active) attitude towards the changes in education[4]. Moreover, part of the difficulty in promoting a clear educational policy stemmed from the fact that education is a political arena on which different interests play out their political power and an ideological struggle for influence takes place (Kozma, 1992). Varying in intensity across countries, the following ideological poles have emerged in Central and Eastern European education as a reflection of the political and civil spheres (Offe, 1997; Pastuovic, 1993): Europeanization versus nationalism; secular education versus religious education; nationalist education versus ethnic or local education; nationalist education versus international education; public education versus private education; monolithic education versus diversified education; centralized structure versus decentralized structure; and formation of human capital versus moral training. These differences have not, according to Mestenhausen (1995), facilitated compromises across groups and categories of people.

Former Yugoslavia is an extreme example of how the above dichotomies have come into full play. In Bosnia-Herzegovina, for instance, the pressure along ethnic lines has resulted in the establishment of three different education systems (Kolouh-Westin, 1999). Another example is the discipline of History; in some countries elements of the content from the pre-war period have been revived but the Communist period is not considered. For instance, Lithuania tried to use textbooks published before 1941 and other countries have introduced descriptions of their great periods in history (Kozma, 1992).

Despite the lack of organized interests such as associations and popular movements, initiatives were in many instances taken at the grassroots level. For instance, where the church or other groups were strong, they established their own schools or took over public schools which had belonged to them before the war or the Communist period. In many cases private and local actions were undertaken before the legal framework was changed (as in the Czech Republic or Romania, for instance) (Florestad, 1997; Rydl, 1998).

At the same time, educational reforms were implemented through a top-down approach, and a standardized policy was applied across all transitional countries, irrespective of country-specific features (Sandi, 1997). International donor organizations, in particular, pushed for fast reforms in all countries.

The policy of equality lost the importance it had enjoyed before 1989; no special arrangements are now made to control access to educational institutions or to control the wage system. According to Mateju & Rehakova (1996), meritocracy has been renewed in the Czech Republic, Hungary and Poland. Pupils are admitted to secondary and tertiary education according to their achievement at lower educational levels, and wages are differentiated according to the amount or type of education that are required for various employment. There are indications that the education systems are put under the double pressure to form human capital and competitive individuals, on the one hand, and to maintain national or ethnic identity, on the other hand.

It is not surprising, then, that the eight, ten or twelve years of comprehensive compulsory education were reduced in several countries, and the structure of educational systems came to vary greatly. Where the conservative influence was strong, education was not seen as an instrument for achieving equality; the comprehensive school was either not maintained, or it was maintained but a parallel system was established similar to the ones in Austria and Germany. All pupils are enrolled in the same schools during the first four years, but then they have the option either to continue to the eight or ninth grade before entering secondary education (3-4 years), or to start in the eight year long secondary education.

It is also worth noting that demographic changes (i.e., smaller cohorts of school age than before) have lowered the number of school age children, at least during the first half of the 1990s, while in several countries, a corresponding decline in the number of schools and teachers did not take place.

The collapse of the central state bodies brought about changes in the governance of educational systems along two main dimensions: (a) central-local initiatives, and (b) public-private initiatives. But the extent to which one or the other pole dominates each dimension varies across countries and across levels of education. The central educational structures were maintained in most of the countries, but the chaotic conditions and the passive attitude of policymakers enabled the emergence of local and private initiatives to establish schools over which central authorities do not have control. There was also a growing demand to re-establish the institutions that had been closed down with the Communist takeover in the 1940s (Kozma, 1992; Offe, 1996). In Russia, the education system remained centralized although a lot of initiatives were taken from below.

There was a commonly agreed upon view that the state monopoly in education was to be abolished, and very few argued for maintaining the comprehensive education system (Kozma, 1992). Populists tended to associate educational privatization with their community school experiments (Ibid.). Conservatives and liberals, majority in some countries, promoted the introduction of very selective systems but also of alternative schools.

Despite the consensus around allowing private education, however, the portion of primary school children in private schools is still quite low, in the single digits. The situation is rather different at the higher education level, where a relatively large proportion of students are enrolled in newly established private institutions (see individual countries below).

Curriculum changes were perhaps the most prevalent and the swiftest in all countries of the region. When the monolithic state ideology was dissolved, religion and/or nationalism entered in the course offerings in Poland, Romania, and some of the republics of former Yugoslavia (Ibid.). Science was given a relatively smaller share than previously.

EDUCATIONAL CHANGE IN SELECTED COUNTRIES

Czech Republic

The 1968 reform movement did not result in a relaxation of Soviet control, as was the case in Hungary after 1956. Once the reform movement had been dissolved, central control was reinforced. The Czech Republic was the only country that included Marxist- Leninist ideology as an independent subject matter in the schools (Ibid.).

During the first decade of Communist rule, the old elites disappeared and a new elite emerged from the Communist party. Education became a channel for promotion and contributed to the formation of cadres for state owned companies and the bureaucracy; a managerial elite emerged and overlapped with the party elite (von Kopp, 1996). According to Mateju & Rehakova (1996), there was heavy state control over education in order to preclude differentiation and inequality from education. The outcome was that social capital (i.e., contacts and social networks) became important for the recruitment to elite positions. In large, the value of education for employment and social mobility declined. Income differences due to educational level were not statistically significant in 1989.

Gradually, the state had to loosen its grip on society. After the collapse of the Communist system and the introduction of market forces, banking and commerce expanded most rapidly. A tremendous demand for economic, administrative and high technology skills emerged. In 1992, differences in hierarchical position, standard of living and occupational prestige were significantly differentiated by educational level, with the exception of differences between secondary and tertiary education (Mateju & Rehako-va, 1996). Compared to 1990, the average monthly salary had increased at various rates for different occupational categories in 1993.

The economy had started to crumble before the Communist collapse, and the deterioration accelerated during the first half of the 1990s. Between 1989 and 1993, the Czech Republic's GNP declined by more than twenty-three percent. Since educational expenditures were maintained at the same level in nominal terms to a larger extent than other spending, the portion of GNP spent on education increased (Rydl, 1998).

In the old system, employment and social security had, to a large extent, been guaranteed by the central state; there was no visible or registered unemployment. In 1994, however, the rate of unemployment had increased to a level similar to that in the Western European countries. The rate of unemployment differed by educational background: in the same year, it reached 10.2 percent among people with basic education or less, 3.7 percent among those with vocational qualifications but without full secondary education, 2.4 percent among those with full technical secondary education, and 1.2 percent among people with higher education (ibid.).

A couple of years after the Communist collapse, a referendum was held and the populations opted not to continue as one common republic but to divide the country into two independent republics: the Czech Republic and the Slovak Republic. These two units of the former Czechoslovak Republic differed linguistically and culturally but also economically. In 1993, GNP per capita was 2,720 dollars in the former, and only 1,950 in the latter (World Bank, 1995).

Education did not become high politics after the collapse of the socialist system. While the National Parliament made decisions, reform initiatives came from different interest groups. The amendments to the Education Act from 1984 enabled the first educational changes in the Czech Republic after 1989. Just as in other countries in Central and Eastern Europe, these amendments made it possible to decentralize the provision and financing of education, and to allow the functioning of private schools.

According to annual opinion polls, education ranked low among the most acute problems. There was a commonly agreed upon view that state monopoly and strong centralization be abolished, but there were different views on what type of system should be created. According to Rydl (1998), "in the field of management, these discussions ranged over the whole spectrum of ideas. Some supported a full application of market principles in education and its complete decentralization, while others advocated a more or less centralized system." Education was supposed to both "repair for the past and prepare for the future" (Parizek, 1995). Multilateral donors and bilateral actors from the OECD countries also attempted to influence the course of development of Czech education.

The share of educational expenditures in GDP increased rapidly during the first half of the 1990s, due partly to the fact that many new and small schools were established.[5] Table 5.7 below shows the evolution of educational expenditures from 1989 to 1994.

The main features of the transformation in the area of education correspond to the general principles of liberalization. Local communities and private interests were the main initiators of changes in public schools or in establishing private schools. Often these initiatives were carried out before the legal framework allowing such transformations was in place at the central level.[6] In 1995, many actions and new establishments, especially concerning non-profit schools, had not been regulated by law. But despite the permissiveness of the Czech state with respect to reform in education, there are indications that only one fifth of all important actors within the educational field strive for innovations.

According to Rydl (1998), the key features and principles of educational transformation in the Czech Republic may be summarized as follows:

1. De-politicization of education and training, and the end of ideological control.

2. Recognition of the right of students and parents to choose a school.

3. Breakdown of the state monopoly in education by allowing private and denominational schools to be established.

4. Decentralization of educational management.

TABLE 5.7 EVOLUTION OF EDUCATIONAL COSTS IN THE CZECH REPUBLIC, 1989–1994

Educational Costs as:	1989	1990	1991	1992	1993	1994
% of GDP	4.0	4.1	4.3	4.8	5.7	5.9
% of state budget	13.8	14.4	13.1	15.3	14.8	14.8
% of educational expenditures on basic education	28	25	23	24	29	29

Source: Rydl (1998).

A large portion of the decision-making has been maintained at the central level, but the regional bodies that had been important during the communist period were dissolved. Instead, the municipalities have become autonomous units. After a legal amendment in 1995, District School Offices have been established. Schools have also attained a certain degree of autonomy. The previous system of nine years of compulsory education was maintained in the Czech Republic. No overall structural reforms were carried out during the first years of the 1990s. With the promulgation of new laws and amendments to existing ones, the comprehensive school was divided into two cycles— lower primary (grades 1-5) and upper primary (grades 6-9). The most important changes have taken place in secondary education, which was divided into the following branches: general upper secondary school (gymnasia), secondary technical school, and secondary vocational school. In secondary and tertiary education, the structure as well as the content have been reformed. The distribution of secondary pupils in various branches has changed considerably during the 1990s, shifting from secondary vocational to secondary technical and gymnasia. The proportion of pupils in the first mentioned decreased from sixty-one to forty-seven percent and in secondary technical increased from twenty-four to thirty-four percent (Rydl, 1998).

After 1989, private and non-state schools were allowed to function to contribute to the diversity of educational services in order to meet the interests of the students and to respond to labor market demand. Also, competition between schools was seen as an important means to improve educational quality. Private schools are subsidized and receive 90 percent of the cost per pupil at the corresponding level in public education.

During the first chaotic years, individual persons started schools as a means to make a profit. However, certain regulations were then introduced which favoured non-profit schools. For instance, for-profit schools faced more stringent requirements such as not being permitted to charge high tuition or administrative fees, and restrictions on the magnitude of their economic surplus. Private schools have been established mainly at the secondary education level. In the middle of the 1990s, approximately three percent of the pupils at the basic school level attended private schools.

After 1989, fundamental changes were made in the financing of education. Resources from the central budget are distributed to School District Offices and then to schools. The amount of funding that a school receives depends on the number of pupils enrolled in the school. The average costs per pupil are estimated according to an index based on the economic level of the district, demographic factors, etc. At present, most of the funding for education still comes from the central budget. Only one fifth of the costs for pre-school and basic education is covered by the municipalities themselves (World Bank, 1997). And, in general, it has been difficult to convince private companies to sponsor schools, in sharp contrast to the financing arrangements established between state-owned enterprises and vocational schools before 1990.

The number of pupils per class in primary education decreased from 26.9 in 1989–1990 to 22.4 in primary education, and from 34.9 to 30.0 in secondary education. (Rydl, 1998). A corresponding decrease in the number of pupils per teacher also took place. The decrease is due to smaller cohorts than before but also to the fact that more schools have been established, mainly through private initiatives. For secondary education, the enrollment figures did not change but a shift took place, as mentioned above. On the other hand, a dramatic increase has occurred in the number enrolled in higher education, from 23,000 in 1989–1990 to 33,000 in 1994–1995. In 1995–1996, the percentages of pupils in private schools were less than one in basic education and approximately eight in the *gymnasium*, ten in secondary vocational education and seventeen in secondary technical education.

Hungary

Hungary had 10.3 million inhabitants in 1994 and the population has been decreasing since the 1980s. Apart from the majority of Hungarians, there are small minorities of Gypsies, Germans, Croats, Slovaks and Romanians. Between 1949 and 1990, the percentage of children below the age of fourteen decreased from twenty-five to twenty-one, a fact that had consequences for educational planning (NIPE, 1996).

After the 1956 upheaval, the Hungarians were able to reform their economic and educational systems to a greater degree than other communist countries. The economy was gradually transformed from 1968 onwards. In the 1970s, the management of state enterprises started to be decentralized and some market mechanisms introduced; increased efforts were made in the late 1970s to stabilize macroeconomic variables. However, Hungary's economy was affected by the worldwide recession, and it entered a period of crisis. Government expenditures exceeded government income beginning in the mid-1980s. The country started to borrow money to cover the foreign trade and budget deficits (NIPE, 1996). But the 1980s also brought along the development of the private sector (Héthy *et al.*, 1994; Offe, 1996), when it became common for people to work apart from their employment in the state sector, or to create their own small companies. Despite the growth in the private sector, however, industrial production declined continuously until 1992.

The collapse of the communist system resulted in massive employment transfers across sectors and branches of the economy, an increasing social stratification, and the strengthening of meritocracy. The category of semi-skilled and unskilled workers, as well as the number of workers in industry and construction decreased considerably after 1989, while the category of managers, intellectuals and self-employed increased. Many individuals started their own companies or took over agricultural units.[7] The share of different categories in total number of earners in the economy changed substantially between 1990 and 1993. The percentage of white-collar workers increased from thirty-three percent to thirty-nine and self-employed from five to eleven per cent, while the percentage of workers in industry and construction decreased from thirty-eight to thirty-one percent (NIPE, 1996). At the same time, unemployment—which was negligible in the socialist period—began to increase: in 1993, it reached thirteen percent, and decreased slightly to around ten percent in the mid-1990s (ibid.).

Hungary differed from other Eastern European countries in its ability to gradually adapt its educational system in response to its needs. Perhaps as a result of this, in international comparisons (IEA) Hungarian pupils score high on academic performance tests, among the highest in the world still in the late1980s. The Hungarians were proud of the education system. However, surveys conducted in the 1980s show that a dramatic drop in the confidence of the population in the education system occurred between 1986 and 1988. In 1981, ninety-eight percent of the Hungarians believed that their education system was better than those of the Western countries. In 1986, this proportion had dropped to eighty-seven percent, and in 1988 to forty-six percent (Swain, 1992).

From 1970 to 1990, the policy goals with direct impact on education were (i) to maintain free social services including education, (ii) to keep labor demand and supply in balance through planning, (iii) to adapt the education system to demographic fluctuations (the cohorts during the 1970s and the first half of the 1980s were larger than previous cohorts), and (iv) to improve the cost-effectiveness of the education system (Héthy *et al.*, 1994).

Education was always a high priority sector in Hungary, and the share of GDP spent on education increased steadily during the 1980s and 1990s (see table 5.8). However, since GDP declined by twenty percent between 1990 and 1996, the increasing percentages spent on education meant in reality that the level of educational spending was more or less maintained during this period.

TABLE 5.8 EDUCATIONAL EXPENDITURES AS PERCENTAGE OF GDP IN HUNGARY

Year	1973	1978	1983	1987	1989	1990	1991	1992	1994
% of GDP	3.4	3.8	4.2	4.7	5.1	5.6	6.2	6.7	6.4

Source: Data for the period 1973-1989 are from Héthy *et al.* (1994), and data for 1990-1994 from NIPE (1997).

As in other socialist countries, primary education was granted the utmost importance. Its share in total educational costs was large already in the 1960s; it increased gradually from 1973 to 1983 (also due to the larger cohorts that entered the system until the middle of the 1980s)[8], and then slowly declined (Héthy *et al.*, 1994). In 1994, only thirty-one percent of the educational budget was dedicated to basic education (NIPE, 1996).

Although educational administration had been centralized as in other Eastern European countries, control was gradually relaxed and the financing of education was delegated to lower levels. The principal amount of funding continued to come from the central budget, but funds were increasingly channelled through local councils. Moreover, parental contributions have increasingly become a source of private contributions to compulsory education. For instance, in 1971, the central level of the administration covered more than forty percent of the recurrent costs and the remaining part was distributed on local council and private sources. In 1984, the share from the central level had creased to thirteen percent and the private share was almost the same as in 1971 (Héthy *et al.*, 1994).

Although Hungary introduced gradual changes of the education system during the last two decades before the Communist collapse, drastic changes have taken place after 1990.

For instance, in 1989, a process of relaxation began in that the central planning of school admission was gradually abolished and private schools were allowed to function.

Starting in 1993, admissions are decided upon by the municipalities and the schools, and

> In 1994, the Ministry of Culture and Education signed an agreement with the Churches on public education. According to this agreement, they are entitled to state support if they provide public provision, but they are not allowed to request tuition fees. (NIPE 1996:39)

In 1990, although no new Education Act was adopted, amendments made to the Act of 1985 introduced the first decentralization and privatization provisions. The Churches and the private sector regained the right to maintain schools. As a result, churches—which had owned and governed 60 percent of the schools in basic education before 1948—were now allowed to reclaim their property. In 1993, a new Education Act was enacted. According to the National Institute of Public Education in Hungary (NIPE, 1996), the most important provisions of this act are:

* The responsibility to provide education was conferred upon the municipalities; the Education Act regulates the division of responsibilities among municipalities to perform this task. Much of decision-making and finance were decentralized to the municipality or school levels. The boards of the municipality councils are now elected bodies. Municipalities make decisions concerning establishment, closure and profiles of the schools, and they determine the budgets and employment of staff. In order to guarantee social control over schools, the Education Act introduces the institution of the school board, on which the parents, the school and the maintaining authority are represented.

* A lump sum estimated according to certain criteria (such as average income, demographic composition, etc. of the area) is provided each municipality by the central government.

* A new core curriculum was implemented in 1998. Within a centrally established framework, the municipalities are free to adapt the curriculum to local conditions, and minorities will have the option to have instruction in their mother tongue. The regulation of curricula is carried out at two levels. The state issues the National Core Curriculum (NCC), which is a framework curriculum. On the basis of the NCC, the schools develop their own local program suited to the specific needs of their clients. The local curriculum is (also) a document of financing, which is to be approved by the local authority.

* The Act prescribes national examinations to be administered at the end of the period of mandatory schooling and at the end of secondary education. These examinations are linked to the implementation of the two-level curriculum control.

* The obligation to participate in full-time general education was extended from 14 to 16 years of age.

In practice, the major outcomes of the educational policies implemented after 1989 concern the decentralization of decision-making and financing, and the establishment of private schools. In addition, automatic promotion was abolished and lower priority was given to equality.

Beginning in 1961, the education system included eight years of compulsory education and two principal branches of secondary education (general and vocational). In the late 1980s, approximately one fifth of the students were enrolled in the general branch, and three fourths in the vocational branch (Héthy *et al*, 1994).

Nowadays, the system is composed of general basic education of 8 years (4 years of lower basic education and four years of upper basic education) and upper secondary education, divided into three branches. After the fourth grade, the pupils may enter the eight year cycle of general secondary education or complete eight years of basic education and then enter one of the three branches of upper secondary education. Some restrictions in this aspect were introduced in 1995 with an Amendment to the Education Act of 1993: there should be exceptional reasons for transferring from basic education to secondary education already from the fourth grade (NIPE 1996).

From 1985 to 1995, the proportion of primary school leavers that continued in secondary education increased from approximately ninety-four percent to ninety-nine percent, and there was a shift in secondary education enrollment from vocational schools to general secondary education or secondary vocational education.

The number of private schools in general basic education increased from eighty-three in 1992 to one hundred sixty in 1995. Most of them are in the ownership and governance of churches. In 1995, however, only three percent of enrollment in basic education was in private schools.

Educational expenditures have been maintained despite economic recession. The cost per pupil has increased in primary and secondary education during the 1990s due to the increasing number of private schools, the maintenance of small schools in rural areas, and a decreasing number of pupils in basic education.

Apart from the lump sums that the municipalities receive from the central government, they themselves have to cover a portion of the costs, and "many municipalities have run into debts in order to be able to maintain their schools . . . " (NIPE 1996). Schools are allowed to find money from sponsors but they are not allowed to charge fees.

National as well as international (IEA) tests show that the level of academic achievement has declined in Hungary since the end of the 1980s, and that differences across schools have increased, especially between urban and rural schools (Balazs, 1997; NIPE, 1996). According to Balasz (1997), much of the decline in achievement is due to the unequal distribution of resources in relation to geographical area, as well as to differences in the socio-economic composition of the student body; some schools were able to maintain their level of academic performance while others were not.

Poland[9]

The Catholic church in Poland was strong morally and administratively and it was left relatively autonomous by the Communist party (Misztal, 1995). According to Roskin (1994), the Catholic church "stood as a bastion of traditional and human values." The contribution of the Solidarity movement to the collapse of Communist system (not only in Poland but also the other Eastern European countries as well) is hard to assess. However, Wesolowski (1995) argues that Solidarity's strategy became inappropriate when the system had collapsed and a market economy had been introduced. Solidarity was transformed into a political party, but it seems not to have been able to channel the divergent pressures and demands that emerged when the Communist monopoly was over.

The ideological divisions mentioned in the previous sections of this chapter are highly visible in Poland, where a large number of political parties have been established. They represent all the poles of national vs. universal, confessional vs. secular, authoritarian vs. democratic, marketist vs. interventionist, populist vs. elitist, market and human capital oriented vs. humanistic and religious oriented, and so on. According to Wesolowski (1995), this diversity of parties may also be seen as a response to the lack of intermediate groups that link society and state organs in a democratic way.

The free elections of 1989, which brought the first non-communist government in postwar Eastern Europe to power, set Poland at the forefront of the countries making the transition to democracy and a market economy. The introduction of a shock program of economic reforms in the autumn of that year did not translate into a growth in GDP until 1992, when Poland became the first of the Eastern European countries to record a growth of over four percent (RPMNE, 1995).

While in the socialist system wage differentiation was related to the bargaining power of particular branches of the economy, in the market system occupational qualification has assumed more weight. By 1993 over sixty percent of the Polish workforce was engaged in private sector activity (*Europe Review*, 1993/94), and incomes had become more susceptible to meritocratic reward. Important shifts took place also in the composition of employment by sector: in the period from 1993 to 1996, employment in industry as a whole registered a decline of more than three percent, while that in agriculture and transport recorded the largest increases (8.6 and 5.4, respectively). Employment in education increased by 5.4 percent, from 813,000 to 857,000 people, in the same period (IMF, 1998b).

Disillusionment with economic reforms, which contributed to unemployment, greater wage differentials and high inflation, was registered early and contributed to a splintering of support for the Solidarity party, with nearly thirty political parties being represented in Parliament at the end of 1992. The Catholic church, which had been instrumental in achieving the downfall of the communist regime maintained influence in parties such as the Catholic Election Action Party and the Christian National Union; for a time, national attention was drawn to the issue of introducing prayer in public schools. However, the heavy-handed lobbying for power by the church attracted the opposition of intellectuals and its initiatives were not successful.

The fragmentation in the political sphere had repercussions for the course of educational reforms. Within the first six years after the fall of communism, there were seven ministers of education. Diverse political and social groups proposed changes in the educational system which were conflicting and unclear. What was clear, however, was that the value of education was perceived to be greater under the new system: education came to be seen as a significant factor in career success (Mieszalski,1996; Koucky, 1996). In 1987, a higher education diploma translated into income seven percent above the national average; in 1993 this diploma translated into a thirty one percent advantage (RPMNE, 1995).

The share of public expenditure on education in GDP went up after 1989, and taking into the account the initial falls in GDP, by 1994 a real increase of expenditure on education was observed (Koucky, 1996). By 1995, public expenditure reached 4.6 percent of GNP (World Bank, 1998).

While the basic structure of the educational system, in terms of years of study, has remained the same after the societal transformation, the demands on the system have been altered significantly. Demand for post-primary, basic vocational schooling (generally three years) has decreased, while that for secondary schooling in general education and vocational education (where instruction lasts four years) has increased. General secondary education is becoming more universal.

The educational system has also changed markedly towards a more decentralized one. The process of decentralization had its roots in the Solidarity period, when in 1980 a "commission of experts" was created to look into ways of promoting teacher involvement in curriculum design. Although abandoned in the martial law period, the movement to decentralize was renewed in the late 1980s. Under the Educational System Act of 1991, both public and non-public schools exist. Public schools are state or local self-government schools. State public schools are run by the *voivodship* education superintendent, and are gradually being handed over to the communes to be run as local self-government schools. The non-public schools may be run by voluntary organizations (now known as community schools), religious organizations (considered community or private), or natural persons (private schools).

Most non-public schools are in the first category, with the Community Education Association operating the greatest number of community schools. Although schools operated by religious organizations had existed under the communist system, the number has grown since 1990. Schools run by natural persons are private schools, generally commercial in nature, and charge the highest tuition fees. While public schools enroll the vast majority of students, the number of non-public schools is growing. Particularly at the secondary level, the choice of non-public schools is more significant. At the primary level, 99.6 percent of students are enrolled in public schools; at the secondary level 96.2 percent are so enrolled. Non-public secondary schools are observed to offer smaller classes, and generally employ more qualified teachers. Emphasis on intensive instruction in foreign languages or in computer skills is considered an advantage in attracting students.

Science had a larger portion of the curriculum in Poland but the Polish schools were also allowed to teach Christian values. The role of science in the curriculum declined after the shift in 1990 (Kozma, 1992). Initially there existed some reluctance among educational policy-makers and administrators to internationalize education, since internationalism had for a long time meant Russification.

Curriculum for primary and secondary schools must be consistent with core curricula drawn up by the Ministry of Education. Changes in curriculum have largely involved elimination of Marxist-Leninist ideology, a favoring of English, rather than Russian, as a foreign language, and increased emphasis on computer science. The Educational System Act of 1991 includes provisions to support minority pupils' national, ethnic and linguistic identities. Under these provisions, instruction in German as a mother tongue began in 1991 in the provinces of Katowice and Opole, Belorussian is taught in Bialystock, Ukranian in eight voivodships, and primary school curricula for Lithuanian, Slovak and Romanian minorities have been drawn up (Republic of Poland Ministry of National Education, 1995).

Legal provisions for greater autonomy in higher education institutions in Poland preceded those of other Eastern European countries, and have resulted in a system with both public and private sectors and multiple tiers. In addition to the traditional full-time, five-year program of study leading to the *magister* degree, many institutions now offer short–cycle programs, such as three-year courses leading to a *licencjat* degree. *Licencjat* degree courses in business studies and foreign language teaching have been introduced to help meet the demand for professionals with skills suited to the new economic and societal circumstances. Short–cycle post–secondary and post-graduate programs also answer the call for educational choices which lead to careers in the new economy (Sörensen, 1997).

Romania[10]

After the collapse of the socialist system in Romania, numerous parties emerged to fill the remaining political vacuum; in 1996 there were about 200 such parties. In the first "free" elections, organized in May 1990, the National Salvation Front (a left-wing party considered to be comprised mostly of the ex-communists and nomenklatura members) won a resounding victory. New elections took place soon after, in 1992, and brought to power a left-wing coalition. This second round of elections did not yield much change, neither in the composition of the Parliament, nor in the economic and social reform policies implemented by the government. With the elections in 1996, a seemingly more reform-oriented Parliament was elected and a new government was instituted.[11]

Education was not a political campaign issue, despite the clear ideological distinctions among the major players on the Romanian political arena. But the coalition government of 1996 set forth a program entitled "The Model of Romania's Rebirth Through Education," which re-emphasized the importance of education to national development (Birzea and Badescu, 1998). This was followed by a surge in public interest in education (Birzea, 1997). Nontheless, even at present no party has a clear political program regarding education; only occasionally one party or another will take a stance with respect to some crisis in the field of education (such as that regarding the educational rights of minorities in Romania, for instance—see below). And very few educational issues, regardless of the level (primary, secondary or higher education), seem to have become the object of public debate, at least until recently.

The Romanian Democratic Union of Hungarians (RDUH) was the most vociferous on educational policies among the political parties. The Education Law adopted in 1995 was arduously challenged by this ethnic group on the grounds of insufficient educational rights for minorities, particularly in post-secondary education. This issue came to the foreground again at the end of 1998, when political ideologies became polarized around the issue of establishing a state university with teaching in the Hungarian language. The government instated in 1996 had promised to meet the RDUH's demand for permitting the founding of Hungarian–language public higher education institutions (in addition to the sections in existing public universities), in return for the participation of the RDUH in the coalition. In September 1998, the government issued a decision regarding the funding of a multicultural university with "Teaching in the Hungarian and German Languages." This decree was vigorously opposed by different interest groups or individuals, including the Social Democratic Party of Romania and the chair of the Parliamentary Committee for Education, a member of the National Christian Democrat Peasant Party (Adevarul, 1998). The Ministry of National Education judged the decision of the government as "illegal" (Vergu, 1998a).

The social and economic background for the evolution of the educational system in Romania after 1989 may be summarily characterized by the accentuated economic crisis, the emergence and growth of the private sector in the economy, significant sectoral shifts, important changes in the labor market, and demographic changes in the population (Romania, Ministry of National Education, 1998).

The first four years of this period were characterized by a drastic decline of GDP; after 1993, however, the economy rebounded slightly such that a positive rate of growth was recorded (with the exception of 1997) (Jigau et al, 1998). The share of the private sector in GDP increased from almost twenty-four percent in 1991 to over fifty-two percent in 1996 (Romania, National Commission for Statistics, 1997). At the end of 1996, agriculture was contributing the most among all sectors of the economy (62.3 percent) to the private sector share of GDP;[12] the highest level of private ownership was also recorded in agriculture (IMF, 1997). The private sector's share of GDP increased from 24 percent in 1991 to 45 in 1995 (Ibid.). Important structural changes took place such that the share of agriculture in total employment decreased from 49 percent in 1970 (World Bank 1998) to 35 percent in 1996. Employment decreased in all sectors and branches except construction and education (Romania, National Commission for Statistics, 1997).

Along with the decline in production and GDP, the unemployment rate peaked at 8.2 percent in 1991, and as of mid-1998 it had reached 7.4 percent (Jigau *et al.*, 1998). But the most affected by unemployment are young people between the ages of 15 and 24, among which the unemployment rate was estimated at 20.9 percent at the beginning of 1998.[13] By educational level, the most vulnerable group was that of high school graduates, which accounted for 33.9 percent of the total number of unemployed in Romania. In relation to educational background, unemployment is largest among those who have high school education, especially the 15-24 years old (Jigau *et al*, 1998).

Romania's population declined from 23.21 million in 1989 to 22.57 million in 1997 (IMF, 1998a), mostly as a result of emigration and diminished birth rates.[14] And while the total school age population declined steadily as well from 1991 to 1996, the dynamics varied across different age groups: the number of children of high school age increased through 1994, after which it began to decline again, the opposite pattern from that exhibited by the category of those aged 20 to 24.

In addition to the contraction in the school age population, the overall enrollment ratio declined in the last ten years, such that at present only 20.7 percent of the population overall is enrolled in some form of education (compared to 24 percent in 1989) (Romania, Ministry of National Education, 1998). Between 1989–1990 and 1996–1997, enrollment increased from 92 percent to 99 in primary education and from eight to 22 percent in higher education. On the other hand, there was a decrease from 91 to 69 percent in upper secondary education (UNESCO, 1997).

The share of educational expenditures in GDP, although it increased from the meager 2.2 percent in 1985, stayed well below the four percent threshold established by law. The structure of educational expenditure also changed over time; the increase in current educational expenditure on higher education was offset mostly by cuts in the spending on pre-primary and primary education (Sapatoru, forthcoming). Overall, educational spending per pupil varied greatly over the past nine years, as a result of the interaction of the evolution of public expenditure on education and that of actual enrollment levels. While from 1991–1992 to 1995–1996 there was an upward trend in overall spending per pupil, this was discontinued the following year.

Educational reform policies

Birzea (1997) distinguishes four types of educational reforms implemented in central and Eastern Europe, more generally, and in Romania, specifically. These include corrective, modernization, structural, and systemic reforms. The first category pertains to measures which have immediate objectives of reparing in education, such as the discontinuation of political indoctrination, of excessive bureaucratic centralization, of personal and institutional police control, and of improving work conditions for teachers (including the reduction of class size to a maximum of thirty-six and of teaching loads). These were undertaken in the first months of 1990 in Romania. The second category of reforms concern changes in curricula, textbooks, teaching and learning methods, and educational standards, measures that aim to reduce the gaps between Eastern and Western structures and institutions. Several of such measures as implemented in Romania are discussed below, but modernizing reforms are still undergoing. The third category, of structural reforms, refers to the legal and managerial framework of education. Important laws and other legislation regulating the operation of the educational structure were passed. And, finally, the fourth type of reforms, the systemic reforms, introduce a real paradigm shift which affects the inner logic of the system by changing the fundamentals of the educational system. According to Birzea (1997) these reforms have not been pursued yet in Romania.

Although more significant educational restructuring began in 1993 with the drafting of the Education Law, and mostly under pressure from international organizations (such as the World Bank, the Council of Europe, and the EU-PHARE program), this did not have a major impact on the system as a whole (Birzea, 1997). Debate around educational issues and an acceleration of reform began in 1997 with the appointment of a new Minister of Education, Andrei Marga. According to Marga, new reforms were necessary at that time because the educational system lacked clear purposes, qualification standards, and evaluation criteria. Moreover, he believed that the system contained too many "original features" which were falsely promoted as the expression of national development, but in fact were meant only to mask corruption. Marga also advocated the idea that, while it was not necessary to invent new forms and structures, if the "Romanian traditions" in education are to be effective, they must be re-thought and adapted (Marga, 1998).

Most of the reform programs proposed and adopted in 1998 fell into the category of modernization reforms. According to the MNE, these were necessary because of the deficiencies inherited from the old system, the necessity to adapt to international standards, the need to anticipate the cultural, social and economic changes in the society, and the desirability of participation in European projects in education (Romania, Ministry of National Education, 1998). That does not imply, however, according to the present Minister of Education, that the tendency is to return to an "educational materialism" where the main responsibility of the educational system is to provide the labor force in the economy (Iordanescu, 1998).

Six months after the appointment of the new Minster for Education, the main reform directions for 1998 envisaged "curricular reform, increasing the links between education and the economic, administrative and cultural environment, improving the educational infrastructure, eliminating paternalism and populism from educational management, and enhancing international cooperation in education" (Marga, 1998). In addition, other important objectives of the government were increased support for private education, and financial and managerial decentralization at all levels of education (ibid.).

Despite the progress made, however, at present there is no unitary program of reform in Romania, but rather a collection of reform packages in most of areas and levels of education (Romania, Ministry of National Education, 1998). According to Negucioiu (1998), the implementation of educational reform in Romania is not occurring at an appropriate speed. Among the five principal factors cited by the author, high on the list is the slowness in developing the legal system. In general, the Parliamentary Committee for Education did not cooperate very well with the Ministry of Education and promoting particular components of the educational reform, including the legal framework, impedes the implementation of proposed changes and the development of the private educational in approving the legislation necessary for reforms. Negucioiu (1998) claims that in many cases appointments and promotions were made according to political criteria or personal interests, rather than on a professional merit basis. The financing of education in Romania is inadequate, much below that slotted for education in most developed countries and many transition and developing countries (Negucioiu, 1998). In this case, even if there were no legal or other impediments for implementing certain reform measures, often the government or individual institutions lack the financial means to do so (Bulic, 1998).

One of the first measures of the post-1989 government was to reduce the level of compulsory education from twelve to eight years. This measure passed without any public discussion, possibly as a populist measure meant to reduce the strain of high school admission examinations for secondary school graduates. In 1998, the Romanian Parliament approved the Ministry of National Education's proposal to increase compulsory education to nine years, and to end with period with "capacity examination" (Vieru, 1998) (in place of the current baccalaureate examination after eight years of school).[15] Another structural change approved by the Parliament concerns the new structure of educational levels in the pre-university system. While primary and upper secondary education will continue to be four year long cycles, the duration of lower secondary education will be reduced to three years (Vieru, 1998). Despite the changes in the labor market and the reform policies introduced by the government, particularly those regarding requirements for graduation and the structure of the educational system (i.e., the introduction of new forms and levels of education), the composition of total enrollments has remained relatively stable over time.

The first transformations in Romania's educational system, the corrective or "destructuring reforms," were legalized by a 1990 Government Decision and enhanced by another decision in 1991. And the December 1991 new Constitution of Romania further consolidated these changes and set the ground for further reform by sanctioning alternative teaching methods and the private provision of education, among others (Birzea, 1997).

In 1992, after the second round of elections, education was declared an issue of "national priority," and a series of ambitious reforms were to be initiated. Some political debate commenced at that time with the discussion in Parliament of a new Education Law, particularly around the issue of educational rights for minorities in Romania. Naturally, the Romanian Democratic Union of Hungarians (RDUH) took an active role in this debate. Moreover, the conservatives opposed the reforms proposed, arguing that the pre-1989 educational system was sound (Marga, 1998), and that only the anarchic development of the country after 1990 was to blame for the current problems in education.

Nonetheless, the new Education Law was passed in 1995. The new elements of the Law were the suppression of the state monopoly in the organization of education (by allowing private schools and universities to function), the interdiction of political activities in educational institutions, the guarantee of education for pupils with special needs, the guarantee of education in minority languages, and the official declaration of education as a national priority and the allocation of a minimum share of four percent of GDP for education.

Other decrees and laws concerning education were passed in the period of 1993 to 1995, of which the most important are the Law on the Accreditation of Higher Education Institutions and Diplomas (1993).[16] Nonetheless, the legislative framework for education is still insufficiently developed and contradictory. Educational reforms are hindered because the amendments to the Education Law have not yet been discussed and approved (Romania, Ministry of National Education, 1998).

According to Negucioiu (1998), one issue that needs immediate attention is the amendment of the legal provisions which govern education. The laws and regulations concerning the functioning and accreditation of private educational institutions, especially at the higher education level, are in many instances contradictory; in addition, they reduce the incentives of faculty to keep a full-time job in private institutions, and create insurmountable hurdles for academic accreditation (Negucioiu, 1998).[17]

Changes were very limited in the governance of education in Romania. There is still a central budgetary institution—the MNE—which is responsible for managing preschool, primary, secondary and public higher education, and for accrediting private institutions. Moreover, the vast proportion of financing for public education comes from the central budget, although schools have increasingly started to use fund-raising as a means of supplementing their income from the state.

At the local level, schools are subordinated to the *judet* school districts (or *inspectorate*, as they are called in Romanian), whose management is appointed by the MNE. Teacher salaries, textbooks, student financial aid, and investments are covered from the central budget funds, while the local school districts and the city halls are responsible for maintenance expenditures, current repairs and subsidies for the dorms.[18] Managerial decentralization began in the mid-1990s, the first year when schools were free to choose among alternative textbooks. Moreover, the Ministry of Education recently has granted permission to schools in choosing elective courses to be offered from particular categories of courses and within the limits set by the Ministry of National Education (see below). However, teachers are not allowed to choose their own auxiliary teaching materials, but only those specifically approved by the Ministry of Education (Popa, 1998a). The primary and secondary levels of education did not encounter much change in terms of financing or governance. Profound decentralization of financing and management occurred, nonetheless, with the emergence of private education as part of the structural reforms implemented. Particularly at the higher education level, a large number of private universities emerged.[19] At the lower levels, however, the pace of establishing private schools was much slower. For instance, in the 1996–1997 academic year, private education was represented by the twenty-six pre schools, three high schools, twenty secondary vocational schools, thirty-five post-secondary vocational schools, and one hundred sixty-one higher education departments (programs) (Romanian National Commission for Statistics, 1997). This translates into varying shares of the private sector in the number of educational institutions by level: while private pre- university education is almost insignificant,[20] private post-secondary vocational and higher education have gained a significant stake in the number of schools and universities, respectively.[21] In addition, private schools tend to be smaller than public ones at most levels of education, with the exception of vocational education (secondary and post-secondary). In 1997, seventy-three percent of the educational financing derived from the central level, 14 from the local level och 11 percent from schools´ own revenues (Romania, Ministry of National Education, 1998).

The lower levels of enrollment in private institutions further reduce the share of private provision of education in the total as measured by the number of students attending a private school or university. Some measures to reform school and university curricula have already been implemented, and they consisted mostly of eliminating several outdated subjects and introducing new ones, authorizing "alternative textbooks," and sanctioning alternative teaching methods.

The monopoly of the subsidized state-owned single publisher of textbooks was dismantled, and new publishers were allowed to enter the textbook market. At present there are alternative textbooks for all subjects and all grades at the pre-university level, facilitated by a conditional loan from the World Bank. Nonetheless, schools are not entirely free in choosing alternative textbooks for their pupils. They are restricted among three textbooks which are included on a short list comprised by the Ministry of National Education as a result of an open tender for textbooks. All the books which enter the tender must abide by the curricular criteria established by the Ministry.

According to the present Minister of Education, however, there are at least four principal reasons for embarking on further curricular reform in Romania. These include the need for increased academic performance, the over-burdening of the students on the current curriculum, the existence of a parallel system of education (private tutoring) which needs to be eliminated, and the need for compatibility with European curricula. The curricular reform proposed by the Ministry of Education encompasses not just changes in the structure of course offerings, but also in the system of academic evaluation, in the organization of the academic year, and in the statute of teachers and students.

In mid-1998, the Ministry of Education organized a large public debate around the issue of changes in the structure of school curricula and the so-called "framework curriculum." According to the Ministry's proposal, the basis for amendments to the 1995 Education Law, the Ministry develops a core curriculum, characterized by a minimum number of hours in particular subjects for each grade, which would be compulsory for all schools. This would represent seventy or seventy-five percent to one hundred percent[22] of any given school's program. A school may adhere to this core curriculum, or extend its course offerings—to fill the remaining twenty to twenty-five percent allowed (up to the maximum number of hours determined by the Ministry of Education).

In 1998, at the international evaluation in sciences and mathematics, Romanian pupils were ranked 33rd in sciences and 31st in math, among the forty-one countries participating. Only 0.5 of the student population makes it to the school olympics (Negucioiu, 1998).

CONCLUSIONS

The gradual social and economic changes taking place before the second World War were to some extent "frozen," first with the outbreak of the war and then with the installation of the Communist regimes (Offe, 1997). When these regimes collapsed, there existed two principal alternatives: (i) return to the past (the pre-war situation) and restore what still existed and revive other aspects, and (ii) adapt to Western Europe, where forces of world wide competition, human capital thought, educational restructuring and demand for civil initiatives had dominated for some time. The countries described in this chapter have tried to combine both alternatives.

The education systems of central and Eastern Europe, when free from the Soviet pressure, had to adapt to the same forces as those in West: on the one hand, internationalization, globalization and competition, and, on the other hand, national as well as subnational (ethnic or local) demands. In addition to this, educational policies also were formulated to eliminate what were seen as undesirable remnants from the Communist period, but at the same time maintain what was good in the old system.

NOTES

[1] Unfortunately, no data is readily available to illustrate the differences in economic structure among the countries of Central and Eastern Europe.

[2] Since heavy emphasis was placed by the state and party on industrialization, more so in certain countries of the region which had been left behind earlier (such as Romania, for instance), education (and in particular higher education) was geared to respond to the needs of heavy industry. However, despite the alleged scientific planning of education in response to labor market demand, there was an overproduction of engineers and technically trained graduates. As employment was guaranteed upon graduation, this compounded the problem of labor hoarding in the economy.

[3]   Romania first introduced ten years of compulsory schooling (equivalent to the first high school cycle) in the late 1980s; in late 1989, Ceausescu announced that the level of compulsory education would be further raised to twelve years (the equivalent of a full high school education). However, this measure was never put into practice.

[4]   It might be that they were fully preoccupied with the construction of the new state and therefore no resources remained for educational reforms. It is also possible that education was, to a large extent, consciously left to "civil forces."

[5]   While the number of pupils has declined, the number of schools has increased; between 1989–1990 and 1994–1995 the number of pupils dropped by eighteen percent (Rydl, 1998).

[6]   The delay in creating the legal framework seems to have been due more to administrative overload and bureaucratic inertia than to conscious political or ideological reluctance.

[7]   The share of state farms and cooperatives in the total area of agricultural land decreased between 1989 and 1995 from 82 percent to 31 percent (Morell, 1997).

[8]   The share of expenditures in primary education in the educational budget rose from 34.6 to 46.9 percent in this ten year period.

[9]   Dr. Karen Sörensen, Institute of International Education, Stockholm University, Sweden, contributed to this section.

[10] This section on Romania was written by Dana Sapatoru, Stanford University, United States, with the cooperation of Luminita Nicolescu, Academy of Economics Studies, Bucharest, Romania.

[11] The coalition, albeit fragile, that won significant seats in Parliament in 1996 includes the Democratic Convention of Romania, the DP and the RDUH. The Social Democratic Party of Romania (SDPR), the ex-FDNS, and the other parties in the previous coalition in power are now in opposition.

[12] Young people have a lower than average duration of unemployment, however (i.e., 12.9 months compared to the overall average of 16.9 months) (Jigau *et al*, 1998).

[13] In 1997 there were almost 40 percent fewer births than in 1989 (*Romania*, Ministry of National Education, 1998). These drastically reduced birth rates will continue to affect educational demand in the years to come.

[14] The first cohort to enroll in the compulsory nine years of education and to take the "capacity examination" is the entering class of 1998–1999.

[15] See Sapatoru (forthcoming) for a brief description of the main provisions of this law.

[16] Moreover, there are inconsistencies between the legal framework in education and that in other areas of the economy: for instance, the existing public finance laws preclude the implementation of proposed changes in the compensation of statute of school teachers (Vergu & Popa, 1998a).

[17] See Birzea (1997) for a more detailed description of responsibilities at the central, local and institutional levels.

[18] Private higher education institutions must submit to an accreditation process by the National Council for Academic Evaluation and Accreditation (NCAEA). For a discussion of the accreditation process, see Sapatoru (forthcoming).

[19] The share of private pre-university schools in the total number of schools in Romania is 0.2 percent for pre-schools and high schools each, and 2.5 percent for secondary vocational schools. There are no private schools at the primary and lower secondary levels.

[20] These represent 7.1 percent and 33.2 percent of the total number of post-secondary vocational schools and higher education programs, respectively.

[21] The maximum number of hours (100 percent) permitted under this proposal is identical to the number of hours children spend in school at present, for each grade respectively.

REFERENCES CITED

Balasz, E. (1997). "Educational Reform in Hungary." Paper Presented at the CIES Conference in Mexico City, Mexico, March 1997

Birzea, C. (1997). "The Dilemmas of the reform of Romanian Education: Shock Therapy, the Infusion of Innovation, or Cultural Decommunization? " <i>Higher Education in Europe.</i> vol. XXII, no. 3.

Birzea, C. and M. Badescu (1998). Financing the Public Education in Romania. Policy Issues and Data Availability. Bucharest: Editura Alternative.

Czeckia (1993). <i>The Educational System of the CFSR.</i> Prague: Institute of informatics in education

Filer, R. K. (2000). Education Reform in the Post-Communist Czech Republic. Paper presented at the International Conference on Choice in Education, Michigan State University, March 15–17, Lansing, USA.

Florestad, K. (1997). "Legal Issues in the Decentralization of Education." Paper presented at the CIES Conference in Mexico City, Mexico, March 1997.

The Europe Review 1993/94, Seventh Edition. The Economic and Business Report. London: Kogan Page and Walden Publishing.

Freeman, C. and L. Soete (1994). <i>Work for all or Mass Unemployment.</i> London: Pinter.

Hanley, E. and M. McKeever (1997). "Persistence of Educational Inequalities in State-Socialist Hungary: Trajecting verses Counterselection." <i>Sociology of Education</i>, Vol 60, No 1.

Héthy, J. <i>et al.</i> (1994). "Human Resource Development Responses to Economic Constraints: A Hungarian Case Study." In J. Samoff (ed.). <i>Coping With Crisis. Austerity, Adjustment and Human Resources.</i> Paris: Cassel/UNESCO.

IMF (1997). International Monetary Fund. Staff Country Report 97/46. Romania: Recent Economic Developments. June 1997.

IMF (1998a). International Monetary Fund. International Financial Statistics Yearbook.

IMF (1998b). International Monetary Fund (1998b). Staff Country Report no. 98/51. Republic of Poland: Selected Issues and Statistical Appendix.

Iordanescu, M. (1998).). "Romania may find a factor for economic re-launching in education." Interview with the Minister of Education, Andrei Marga published in the weekly magazine <i>Economistul.</i> Bucharest, 12 May 1998.

Jigau, M., M. Jigau, C. Novac, and S. Pert (1998). <i>The Professional Integration of Vocational and Secondary School Graduates.</i> Bucharest.

von Kopp, B. (1996). "Elite and Education in the Process of Post-Communist Transformation." Paper presented to the 9th World Conference of Comparative Education, Sydney, Australia, <i>July 1996.</i>

Koucky, J. (1996). "Educational Reforms in Changing Societies: Central Europe in the Period of Transition." <i>European Journal of Education</i>, vol. 31, no. 1.

Kozma, T. (1992). "The Neo-Conservative Paradigm: Recent Changes in Eastern Europe." In R. F. Arnove, P. G. Altbach and P. G. Kelly (eds.). *Emergent Issues in Education. Comparative Perspectives.* New York: SUNY Press.

Lowe, J. (1997). "Curricular reform in Poland: Proud past-uncertain future." Paper presented at the Oxford Conference on Education, Oxford, UK, September 1997.

Marga, A. (1998). "Minster Andrei Marga Presents His Program: Reform for the National School." Interview published in the daily *Azi*. Bucharest: *Azi*. 20 May 1998.

Mateju, P. and Rehakova, B. (1996). "Education as a Strategy for Life Success in the Post- Communist Transformation: The Case of Czech Republic." *Comparative Education Review*, vol. 40, no 2.

Mestenhausen, J. A. (1995). "Neglected: Inter-cultural Perspective on Educational Transition as Intercultural Task." In C. Wulf (ed.). *Education in Europe. An Intercultural Task.* New York: Waxman.

Mieszalski, S. (1996) "Polish School System and Adult Education in the Process of Transformation." Paper presented at the 9th World Congress of Comparative Education Societies, Sydney, July 1st-6th, 1996.

Misztal, B. (1995). "The Uses of Freedom: Post-Communist Transformation in Eastern Europe." M. Darnovsky, B. Epstein and R. Flacks (eds.). *Cultural Politics and Social Movements.* Philadelphia: Temple University Press.

Mulhearn, C. (1996). "Change and Development in the Global Economy." In C. Bretherton and G. Ponton (eds.). *Global Politics. An Introduction.* Oxford: Blackwell Publishers.

Negucioiu, A. (1998). "Education—a Priority of Priorities of the Romanian Society." Bucharest: Economistul, 17 August 1998.

NIPE (1996). Education in Hungary 1996. Budapest: National Institute of Public Education.

Offe, C. (1996). *Modernity and the State. East, West.* Cambridge, Mass.: The MIT Press.

Offe, C. (1997). *Varieties of Transition. The Eastern European and East German Experience.* Cambridge: The MIT press.

Parizek, V. (1995). The Vision of Education in the Czeck Republic. In C. Wulf (ed.). *Education in Europe. An Intercultural Task.* New York: Waxman.

Pastuovic, N. (1993). "Problems of Reforming Educational System in Post-Communist Countries." *International Review of Education.* vol. 39, no. 5.

Ponton, C. (1996). "The End of the Soviet Era: Implications for Global Politics." In C- Bretherton and G. Ponton (eds.). *Global Politics. An Introduction.* Oxford: Blackwell Publishers.

Popa, D. (1998a). "Schools may use only auxiliary teaching materials approved by MNE." Bucharest: *Adevarul*, 15 October 1998.

Popa, D. (1998b). "The Rectors Council Does Not Agree with the Diminished Standards for the Accreditation of Private Universities." Bucharest: *Adevarul*, 20 October 1998.

RPMNE (1995) Republic of Poland. Ministry of National Education. *Education in a Changing Society.* Warsaw: Tepis Publishing House.

Romania, Ministry of National Education (1997). *The Evolution of the Educational System in Romania: Statistical Data.* Bucharest.

Romania, Ministry of National Education (1998). *The White Book of Educational Reform in Romania.* Bucharest : Editura Alternative.

Romania National Commission for Statistics (1997). *Romanian Statistical Yearbook.* Bucharest.

Roskin, M.G. (1994). *The Rebirth of East Europe.* Englewood Cliffs, N.J.: Prentice Hall.

Rydl, K. (1998). "Educational Restructuring and Tradition in the Czech Republic." In H. Daun and L. Benincasa (eds.). *Restructuring Education in Europe. Four Country Studies.* Report No 109. Stockholm: Stockholm University, Institute of International Education.

Sandi, A-M. (1997). "Central and East Europe: Educational Reform—How Far." Paper presented at the Oxford Conference on Education, Oxford University, September 1997.

Sapatoru, D. (forthcoming). *Higher Education Choices in Romania: Public or Private?* Stanford: Stanford University, School of Education.

Slomczynski, K.M. and G. Shabad. (1997). "Continuity and Change in Political Socialization in Poland." *Comparative Education Review.* vol 41, no. 1.

Sorensen, K. (1997) *Polish Higher Education En Route to the Market.* Institute of International Education. Stockholm: Stockholm University.

Swain, N. (1992). "Global Technologies and Political Change in Eastern Europe." In A. G. McGrew and P. G. Lewis (eds.). *Global Politics.* Oxford: Polity Press.

Szebenyi, G. (1992). "Change in the Systems of Public Education in East Central Europe." *Comparative Education.* vol 28, no. 1.

Tomiak, J. (1992). "Education in the Baltic States, Ukraine, Belarus and Russia." *Comparative Education.* vol. 28, no. 1.

UNESCO (1991). *World education report.* Oxford: UNESCO publishing.

UNESCO (1995). *World education report.* Oxford: UNESCO publishing.

UNESCO (1997). National Human Development Report: Romania. Bucharest: Unesco.

UNESCO (1998). UNESCO Statistical Yearbook. Washington: Unesco.

Vergu, M. (1998a). "MNE Representatives Warn Again: the Founding of the Hungarian- German University is Illegal." Bucharest: *Adevarul*, 15 October 1998.

Vergu, M. (1998b). "On November 15, MNE Will Report to the Prime Minister that the Problem of the Access of the Hungarian Minority to Higher Education is Resolved." Bucharest: *Adevarul*, 10 November 1998.

Vergu, M. and D. Popa (1998a). "In Our Country, Education Remains State Education." Interview with the Minister of Education, Andrei Marga, published in the daily *Adevarul*. Bucharest, 19 May 1998.

Vergu, M. and D. Popa (1998b). "School Reform at the Hour of Truth. The Framework Curriculum." Bucharest: *Adevarul*, 16-17 July 1998.

Wesolowski, W. (1995). "The Nature of Social Ties and the Future of Post-Communist Society: Poland After Solidarity." In J.A. Hall (ed). *Civil Society. Theory, History and Comparison.* Cambridge: Polity Press.

Vieru, Ana-Maria (1998). "The Ministry of National Education Prepares the Reform.." Bucharest: *Jurentul*, 10 July 1998.

World Bank (1976). *World Development Report.* Washington, D.C.: World Bank.

World Bank (1977). *World Development Report.* Washington, D.C.: World Bank.

World Bank (1980). *World Development Report.* Washington, D.C.: World Bank.

World Bank (1981). *World Development Report.* Washington, D.C.: World Bank.

World Bank (1986). *World Development Report.* Washington, D.C.: World Bank.

World Bank (1991). *World Development Report.* Washington, D.C.: World Bank.

World Bank (1992). *World Development Report.* Washington, D.C.: World Bank.

World Bank (1993). *World Development Report.* Washington, D.C.: World Bank.

World Bank (1995). *World Development Report.* Washington, D.C.: World Bank.

World Bank (1998). *World Development Report.* Washington, D.C.: World Bank.

CHAPTER 6
China's Transition Patterns
JAN-INGVAR LÖFSTEDT AND ZHAO SHANGWU

INTRODUCTION

China recently to celebrated its fiftieth anniversary as a people's republic. As one of few remaining countries still calling themselves socialist or communist, China is looking back upon half a century of extremely radical and sometimes dramatic changes, where new and old, modern and traditional, eastern and western, individualist and collectivist, Marxist and Confucian patterns and cultures have alternated and often coexisted. Over these fifty years, the world has witnessed China's transitions and restructuring—from semi-feudal and semi-colonial to pre-capitalist, from pre-capitalist to pre-socialist, and from pre-socialist to market socialist.

Although often isolated—or isolating itself—from the rest of the world, China has, in the capacity of the very size and history of its population and culture, always received—and deserved—the attention of other countries. Whatever happens in China will sooner or later have great repercussions in the world. In an era of more intensive and compelling globalization, Chinese development will concern the others.

In this chapter we try to glimpse something of the trends and forces that in the last fifty years have moved China, sometimes through pendulum swings and abrupt policy shifts, from backwardness and deep-rooted tradition to modernity—struggling at the same time to resolve the contradictions between authoritarianism and democracy, superstition and science, self-sufficiency and interdependence, among others.

AN OVERVIEW OF POLITICAL AND ECONOMIC PARADIGM SHIFTS

China has a population of about 1.24 billion (1997). It is expected to be around 1.3 billion by the turn of the century. Approximately 92–93 percent are Han Chinese, but there are altogether fifty-six different ethnic groups, such as Mongolians, Tibetans, Koreans, Hui, and so on. The minority population inhabits nearly sixty percent of China—mainly the western parts.

Life expectancy at birth in 1990 was 68 years for males and 71 years for females. Both mortality rates and birth rates have dropped markedly over the last decades. The annual population growth was around 18 million in the 1980s, but was down to 12.37 million by 1997 (People's Republic of China, 1998). As late as the early 1990s, around 80 percent of the population lived in rural areas. By 1997, the figure had gone down to seventy percent, and the population is growing continuously.

China as a whole is regarded as a poor country in terms of per capita production, but the eastern coastal provinces have reached levels of development that compare well with—or even surpass—those of Southern Europe. Conflicting trends can be observed since the introduction of market economy and the intensification of international contacts and exchange in the early 1980s, and whereas some regions prosper others remain in poverty. In absolute terms the number of poor people without enough food to eat, according to official figures, dropped from 200 million in the late 1970s to around 70 million a decade later, but at the same time regional disparities and unequal distribution of consumption and production increased rapidly.

According to official history (as, for instance, reflected in the *Constitution*), China was a feudal country which in the mid-nineteenth century gradually turned into a semi-colonial and semi-feudal system. The 1911 revolution toppled imperial rule and the feudal monarchy and gave birth to the Republic of China. Considerable foreign influence and control were not terminated, however, until after World War II. The civil war between the Guomindang Nationalists and the Communists ended in communist victory in 1949.

One way of getting an overview of the paradigm shifts since 1949 is to compare the political and economic strategies of three generations of Chinese communist party leaders, that is the first generation (Mao Zedong; 1949–1976), the second (Deng Xiaoping; 1977–1989) and the third generation (Jiang Zemin; 1989–). There were, however, considerable changes also within the "Mao era" with moderate policies in the mid 1950s and the early 1960s and radical—or even extremist—policies in the late 1950s, of Great Leap and the era of the "cultural revolution" of 1966–1976.

The First Generation: Mao Zedong (1949–1976)

During the 1950s, China initiated a rapid transition from a "New-Democratic" to a socialist society with public, or state, ownership of the means of production and centrally planned economic and social development led by the communist party. The early 1950s was characterized by land reform, redistributing land to 300 million poor peasants, and nationalization of the economy. Then followed the application of the Soviet development strategy with emphasis on heavy industry and modern technology and gradual collectivization of agriculture, even beyond the Soviet model, with the establishment of the "people's communes" in 1958—one of the factors that precipitated the break with USSR in 1960. The extremely ambitious industrialization program launched in the 1950s was assisted by the USSR, which at first welcomed China to the socialist camp. Towards the end of the 1950s, however, Mao Zedong rejected the rather one-sided emphasis on industry, advocated by the Soviets, and proposed a more sound balance between industrial and agricultural development. In the late 1950s, the new development strategy was introduced, the most conspicuous elements of which were the "Great Leap" intensification of rural industrialization and the "Commune" reform which was seen as a step toward an ideal communist classless and collectivist society. The commune reform had followed the "anti-rightist" campaign which was the beginning of the Maoist radical period with struggle against the moderates within the communist party and bourgeoisie intellectuals in society at large.

One important slogan in the new campaigns was "walking on two legs," which meant simultaneous development of industry and agriculture, of national and local industries, of large and small enterprises, and of the application of both modern and indigenous or traditional methods of production. In political terms the new strategy included sharpened class struggle and struggle against "revisionism" and bourgeoisie ideology. The new line was not acceptable to the Soviet side and as a result of this, as well as of other ideological differences, all USSR assistance was terminated. Since the Korean War, China had been subject to blockade by the West and after 1960 it was also ostracized by the other Socialist countries, except Vietnam and North Korea.

After the period of transition in the 1950s, China was officially a "socialist state under the people's democratic dictatorship led by the working class and based on the alliance of workers and peasants." (People's Republic of China, 1982)

The excesses of the "Great Leap" period and the discontinuation of Soviet support led, however, to economic crisis and isolation from the rest of the world. The more moderate forces within the communist party (Liu Shaoqi) took over the leadership from Mao Zedong and introduced economic liberalization with free markets and private plots of land for the peasants. Military confrontation with India helped to unite China's internal political factions. But the economic crisis lasted for several years and led to widespread starvation in the end of the 1950s, and also caused a political crisis and loss of confidence in Mao Zedong's line. It has been estimated that the "Great Leap" and the commune reforms, with, among other ingredients, the massive backyard steel production campaign and the concomitant neglect of agricultural production, led to a great famine which caused the death of more than 30 million people (UNDP, 1996).It took China several years of reconstruction and moderate liberalization of the political and economic systems to get back on its feet.

After his defeat in the early 1960s, Mao managed to stage a comeback by mobilizing forces, mainly outside the communist party and especially the students, in a head-on struggle against "Soviet revisionism" and the "capitalist roaders" who were betraying the party and were forgetting about class struggle. This led to a new "radical" and chaotic period of the "cultural revolution" (1966–76). During this period many political and economic structures were destroyed in the both ideological and physical struggle against the disguised "capitalists" inside and outside the communist party and against bourgeoisie intellectuals including teachers. Nearly the whole educational system came to a standstill at least for some years, and then became an experimental laboratory for utopian socialism.

The Second Generation: Deng Xiaoping (1977–1989)

It was not until the late 1970s, with the death of Mao Zedong and the fall of the leading group of the "cultural revolution," Gang of Four, that the chaotic period was over and correction and reconstruction could be initiated. The second generation of leaders began to take over and started to prepare for broad structural changes and reforms. A marked break with the first generation socialism in China was made, and Deng Xiaoping introduced "socialism with Chinese characteristics." Important elements of the new strategy were radical economic reform, allowing for a certain amount of capitalist management and private enterprises, "the four modernizations," and the "opening up to the outside world." Deng's slogan *"Education must be geared to modernization, to the world, and to the future"* was widely publicized in China.

The open-door policy had far-reaching effects economically and politically but also in the fields of education and research. During the period from 1978 to 1983, more than 18,000 students went abroad with public support, and more than 6,000 foreign students studied in China. By the end of 1983, more than 600 Chinese institutions had signed agreements with over 200 institutions of higher education in other countries. By 1987, the total number of Chinese students who had gone abroad had reached 30,000 (*Beijing Review*, No.45, 1988).

Of great importance in the new strategy was also the decollectivization of agricultural land which was distributed to the households for contracted individual and joint production. Deng's model combined elements of a market economy with strict communist party control over education and mass media. The concept of human rights was still rejected.

In the new economic construction and modernization, more emphasis was given to the consumer goods industry, the energy and transport industries, international contacts and exchange, and the role of the professionals and specialists rather than the cadres and the political levels.[1] All local (e.g. provincial) governments are under the leadership of the central level. But at the same time, according to the party constitution, the communist party exercises absolute leadership at central and all other levels. All major decisions are taken within the party and then passed on to state officials.

The program for economic reform announced in 1984 called for more rational (read: market oriented) price policy, enterprise responsibility for accountability and loss and profit, less mandatory central planning, and the adoption of more indirect instruments of macroeconomic regulation (Löfstedt 1990:10).

By the mid-1980s, China's economic structure had changed radically. Heavy industry had increased its share of the national gross output from slightly over 15 percent in the early 1950s to nearly 35 percent in 1986, and during the same period, agriculture had decreased its share from close to 57 percent to just over 35 percent. Simultaneously, rural industrial output had increased and by 1986, for the first time, the value of this output exceeded that of agriculture. The rapid industrialization of rural areas, however, also meant that large numbers of people had to be retrained from agrarian to industrial skills, and it also resulted in serious soil and air pollution (Löfstedt, 1990).

The thirteenth national congress of the communist party in 1987 defined the concept of "primary stage of socialism" typical of the Deng Xiaoping period in the following way:

> (1) concentration on modernization and development of the productive forces; (2) comprehensive reform of production and the superstructure (e.g. culture, the legal system, education, and norms and values); (3) continued adherence to the "open door" policy, i.e. trade and international contacts, including foreign investments in China; and (4) rapid expansion of a planned commodity economy with public ownership playing the dominant, but not only, role (cited in Löfstedt 1990).

The same party congress in 1987 also presented guidelines for political reform calling for

> (1) separation of party and government; (2) delegation of powers to lower levels; (3) reform of government organs; (4) reform of the personnel (cadres) system; (5) the use of consultation and dialogue; (6) the improvement of socialist democracy; and (7) strengthening of the socialist legal system. (ibid.)

The concept of "socialism with Chinese characteristics" has to be understood in contrast to the "traditional model of socialism" of the USSR. "Socialism with Chinese characteristics" is a combination of public ownership, with individual, private, and foreign-invested sectors. Already by 1989, nearly 82 percent of China's 87,000 small and medium-sized commercial enterprises were operated on contract, had been leased out, or had been transferred to non-state ownership (*Beijing Review*, No.52, 1989, p.17). The scope of mandatory central planning was reduced. The number of industrial products subject to mandatory planning fell from 131 in 1980 to 14 by 1989, and the corresponding agricultural products from 117 to 9 (ibid.). Around 1993, China had 14 million individual households engaged in industrial and commercial activities, 120,000 private enterprises, and more than 60,000 firms with foreign investments. A typical feature of Chinese socialism is thus the opening up to the outside world with foreign trade, foreign investments, and joint enterprises.[2]

In spite of these intensive reforms, the state in China is still, as noted above, completely controlled by the communist party, but there are a number of organs which exercise state power at different levels, such as the National People's Congress and the local people's congresses. An expression of the united front concept in China is the

Chinese People's Political Consultative Conference, which according to the 1993 PRC *Constitution* is a:

> broadly based representative organization of the united front which has played a significant historical role, [and] will play a still more important role in the country's political and social life, in promoting friendship with other countries and in the struggle for socialist modernization and for the reunification and unity of the country. Multi-party cooperation and the political consultation system under the leadership of the Communist Party of China shall continue and develop for the extended future (People's Republic of China, 1993).

The Third Generation: Jiang Zemin (1989–present)

Deng's strategy thus did pave the way for the third paradigm shift—"the socialist market economy"—even before his death in 1997. Now most prices of goods are determined by supply and demand with little state interference, and the private sector has expanded rapidly to contribute about forty percent of GNP. Foreign investments have reached new highs, and foreign trade has expanded very fast to reach a level of around 250 billion in US dollars annually (An Bin, 1998b).

In the period of 1980–1993, the annual growth of GNP per capita was 8.2 percent, almost doubling the rate of 4.3 percent from the earlier period of 1952–1980, and GNP per capita rapidly increased from $280 in 1980 to $530 in 1994 (World Bank, 1996). Except for the early 1950s and the period 1962–1965, when the economy was recovering from war or famine, at no time in the history of the PRC has the economy grown as fast as in the 1980s and the first half of the 1990s. Although the growth rate declined to 4–5 percent in 1989 and 1990 due to the efforts to deal with high inflation and turmoil, the rates increased again to 7 percent in 1991, to 14 percent in 1992 and in1993, 11 percent in 1994, and to 10 percent in 1995 (*Beijing Review*, No. 14, 1996).

Recent data from the State Statistical Bureau of China show that in the last 19 years, the Gross Domestic Production (GDP) increased from 1979 to 1998 with an average annual growth of 9.8 percent. (*People's Daily* Overseas Edition, 1998-09-23). Table 6.1 puts China's economic growth in the first half of the 1990s in an international perspective.

China's economic growth rate in comparison with low/high income countries is shown in table 6.2. It has been calculated that the number of poor people declined by one percent for every one percent increase in real GDP in its rapid progress in both economic growth and poverty reduction between 1978–1984. According to World Bank figures, the number of people living under the national poverty line (60 cents a day per capita) decreased from 260 million in 1978 to 97 million in 1985, or from 33 percent to 9.2 percent.

TABLE 6.1 ECONOMIC GROWTH RATES IN SOME OF WORLD'S MAJOR COUNTRIES
AND REGIONS (%)

	1990	1991	1992	1993	1994	1995*
World Average	2.2	0.8	1.4	2.3	3.1	3.6
Developed countries	2	0.3	2	1.8	2.7	2.7
USA	0.8	-1.1	2.6	3.1	3.7	2.5
Japan	4.8	4.1	1.3	0.1	0.7	1.9
Developing countries	3.5	3.9	5.6	6.1	5.6	5.6
China	3.9	8	13.6	13.4	11.8	10
India	4.9	1	4.6	4.5	5.2	5.5
Indonesia	7.2	6.9	6.3	6.7	7	7.2

* Estimated figures

Between 1991 and 1996, the number of people below the poverty line fell from 94 to 65 million. Since 1980, the number of poor in rural areas, according to official sources, decreased from 250 million to 58 million, which is still a very high number.[3]

TABLE 6.2 COMPARISON OF AVERAGE ANNUAL GROWTH RATE OF GNP AND GNP PER CAPITA, 1996–97

World	Low Income Countries	Middle Income Countries	High Income Countries	East Asia & Pacific	China
		Average Annual GNP			
3.2	5.0	4.9	2.8	8.8	8.9
		GNP per capita			
1.8	2.8	3.8	2.2	5.6	7.8

(Source: *World Development Report 1998/99* http://www.worldbank.org/wdr/contents.htm)

In 1996, China ranked first among the *low income economies* with a GNP per capita of US\$ 750 but far behind the *high income economies* such as for instance Japan (third) with close to US\$ 41,000 (World Bank, 1998). The projected output of some major agricultural and industrial products are given in Figure 6.1 below.

Important changes in China's development strategy in the mid-1980s led to increasing regional and urban-rural disparities. Major components of the new strategy were a shift of emphasis from agriculture to export-led industrialization, and a number of economic measures favoring the eastern coastal provinces and cities. One outcome of the new policies was that the income gap between urban and rural residents widened. In 1984, the average per capita income of urban residents was 1.7 times more than the income of the rural residents, whereas in 1997 it had risen to 2.2 times (*People's Daily*, 1998-02-16).

While still a poor country in absolute terms there are signs that China's economic development is at present too fast and creating serious both economic and social problems. Economic observers refer to the overheated economy claiming that the economic growth has accelerated beyond a sustainable rate and that it is necessary to cool the economy and stem inflation (Harrold & Lall 1993). The expansion of the private sector in the economy in combination with increased imports from abroad has also increased the competitive pressure on the state owned enterprises (SOEs) and this has revealed serious weaknesses in them (Broadman 1995) and sometimes led to collapse and increased unemployment.

According to official figures, 44 percent of the SOEs are running at a loss. In order to avoid that more labor are laid-off increasing unemployment, many SOEs continue to produce goods which will never be sold because they are of less quality than goods imported or produced by collective or foreign funded enterprises (see for instance Smadja, 1998). Still it is estimated that out of the 120 million people employed in State enterprises, at least 30 million, or 25 percent, will be made redundant if the SOEs are going to become economically sound. By 1997, a major economic problem was still enterprise losses.

Regional and urban-rural disparities continues to constitute a serious problem. The differences in living standard between the rich eastern parts and the poor western regions is a serious problem that also overlaps with the problem of the strained relationships between the Han majority and the ethnic minorities most of whom inhabit the western regions. Limited demands for independence are found especially in Tibet and among the Central Asian Moslems in Xinjiang. The urban-rural disparities are illustrated by the fact that the average annual per-capita net income of rural residents in 1997 was 2,090 *yuan* compared to 5,160 *yuan* in urban areas (People's Republic of China, 1998). Among the social problems taking on new importance are crime, prostitution, AIDS and corruption. Hu Ruiwen (1994), Director of the Shanghai Institute of Human Resource Development, defines some of the new problems in the following words:

The traditionally functioning social control system in which a social organization (work-unit) has held control over its members through the system of social administration and household registration, has been weakened. The weakening of this highly specified organizing function, the rise in the social mobility rate, and changes in values held by the members of society, have lessened the binding effect of the traditional moral concepts. Under such circumstances, the sharpening of class interests, the temptations of the life style of "the new rich" (dakuan in Chinese), consisting of the owners of private enterprises and employees in foreign-invested ventures, as well as the unfavourable stimulation caused by the uneven social distribution, have all worked together to sharpen the sense of deprivation, the eagerness to become rich, and a utilitarianism on the part of a certain proportion of society's members.

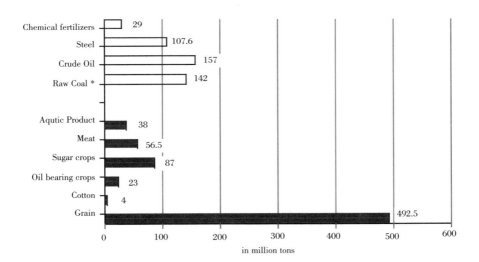

FIGURE 6.1: PROJECTED OUTPUT OF MAJOR PRODUCTS IN 1998
(source: Chen Jinhua (1998) "Report on the Implementation of the 1997 Plan for National Economic and Social Development and on the Draft 1998 Plan." Beijing Review, No.15, 1998.)

On the human rights issue, there are some–although perhaps slow-coming–signs that official policy will change. According to the Amnesty International (1997):

Human rights related legislation during the 1990s in China indicate two opposite tendencies. One is aimed at increasing the legal protection for certain rights, bringing some aspects of the Chinese legislation more in line with international rights standards. The other one has expanded the State's legal tools of repression, further restricting fundamental freedoms and criminalizing activities involving the peaceful exercise of basic rights. New laws introduced in 1996 reflect these two tendencies.

It should be noted, however, that the Chinese government signed the *International Covenant on Economic, Social and Cultural Rights* in October 1997 and the *International Covenant on Civil and Political Rights* recently (October 1998). This testifies, according to official sources, to the resolve of the Chinese government on promoting and protecting human rights (*Beijing Review* 1998, No.41).

The question of democracy will have to wait for a possible solution. The Chinese policy with regard to dissidents and the crackdown on the students' movement in 1989 have been serious setbacks for democracy in China, as has China's policies with regard to the demands from some ethnic minorities for increased autonomy. According to some observers, the democratic movement has in fact suffered from the improvement in people's living conditions that resulted from the "commercial wave" initiated by Deng Xiaoping in 1992. Some of the conservative leaders in China see a conflict between economic growth and democratization. There are signs, however, that the National People's Congress (NPC) is gradually becoming more democratically representative in the sense that NPC delegates are elected with less party interference, and more independent of the communist party and the government in the ballots. Starting in the late 1980s, nay votes against the government became increasingly common in the NPC. When Yang Shangkun was elected President in 1988, there were 158 nay or abstain votes, and in 1989—the year of the TianAnMen Square disaster—36.6 percent of 2,600 delegates voted against the appointment of Jiang Chunyun as the Vice-Premier of the State Council.

RESTRUCTURING AND CHANGE PATTERNS IN CHINESE EDUCATION

The Present Structure of the System

Education in China is divided into four categories that is Basic Education, Secondary Vocational and Technical Education, Regular Higher Education and Adult Education.

Three systems coexist for primary and lower secondary education: the 6 + 3 system, the 5 + 4 system and the nine-year comprehensive system, with the 6 + 3 system predominating in most areas. Thus the length of schooling for primary education is six or five years, and for lower secondary education four or three years. Children start school at the age of 6 or 7, and enter lower secondary schools at the age of 12 or 13.

Basic Education includes pre-school education, primary education and general secondary education. Primary education usually lasts six years. Secondary education is divided into lower secondary and upper secondary; each usually takes three years to finish. Primary education has been universalized in areas inhabited by 91 percent of the entire population of the country. In 1996, there were 645,985 primary schools with a total enrollment of 136.15 million pupils. In 1997, enrollment had grown to around 140 million The net enrollment rate of school-aged children reached 98.9 percent that year.

Secondary Education is being steadily universalized in big cities and economically developed areas. In 1966, there were 67,600 lower secondary schools with a total enrollment of 50.48 million students (52.50 million in 1997). In 1997, 8.5 million students were enrolled in 13,880 regular upper secondary schools, whereas nearly 11 million students were enrolled in vocational or technical schools. Secondary Vocational and Technical Education is provided by Regular Specialized Secondary Schools (e.g. Secondary Technical Schools and Normal Schools), Skilled Workers Schools, and Vocational Schools. Secondary Vocational and Technical Education has been developing rapidly since the 1980s. The proportion of students in technical/vocational schools rose from 18.9 percent in 1980 to 56.2 percent in 1997. Promotion rate from primary to lower secondary has increased from nearly 82 percent in 1993 to more than 90 percent in 1995. In the same period, promotion from upper secondary to higher education increased from around 43 percent to almost 50 percent.

Regular Higher Education mainly refers to the normal (4-year)and short-cycle (2-3-year) programs offered by regular higher education institutions. Most normal cycle undergraduate programs take four years to complete, while a few take five or even six years. Postgraduate studies include the master's program and the doctoral program. The former requires two to three years and the latter is of three years duration. In 1997, there were 1,020 general universities with a total enrollment of 3.2 million, and 735 postgraduate institutions with 180,000 students (People's Republic of China, 1998).

TABLE 6.3 ENROLLMENT RATES IN INSTITUTIONS OF HIGHER LEARNING IN 1992 (%)

China	1.6	*World's Average*	*13.9*
Developed Countries	*15.8*	*Developing Countries*	*4.1*
USA	76.2	The Philippines	27.8
Japan	31.5	Indonesia	10.1
Britain	28	India	6.1

In spite of impressive expansion of higher education China still ranks very low in international comparisons in terms of enrollment rates. Table 6.3 gives the percentages of the university age population enrolled in higher education in an international perspective for 1992 and shows for instance that China is still far behind developing countries such as Indonesia, and India. The number of higher education institutions has grown from 207 in 1949 to 1,054 in 1995 (5.1 times), with a total enrollment of 2.9 million students (nearly 25 times the number in 1949).

According to official sources, significant progress has been made particularly through the reform and readjustments since 1978. The educational structure has become more rational, and the quality of education and training as well as the efficiency of higher education institutions have noticeably improved to be more responsive to the needs of economic and social development of the nation.

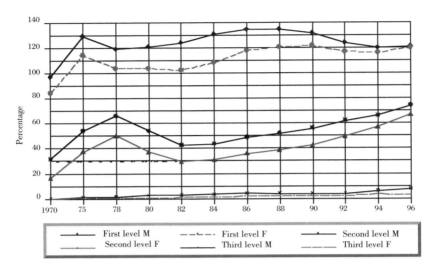

FIGURE 6.2 GROSS ENROLLMENT RATIO BY LEVEL 1970-1996
(ADAPTED FROM UNESCO STATISTICAL YEARBOOK 1997)

Adult Education includes literacy work, all types of in-school and extra mural educational programs and activities designed for working adults. In primary schools for adults, Chinese language and mathematics are taught for one to two years. In secondary schools for adults who study full time, the length of schooling is the same as for regular secondary schools; adults who attend part time normally are expected to study for one additional year. Total number of hours of instruction in institutions of higher education for working adults is slightly less than in regular higher education institutions. (In 1996, there were 1,138 tertiary adult education institutions and about 800 regular higher education institutions which offered adult education programs. Total enrollment reached nearly 2.7 million.)

The Educational Level of Human Resources in China

In spite of all attention that has been paid to educational development, the educational level of the Chinese population is still very low. According to the 1995 Sample Census, people who had received college education accounted for only about 2 percent (according to other sources 5 percent) of the total population, which is very low compared with other countries.

In 1990, there were 180 million illiterate and semi-literate citizens (15+), representing 15.9 percent of the total. Chinese illiterates account for about 30 percent of the world total. By international standards, China has, however, reached a high level of literacy. In 1995, the literacy rate was 81.5 percent—well above the average for developing countries. It is noteworthy, however, that the literacy rate for females fell considerably between 1990 and 1995. Total literacy rate is expected to have reached 85 percent by year 2000. The educational level of the Chinese people is still far from meeting the needs of economic and social development.

The Financing of Education

In spite of the importance attached to education in China in the last twenty years, it has not been provided as much economic support as in industrialized countries. The Chinese government allocation to education as a proportion of the entire state budget has been very low. According to a UNESCO survey in the late 1980s, China ranked 130th among 149 nations in terms of the percentage of GNP allocated to education. According to statistics, per capita education spending allocated by the Chinese government is about ¥ 40 (US$ 7) a year, which ranks next to last in the world (Zhao, 1993). A comparison with India and Egypt shows that China in spite of a superior annual growth rate of GNP per capita spends much less on education in terms of percentage of GNP.

State budget expenditure on education in China accounted only for 1.5 percent of the world total educational spending, while the total population receiving certificate education in China accounted for twenty-five percent of the world total.

At present, educational expenditures come from government grants, which are derived from both the national and local governments' budgets. Generally speaking, local governments at various levels are responsible for financing those educational institutions that they administer, whereas the central government is responsible for financing institutions under the State Education Commission and other ministries. In addition, the central government is also responsible for providing grants earmarked for specific purposes.

Provincial and county governments may collect supplementary funds for education every year. Most schools are financed mainly by government funds, but many schools also obtain funds through other channels.

China deems it necessary to raise funds through various channels, and the central government has implemented the educational policy of "Walking on two legs" and thus depends on diversified funding. Additional sources at present include: the levying of education taxes by local governments; subsidies from enterprises and other commercial organizations; endowments or contributions by voluntary organizations and individuals; sundry charges collected from students; income derived from work-study programs run by schools; and so forth (table 6.4 below).

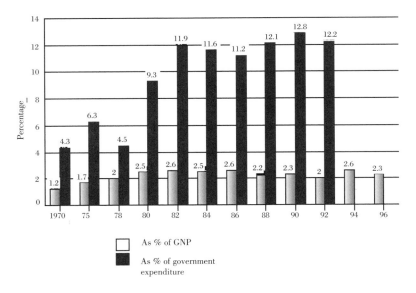

FIGURE 6.3: PUBLIC EXPENDITURE ON EDUCATION
(SOURCE: PEOPLE'S REPUBLIC OF CHINA, 1998)

TABLE 6.4 EDUCATIONAL FUNDS BY TYPES 1994–1995 (IN BILLION ¥ RMB)

	1994	1995	1995/1994 (%)
State financial allocation (Government Budget)	88.4	102.8	116.34
Levying of education taxes by local governments	13.28	18.91	142.41
Funds from industrial enterprises	8.91	10.49	117.69
Income derived from work-study programs run by schools	6.07	7.68	126.62
Other state allocated funds	0.82	1.23	150.43
Endowments or contributions by voluntary organizations and individuals	1.08	2.04	188.96
Funds collected within community	9.75	16.28	167.1
Tuition and sundry charges collected from students	14.69	20.12	136.97
Other funds	5.89	8.2	139.21
Total	148.9	187.8	126.14

Source: People s Republic of China, 1996

According to the *Outline for Reform and Development of Education in China*, the government's expenditures for education will be gradually increased (including allocations from governments at all levels, urban and rural education surtax, funds from enterprises for developing education in primary and secondary schools, etc.), to account for four percent of GNP by the end of the century. The percentage of GNP allocated to education has, however, fluctuated around two percent or a little higher since the 1970s (see figure 6.3).

During the 5th session of the Chinese People's Political Consultative Conference in March 1997, delegates worried about the poor educational funding and urged the government to increase the expenditures for education in order to reach the goal of four percent of GNP by the end of the century (*China Daily*, 1997-03-08).

Shifts in Educational Policy

The third generation restructuring and paradigm shifts in the political and economic systems in China have also been reflected in education. The Mao period of educational development (1949–76) was characterized by fluctuations between moderate ("Soviet-revisionist") and radical (Maoist) policies. The tensions between the 'moderate left' and the 'radical left' in China centered on a number of policy issues or choices of emphasis such as: theoretical/academic and practical/vocational orientation; central versus local control; full-time versus part-time schooling; quality versus quantity; 'red' (political) versus 'expert' (professional) emphasis; education for economic development versus ideological education; professional (formally trained) versus amateur (barefoot, *minban*) teachers; Chinese characteristics versus foreign (e.g. Soviet) models; industrial versus agricultural culture; generalist versus specialist training; and many others (Löfstedt, 1980).

The "key school" ("bet on the strong") concept, for instance, and the "two-track" system with parallel academic and vocational streams were advocated by the 'moderate left' and influenced educational policy in the early 1960s, when Mao Zedong had temporarily lost much of his power and political influence. Anti-intellectualism, refutation of Soviet pedagogy, expansion of *minban* (locally funded) schools, emphasis on 'worker-peasant students', "open-door" (i.e. open to the rest of society) education, on the other hand, are examples of 'radical left' priorities which influenced educational policy during the "Great Leap" period in the late 1950s and, above all, the "cultural revolution" period (1966–76). The educational policy during the radical periods was characterized by mass participation, working class control, basic education for all, politicization of education, egalitarianism, and the combination of education and production even to the extent of transferring administrative control over schools to production units (Löfstedt, 1990).

The second generation of Chinese leadership reversed the policies of the radical periods. Modernization was the strategic goal and should be promoted by, among other things, education which received a greater share of investments. Politicization was gradually replaced by economism. Ideology was less important than competence. Some of the important trends of the early 1980s were: upgrading of higher education; more academic and theoretical curriculum with less productive labor in schools; more stress on teacher authority and professionalism; "the betting on the strong" policy of more support to advanced ("key") schools; a more selective system and university entrance exams instead of political recruitment of students. (Ibid.) Important priority areas were: universal primary education and the introduction of nine year comprehensive education; expansion of secondary technical/vocational education; expansion and more diversification of higher education with less narrow academic (Soviet type) specialization; and decentralization of planning and administration. Other important reform measures in higher education were expansion of the humanities and social sciences faculties; expansion of postgraduate education, the introduction of academic degrees; and the introduction of short-cycle (more vocational) higher education.

Major reforms affecting education took place in the mid-1980s. One was the decentralization of basic education, and the other was the marketization of higher education. The decentralization basically meant that financial responsibility for nine-year basic education was given to the local levels of village (*cun*) for primary education, townships (*xiang*) for junior secondary education, and county (*xian*) for secondary schools. Individuals, various groups, local industries, and units were also allowed to make donations to schools. The local resources should cover the *minban* teacher salaries. The non-qualified "community teachers" still constitute about forty percent of all rural teachers. According to official sources, nearly ninety percent of total public expenditure on education in 1993 came from the local governments (county and below). In the same year, around forty percent of total educational expenditure came from non-government sources. The increased reliance on local resources has—not surprisingly—led to widening disparities in educational quality between prosperous and poor regions.

Secondary education underwent considerable restructuring or vocationalization during the 1980s. The enrollment ratio between technical/vocational and general academic education changed from 1:4 to 1:1 between 1980 and 1992.

The current third phase of Chinese restructuring in education during the 1990s has been characterized by continued decentralization of finance and administration and control in general, growing impact of market mechanisms, increased pressure for efficiency and effectiveness, privatization, and more individualization. The latter refers for instance to the fact that the previous system of state assignments of jobs for university graduates has been replaced by a system where students are more free to seek jobs, and enterprises are more free to recruit graduates themselves. In the 1980s, a new policy was implemented according to which the most qualified students would receive free higher education whereas those who did not do so well in the entrance exams would have to pay their own tuition. Today most students have to pay for higher education, and many observers are warning that the cost of higher education will soon be too high for the poor.

According to the present policy of cost-sharing, compulsory education is free whereas at the levels of non-compulsory education, the system of tuition fees is being adopted.

Privatization has led to the setting up of a number of non–government sponsored educational institutions. A major difference between these and government-sponsored institutions is that the principal of a government school is appointed by the educational authorities whereas the non–government schools usually adopt a principal-responsibility system under the leadership of the Board of Trustees. Another difference is that government schools are mainly financed by government allocations and no tuition is charged for compulsory education. Non–government schools, on the other hand, are funded mainly by their sponsors. They may charge tuition upon approval by the authorities.

The perhaps most conspicuous educational changes and reforms in the last decades have occurred in higher education. According to Yin and White (1993), the term marketization (*shichanghua*) "denotes a process whereby education becomes a commodity provided by competitive suppliers, educational services are priced, and access to them depends on consumer calculations and ability to pay."

In the 1980s, China's colleges and universities were managed by the State Education Commission, various Chinese ministries, and local governments. "This approach created a large number of single-field institutions whose administrations were unable to meet the needs of a growing market economy." (Zhou Zuoyu, 1998). In the mid-1990s, many institutions of higher education were merged into comprehensive universities in order to broaden the subject majors and raise the academic levels.

One aspect of the marketization is the privatization of higher education. The 1982 *Constitution* of China stipulated that "the state encourages collective economic organizations, governmental enterprises and other social groups to initiate and administer various kinds of educational activities according to laws." The first *minban* (people-run; non-public) higher educational institution had been set up in Beijing already the same year, and more than one hundred then followed suit.

The year 1992 saw a "second spring" for private higher education. Presidents of *minban* institutions met in Beijing and worked out a program for the development of private higher education. The next year, the State Education Commission enacted the "Provisional Regulation for the Establishment of People-Run Schools for Higher Education," which provided the legal basis for private higher education. In 1993, the *Outline for Reform and Development of Education in China* declared that the government was not obliged to provide higher education and that students should pay tuition fees. According to the 1993 *Constitution*, the State still has overall responsibility for basic education and the establishing and administering of schools of various types and the universalization of compulsory nine-year education.[4]

The previous system of state owned enterprises running their own schools is being changed. In an effort to establish modern administration, the large and medium sized SOEs will gradually close down their primary and secondary schools. All enterprises, however, will conduct vocational education and training.

In order to strengthen monitoring and assessment of educational development a State Education Inspectorate has been set up supervising mainly primary and secondary education. Local governments have also set up similar agencies. Departments of inspection now exist in thirty provinces, autonomous regions, and municipalities under the central government.

Although China ranks high among developing countries in terms of distribution of education and level of literacy, education is also facing many problems at present. Some local authorities are more interested in economic development than in educational investments, and there are cases where allocations to basic education were reduced or diverted and where teachers did not receive their salaries on time. There is a general feeling among educators in China that the reform of the educational system lags behind the reform of the economic system. The new system of diverse funding (allocations, taxes, levies, fees, donations, etc.) has not remedied the situation, and the number of neglected school buildings on the verge of collapse has in fact actually increased (Chen Guoliang 1994).

CHINA IN THE GLOBAL SYSTEM

As noted above, China has in the last two decades intensified contacts and relations with the rest of the world and has become increasingly active both economically and politically on the international arena. Foreign trade has developed rapidly and by 1997 the total volume of export and import reached US\$ 325.1 billion which was about twelve percent more than the previous year. The trade surplus was more than US\$ 40 billion. Direct foreign investment in China was US\$ 45.3 billion in 1997 which was 8.5 percent above the corresponding figure in 1996 (People's Republic of China, 1998).

China has defined its foreign policy as an independent policy of peace and persistent development of relations of friendship, equality and mutual benefit with other countries on the basis of the *Five Principles of Peaceful Coexistence* (see below), strengthening unity and cooperation with Third World countries, and opposing hegemony and safeguarding world peace.

The *Constitution* adopted in 1982 stated that:

> China's achievements in revolution and construction are inseparable from the support of the people of the world. The future of China is closely linked to the future of the world. China consistently carries out an independent foreign policy and adheres to the five principles of mutual respect for sovereignty and territorial integrity, mutual non-aggression, non-interference in each other's internal affairs, equality and mutual benefit, and peaceful coexistence in developing diplomatic relations and economic and cultural exchanges with other countries; China consistently opposes imperialism, hegemony and colo-

nialism, works to strengthen unity with the peoples of other countries, supports oppressed nations and developing countries in their just struggle to win and preserve national independence and develop their national economies, and strives to safeguard world peace and promote the cause of human progress.

Since the 1980s, the Chinese government, while carrying out its policies of openness and reform, has been more active in the UN and its organizations (FAO, UNESCO, UNDP, WHO, etc.) devoted to world peace and development. China has joined more and more international organizations and has made great efforts to cooperate in all areas with the UN and the rest of the world and has furthermore been very active in pushing forward the North-South dialogue and South-South cooperation. China has in recent years taken many measures to promote, economic contact with the outside world, including the policy of "one country–two systems" (the coexistence of socialism and capitalism, referring to Hong Kong and Taiwan); the establishment of special economic zones in parts of China; the permission of foreign investments; and the return to the World Bank and the International Monetary Fund. In 1986, China formally applied for the restoration of its position as one of the founding members of GATT (General Agreement on Tariffs and Trade, now called the World Trade Organization), the world's largest international economic and trade organization. This aims to expand exports, develop foreign trade and raise China's international status.

There has also been a gradual expansion of international cooperation and exchange in education with the implementation of the policy of opening to the outside world. According to the State Education Commission, the cumulative number (from 1978 to 1996) of students/scholars going abroad for advanced studies had exceeded 200,000 and the number of faculty members teaching in foreign institutions under bilateral agreements between governments had reached 1,260. More than 12,000 foreign experts had been employed by Chinese higher education institutes.

In 1996, China sent more than 10,000 people to study abroad in about 100 countries and regions, and 267 regular higher education institutions received around 33,000 students from 160 countries enrolled in either long-term or short-term programs. The intensified contacts with the outside world has made it possible for Chinese educators to learn from the experiences of other countries and has promoted the reform and development of education in China.

An important role in China's interaction with the rest of the world is played by Internet. So far, 45 Chinese media units have been connected with Internet, which is also a vehicle for publicity of 17 provinces, autonomous regions and municipalities. According to the Information Office of the State Council, these units include the China Net Information Center (CIC), People's Daily, Xinhua News Agency, Beijing Review, China Daily and China Central Television. With the development of the Internet, the Chinese media is placing much stress on publicizing the country's culture, reform and the opening up through the new communications medium. It has become very popular with users for its convenience and timeliness, as well as its interchangeable Chinese and foreign language versions. Since the founding of CIC more than one year ago, the average number of daily visitors has exceeded 80,000, with 88 percent being foreigners, who have access to data totaling about 100 million words.

CONCLUSIONS

China has over the last fifty years taken several important steps from a poor, semi-colonial and semi-feudal, and predominantly agricultural stage to a relatively developed and industrialized stage. The poverty problem still has to be definitively resolved but considerable economic and technological progress together with the high levels of literacy and life expectancy place China well ahead of most developing countries. Although still a *low income* country in per capita terms, China is now a semi-developed country half way between the South and the North.

Politically China has over the fifty years been a one-party socialist country. During the first three decades after 1949 the overriding policy question was how to interpret Marxism in the Chinese context and translate it into a Chinese development strategy. At present the main problem seems to be how to interpret capitalism and apply it to China.

One important issue in the early years was how to relate to the Soviet development model with its emphasis on heavy industry and enforced collectivization of agriculture, which was first tried and then rejected by the radical left headed by Mao Zedong. The pendulum swings between Moderate and Radical left policies characterized the first thirty years, but there was at the same time a strong element of continuity in policy making from the mid-1950s, through the early 1960s and up to the immediate post-Mao period in the late 1970s, and the convulsions of the "Great Leap" years and the "cultural revolution" seem more like Maoist parentheses. Before the "cultural revolution" the conflicts between the Moderates and the Radicals in most cases resulted in compromise, but in the late 1960s they turned totally antagonistic. It was only after the death of Mao in 1976 that the Moderates could topple the "Gang of Four" and end the radical period.

It is interesting to note that it was in fact members of the First Generation leaders (especially Deng Xiaoping) who paved the way, in the late 1970s and early 1980s, for a Second Generation shift from a centrally planned to a socialist market economy. Deng Xiaoping, of course, belonged to the Moderate faction in the First Generation from the very beginning. To the Radicals the main ideological issue was that of class relations and they maintained that the main contradiction in China during the first decades was between the proletariat and the bourgeoisie, whereas the Moderates adhered to the "theory of productive forces" which meant that the main contradiction in China was between the (politically) advanced socialist system and the economically backward productive forces. It was, of course, this stand that paved the way for the economistic and consumerist policies of the Second and Third Generations.

In education the early Moderate line was to copy Soviet methods especially in higher education which was greatly influenced by the Soviet experts who came to China in the 1950s. Although literacy and mass education were considered important, the main emphasis was on secondary and tertiary education and the training of specialists for socialist construction.

When the Radicals gained more influence in the late 1950s one of the most important reforms was the introduction of productive labor and practice in schools and the integration of education and production. The ideological rationale behind the reform was that (1) socio-cultural differences between workers and intellectuals should be eliminated and socialist consciousness promoted; (2) the teaching-learning process should be more effective; (3) a more harmonious all-round human development should be promoted; (4) educational costs should be reduced; and (5) students should be better prepared for working life.

With the Moderate policy swing in the early 1960s it was instead stipulated that the focus in the schools must be on teaching, and that classroom work was the main form of teaching and learning. The "education-with-production" movement was, however, revived again on the eve of the "cultural revolution" towards the mid-1960s, when a variety of arrangements were introduced, such as schools being run by factories and schools having contracted cooperation with enterprises or running their own factories or farms.

In the last years of the 1960s, the diversified study-work system was implemented in many parts of China. As much as twenty to forty percent of the school year could be devoted to manual labor. The rationale this time was that students should be ideologically reformed through labor and contact with the laboring people. After the "cultural revolution," however, it was for instance stipulated that 2.2 percent of the classroom work should be devoted to labor in primary schools, and 6.8 percent at the secondary level. (Renmin Jiaoyu, 1986)

The economic reforms of the 1980s and 1990s have led to a fundamental restructuring of Chinese society and also to changed relations with the rest of the world. As in many other countries marketization in the economy–and also in education–and open borders have led to increased competition, improved efficiency and effectiveness and increased output but has also caused a number of problems such as inequalities and disparities, crime and irregularities, drugs and prostitution, and deterioration of the environment.

The present Chinese leadership seem to adhere to the rather positivistic notion that development is a linear process of economic growth which can be measured in quantitative and material terms of output and consumption rather than in terms of quality of life and the quality and well-being of the population and the environment. The economic reforms have not yet been accompanied by the corresponding reforms regarding political democracy and human rights including the rights of the ethnic minorities. There are signs, however, that a parliamentary system with more democratic influence is on its way. The prospects for ethnic equality, on the other hand, seem more bleak, not to mention autonomy or independence.

NOTES

[1] The political side of Deng's model may be illustrated with the 1982 *Constitution* and the *Charter of the Chinese Communist Party* (People's Republic of China, 1982). According to the *Constitution*, central political power is in the hands of the National People's Congress, the President, the State Council, the Central Military Commission, the Supreme Court, and the Supreme Procurator.

[2] The 1993 *Constitution* states: The People's Republic of China permits foreign enterprises, other foreign organizations and individual foreigners to invest in China and to enter into various forms of economic cooperation with Chinese enterprises and other Chinese economic organizations in accordance with the law of the People's Republic of China (People's Republic of China, 1993).

[3] According to UNDP (1996) figures, the number of people lacking the basic living necessities of food, clothing and shelter fell from 250 million in 1978 to 80 million in 1995.

[4] It also repeats what was stipulated in the 1982 *Constitution* (People's Republic of China, 1982) that the State *"encourages the collective economic organizations, state enterprises and institutions, and other sectors of society to establish educational institutions of various types in accordance with the law."* (Article 19).

REFERENCES CITED

Amnesty International. (1997). *China: Law Reform and Human Rights*. Report - ASA 17/14/97, March 1997.

An Bin. (1998). "China's State Structure: Origin, Current Conditions, and Challenges." http://www.chinasi.org/lib/csr/I/csr4/2.htm.

———. (1998). "Report from China: ASocialism with Chinese Characteristics@ and Its Challenges." http://www.chinasi.org/lib/csr/I/csr1/3.htm.

Beijing Review, 1988/45.

Beijing Review, 1989/52.

Beijing Review, 1996/14.

Beijing Review, 1998/41.

Broadman, H. (1995). *Meeting the Challenge of Chinese Economic Reform*. World Bank Discussion. Paper No. 283.

Chen, G. L. (1994). "Education Restructuring and Institutional Innovations: Chinese Education Reforms in the 1990s." Background Report for the *Fourth International Conference on Chinese Education for the 21st Century*, Shanghai.

Chen, J. (1998). "Report on the Implementation of the 1997 Plan for National Economic and Social Development and on the Draft 1998 Plan. *Beijing Review*. No. 15, 1998.China Daily, 1997-03-08.

Harrold & Lall (1993). "China: Reform and Development in 1992-93." Discussion Paper, World Bank–Washington, D.C.: World Bank.

Hu, R. W. (1994). "Chinese Education: Development and Perspectives. "Background Report for the *Fourth International Conference on Chinese Education for the 21st Century*, Shanghai.

Löfstedt, J-I. (1980). *Chinese Educational Policy*. Stockholm: Almqvist & Wiksell International.

Löfstedt, J-I. (1990). *Human Resources in Chinese Development*. Paris: International Institute for Educational Planning.

Mok, K. H. (1996). Privatization and Quasi Market: Educational Development in Post-Mao China. Paper presented at the Ninth World Congress of Comparative Education. Sydney: July 1996. Outline for Reform and Development of Education in China.

People's Daily (Overseas Edition), 1998-02-16.

People's Daily (Overseas Edition), 1998-09-23.

People's Republic of China (1954). *Constitution of the People's Republic of China*. Peking: Foreign Languages Press, 1954.

———. (1982). *Constitution of the People's Republic of China*. Peking: Foreign Languages Press, 1982.

———. (1993). *Constitution of the People's Republic of China*. Peking: Foreign Languages Press, 1993.

———. (1996). China Educational Funds, Annual Report 1996. Peking: State Statistical Bureau of the People's Republic of China.

———. (1998). *Statistical Communique on Socio-Economic Development in 1997*.

Renmin Jiaoyu (People's Education), 1986/12

Smadja, C. (1998). *World Economic Forum*. http://www.edu.cn/undp/shd/poverty.htm.

UNDP–China. (1996). Elimination of Poverty. http://www.edu.cn/undp/shd/poverty.htm.

UNESCO (1998). *UNESCO Statistical Yearbook 1997*. Paris: UNESCO.

UNESCO (1999). http://Uneb.edu/educdb/db_idx.htm.

World Bank (1996). *The World Bank Atlas*. Washington: The World Bank.

World Bank (1999a). *World Development Indicators 1998*. Washington: The World Bank.

World Bank (1999b). *World Development Report*. Web site: Http://www.worldbank.org/ wdr/contents.htm

Yin, Q.P. & White, G. (1993): The Marketization of Chinese Higher Education: A Critical Assessment. Discussion Paper, Institute of Development Studies. Brighton, United Kingdom: University of Sussex.

Zhou, Z.Y. (1998). Reforming China's Higher Education. File:///A/98-1-11.html.

CHAPTER 7

Arab Countries
Oil Boom, Religious Revival and Non-Reform

HOLGER DAUN AND REZA ARJMAND

INTRODUCTION

The role of the Arab countries in the world changed considerably from the 1970s, when growing export revenues began to be used for diverse purposes. For instance, some of the countries invested heavily in industry and education; economic support to development projects in Africa was also increased. Apart from the revenues created with the oil boom, Islamic revival contributed to the changed role of the Arab countries.

Educationally, the Muslim countries in the Middle East differ in at least two ways from other countries in the world: (i) their school curricula contain a larger proportion of religious subjects; and (ii) they have very centralized education systems but have not implemented restructuring measures, that is decentralization, to the same extent as other countries have. With a few exceptions, they were also very late to introduce the modern type of schools and in many cases, education is not compulsory. In Oman, for instance, the first modern school was established in 1940 and as of 1969–1970, only ninety pupils participated in primary education (Morsi, 1990). The educational policies and education systems differ between the Arab countries in at least the following aspects: rates of literacy; curricula and content of education; costs; and rates of enrollment.

Educational restructuring of the type carried out in Africa, Europe and North and South America during the 1980s and 1990s, has not been implemented to any large extent in the Arab countries.

This chapter deals with some of the countries and their educational development in the Middle East.

BACKGROUND

In order to understand the role of primary education in the countries in question, it will be necessary to look at some principal features of Islam and the Muslim community. The unity of people professing Islam form the 'umma (the Muslim community, the Muslim world). Varieties of Islam have emerged from the dialectics between the Islamic cosmology and different societal realities (Al-Ahsan, 1992).

Koranic education accompanied the spread of Islam. With the expansion to new areas, the need for written norms and laws and for educated administrators increased. A large number of written sources and oral traditions about the Prophet Mohammed and his successors and their conduct were collected. The sources that seemed to be the most reliable, were eventually known as the Sunna (El-Garh, 1971) came from four scholars living in different places and periods. The Sunna were standardized and formalized, and each scholar founded his own legal school and one legal school was founded in the name of each scholar known as *Hanafi, Hanbali, Maliki* and *Shafe'i*. *Shi'a* in turn established the school of their own called *J'afari*, attributed to the sixth Imam of *Shi'a*.

The emergence of a class of learned men—'ulama—was the result of the spread of education and the societal needs for Islamic experts in various domains. The religious experts, experts in jurisprudence and teachers in different levels. The juridical experts came to play an important role in the political administration of the Muslim caliphates and states (El-Garh, 1971). In time, a differentiation into "sub-sects" took place in addition to the Sunni–Shi'ite schism.

Islam is not only a religion but also a way of life (Saadallah, 2000). Islamic law is considered a type of sacred law and the authority of the jurist or *faqih* in Islam an exclusively declarative authority, the authority to declare divine law. The Muslim jurist was very much bound to formal sources. His authority depended more upon his skills as an interpreter of texts than upon any inherent wisdom. The earliest Muslim jurists relied heavily on their own sense of equity and propriety, on their views and opinions (*ra'y*), but even then they appear to have been mindful of being in some sense subservient to the divine will (Weiss, 1998: 114).

ISLAMIC COSMOLOGY

Some elements of the Islamic cosmology may be described from an abstract level down to the level of concrete norms and rules of conduct. This will allow us to better understand the context in which education in the Muslim world is taking place.

All aspects of the world are united: God is a unity, unity between God and man, unity between men, man as a unit and unity between the sacred and the profane. The relationship (the unity) between God and man is complex. The *Shari'a* is the divine law and it is, among other things, the guiding principles that the individual has to follow in order to be regarded as a Muslim (Hjärpe, 1979; Nasr, 1975). In short, *Shari'a* is the concrete laws and norms that every Muslim has to follow if he or she is to have a min-imum unity with God. The *Tariqa* contains two fundamental elements: a metaphysical doctrine and a spiritual education in the stages of the way to God (Nasr, 1975:148). The *Haqiqa* is the inner core of Islam; it is the Truth itself. This doctrine could be traced through Islamic Mysticism. The Truth will not come automatically to man, he has to strive and struggle *(jihad)* for it. The intellect is an instrument in this struggle; only the intellect can understand the metaphysical aspects of Islam. To understand is to have a "contemplative vision" of things by the means of intellectualization, while reason is just a mental representation of things. Very few are able to reach Truth.

Man needs a *Shari'a* that guides his actions and a *Haqiqa* (essential truth) which gives his actions and his life a higher meaning (Yahia 1975:a,b). There is unity between all individuals who follow the *Shari'a* strictly. Mohammed's behaviour and actions as they are described in the Koran, the *Sunna* and the *Hadith* (the traditions) are the prototype for human conduct (Dodge 1962; Nasr 1976; Watt 1968). Basically, Islam does not distinguish between the sacred and the profane; everything is sacred or has to be subordinate to the Truths. The State, for instance, is embedded in or an instrument for sacred forces. In reality, a large number of secular rules and laws have been derived from the *Shari'a* and exist somewhat autonomously in the secular sphere (i.e. commercial and similar laws). Morals and ethics have their source in the Koran, the *Sunna*, the *Hadith* and the *Sira* (the "conduct and way of living" of Mohammed). The *Hadith* is divided into sections that deal with a particular sphere of everyday life, and together these are taught as a subject in Islamic education. The divisions comprise the sayings of the Prophet concerning government, legal procedure, (military law, land ownership, financial instructions, ritual purity, and marriage, divorce and inheritance (Dodge, 1962:54-55).

Religion and Culture

Muslims differ due to a series of conflicts that took place from the first centuries after Mohammed's death up to the present time. The majority of Muslims are Sunnis, while Shi'its are in the majority in Iran, Iraq, southwestern Afghanistan, parts of Pakistan and south of Lebanon. As to state and leadership, some differences between the two principal sects may be mentioned.

Shi'îtes believe that the *Shari'a*, which is seen as directives set forth by the Prophet, should be followed strictly. Imams are the source of understanding and interpretation of *Shari'a*. There is a hierarchy of religious scholars, but all leadership is religious; therefore, no state leadership can exist apart from Islam. Consequently, education should be predominantly Islamic. For the Sunnis, on the other hand, Shari´a is the *Haqiqa* (the essential knowledge), and there is no need to add anything further or to interpret *Shari'a*. The forces of Islamic faith are the Koran and the Sunna. Leadership is divided into spiritual leadership (imam) and political leadership (malek or sultan), an arrangement that legitimizes the existence of a state. Therefore, education can be both religious and profane.

Across the categories mentioned, Muslims have to varying degrees been exposed to modernization and education of the type prevailing in the Western countries (Ahmed, 1992; Ayubi, 1991). Modernization came with colonialism. It was accepted to the extent that it brought economic growth and a better material standard of living. However, the price for material progress tended to be increased economic and political differentiation, stratification, individualization and secularization (Kramer, 1997; Tibi, 1995). "Modern" was translated by many Muslim leaders as a drive to acquire Western education, technology and industry and to accept or adapt to the tendency toward secularization, individualization, and privatization. These features came to be perceived as Westernization and were, therefore, rejected (Ayubi, 1991:33).

The relativization implicit in or resulting from globalization threatens the Muslim way of life and make it necessary for Muslims to defend their values and belief systems (Appadurai, 1991). A more efficient and orthodox education might be a means in these efforts. Another type of differentiation took place, not only between the countries included here but also within them: Contradictory processes of secularization, on the one hand, and revitalization of particularistic sub-cultures and fundamentalism, on the other hand (Ahmed, 1992; Massialas & Jarrar, 1991). This contradiction is to some extent mirrored in education at the elementary level.

Waters (1995) identifies two different types of responses to globalization processes: (i) translation of the ideas and beliefs that accompany globalization, which results in syncretism; and (ii) reinforcement and revival tradition as a defense against globalization impulses, which results in fundamentalism. According to Turner (1991), "fundamentalisms provide traditional defense of modernity . . . " (169) but is also " . . . a reaction against cultural and social differentiation and fragmentation" (161). It "promotes modernity and is a defense of it against postmodernism, a response also to modernization"(165).

Fundamentalism does not necessarily imply traditionalism; it might simply imply a return to the original texts, while traditionalism is a return to the traditional way of life (Saadallah, 2000). The Islamic fundamentalists reject the secular aspects of modernization, and their reason for doing so is that, in their view of Islam: (i) there should be equal distribution of resources, (ii) *Shari'a* should serve as the legal base, and (iii) education should be organized according to Islamic values, beliefs and practices (Turner, 1991:173, 175). The fundamentalists are, according to Turner, (1991) anti-consumerist.

Globalization has resulted in intense encounters between, and mutual penetration of, world religions such as Islam, religions that more than ever before, compete and challenge one another, each one with its claim to possess "exclusive and largely absolute truths or values" (Turner, 1991:173). Originally, the *'umma* was not only a religious community but a whole community of Muslims (Ayubi, 1991:6). However, with the secularization it has most often become a community of a religious nature; it is all the Muslims wherever they live (Beeley, 1995). Expansion of Islam implies an expansion of the *'umma*. Turner (1991:177) sees a paradox in the relationship between globalization and Islam. The global system of communication has made it possible for Islam to reach many people around the world with its message but at the same time it is "also exposing the everyday world of Islam to the competition of pluralistic consumption and the pluralization of lifeworlds . . . "

The fact that the new information technology is both a part and a cause of the globalization processes has implications for Islam that have been described in a dramatic way by Ahmed (1992):

> Nothing in history has threatened Muslims like the Western media; neither gunpowder in the Middle Ages . . . nor trains and the telephone, which helped colonize them . . . The Western mass media are ever present and ubiquitous; never resting and never allowing respite. They probe and attack ceaselessly, showing no mercy for weakness or frailty (Ahmed, 1992:223).

On the other hand, Islam may be seen as a globalizing force in that it is spreading geographically (Haynes, 1999). During the 1970s, Islamic organizations were created in the Arab countries in order to reinforce Islam around the world and to create a front against what was perceived as Western cultural imperialism (Brenner, 1993).

The Islamic Organization for Education, Science and Culture (IOESC) was formed with the principal aim to establish an arabo-islamic culture as an uniting force, and to establish opposition against Western cultural imperialism. It supports educational projects not only in Africa, Asia and Latin America but also in the industrialized countries, including adult education, teacher training in the Arabic language, support to Arabic schools, and so on. The first World Conference on Muslim education was held in Mecca in 1977.

Muslims react differently to the capitalist lifestyles and to education of the type provided in modern schools. Different attempts have been made to classify the Muslims according to their view and acceptance or rejection of modernity. Ahmed (1992:157ff.) makes a distinction between modernists, traditionalists, and radicals, while other authors sometimes add "reformist", for instance. Instead of relying on particular terms, ideal types are used in table 7.1 in an effort to emphasize some differences among Muslims around the world.

Six topics that are relevant in this context have been included: Religion, Westernism, modernization, the state, globalization and education. The Muslims are classified according to the beliefs, value orientation and attitudes they seem to hold in relation to these issues.

* Highly educated individuals in categories II and III make efforts to maintain and improve Islamic education. They want to make it efficient in transmitting Islamic issues as well as elements of natural science (Ali, 1987; Ashraf, 1987).

* The majority of Muslims probably belong to category II, while category I constitutes scattered minorities living in Western countries or in urban centers in Muslim countries. Category IV is a minority in the Muslim world.

* The Muslims that constitute minorities in the former Soviet Union, former Yugoslavia and India are probably over-represented in categories I-II.

* As with other types of knowledge and education, the Islamic education is stratified. Very few people are perceived to be able to attain the highest levels of knowledge (Eickelman, 1978; Nasr, 1975). However, the Islamic knowledge among the masses might be improved and some representatives make efforts to educate and inform those who have less knowledge

Finally, before the 1970s, the *'ulama* (the learned men) were well represented among the most militant Muslims. Today, the situation is different: the most militant Muslim groups tend to have a low level of Islamic education in combination with a low level of Western education or none at all (Ayubi, 1991). The role the 'ulama has in educational and other matters varied with the rate of modernization of each country; the more rapid, the more Islam is revived and the 'ulama in a position of greater power (Ayubi, 1999:91).

TABLE 7.1 IDEAL TYPES OF MUSLIMS

Issue	I	II	III	IV
Religion	Is a private affair	Is a family and/or community affair	Is a community affair	Is a community affair
West	Indifferent	Critical	Reject Westernism	Reject Westernism
Modernity	Affirm modernity	Affirm modernity	Accept modernity	Reject modernity
State	See the State as an instrument for secular affairs	See the State as an instrument for religion	See the State as subordinate to religion	Perceive the State as irrelevant
Globali-zation	Are involved and accept	Are involved, feel threat, have a missionary attitude and want to impose *Shari'a*	Are involved, feel threat, have a missionary attitude and want to impose *Shari'a*	Make efforts to escape globalization forces and reject them. Withdraw
Education	Tend to have modern *and* Islamic education. Education tends to be an individual affair.	Tend to have modern or Islamic education. Education tends to be an individual and community affair.	Tend to have Islamic education only. Education tends to be a community affair.	Tend to have Islamic education only. Education tends to be a community affair.

Based on information from Ashraf, 1987; Ayubi, 1991; Ahmed, 1992; Budie, 1986; Gellner, 1994; Nasr, 1975; Saadallah, 2000; Turner, 1991; Watt, 1968; Waters, 1995).

Economy: Oil Boom or Poverty?

Economic differences between the Islamic countries existed early on, but were reinforced by the oil boom; countries that exported oil were able to raise their material standard of living (i.e., Iraq, Kuwait, Oman and Saudi Arabia), while other countries remained among those with the lowest standard in the world (i.e., Yemen) (Massialas & Jarrar, 1991; Ohlin, 1995). Oil revenues meant tremendous changes for some of the countries; their GNP per capita multiplied and enrollment in modern education increased rapidly.

The production of oil has been important during the whole period in Kuwait, Oman and Saudi Arabia. Of the countries in Table 7.2, Algeria and Tunisia do not produce oil to any large extent. The rates of GDP growth were highest in the oil-producing countries in the 1970s, although Iraq had high rates already during the 1960s. All of the selected countries except Oman continued to have strong growth during the 1980s. Generally, most of the growth derived from merchandise export or service-sector growth.

The GNP per capita differed considerably between the countries in 1977 and the gap increased from the 1970s to the 1990s. The differences in economic level and the sectors of production are mirrored in the degree of urbanization. While Oman had ninety percent of its population living in rural areas, Jordan forty percent and Kuwait only five percent, for instance.

Table 7.2 Annual GDP Growth in Selected Arab Countries

| | GDP Growth | | |
	1960-1970	1970-1979	1980-1992
Algeria	4,6	5,8	2,1
Iraq	6,1	10,5	..
Jordan	6,6	..	-5,4
Oman	..	..	7.6
Saudi Arabia	..	11.1	0.4
Syria	5,7	9	..
Tunisia	4.7	7.6	3.7

Sources: World Bank 1979, 1981, 1986, 1995. Information on Kuwait was not available.

In 1960, agriculture played an important role not only for production but also for employment in all countries except Kuwait, which had only one percent of the active population engaged in this sector. Between 1960 and the beginning of the 1990s, industry grew in Algeria and Tunisia, while the service sector grew most in the other countries, especially Iraq and Saudi Arabia.

TABLE 7.3 DEVELOPMENT OF GNP PER CAPITA IN THE SELECTED ARAB COUNTRIES

	Algeria	Jordan	Kuwait	Oman	Saudi Arabia	Syria	Tunisia
	GNP per capita						
1977	1,110	710	12,270	..	6.040	910	860
1979	1,590	1,180	17,100	..	7,280	..	1,120
1984	2,410	1,570	16,720	6,490	10,530	1,620	1,270
1993	1,730	1,120	19,360	4,850	7,510	..	1,720

There has always been a shortage of labor in the oil-producing countries and, therefore, immigration is high (Morsi, 1990).

Economic aid to countries in Africa and Asia expanded rapidly with the oil boom. A certain portion of this economic support was clearly linked to religious projects such as the building of mosques, establishment of Islamic schools, and so on (ISESCO, 1986). Later, when the oil prices stagnated and the revenues from oil exports tapered off, the international aid also decreased.

The world-wide economic recession during the 1970s and 1980s was severely felt in the Arab countries, especially in those that did not produce oil (Tunisia, for instance). They had to take loans on the international market. Algeria had in 1970 a debt equal to nineteen percent of the GNP; in 1991 the debt had increased to seventy percent. For Tunisia, the external debt was sixty-six percent of the GNP in 1991 (World Bank, 1977, 1981, 1986, 1995).

STATE FORMATIONS

Although sultanates and other political units have existed for centuries, most of the modern states were constructed by the colonial powers and they followed secular laws. In the Muslim countries, the state and its role cannot be understood in isolation from *umma, justice* and *leadership* (Ayubi, 1991). Independence from the colonial powers, none of the states replaced the secular legal system by he full range of Sharia elements. The only exceptions are Iran, Libya, and Saudi Arabia, countries in which the Shari´a more than secular laws is applied (Badie, 1986). None of the countries have a multi-party democratic system of the Western liberal variety. Algeria held elections in the mid-1990s but the winning party was not allowed to form a new government. Instead, the military intervened. As mentioned before, the Muslims differ in their view on the role of the state and public education. Ideally, there should be a balance between *din* (religion) and *dunya* (the world or life), and *dawla* (the state) according to Islam (Ayubi, 1991; Ahmed, 1992:117). The state should be an element of the religion or at least serve religious interests; law (*Sharia*) precedes the state (Ayubi, 1991:22).

The more secular the state is, the more the Muslims of types II-IV exit from it (Budie, 1986). The main values of the Muslim state are not freedom and equality but justice (Ayubi, 1991:24). That is, there may exist inequalities but they might be seen as given by God and are, consequently, fair. According to Muslims in categories III and IV, individual freedom is unthinkable since the individual is an element of the *umma*, the brotherhood or another collectivity (Ayubi, 1991). If we accept the most common definitions of civil society, there is no such society in countries with strong Islamic influence; Islamic collectives exert a "totalizing" influence and put total demands on the individual (Gellner, 1994). They compete with the state for the population's loyalty. However, Islamic associations may fulfill certain functions normally assigned to civil society (Mardin, 1995; Kramer, 1997); since the mid-1980s, for example, projects such as hospitals and schools have been created by Muslim associations in Egypt and other countries (Ayubi, 1991).

The religious sources and their interpretations describe the ideal situation, but the religion does not define power relationships (Gellner, 1994). That is, power relations emerged that the Islamic sources do not comment upon, since many phenomena did not exist at the time the Koran was revealed. This leaves space for different interpretations and for the priority of interpretations offered by those in power positions. The state tends to be an arena of struggle for reproduction of existing power relationships and class interests. The Koranic schools are, according to Talbani (1996), an instrument for this reproduction. The reproduction not only of local power relations but their total impact is a legitimation of power relations in each country.

Islamic and Western Education

As previously mentioned, the primary schools in the Muslim countries teach more religion than primary schools elsewhere. Yet, Koranic schools function as a complement to modern primary schools. There are also a few private institutions that include more religious subjects than in public schools, from primary up to tertiary level. In addition, these schools do not teach music or art (Morsi, 1990) in its western sense. Among Muslims the recitation of the Koran is considered to be both music and calligraphy. These are thought of as Islamic art subjects and can be taught as optional or extra-curricular subjects in some schools.

Islamic Education

In the Islamic conceptualization of knowledge, a distinction is made between acquired knowledge; and revealed knowledge. The latter type of knowledge is sacred and available to only a few adherents. The former type of knowledge is either transmitted traditions or rational knowledge, achieved through reason (Talbani, 1996). Thus, education is a twofold process dealing with the acquisition of external knowledge that improves the faith, and the internal realisation of intrinsic meaning. Education "is a way of approaching the absolute values represented by God and a means for integration into society" (Ali, 1987; Ashraf, 1987). In practice, man has to discipline his nature in order to act in accordance with the arbitrary code of conduct laid down by God, and to refer to particular Koranic verses in appropriate contexts (Eickelmann, 1978:494).

Koranic education is "confined to the transmission of traditions and dogma, and is hostile to research and scientific inquiry" (Talbani, 1996:69). The basic stock of Islamic knowledge has remained constant over time and throughout Muslim areas, and the paradigm for all such knowledge is the Koran. On the basic level of education, knowledge always flows from the teacher to the pupil in a one-sided process (Eickelmann, 1978:492). Talbani (1996) sees Koranic knowledge as instrumental to the reproduction of existing power relations:

> For the traditionalists, the Koran is the source of perennial knowledge and provides guidance for all matters. . . . Political power lies in the control over religious interpretation and the discourse that the religious groups use to exert such control (Talbani, 1996).

The goals of Islamic education are to equip the pupils with knowledge about and for this world and the next and to lead "each individual and society as a whole, to the Ultimate Truth" (Ali, 1987:36). Education is regarded as the way of receiving knowledge that is required in order to live in accordance with the will of God and to ensure a good next life. The Koran contains the core content of basic Islamic education and textbooks are seen as deviation from the correct way (Hurst, 1985).

Islamic education can be classified into three levels: elementary (Koranic), post-elementary (post-Koranic), and higher education. There are no formal grades, forms or stages in the Koranic schools. Anyone is free to start and to finish whenever he or she wants. The pupil is expected to learn the Koran by heart, and he or she learns at his or her own rate. Questioning of or critical reasoning in relation to Islamic principles is not allowed. The goals of post-elementary education are to create "experts" in, first and foremost, Muslim law, the Islamic religion and the Arabic language. These experts are supposed to have perfect knowledge in the domain in which they have specialized. For a long time, the majority of the *'ulama* and other leading members of the Muslim world opposed the translation of the Koran into other languages and were able to prevent it (Dodge, 1962:31-32). Post-Koranic education, at least among Shi'a is taught in theological seminaries following a curriculum designed for the purpose of religious experts.

The student must pass through three stages in order to attain the rank of an expert. The order of the curriculum is as follow:

* Preliminary Course: prerequisite courses on Arabic grammar, syntax, composition, logic, rhetoric, and ability to understand and explain the Koran and other religious texts.

* Intermediate Course: principles of Islamic jurisprudence, laws of Shari'e, mastery in intellectual reasoning, mastery over jurisprudence.

* Advanced Course: Mastery over jurisprudence, interpretation of the Koran, and the ability to reach a proper conclusion in required cases and issue a religious verdict. In this stage the student can touch the religious authority through the ability of reasoning in different questions.

* Extracurricular Studies: the student can participate in different courses including Islamic Philosophy, Arabic Literature, Biography, Scholastic Theology, peripatetic thinking and gnosticism.

Western Education

Western-style education was introduced by the colonizers, but Iran and Saudi Arabia, which were never colonized, also established this type of education. The structure of the education system has to a large extent remained the same as it was during the colonial period, while the content has changed considerably. The Arab countries have made many attempts to coordinate cultural and educational activities. The first World Conference on Muslim education was held in Mecca in 1977.

With a few exceptions educational aims are based on Islam (Hussein, 1994; Morsi, 1990; Ben Jaballah, 1994). The Charter of the Arab Cultural Unit established in Baghdad in 1964 states that the Arab countries should have the same educational goals and objectives. However, despite the efforts to homogenize education, the educational policies, education systems and educational indicators differ between the Muslim countries in at least the following aspects: rates of literacy; curricula and content; costs; and rates of enrollment. It should also be mentioned that educational restructuring has not been implemented by any of the countries to the same extent as in other parts of the world.

There are some similarities between the countries: all systems are highly centralized, although attempts have been made by Oman and Saudi Arabia to delegate some decision-making to the regional level; the proportion of religious subjects is comparatively large; all the countries allow and subsidize private schools (international or Muslim); and the cost per pupil is comparatively high (Morsi, 1990; World Bank, 1995). In Kuwait, Qatar and Saudi Arabia, private schools have to use the same curriculum, teaching methods and examination systems as those used in public schools (Morsi, 1990). Apart from Kuwait, where one third of all primary school pupils attend private school, the rate of private enrollment at the primary level is very low—three percent in Saudi Arabia and one percent in Qatar. Some countries have separate schools for boys and girls. For instance, in 1990, seventy percent of all primary school pupils in Oman attended separate schools (ibid.).

In 1960, the rate of literacy was only three percent in Saudi Arabia, while it was forty percent in Kuwait. Saudi Arabia started to modernize very late, when oil was extracted. However, the rate of literacy has increased rapidly, especially between the mid-1970s and the beginning of the 1990s. Iraq (not included in table 7.4) is the only country that has had a decline in the rate of literacy. It may be assumed that the war and the subsequent international blockade of the country are the principal causes of this decline.

As far as primary school enrollment is concerned, all selected countries except Saudi Arabia had comparatively high rates (gross as well as net) in primary education enrollment in 1960. Saudi Arabia started from twelve percent in the beginning of the 1960s and then had a rapid growth. In Algeria, Iraq, and Kuwait the trend was broken in the 1980s or 1990s. All three countries have been or are involved in armed conflicts. The rates of net enrollment follow a similar trend but Oman had a decrease in the end of the 1980s. Female enrollment rates follow the general trend. The interruption in the upward trend in Kuwait was stronger for girls than for boys.

TABLE 7.4 ADULT LITERACY RATE, ARAB COUNTRIES

	1960	1975	1990	1995
Algeria	10	25	50	57
Jordan	..	59	..	87
Kuwait	47	60	70	77
Oman	..	..	30	..
Saudi Arabia	3	9	60	61
Syria	..	53	..	71
Tunisia	16	55	65	67

Sources: World Bank, 1979, 1980, 1986, 1991, and 1999

As regards the contents of the curriculum, data has not been available for all the countries selected for this chapter. There are considerable differences between the selected countries. While in Yemen pupils spend nearly one third of school time on the Koran and Islamic studies, pupils in Lebanon spend none. Arabic is given a more important role in Yemen than in other countries. Foreign languages are not studied at all in Yemen and Egypt, while they are given about one third of the time in grades 3-6 in Morocco and Lebanon.

TABLE 7.5 PERCENTAGES OF TIME SPENT ON VARIOUS SUBJECTS IN PRIMARY EDUCA-
TION, SELECTED ARAB COUNTRIES

	Koran and Islamic studies	Arabic	Foreign Language	Mathe- matics	Science	Math and Science
Grades 1-2:						
Oman	20	36	0	17	7	24
Yemen	28	31	0	17	10	27
Egypt	11	36	0	22	7	29
Morocco	18	50	0	20	4	24
Lebanon	0	26	26	16	6	22
Saudi Arabia	50	..	..	..	..	..
Grades 3-4:						
Oman	18	27	0	17	10	27
Yemen	28	31	0	17	17	34
Egypt	10	31	0	20	20	40
Morocco	14	25	36	15	15	30
Lebanon	0	27	27	17	17	34
Grades 5-6:						
Oman	17	20	0	17	10	27
Yemen	27	30	0	17	10	27
Egypt	8	23	0	15	10	25
Morocco	15	25	38	16	4	20
Lebanon	0	25	28	18	11	29
Saudi Arabia *	31	30	0	..	.	39
Grades 1-6:						
UAR	12	25	0	..	..	63
Kuwait	10	35		..	..	55

Note: Figures for Oman are based on information from Ohlin (1996) and other figures on information from Massialas & Jarrar (1991). For the last section (Grades 1-6), data has been obtained from Morsi (1990:100). * For Saudi Arabia, grades 6-9, figures derive from Al-Baadi (1994).

There are considerable differences between the selected countries in regard to spending on education. Some countries, Algeria, for instance, have spent significantly more than others (see table 7.6). Iraq was a big spender in the 1960s but since then it has had the lowest percentage.

However, there is no correlation between expenditure and the number of pupils per teacher. Saudi Arabia has during the whole period had the lowest number of pupils per teacher at the first level, but its expenditure on education is average. The low pupil/teacher ratio is to a large extent explained by two factors: primary education is divided so that there are separate schools for boys and girls; and a comparatively large portion of the population are nomads (al-Baadi, 1994). Algeria has had the highest number of pupils per teacher.

TABLE 7.6 TOTAL EXPENDITURE ON EDUCATION AS % OF GNP

	1960	1980	1986	1988	1992
Algeria	5.6	7.8	6.1	9.9	8.1
Iraq	5.8	3.0	3.7	3.8	3.8
Jordan	..	..	..	..	6.5
Kuwait	..	2.4	4.6	5.5	6.1
Oman	..	2.1	6.6	4	3.8
Saudi Arabia	3.2	5.4	10.6	7.5	6.4
Syria	..	4.6	..	..	4.2*
Tunisia	3.3	5.4	5.0	6.3	6.3

Sources: World Bank, 1977, 1981, 1990, 1995 and 1999. * In 1996.

CASE STUDIES

Saudi Arabia

Before the discovery of oil, Saudi Arabia was a poor country, inhabited by a large number of nomads. It had 17.4 million inhabitants in 1993. Through oil exports, the country has attained one of the highest economic positions in the world (as measured by GNP per capita). The agricultural sector now plays a very small role, while industry and service contribute most to production and employment. Due to the shortage of Saudi labor, the industrial sector to a large extent relies upon immigrants, which constitute more than one forth of the population (al-Baadi, 1994).

The great majority are members of the Sunni sect Wahabis—the puritan fundamentalists—whose intent is to "return to the true faith". Only an estimated five percent of Saudis are Shi'a, inhabiting the southern part of the country. The public discourse is based on Islam but sections of the population contend that the politics are Westernized (featuring individualism and secularization, among other characteristics) (Ayubi, 1991). According to Turner (1991:174), "Fundamentalists see the Saudi government as corrupted by Western consumerism" and adhering to the foreign policy objectives of Western societie. In 1979, a group of armed Wahab sect members took over the mosque at Mecca in protest against the Westernization and secularization of the country (Ayubi, 1999).

The oil revenues have to some extent been used for domestic investments such as in the health, social services, and educational sectors, but a large. According to the 1990–1995 development plan, efforts are to be made to improve the competence and skill among the Saudi population so as to "Saudinize" the labor force. Socioeconomic differentiation due to modernization exacerbates traditional forms of differentiation, and this is mirrored in education.

Until 1926, educational efforts were mostly limited to kuttab (Koranic schools) (Al-Baadi, 1994). A number of government and private schools of the modern type had been established but they were not supervised by the government (Twitchell, 1953).

Several features stand out in relation to the Saudi system of education. First, there are two different educational systems, one for boys and one for girls. The education of girls is not placed under the Ministry of Education, but is in the hands of a council of *ulama*. The first public school for girls opened in 1981, and since this time, many girls have graduated from school and entered university. After completion of their studies, females participate in the system for the most part as teachers or authorities for women in universities or schools.

Secondly, as is common in other Arab countries, Islamic subjects occupy a large proportion of the curricula. In Grade 1, for example, fifty percent of the teaching time is spent on religious matters, and in grades 6-9, this is reduced to over twenty percent.

There are two different types of schools: (i) public primary schools; and (ii) primary schools for learning the Koran. Apart from an even greater proportion of religious subjects than in public primary school, schools in the latter category follow the same national curriculum as the former. No measures of the restructuring type have been implemented. In 1989–90, 4.3 percent of all students were enrolled in private schools, to which the parents were obliged to pay fees (Al-Baadi, 1994), and this proportion has not changed. The education system is also more decentralized (through delegation) than those of the other Arab countries (Morsi, 1990:62) but from an international comparative perspective it is still rather centralized.

Educational expenditures as a percentage of government expenditures increased from 6.3 in the 1950s to 16.0 in 1989–1990 (Al-Baadi, 1994). After an increase from the 1940s to the 1960s, spending on education fluctuated considerably. Since the GNP and government budgets have increased substantially in the last few decades, however, spending on education has risen in absolute terms.

Oman

Oman, with a population of two million in 1993, is a Sultanate ruled by a king. The population is predominantly Sunni. Until the beginning of the 1980s, the country was principally agricultural, but the exploitation of oil has made Oman a leading oil exporter, with an economy dominated by the petroleum industry. Rapid economic growth and social change since the 1970s has resulted in a lack of Omanis that are qualified for jobs in modern sectors. In this respect, the country has to rely upon immigrants from Asia (Shanfari, 1994). In the mid-1990s, approximately 69 percent of the employees in banking, more than 90 percent of those in construction and more than 80 percent of those employed in commerce and trade were immigrants. Although the first teacher training center has been in operation since 1977, there continues to be a shortage of teachers; two-thirds of all teachers are foreigners, recruited principally from the Asian countries (Ohlin, 1995).

Until the beginning of the twentieth century, Omani children received Islamic education in kuttabs, small Koranic schools. The first public elementary school was established in 1914, and the first school in the modern sense of the word was established in 1940. Today, there are separate public schools for boys and girls. In the mid-1990s, there were 382 primary schools—34 percent of them for boys, 43 percent for girls, and 23 percent coeducational (ibid). The rate of enrollment in primary education increased from practically zero in the beginning of the 1960s to nearly eighty percent in the mid-1990s (UNESCO, 1995). Education is based on Islamic and Shari'a principles.

There are two types of private schools: those run by Omanis and those run by foreigners. The latter cater to the children of the many expatriates. Apart from delegation of school inspection to the regional level, no other restructuring measures have been implemented in education.

Syria

Islam is the predominant religion practiced by ninety percent of the population, or fifteen million inhabitants. The majority, 74 percent, are Sunnis while the remaining 16 percent belong to different Islamic sects. Approximately 10 percent of the entire population are Armenians, Asyrians and followers of other religions (The World Factbook, 1999). The Ba'ath socialist party has been ruling the country since the end of the 1950s and socialism was made the official ideology in 1958. Vital sectors of the economy are owned or controlled by the state, which also regulates private business. However, since the 1980s, the government encourages private initiatives and savings and investment by citizens of other Arab countries (Encyclopedia Britannica, 1994).

The process of industrialization started in the early 1960s, resulting in changes in the distribution of employments. The Syrian economy is based on agriculture and industry (mainly oil and phosphate), and the agricultural sector provides jobs for many people from rural to urban areas (The World Factbook, 1999). Petroleum constitutes 65 percent of the value of all exports but its share of the exports is declining.

During the Ottoman occupation, Syria had more schools than other Arab provinces, but expenditures on Syrian education were very limited. By 1945, only five percent of the state budget was allocated to education and most schools were located in towns. Most people at the time remained illiterate, as education was restricted to the sons of privileged people and civil servants. Turkish language was the medium of instruction. After the First World War, Syria was, like many other Arab countries, under French Mandate. In the Constitution of 1928 it was stated that (i) education should be free and the primary level should be compulsory; (ii) arabic should be the official language in the public sector; and (iii) technical education should be imposed as compulsory in order to meet the country's need for technical personnel (Gennaoui, 1994).

In 1980, net enrollment in primary education was close to ninety percent and in 1996, ninety-one percent. The enrollment rate at the secondary-school level was thirty-nine percent in 1980 and thirty-eight percent in 1996 (World Bank, 1999). The factors impeding complete enrollment are nomadism, poverty, and a shortage of facilities in some remote areas having small populations. Educational administration in Syria is very centralized, and the curriculum is uniform and applied nationwide. A detailed syllabus is developed by the central authorities. In primary education, the curriculum includes Arabic, mathematics, religious instruction, elements of science and health education, social and national education, art and physical education (ibid.).

Public spending on education as a percentage of GNP was 4.6 percent in 1980 and 4.2 percent in 1996. For all levels of education, the per-pupil expenditure in units of GNP per capita is among the lowest in the region.

Jordan

Jordan became independent in 1946. The constitution was ratified in 1952. More than ninety percent of the five million inhabitants (as of 1998) of the country are Muslims, the majority of whom are Sunni (Center for Middle East Studies, 1999), while nine percent are Christians and the remainder adherents of other religions. In 1980, sixty percent and in 1997, 73 percent of the population were living in urban areas (World Bank, 1999). The population growth rate is very high.

Principal natural resources are phosphate, potash and shale oil and the most important exports are phosphates and fertilizers. Due to economic problems in 1989, the country was inclined to accept some of the IMF recommendations for reform, yet ten years later further restructuring of the economy was deemed necessary and was therefore implemented (The World Factbook, 1999).

As in many other Muslim countries, the expansion of public education started comparatively late. After the Second World War, a very small percentage of all children attended modern schools. In 1946–1947, there were 77 schools with approximately

11,000 pupils. Fifty years later, the number of schools had increased to more than 4,000 and the number of pupils to 1.3 million (Center for Middle East Studies, 1999).

A new Education Act was decided upon in 1994. Modernization (the internationally established features) of the whole education system was planned for implementation in two phases—1989–1995 and 1996–1999. Among the measures taken were centralization of educational planning and decentralization of administration (ibid.).

The educational objectives are strongly based in *Shari'a* and include Islamic components, as in many other Muslim countries. Basic education is compulsory and public schooling is free of charge. In 1996, 76 percent of all primary school students were enrolled in public schools, sixteen percent in private schools and twelve percent in schools run by the United Nation Relief and Work Agency (UNRWA). The last mentioned cater to children of Palestinian refugees (Center for Middle East Studies, 1999). Some of the private schools were established especially for gifted students beyond the ninth grade.

The Ministry of Education covers some 74 percent of the cost of education while UNRWA covers 11 percent, with the private sector contributing approximately 14 percent. Net enrollment at the elementary level was 90.4 percent for boys and 90 percent for girls. In 1991, the rate of adult literacy was 82 percent and five years later the rate was 90 percent for males and 80 percent for females (ibid.). Literacy programs for adults are run by both the Ministry of Education and volunteer organizations, who utilize school buildings after hours. In the 1980s, the education budget was on average, more than three percent of the GNP. The proportion of the state budget allocated to education rose from seven percent in 1960, to nearly nine percent in 1990 (Masri & Bermamet, 1994). Curriculum and textbook development is a national activity, administered by the Board of Education. At primary level (6-16 age group), there is a national curriculum, except in the case of non-Muslims, who can run their own private schools with their own curricula. Measures of the restructuring type have not been taken.

Conclusions

The oil-producing Muslim countries had a rapid economic growth until the 1990s. They were able to invest in education and increase the rates of enrollment without drastically restructuring the education systems. The poorer Muslim countries have remained dependent on primary-sector production and their rate of enrollment is among the lowest in the world. In all, the Muslim countries have not responded in the same way as many African, Latin American and Asian countries to the global challenges and the increasing educational costs.

References Cited

Ahmed, A.S. (1992). *Postmodernism and Islam. Predicament and Promise.* London: Routledge.

Arab Countries

Al-Ahsan, A. (1992). Ummah or Nation: Identity in Comtemporary Muslim Society. Leicester: The Islamic Foundation.

Ali, S. A. (1987). "Islam and Modern Education." *Muslim Education Quarterley*, vol. 4.

Appadurai, A. (1991). "Disjuncture and Difference in the Global Economy." In M. Featherstone (ed.). *Global Culture. Nationalism, Globalization and Modernity.* London: Sage Publications

Ashraf, S. A. (1987). "Education and Values: Islamic vis-à-vis the Secularist Approaches." In *Muslim Education Quarterley*, vol. 4.

Ayubi, N. N. (1991). *Political Islam. Religion and politics in the Arab world.* London: Routledge.

Ayubi, N. N. (1999). "The Politics of Islam in the Middle East with Special Reference to Egypt, Iran and Saudi Arabia." In J. Haynes (ed.). *Religion, Globalization and Political Culture in the Third World.* London: Macmillam Press Ltd.

Baadi-al, H.M. (1994). " Saudi Arabia: System of Education." In T. Husén and N. Postlethwaite (eds.). *International Encyclopedia of Education.* Oxford: Pergamon

Badie, B. (1986). "'State' legitimacy and Protest in Islamic Culture." In A. Kazancigil (ed.). *The State in Global Perspective.* Paris: Gomer/Unesco

Beeley, (1992). "Islam as a Global Force in Global Politics." In A. G. McGrew and P. G. Lewis (eds.). *Global Politics.* Oxford: Polity Press.

Ben Jallah, H. (1994). "Tunisia: System of Education." In T. Husén and N. Postlethwaite (eds.). *International Encyclopedia of Education.* Oxford: Pergamon

Benhabib, S. (1998). "Democracy and identity. In search of the civic polity." *Philosophy & Social Criticism*, vol. 23.

Birl, J. B. (1995). "Revolution for Children in Saudi Arabia." *Children in the Muslim Middle East.* Austin: University of Texas Press.

Brenner, L. (1993). "La culture arabo-islamique au Mali." In R. Otayek (ed.). *Le radicalisme islamqiue au Sud du Sahara.* Paris: Karthala

The Centre for Middle East Studies (2000) University of Texas, USA. http://menic.utexs.edu.

Coulon, C. (1993). "Les nouveaux oulémas et le nouveau islamique au Nord-Nigeria." In R. Otayek (ed.). *Le radicalisme islamqiue au Sud du Sahara.* Paris: Karthala.

Dodge, B. (1962). *Muslim Education in Medieval Times.* Washington: The Middle East Institute

Eickelmann, D.F. (1978). "The Art of Memory: Islamic Education and Its Social Reproduction." *Comparative Studies in Society and History*, vol. 4, no. 1.

El-Garh, M.S. (1971). "The Philosophical Basis of Islamic Education in Africa." *West African Journal of Education*, vol. 15.

Encyclopedia Britannica (1994). Chicago: Encyclopedia Britannica Inc.

Gellner, E. (1994). *Conditions of Liberty. Civil Society and Its Rivals.* London: Harnish Hamilton

Gennaoui, A. (1994). "Syria: System of Education." In T. Husén and N. Postlethwaite (eds.). *International Encyclopedia of Education.* Oxford: Pergamon

Haynes, J. (1999). "Introduction." In J. Haynes (ed.). *Religion, Globalization and Political Culture in the Third World.* London: Macmillam Press Ltd.

Educational Restructuring

Hjärpe, J. (1979). *Islam, lära och livsmönster.* (Islam, Faith and Life Patterns). Stockholm: Almqvist & Wicksell.

Hurst, H. (1985). "Critical Education and Islamic Culture." In C. Brock and W. Tulasiewicz (eds.). *Cultural Identity and Educational Policy.* London: Croom Helm.

Hussein, M. G. (1994). "Kuwait: System of Education." In T. Husén and N. Postlethwaite (eds.). *International Encyclopedia of Education.* Oxford: Pergamon.

Kramer, M. (1997). "The Middle East, Old and New." In *Daedalus,* vol. 126, no. 2.

Massialas, B.G. and S.A. Jarrar (1991). *Arab Education in Transition. A Source Book.* New York: Garlands Publishing, Inc.

Mardin, S. (1995). "Civil society and Islam." In J.A. Hall (ed.). *Civil Society. Theory, History, Comparison.* Cambridge: Polity Press.

Marsi, M. and T. Bermamet (1994). "Jordan: System of Education." In T. Husén and N. Postlethwaite (eds.). *International Encyclopedia of Education.* Oxford: Pergamon.

Morsi, M.M. (1990). *Education in the Arab Gulf States.* Qatar: University of Qatar.

Nasr, S. H. 1975. *Islam, perspectives et réalités.* Paris: Editions Buchet/Chastel.

Quilliam, N. (1999). *Syria and the New World Order.* London: Ithaca Press.

Saadallah, S. (2000). *Banners of Faith. The Islamic Presence in Sweden Analyzed.* Unpublished MA thesis. Stockholm: Stockholm University, International Graduate Programme.

Shanfari, Al, A, M. (1994). "Oman: System of Educaiton." In T. Husén and N. Postlethwaite (eds.). *International Encyclopedia of Education.* Oxford: Pergamon Press.

Talbani, A. (1997). "Pedagogy, Power, and Discourse: Transformation of Islamic Education." *Comparative Education Review,* vol. 40, no. 1.

Tibi, B. (1995). "Culture and knowledge: The politics of islamization of knowledge as a postmodern project? The fundamentalist claim to de-westernization." *Theory, Culture & Society,* vol. 12.

Turner, B.S. (1991). "Politics and culture in Islamic Globalism." In R. Robertson and W. R. Garret (eds.). *Religion and Global Order.* New York: Paragon House Publishers

Twitchell, K. S. (1953). *Saudi Arabia.* Princeton: Princeton University Press.

UNESCO, (1995). *World Education Report.* Paris: Unesco.

Waters, M. (1995). *Globalization.* London: Routledge.

Watt, W. M. (1968). *What is Islam?* London: Longmans.

Weiss, B. G. (1998). *The Spirit of Islamic Law.* Athenes and London: The University of Georgia Press.

World Bank (1977). *World Development Report 1977.* Washington, D.C.: World Bank.

World Bank (1979). *World Development Report 1979.* Washington, D.C.: World Bank.

World Bank (1980). *World Development Report 1980.* Washington, D.C.: World Bank.

World Bank (1981). *World Development Report 1981.* Washington, D.C.: World Bank.

World Bank (1986). *World Development Report 1986.* Washington, D.C.: World Bank.

World Bank (1990). *World Development Report 1990.* Washington, D.C.: World Bank.

World Bank (1991). *World Development Report 1991.* Washington, D.C.: World Bank.

World Bank (1992). *World Development Report 1992.* Washington, D.C.: World Bank.

World Bank (1993). *World Development Report 1993.* Washington, D.C.: World Bank.

World Bank (1994). *World Development Report 1994.* Washington, D.C.: World Bank.

World Bank (1995). *World Development Report 1995.* Washington, D.C.: World Bank.

World Bank (1999). *World Development Report 1999.* Washington, D.C.: World Bank.

The World Factbook 1999. www.cia.gov.

Yahia, O. (1975a). "La finalité de l'Islam." In J. Berques and J.P. Charnady (eds.). *Normes et valeurs dans l'islam contemporain.* Paris: Payot.

Yahia, O. (1975b). "La condition humaine en Islam." In J. Berques and J.P. Charnady (eds.). *Normes et valeurs dans l'islam contemporain.* Paris: Payot.

CHAPTER 8

Nationalism and Educational Transition in Central Asia

ALEXANDER KANAEV AND HOLGER DAUN

INTRODUCTION

Central Asian countries that were part of the former Soviet Union inherited a highly developed educational system and high rates of literacy and enrollment. With the collapse of the USSR, educational restructuring and declining educational indicators followed. Afghanistan has all the time lagged behind its neighboring countries and its situation became worse during its civil war. This country has not followed the global trend of educational restructuring but has, with the *Taliban* government, opted for its own way within the Islamic framework. It has withdrawn from education which is now completely organized by NGOs.

BACKGROUND

Large areas of Central Asia were Islamized long before being integrated as republics of the Soviet Union. These areas experienced a rapid transformation and development of welfare. With the collapse of the union, a period of transformation to a capitalist system started. In education, most countries took restructuring measures in a similar fashion and the short-term result has been stagnation on most educational indicators. Geographically and culturally, Afghanistan belongs to the same sphere as the other Central Asian countries but it has never belonged to the Soviet Union. The country has gone through a development of a completely different type. This country is included for the sake of comparison and in order to show the educational diversity that exists in this area.

  The countries, which replaced the republics of the Soviet Union, have similarities as well as differences. On the one hand, they all inherited a similar economic system, an extended social security network and a well-developed educational system. The political structure, as well as the communist ideology, thus form a common denominator.

The distribution of natural resources varies significantly from country to country, Kyrgyztan being the poorest republic, as opposed to Turkmenistan, which has large reserves of gas and oil. The size of the population differs considerably between the countries. The GDP level per capita varied in 1960 and the countries with the highest level continued to maintain their rank just before the collapse of the Soviet Union. All countries except Tajikistan had a rather high rate of GDP growth during the 1970s, and their economies then slowed down during the 1980s, with the exception of Kyrgyztan. Specialization within the USSR economy, level of industrial development, ethnic and cultural differences and distinct approaches to the creation of new states—all these factors affect the present development possibilities (Wheeler, 1969).

After independence, all the countries have to a varying degree liberalized their economies and privatized state enterprises. With the introduction of the private market and the breakdown of old economic links, all countries experienced a dramatic decrease in GDP per capita due to the forced and pressing restructuring that resulted from the collapse of the old system (table 8.1).

TABLE 8.1 SOME CHARACTERISTICS OF SELECTED CENTRAL ASIAN COUNTRIES

	Kazakstan	Kyrgyzstan	Tajikistan	Turkmenistan	Uzbekistan	Afghanistan
Population in 1993, millions (a)						
	17.0	4.6	5.8	3.8	21.9	13.0
GDP per capita						
1960	793	435	384	858	357	775
1970	1,255	655	577	1,105	532	..
1980	1,761	814	723	1,218	734	819
1990	1,720	1,075	685	1,316	822	..
1994	918	497	281	..	612	..
% of population in rural areas, 1992 (a)						
	58	38	32	45	41	80
Largest ethnic/linguistic groups (b):						
	Kazak 42	Kyrgyz 52	Tajik 65	Turkmen 73	Uzbek 71	Pushtun 50
		Russian 22	Ukrainian	Russian 10	Russian 8	Tajik 25
		Uzbek 13	25	Uzbek 9	Tajik 5	
Human Development Index 1994 (a)						
	0.709	0.635	0.580	0.723	0.662	0.228*
Rate of Adult Literacy 1994:						
	97.5	97.0	96.7	97.7	97.2	28.9*
GNP growth:						
1970-80	4.6	4.4	-5.1	..	6.3	..
1980-93	-0.6	1.9	-0.8	..	2.2	..
Contribution from agriculture to GDP, %, 1993:						
	29	43	33	..	23	..
Rate of Gross enrollment in primary education, 1992:						
	86	..	85	..	80	..

Sources: (a) UNDP (1997a); (b) Kaneav and Fägerlind, 1996; World Bank (1981, 1993a; 1995); (d) UNESCO (1995). * = 1992

The typical socialist educational system had the following features: (i) a high rate of enrollment in preschool institutions and primary and secondary education; (ii) vocational components that made the students adapt gradually to the life of work; (iii) students were more or less guaranteed an employment when they finished secondary school; and (iv) a large portion of political education.

Restructuring of education is a hot topic for all the countries in the former USSR. The degree in which steps are taken to reshape the education system along restructuring lines varies from country to country but all of them express the will to decentralize their education systems.

Central Asian Societies

Before many of the Central Asian areas were conquered by Czarist Russia, they were dispersed tribal societies in the crossroads between Chinese, Russian and Muslim cultural influences. Some of them were for a long period ruled by the Turks, among others (Wheeler, 1969). Then many of these countries were economically integrated into the whole Soviet economy. Politically they had a certain degree of autonomy as compared to other areas that did not have this status of autonomous republic. Five of these are Kazakstan, Kyrgyzstan, Tajikistan, Turkmenistan and Uzbekistan. Being republics of the Soviet Union meant a comparatively rapid economic growth, at least until the 1980s, a comparatively extended social security guaranteed by the state and nearly one hundred percent literacy rate. The differences between these former socialist countries—economically, ethnically, and so on, became evident when they became independent nation-states in the beginning of the 1990s.

Afghanistan never became colonized but was an Islamic kingdom that became a Soviet republic in the 1950s, based on a tribal and clan society. Communists supported by the Soviet Union came into power in the end of the 1970s. This provoked a civil war, invasion from Soviet Union and a long war of resistance. Finally, Islamic fundamentalists, the *Taliban*, took control of the country in the mid-1990s.

The degree of urbanization was comparatively low in all of the socialist countries, since the in the Soviet Union, a large proportion of the population was employed on the collective farms. Mobility of the work force was low also because of the bureaucratic control and the planned economy. However, migrations started to take place in the beginning of the 1990s, not only between the countries but also within each country from rural to urban areas.

The level of literacy is very high in all of the countries, as compared to other countries with the same level of GNP per capita. After 1990, the rates of enrollment started to decline and rates of drop out, especially in the higher grades, to increase. Afghanistan, on the other hand, has one of the lowest rates of literacy in the world.

The views on compulsory education, society and so on, differ considerably within each country. There are divisions between: traditional and modern views (whether education should reinforce traditional or more modern values); Muslim versus Christian or atheistic views; broad development of the students versus human capital and skills formation; whether private educational institutions should be allowed or not; and so on (Tinanbaev, 1998; Kaana, 1998; Tibi, 1995; Turner, 1991).

CASE STUDIES

Turkmenistan

The country's history goes back to the trade traditions of the Silk Road. The mixture of invasions, conquests and domination over the centuries by the Persians, Alexander the Great, the Muslims, Genghis Khan, Tamerlane, and eventually the Russians, gradually shaped its borders, which were finally established as part of the Soviet Union in the 1920s.

Turkmenistan proclaimed its independence in 1991, to join the CIS in December of the same year (World Bank, 1993). With 3.5 million inhabitants, it is one of the most scarcely populated. Desert occupies around ninety percent of the surface. The vast majority of the population live on a narrow 100–kilometer strip close to the mountains which separate the country from Iran. Production of gas and oil, as well as cotton production, compose the bulk of a heavily specialized economy, which was, under the USSR, heavily dependent upon trafe with other republics. For example, eighty-four percent of natural gas was exported to other republics in 1991 (World Bank, 1993c:5).

Resources are vast and abundant, and the infrastructure is well-developed. The country has very little ethnic conflict, especially compared to neighboring republics. The comparatively small population and vast deposits of natural gas and oil were supposed to be enough, after 1991, to turn Turkemenistan into the 'second Kuwait'.

To take steps to increase trade, steps have been taken to promote cooperation with Turkey, (viewed by many Central Asian states as a model for successful development) and toward Iran, an immediate neighbor. The new cooperation was not only economic, but included increased political contacts, as well as a extensive program of cultural cooperation, including exchange of students and the creation of joined schools and universities.

Along with other countries of the sub-region, Turkmenistan has inherited an educational and professional training structure, which was tightly linked to the planned economy. Future employment was predictable and guaranteed for students with certificates from tertiary educational institutions. The liberalization of the economy, and growth of the private sector were followed by unemployment shifts in the employment structures, and an increased role of re-training (Deutsch, 1993; Kautsch, 1999).

Turkmenistan experiences the following difficulties, due to specifics of the country:

* The increase in the number of schools does not keep pace with strong population growth. This results in over-utilization of the existing school infrastructure (double shifts in the majority of schools, for instance) both in the cities and in the countryside

* A significant percentage of schools do not have adequate funding, and are in need of repairs and basic maintenance; and

* The low level of teacher income, as well as the decreasing prestige of the work, result in a high mobility of teachers.

Under the USSR, a significant percentage of preschool institutions were built, financed and maintained by factories and organizations. With the crisis of the economy, these institutions are receiving less and less financing and attempts are made to transfer them to the state. This is problematic because of the reduction of the state allocations for education in general. The country had 1,600 preschool institutions, with 220,000 pupils in 1992, which is around twenty-five percent of the children.

Primary and secondary schools, specialized schools

Primary school covers grades from 1 to 3, secondary—from grade 4 to grade 8. The majority of schools (seventy-seven percent) are located in rural areas. Eight years of schooling are compulsory and then the students have a choice to continue upper secondary education or enter a vocational training institution (around 10 percent of the students). The latter institutions suffer decreasing rates of enrollment, primarily due to the loosing link with the requirements of the economy, despite the fact that the duration of this education has been shortened from three to two years.

A significant effort has been invested in changing the goals, structure and the curricula inherited from the USSR. A structural reform, aiming at nine years of education is under way. A range of new subjects have been introduced, directed at the creation of the specific Turkmen national identity. This includes a new approach towards national history, and the introduction of subjects which give students information about the traditions, customs, and culture. The teaching of Islam, knowledge of the Koran and religious values is also part of the compulsory education.

They attempt to supplant the old Soviet ideological values with national cultural heritage, the Turkmen language is viewed by the government as one of the ways to get away from the Russian influence. The new alphabet, based on Latin script, is gradually introduced both as a discipline, and as the common medium used by mass media and the public authorities. Despite the difficulties resulting from the high costs and theproblems of changing the alphabet within a short period of time, the trend is promoted as part of the national policy, with political aims as well (Kanaev and Fägerling, 1996).

The multi-ethnic composition of the population necessitates teaching in the Turkmen, Russian, Uzbek, and Kazakh languages (World Bank 1993c: 120). Compulsory testing has been introduced in grade one and in the specialized schools. The thirty-six 'specialized' schools use a modified curriculum, emphasizing a subject such as mathematics, physics, or languages. They enroll students after grade 8, and provide four years (two more than the normal schools) of education. Usually they are closely linked to a specialized Ministry that provides additional funding and facilities for the school functioning.

Tertiary education

Nine higher education institutions and the Ashgabat State University provide advanced specialized education for around 50,000 students. Tuition fees have been introduced, for both preparatory faculties and full-time, remote, and evening studies. There are declining rates of returns for higher education and enrollment rates are decreasing.

Although the country has proclaimed its neutral status and declared devotion to democracy and a free market, the conservative nature of political developments is a reality, reinforced by strong and almost unlimited presidential power. This has also had an influence on educational development, especially in the formulation of goals of civic disciplines, and the overall orientation of the curricula.

Kazakhstan

Almost five times the size of France, Kazakhstan is the largest former republic. The country has an estimated population of 17 million inhabitants (July 1997). The geography is dominated by vast steppes in the center and the west, desert in the south, and the Kazak Hills that are actually a spur of the Himalayas rise in the east. Kazakhstan was conquered by Genghis Khan and still retains some features of Mongolian language and customs.

The country inherited a well-developed agricultural base and industry. It was of one of the most prosperous countries of the CIS, with huge reserves of gas and oil. The current economic crisis has caused mass emigration of the skilled workforce. Added to that, the country is suffering from ecological problems to a larger extent than its neighbors.

The economic crisis also affects education, which suffers from inadequate funding and a deteriorating infrastructure. Kazakhstan was one of the first countries to undergo a radical decentralization program but at the same time the administrative control over schools and universities remained within the Ministry of Education. Thus, the reform might be viewed as an attempt to decentralize financing more than decision-making opportunities. The trend is similar for all of the countries of Central Asia, but Kazakhstan was the first one to realize the inefficiency of the budgetary decentralization and began re-centralizing financing in 1996 (Atchoarena and Prokhoroff, 1996: 2).

Kazakhstan adopted a number of laws directly dealing with the reform of the education system in 1992 and 1993. The attempt was made to set up a legal framework for the functioning of private-owned educational institutions and, decentralize school management and financing. New alternative ways of financing schools were introduced, along with the introduction of recruiting students on a contractual basis.

Preschool institutions

The number of children in the 8,743 daycare centers and kindergartens—more than one million—had decreased to half in 1995. An alternative network of private and mixed-ownership kindergartens and nurseries developed at the same time. The latter had 80,000 children enrolled in the mid-1990s. A greater diversification of the languages used has been developed, including, for instance, Kazakh, Russian, English, Ukrainian, Turkish and some minority languages. Most of the closed preschool institutions consist of those formerly owned by factories and enterprises, which are unable to support them in market economy conditions.

Primary, secondary and specialized secondary education

Schools have received the right to use their own curricula based on the basic curricula, formulated by the Ministry of Education. Instruction takes place in seven languages (Kazakh, Russian, Uzbek, Uighur, Tadjik, Turkish and German). The number of schools using Kazakh as the language of instruction increased from 3,216 in 1991 to 3,364 in 1995.

There is a great shortage of teachers. According to the 1995 National Report, the country was lacking more than 22,000 teachers, especially primary school teachers, and teachers in the Kazakh language, literature and foreign languages. Twenty-five schools in the country are privately owned, operating on the basis of tuition fees. At the same time, specialized professional education is losing terrain; the number of schools was halved during the period 1991–1995. In 1995, there were 404 vocational schools with 140,000 students, providing both secondary education and professional training. Secondary specialized education has been gradually transferred from various ministries to the Ministry of Education, the number of specialties has been lowered and the curricula have been revised (Deutschland, 1993). At the same time, the enrollment figures have drastically declined. In 1995, specialized institutions were training 214,000 students in 203 specialties.

Tertiary education

Higher education institutions are probably the most affected by both structural change, as well as the content of training they provide. With universalization as the cornerstone, the reform of higher education institutions has led to the appearance of twelve new universities in the period 1991–1995. The combination of universities and secondary specialized schools has been promoted as the way to establish 'educational complexes.' The number of privately owned higher education institutions is increasing, with 35 in 1995.

Kyrgyzstan

Kyrgyzstan is a comparatively small country, bordered by Kazakhstan, Uzbekistan, Tajikistan and China. Only a small percentage of the area is suitable for agriculture, and about forty percent of the total area is used as pastures for cattle and sheep. Natural resources include small amounts of coal, natural gas, oil, rare earth metals, and hydroelectric power. The country was part of pre-revolutionary Russia and became an autonomous republic within the Soviet Union in 1936. Despite a considerable degree of economic and social development (including educational development) and subsidies from Moscow, Kyrgyzstan remained one of the areas in Soviet Union that had the lowest GNP per capita and the lowest degree of industrialization. However, the country was one of the first of the former autonomous republics to initiate a program of structural reform of the economy and to introduce a multi-party system (Asian Development Bank, 1996a; World Bank, 1993b).

In 1995, the country had 4.3 million inhabitants (Asian Development Bank, 1996b). The degree of urbanization was low at the end of the Soviet period: thirty-eight percent of the population in urban areas in 1980 and same percentage in 1991 (World Bank, 1993b).

The dissolution of the centrally planned system resulted in a tremendous migration. A large number of Russians, Germans, Ukrainians and other people have left the country and Kyrgystanis living outside Kyrgyzstan itself have moved to this country. During the period 1989–1996, the percentage of Kyrgyzstanis in the population increased from 52 to 60 percent and that of Uzbeks from 13 to 14 percent, while that of Russians decreased from 22 to 16 percent (UNDP, 1997c). Some of the most important migrations are shown in Table 8.3. The Russians and Germans included the most highly-skilled persons in the country.

TABLE 8.2 EMIGRATION FROM AND IMMIGRATION TO KYRGYZSTAN DURING
THE FIRST HALF OF THE 1990S

	Kyrgyz	Russians	Germans	Ukrainians
Net flow	+ 15,343	-210,284	-103,086	- 30,823

Source:UNDP (1997c).

The economy of Kyrgyzstan was "one of the most backward" within the Soviet Union (UNDP, 1997c:10). Due to the annual deficit in external trade, Kyrgyzstan was frequently given subsidies from the Soviet Union (World Bank, 1993b:xv).

The transition of the economy included liberalization of prices, with the subsequent inflation processes; re-orientation of export and import, with the disruption of traditional economic links to Russia and the other ex-republics of central Asia; and privatization and liberalization processes. The country has had a steady decline in its economy since the end of the 1980s. During the period 1991–1995, 5,895 state-owned enterprises (or fifty-nine percent of the total number) were privatized. There were some variations between the sectors and branches; in consumer-service, all state- owned enterprises were privatized (UNDP, 1997c:3). By 1996, the private sector of the economy had grown to employ 750,000 persons and had a 22.3 percent share in the GDP. From 1990 to 1996, the decline in industrial production amounted to approximately sixty-four percent (UNDP, 1997c:5). At the same time, with the help of international organizations, expertise and NGOs, steps were taken to better analyze the potential of the economy, in order to create a full picture of the actions to be taken.

The year 1996 has been seen by many as a turning point in the restructuring of Kyrgyzstan, when, for the first time since 1991, positive signs in the country's macro-economic indicators were noticed. However, by 1997, GDP was forty percent lower than in 1989 (Eversmann, 1999). The consequences of the immigration from neighboring countries add to the internal migration, resulting in rapid growth of population in urban areas.

The restructuring of the economy led to the unequal distribution of the losses in production. Leading industries are metallurgy, light manufacturing and textiles that are organized according to the former centralized economic structure. Traditional export industries, such as energy production and metallurgy, suffered less damage since they were able to either maintain the economic ties to the former consumers or reorient the export towards countries outside the former USSR. Agriculture suffered a drastic recession period, especially from 1993 to 1994. In the beginning of 1970 private farms constituted thirteen percent of all land and had twenty-four percent of all domestic animals but produced more than seventy-five percent of meat, milk and eggs. The re-orientation from collective farms and *sovkhoz* to individual production started to work from 1995.

One of the biggest problems for the stabilization of the economy is the low rate of investment. Lack of investment, especially in the means of production prevents the acquisition of new technologies and results in lower competitiveness of the national economy and the enterprises. By the end of 1996, the total of credits accumulated by the Kyrgyz government amounted to one billion US dollars.

The economic crisis has produced a drastic decrease in the living conditions of the population. The high percentage of skilled laborers in the population is underutilized, but the private sector is not developed enough to be able to compensate. Adding to that, the re-orientation of the country toward export of raw products decreases the need for highly educated employees. The gap between the rich elite and the majority of the population has widened considerably during the 1990s. The polarization of incomes is undermining the middle class.

However, amongst the former Soviet republics, Kyrgyzstan has been less exposed to the decline in output. At the same time, it has, according to the World Bank (1993b:135) become apparent that the "transition process has proven to be more difficult than initially envisaged. In particular, more attention must be paid to the social and political impact of economic policies."

The Soviet system was known for the high percentage of women in the labor market. Formerly, in Kyrgyzstan, a relatively large percentage of women were employed in agriculture, industry and service, but the unemployment has affected them more than the male labor force (UNDP, 1997b:119).

Kyrgyzstan has, more than other countries, maintained cultural patterns and clan and tribe solidarities from the pre-Communist period (Centlivres & Centlivres-Demont, 1998), especially in the southern areas, where such patterns have been revived (Eversmann, 1998). By tradition, networks of clan relationships exist and they function as protection and control of the individuals involved. The loyalties emanating from this system cut across occupational categories, geographical areas, and so on(Kaana, 1997, 1998). Certain loyalties along clan and ethnic lines have been maintained despite seventy years of communist rule and they have been revived after the collapse of Soviet Union (UNDP, 1997c). The predominating religion is Sunni Islam but there are also adherents to the Orthodox church. There are indications that both religions to some extent have been revived after 1990.

Politically, the country declared itself a sovereign state in October 1990 and became independent in 1991 (World Bank, 1993b:1). The new constitution includes provisions for human and civil rights. A multi-party system was implemented in 1991. After the elections in 1996, twelve parties were represented in the Parliament (UNDP, 1997d). The state system with its central, regional and local structures has been maintained, but representatives to regional and local bodies are now elected. A lot of decision-making power and the burden of finance have been transferred to these local bodies. Generally, there was a belief and hope among the population that the new political situation would be easy and without burdens on the population (UNDP, 1997c). According to a survey of attitudes and opinions,

> (i) people in Kyrgyzstan feel positive about the freedom and liberties that have been created after 1990 but they are very dissatisfied with social development; and

> (ii) the younger generation feels more positive about the changes than the older generation (Olds, Jr., 1997).

The rates of enrollment in primary and secondary education have since declined and the drop-out rate has increased. The decline was most dramatic in preschool institutions (see table 8.4).

In 1996–1997, there were 1,007,100 pupils in public schools and 92,100 pupils in private schools, approximately nine percent. At the secondary education level, there were 42 private grammar schools and 28 private lyceums in 1996. In 1997, the numbers had increased to 65 and 33 respectively (UNDP, 1997c:28). Thirteen of the private schools were Kyrgyz-Turkish. According to a UNDP report:

TABLE 8.3 NUMBER OF CHILDREN IN PRE-SCHOOL INSTITUTIONS IN KYRGYZSTAN, SELECTED YEARS 1940–1994

Year	1940	1970	1980	1990	1994
Number of children	5,000	90,000	150,000	211,600	58,900

Source: Asian Development Bank, 1996a

The new schools tend to be characterized by a new philosophy of education based for the most part on the social-humanitarian idea, on elaboration and implementation of non-traditional educational approaches and an integrated program of courses which are atypical of mass schools (UNDP, 1997c:28).

The spending on education has decreased after 1990, but spending is still high in comparison to that of other countries undergoing similar transitions. The figures are still dramatic if we take into consideration that the GDP declined during the same period. Due to the declining level of GDP per capita, shrinking of state activities and budget cuts, school and health facilities have been among the hardest hit. This has resulted in a lowering of the quality of education and the closure of school canteens serving meals free of charge to the pupils; only 2.4 percent of the pupils received free school meals in 1996 as compared to fifty-three percent in 1990 (UNDP, 1997c:30).

TABLE 8.4 GOVERNMENT EXPENDITURE ON EDUCATION AS PERCENTAGE OF GDP

Year	1989	1990	1991	1992	1993	1994	1995
%	8.7	8.7	7.8	3.7	3.9	5.9	6.1

Source: Asian Development Bank, 1996b.

After the collapse of the Communist system, the structure of the education system was not changed to any large extent. Due to the economic situation, an educational reform was not decided upon until 1996. The primary and secondary education is still a 10-year program but it will be prolonged. According to an amendment to the school law in 1992, some changes were made. "Motherland studies" became a new subject in grades 1-9 and studies in a foreign language became compulsory. In grades 5-9 computer science, economy, and marketing were introduced.

The language of instruction in general primary and secondary education was Kyrgyz for approximately sixty percent of the pupils, Russian for twenty-six percent and Uzbek for twelve percent (World Bank, 1993b:117). English was introduced in 1993, despite the lack of teachers of English. Since Russian is the official language and Kyrgyz the national language, no attempts are made to remove Russian from the curriculum. The number of hours in the Kyrgyz language was increased for Kyrgyz-speaking as well as

Russian-speaking students, and the number of hours in Russian was decreased (Asian Development Bank, 1996a: 65).

Parents have the right to choose a school that offers education in their child's mother tongue, whether Russian or Kyrgyz.

In the beginning of the 1990s, private schools were legitimized and educational financing was decentralized. The state does not subsidize private schools; on the contrary, it levies taxes on the money paid by parents as tuition fees (Asian Development Bank, 1996a:67). In the mid-1990s, private schools had difficulties because they had to rent buildings on a commercial basis. Decentralization implies, for instance, that local communities are to finance teacher salaries, despite their limited resources. The shift in the finance of education was considerable; in 1990–1991, two-thirds of the expenditures were allocated by local budgets, and during the period 1992-1994, this share had increased to three-fourths (Asian Development Bank, 1996a: 37) of the total expenditures.

In the subsequent year, a number of legal documents were adopted, focusing on the aims of higher education, the functions of vocational and secondary schools and the abolition of Marxist curricula. Tertiary education institutions have received the right to develop their own curricula and the right to elect the rector. A state-supervised expert assesses the quality of the new curriculum.

In the present period of austerity and crisis, the population does not benefit from the old compulsory system of education. More and more children do not finish primary education, especially in the countryside (Eversmann, 1999). The new economic realities severely devalue education, a fact that may lead to increased illiteracy. At the same time, the possibilities for a small part of the population to study abroad widens the gap between rich and poor, and the literate and under-educated.

Afghanistan

The area of contemporary Afghanistan was never controlled from outside, although the British made attempts to conquer it in the 19th century. Before the Communist seizure of power in 1978 and the Soviet invasion in 1979, Afghanistan had about 13 million inhabitants. There are a large number of ethnic, tribal and kinship groups. Among the largest ethnic groups are: Pushtun, fifty percent; Tajik, twenty-five percent; Aimaq, five percent, and the Hazara six percent. The majority of the Afghans were Islamized in the period extending from the eighth to the thirteenth centuries. All Afghans are Hanafi Sunni except the Hazara, who are Shi'a.

Since the end of the 1970s, the country has been torn apart by a series of wars and a struggle over the state and its role in relation to Islam. Agriculture was and, still is, the basis of the economy, supported by small family farms. Just before the war, the country was agriculturally self-sufficient, importing mainly machinery and other metal products.

The central state was secular and fragmented, at least until the *Taliban* seized power in the mid–1990s. The only other significant social structures below the government are class, tribes, and *qaums,* which are networks based on tribal affiliation. Those who belong the same *qaum* have reciprocal links of solidarity. The effective network of the *qaum* varies in extension, that is, from a number of extended families to the population in many villages (Dupree, 1980). A big minority of the Afghan are nomads or semi-nomads (Dupree, 1980).

In an Afghan village, there is generally one or more mullahs present, who are responsible for the mosque or are teachers in the *madras* (Koranic school). Although common Islamic values are important, people rely upon their tribal affiliation in difficult situations. Islam has its local representatives in the judges, Koranic teachers, holy men and *amirs* (multi-functional leadership which is both tribal and religous).

As in other Muslim countries, there are at least two categories of activists who have received their educations in public schools. The first perceive Islam not only as a religion but also as a political ideology. They do not rely upon the traditional interpretations of events and do not believe in individual efforts as a means to create justice. They argue that it is necessary to conquer the state machinery (through a political party or not) and change the societal structures and moral values. In their opinion, the state education system should be used to reinforce Islamic values. The second group rejects the state and argue that all aspects of life should be guided by the religious leaders. This ideology is articulated in the Taliban government.

When it comes to the state and politics, the rudiments of a centralized power emerged emerge in the end of the eighteenth century, when the first king made attempts to establish his rule over the area. However, the elements of a nation-state did not appear until the middle of the twentieth century. The state has always been fragmented and weak in the penetration of the whole society (physically, geographically, culturally and politically). Despite its fragility, it has made attempts to modernize society and the educational system has been one important means to this end.

That a nation-state has not yet been established, is evident from the current situation in the country. A centralized school system was built during the 1950s, and a number of large-scale development projects were implemented, particularly in the agricultural sector. In 1973 the king was overthrown in a *coup d'état,* and the Prime Minister declared the country a republic. This government was unable to govern effectively in all parts of the country (Carter & Connor, 1989; Oliver, 1986). Dupree (1980:548) wrote in 1980: "Afghanistan is an artificial country, created out of tribal kingdoms as a buffer state British and Russian in the 19th century . . .".

The pre-war economic development and the state interventions in Afghanistan undermined the power of the traditional Muslim scholars and resulted in a category of intellectuals who wanted to reconstruct society through the state machinery and saw modern school education as one important means to this end. The governments during the 1960s and 1970s made efforts to extend the influence of the state: attempts to create an Islamic village representative, to appoint secular judges as a parallel force to the Islamic *qadi* and to expand schooling through the introduction of government-controlled *madras*.[1] The purpose of the latter innovation was not to destroy the old *madras* but to modernize it and make it more efficient in creating national citizens who are less linked to intermediate contexts such as the tribe or clan and wanted modernization and economic growth (Cronin, 1989). The state supported *madrasi* succeeded to enroll only a small proportion of the children.

The legal system was not derived from *Shari'a* but was a secular system of law. Education was to contribute to the creation of a secular, rational and national citizen. Teaching took place in separate schools for boys and girls and it still does in most places. The government made efforts to expand primary education and enrollment increased in urban areas.

When the Communist party seized power, a comprehensive reform program was presented, and it was to be implemented within a short period.[2] The elimination of illiteracy, and a radical change of the education system were two of the pillars of the reform. The old curriculum dealt with Islam and its history but most of it now was to be replaced by natural sciences, civics, and so on (Carter, 1988). Compulsory schooling was prolonged to ten years. The state aimed at creating a modern, socialist, and technologically rational man. This strategy was met with rejection from the population.

The new content of the school curriculum and the textbooks was perceived to be pro-Russian, communist, and anti-Islamic. The reaction to the implementation of the reform was violent in most places. The population reacted first by withdrawing girls from the schools. Then the boys dropped out as well. Finally, the population started attacking teachers and destroying school buildings.

A large number of armed groups emerged to fight the Communist government and the regular army and later the Russians when they invaded the country. These groups called themselves the liberation movement. These groups were joined in the struggle, *Mujahideen*, against the government and the Russians (Saikel and Maley, 1989). Each group was led by a commander and every village came to be controlled by a commander, who, in turn, might be subordinate to a higher commander at the district level (Carter & Connor, 1989; Cronin, 1989).

In many cases, the commanders had not been traditional leaders, a fact that interfered with and came to destroy the traditional relations of authority and power. The process of fragmentation into intermediate categories was reinforced with the emergence of commanders and a large number of Mujahideen groups during the war. These groups differed considerably but they found a common denominator in the struggle against the Communist government. On the one hand, a general transformation of Afghanistan in the Communist, or even nationalist, direction was a threat to the many religious, clan, and other leaders. On the other hand, a continuation of the fragmented networks that now were armed would also threaten the order. Soon after the *Mujahideen* uprisings, NGOs all over the world started to support the movement, within

Afghanistan and in refugee camps in Pakistan. Schools covering most of the provinces of Afghanistan received support from outside the country through the NGOs. The central state remained secular and fragmented, at least until the *Talibans* seized power in the mid-1990s.

Islamic education was and is an important instrument for the reproduction of the power relationships at the local and international levels and the ideology justifying these relationships (Talbani, 1996). Before the war the core of the curriculum dealt with Islam and its history. When the communists came into power, this was replaced by natural sciences, civics, and so on. The system was changed and oriented towards the formation of the competencies needed for rapid and large scale industrialization (Carter, 1988). Compulsory schooling was prolonged to ten years.

With the *Mujahideen* influence, the educational system established by the Communist government in Kabul was changed thoroughly. The content of the programs and the textbooks were the results of compromises between traditionalist and modernist commanders, *mullahs* and politicians. Forty percent of the time in grades 1-3 and twenty-seven percent in grades 4-6 was dedicated to religious education. For comparison, the corresponding figures for Oman were twenty and seventeen percent respectively, and for Saudi Arabia, forty and twenty percent respectively. This education was offered not only within Afghanistan but also in the refugee camps in Pakistan (Elham & Hirth, 1994), although the government replacing the communist government had reformulated the educational policy in 1992. Peace prevailed for a short period and then the *Talibans* started the war of rebellion. In the mid-1990s, they controlled large parts of the country and finally took over the central government. They have given a low priority to education of the modern type. The result is the NGOs runt most of the primary schools, financed principally by the EU and the Swedish Sidav (Mansour, 2000). Paradoxically, the *Talibans* changed the curricula so that they came to have a smaller proportion of Islamic than before. However, many of the NGO-run schools follow the curricula established in the beginning of the 1990s (Luxen, Pehrsson, and Öström, 1997).

Before the communist seizure of power, the country had among the lowest rates of literacy and primary school enrollment in the world, and the rate of female enrollment in primary education was the lowest. In 1980, the rate of illiteracy was one of the highest in the world (66.8 percent for men and 94.2 percent for women) (Lin, 1985). In 1979, twenty-two percent of all school children were reportedly enrolled (but only seven percent of the girls). In 1992, the rate of gross enrollment was thirty-one percent (UNESCO, 1995). The majority of children dropped out between the third and fourth grades or at least before they completed the fourth grade. Girls rarely continue after the third grade. There are indications that nearly half of all boys aged seven years were enrolled in the first grade.

Almost all children attend a Koranic school during a certain period (in general, between 6-10 years of age).

TABLE 8.5 PRIMARY SCHOOL ENROLLMENT IN AFGHANISTAN

	1967–1968 (1)	1968–1969 (2)	1969–1970 (2)	1979 (3)	1992
Number of pupils	497,879	540,737	579,955	1,034,202	..
Rate of primary enr.	..	..	22 (4)		29 (5)
% girls of all pupils	14	11	13	..	33 (4)

Sources: (1) Dupree (1980); (2) Unesco (1982); (3) Unicef (1990); (4) Unesco (1984); (5) World Bank (1995).

CONCLUSIONS

In the 1980s, the countries within the Soviet bloc had highly developed educational systems and practically one hundred percent enrollment in primary education, while Afghanistan remained one of the countries with the lowest rates of enrollment in the world. Since the *Taliban* government has withdrawn from and is hostile to schooling most of the schools are run by NGOs, often in separate schools for boys and girls (Mansour, 2000).

With the collapse of the Soviet Union, all countries formerly belonging to the union started to restructure their education systems according to the international model of privatization, choice and decentralization. The content of education (especially that of history, geography and social science) was nationalized immediately, while the structure of the educational system was gradually changed in some countries from the mid-1990s. Privatization started in the early 1990s, and in some countries even before the laws were changed so as to make private schools legitimate. However, rates of enrollment decreased and dropout rate increased in all countries, at least until the end of the 1990s.

Efforts were made to coordinate educational policies among the Central Asian countries in transition but in reality, each country has come to change its education system in accordance with the sometimes contradictory requiremens from the international agencies, on the one hand, and the national and local demands, on the other hand.

Afghanistan has, due to internal conflicts and fragmentation state, followed its own path. Educational changes have been made according to different interpretations of Islam and not the world model.

NOTES

[1]   Madras in singular, madrasi in plural (See Talbani, 1996).

[2]   Common farmers are to a large extent linked in a semi-feudal relationship to a *pir* who is a religious leader of a clan or tribe or an *amir* is a multi-functional leader of similar unit.

REFERENCES CITED

Asian Development Bank (1996a). Kyrgyz Republic. Education and Training. Master Plan. T.A. 2290-KGZ. Gopa Consult.

Asian Development Bank (1996b). Kyrgyz Republic: Education and Training. Annexes. T.A. 2290-KGZ. Gopa Consult.

Atchoarena, D. and G. Prokhoroff. (1996). "Adjustment or Transition." *IIEP Newsletter*, vol. XIV No. 4 October-December 1996, IIEP, Paris.

Carter, L. (1988). *Assessment of Current Activities and Priorities in Primary Education and Teacher Training for Aghans.* Peshawar: Unesco.

Carter, L. and K. Connor. (1989). *A preliminary investigation of contemporary Afghan councils.* Peshawar: ACBAR.

Centlivres, P. And M. Centlivres-Demont (1998). "Tajikistan and Afghanistan: The ethnic groups on either side of the border." In M.-R. Djalili, F. Grare and. Akiner (eds.). *Tajikistan: the trials of independence.* New York: Plenum.

Cronin, P. (1989). *Afghanistan After the Soviet Withdrawal. Contentions for Power.* Washington: CRI Report for Congress.

Daun, H. (1990). "Swedish Support to Mujahedeen in Afghanistan." Seminar Paper. Stockholm: Institute of International Education, Stockholm University

Deutschland, I. (1993). *Die zentralasiatischen GUS Republiken, Kirgistan, Usbekistan, Turkeminstan, Tadschikistan.* Berlin: German Development Institute

Dupree, L. (1980). *Afghanistan.* New Jersey: Princeton University Press

Dupree, L. (1989). "Post-Withdrawal Afghanistan: Light at the End of the Tunnel." In A. Saikal and W. Maley (eds.). *The Soviet Withdrawal from Afghanistan.* Oxford: Oxford University Press

Elham, M. R. and M. Hirth (1994). *A Report on Afghan Refugees' Islamic Madrassas in the Timergara Area, NWFP, Pakistan.* Peshawar: GTZ, Basic Education for Afghan Refugees

Eversmann, E. (1999). *School Attendance in the Kyrgyz Republic.* Bishkek: Unicef

Imanbayev, S. (1998). Interview, March, 1998. Bishkek: Central Commission on Elections and Referenda of the Kyrgyzstan Republic.

Kaana, A. (1997). "Kygyzstan and international legal norms in the area of human rights." Bishkek: BHMS

Kaana, A. (1998). Interview, Febr. 1998.

Kanaev, A. (2000). *Civic Education in Central Asia. Re-conceptualization of Citizenship in Newly Independent States.* Stockholm: Stockholm University, Institute of International Education.

Kanaev, A. and I. Fägerlind. (1996). *Citizenship Education in Central Asia. Status and Possibilities for Cooperation.* Final Report from a UNESCO sub-regional workshop in Ashgabat, Turkmenistan. Vol. 103. IIE, Stockholm.

Kautsch, I. et al (1994). *Labour Market Policy in Transforming Countries. The Case of Kyrgyzstan.* Berlin: German Development Institute.

Lin, D.- F. (1985). "Afghanistan: System of Education." In T. Husén and N. Postlethwaite
    (eds.). *International Encyclopedia of Education.* Oxford. Pergamon Press

KNSU (n.d.)."Democratization Project." Bishkek: Kyrgyz National State University.

Luxen, J. P.. K. Pehersson and K. Öström (1997). The Swedish Committee for Afghanistan. A
    joint EC - Sida evaluation of support to the health and education sector programmes.
    Stockholm: Sida.

Mansour, A. M. (2000). Girls' Schooling in Afghanistan. (Unpublished paper). Stockholm:
    Stockholm University, Institute of International Education.

Olds, Jr, H.W. (1997). *Public Opinion in Kyrgyzstan 1996.* Washington: International
    Foundation for Election Systems.

Oliver (1986). *Islam and Resistance in Afghanistan.* Cambridge: Cambridge University Press.

Saikal, A. and W. Maley (1989). "Introduction." In A. Saikal and W. Maley (eds.). The Soviet
    Withdrawal from Afghanistan. Oxford: Oxford University Press.

Talbani, A. (1996). "Pedagogy, Power, and Discourse: Transformation of Islamic Education."
    Comparative Education Review, vol. 40, no 1.

Tibi, B. (1995). "Culture and knowledge: The politics of islamization of knowledge as a post-
    modern project. The fundamentalist claim to de-westernization." *Theory, Culture &*
    Society, vol. 12.

Turner, B.S. (1991). "Politics and culture in islamic globalism." In R. Robertson & W. R.
    Garret (Eds.). *Religion and global order.* New York: Paragon House Publishers

UNDP (1990). *Human Development Report, 1990.* Oxford: Pergamon Press/UNDP

———— (1997a). *Human Development Report 1997.* New York: Oxford University Press/UNDP

———— (1997b). *Human Development under Transition in Europe & CIS.* Geneva: UNDP

———— (1997c). *National Human Development Report of the Kyrgyz Republic, 1997.* Bishkek:
    UNDP

———— (1997d). *Political System of Kyrgyz Republic, January 1997.* Bishkek: UNDP

UNESCO (1982). *UNESCO in Asia and the Pacific. Report on the Work and Programme of*
    Unesco Regional Office for Education. Bangkok: Unesco

———— (1984). *Science Eduction in Asia and the Pacific.* New York: UNESCO

———— (1995). *World Education Report,* 1995. Paris: UNESCO.

Wheeler, G. (1969). "Russian Central Asia." In G. WINT (ed). *Asia Handbook.*
    Harmondsworth: Penguin.

World Bank (1981). *World Development Report, 1981.* Washington, D.C.: World Bank.

World Bank (1993a). *World Development Report, 1993.* Washington, D.C.: World Bank

World Bank (1993b). *Kyrgyzstan. The Transition to a Market Economy.* Washington, D.C.:
    World Bank

World Bank (1993c). *Turkmenistan.* Washington, D.C.: World Bank

World Bank (1995). *World Development Report, 1995.* Washington, D.C.: World Bank.

CHAPTER 9

Economic Decline, Religious Revival and Educational Restructuring in Sub-Saharan Africa[1]

HOLGER DAUN

Introduction

After some years of economic growth up until the 1970s, sub-Saharan Africa (SSA) has experienced several major problems and transformations: economic crisis and structural adjustment programs (SAPs), political transitions, accompanied by educational restructuring. A few countries have undergone a steady economic growth, while for others, the economy stagnated or economic growth was tremendous towards the end of the 1990s. As a whole, however, the continent has become marginalized economically, as ten of the world's poorest countries are situated south of Sahara. The informal sector has grown rapidly; serving as employer for a significant portion of the population, it is to a large extent characterized by a culture of collective survival. Local and international NGOs are flourishing on the continent and many of them are highly involved in educational endeavours.

Educationally, there has been an enormous expansion since independence but some countries have, since the 1970s, had a decline in enrollment rates and an increase in drop out. With the SAPs, education systems were decentralized and private arrangements in education became legitimate even in countries were such solutions had formerly been rejected. Throughout much of the continent, the burden of educational costs has shifted from the central state to local communities and parents. Despite these reforms, there are few indications that rates of enrollment, repetition and drop out have improved.

BACKGROUND

Development strategies formulated and applied after independence were conditioned by the mode of production and economic structures, as well as the political ideology, of the new governments. Then with the crisis, most of the countries were compelled to implement SAPs. Although it led to a rapid increase in literacy, among other benefits, the equality-oriented development strategy adopted by socialist countries, had to be abandoned (Carnoy & Samoff, 1990a,b; Groth, 1987).

AIDS has affected Africa more extensively than other continents. This fact has repercussions on children's health and the possibility to attend school and infant mortality has also increased (Odiwur, 2000).

ECONOMIC INCORPORATION OR MARGINALIZATION

The economic conditions of the African countries differ according to economic level when the colonizers left; mode of production; degree of differentiation and class formation; and degree of incorporation into the world economy. Few countries had a capitalist class and, consequently, a force that could bring about economic growth as in the Western countries and Asia existed in a few countries. Instead, the state had intervened and made investments (Glickman, 1987; Mengisteab, 1995; Wilson, 1989).

There were big differences between the countries already in the 1960s and economic differentiation has increased (See Table 9.1). On the whole continent, economic recession became more severe and SAPs were implemented in many countries during the 1980s and 1990s.

TABLE 9.1 DISTRIBUTION OF TOTAL AFRICAN GDP

	1960	1970	1980	1993
Major oil exporters	24.3	32.7	42.1	41.2
Non-oil exporters	74.6	65.8	56.3	58.8
Least developed	18.9	16.4	13.3	10.9

Shaw (1985:10) for the period until 1980. Figures for 1993 are estimated on data from World Bank data, 1995a. Since the numbers are from different sources, it is not possible to establish how comparable they are. However, the trend for the least developed countries seems to continue.

Practically all African countries came to establish import-substituting industries, state control of foreign trade in order to protect their own economy, and emphasize agricultural production for export. The first years of independence generally saw rapid economic growth. Agricultural production and import substitution industry had to increase. Since farmers constitute the biggest category and their contribution to the national economy was and is important, efforts were and are made to stimulate them to produce a surplus for export. For SSA, the portion in world trade had in 1996 fallen to a lower level than 20-30 years prior to that date. No considerable improvement occurred during the first half of the 1990s (Rodrik, 1998; UNDP, 1995). The portion in world trade did not change during the latter half of the 1990s, although in 1996, the continent as a whole had five percent growth, which is the highest rate since the 1970s (Rodrik, 1998). Some examples of the differing economic levels are shown in Table 9.2.

TABLE 9.2 ECONOMIC GROWTH AND GNP PER CAPITA IN SOME AFRICAN COUNTRIES, SELECTED YEARS

	Economic growth			GNP per capita			
	1960-1970	1970-1979	1980-1993	1978	1984	1989	1993
Botswana	..	13.9	9.6	...	960	1600	2790
Cameroon	4.7	8	0	460	860	1000	820
Kenya	6	6.5	3.8	330	310	380	270
Mozambique	4.6	-2.9	1	140	...	80	90
Nigeria	3.1	2.5	2.7	560	730	250	300
Senegal	2.5	2.5	2.8	340	380	650	750
South Africa	6.4	3.6	0.9	1380	...	2460	...
Tanzania	6	4.9	3.6	230	210	120	90

Sources: World Bank, 1980, 1986, 1995a

Most of the countries have experienced economic stagnation or even decline since the 1970s, while a few countries have had a steady economic growth. Botswana, for instace, has had a continuous growth, while Cameroon had a rapid growth until mid-1980s and then there was a considerable decline. Both had and have a growth-oriented development strategy. Mozambique and Uganda experienced economic growth during the latter half of the 1990s after two decades of decline. Nigeria had a very high growth rate during the 1970s due to the oil boom but then the economy more or less collapsed. Both Tanzania and Mozambique applied an equality-oriented strategy until mid-1980s. Tanzania had overall economic growth during the first decade of independence, but from the mid-1970s, the economy has declined. The economy of Mozambique experienced a decline until mid-1990s (World Bank, 1995a). However, during the past five years, the country had strong economic growth (Rodrik, 1998).

There are two principal views on the reasons for the economic decline in Africa: the structuralist and the neo-liberal. The former focuses on factors external to each country, such as the International Division of Labor and worsening terms of trade, while the latter gives priority to factors internal to each country, such as mismanagement, bureaucratization, corruption, and so on (Bgoya and Hydén, 1987; Bienen and Waterbury, 1989; Callaghy, 1988; Colclough, 1991; Herbst, 1990; Higgot, 1986; Hydén, 1988; Krugman, 1995; Shaw, 1985; Streeten, 1987).

Many factors undermined the economic situation, such as increasing competition, repayment of loans as requested in the conditionalities, and a different geographical emphasis in development assistance in the world disfavored the continent. In the 1960s, Africa received thirty-seven percent of all development assistance. During the period 1985-1989 the percentage was fifteen. The corresponding figures for Asia were seventeen and forty-four percent respectively. According to Abedeji (1995:237), Africa has always had a deficit in its transactions with the North: when development assistance, investments, repayments and rent paying are taken together, there has been a net transfer of resources from Africa to the industrialized countries. In 1986 it was 1.1 billion, in 1988 1.2 billion and in 1989 1.5 billion, for instance.

Until the beginning of the 1980s, the World Bank had taken for granted that the state should have an important and active role in development affairs. However, in 1979, the Bank suggested a shrinking of the state for the first time (Mosley, Harrigan and Toye, 1991; Ravenhill, 1986). Conditionalities were then increasingly linked to the credits offered by the Bank, and the fulfilling of conditionalities often implied a restructuring not only of the economy but also of the state and the education system (Herbst, 1990).

The results of the recession and the SAPs on the African economies differ considerably but generally, economic growth rates have improved in very few cases only. Harbeson (1994:7), for instance, states: "The clear evidence is that Africa as a continent has recorded only marginal progress under World Bank/IMF-led structural adjustment regimes." The basis for the SAPs in Africa has also been criticized. Munene (1995), for instance, argues that incentive structures in Africa are embedded in a "complex mixture of personal linkages developed for the purpose of survival" (p. 78) and, according to Hoerner (1995), the informal (sector) is a complex of economic and cultural ties whose primary function is the survival of the group and in this complex, there is no space for a capitalist development.

Women are responsible for seventy-eight percent of food production, eighty percent of food processing, and so on (Chazan *et al.*, 1988:88), and in many places in Africa the inheritance of land is matrilinear (Desjeux, 1987; Dumont, 1986). The colonial states destroyed many female institutions and did not consider women in its dealings with the African societies. This trend continued with the independent governments and the SAPs (Parpart, 1988). Development strategies were male-oriented, and in neo-liberal thought, individuals are seen as undifferentiated relative to social and economic structures. For instance, issues that are privatized are assumed to be taken care of, if not by the market, then by the families, that is, the women (Kabeer and Humphrey, 1991; Parpart, 1986). On the other hand, women have to some extent taken advantage of the situation and have responded to SAPs by forming associations for production, for instance (Tripp (1994:151).

WITHDRAWAL OF THE STATE OR THE POPULATION?

African states were and are comparatively large (Marenin, 1987). The state was, during the first decade of independence, seen as the motor of development. There was, according to Young (1994:39),

> . . . an integral state illusion that was in part a product of a global conjuncture. State socialism, Keynesian theory and development economics shared the conviction that active state management of the economy, guided by extensive planning, would produce rapid economic growth, a secular faith seemingly validated by the . . . historical development in Europe.

The state was expanded also as a way for political leaders to maintain the loyalty of their clients (Bratton and de Walle, 1997). Despite the SAPs, African state apparatuses use a relatively large portion of the GNP (Marenin 1987; Mengisteab, 1995). One indicator of the extensiveness of the state is the share of the public sector of the GNP. The public sector's share of GNP was fifteen percent in Africa, twelve percent in Latin America and three percent in non-socialist Asia (Mengisteab, 1995:103). At the end of the 1980s, in Africa, fifty-four percent of all workers employed outside agriculture had public sector jobs, and the corresponding percentages for Asia and Latin America were thirty-six and twenty-seven percent respectively (Bienen and Waterbury, 1989:622). This means that, apart from the informal sector, the state is still the most important employer.

Mbembe (1988:127) maintains that the state was striving for monopoly in the description and naming of Africa's present and historical realities. This was visible in the curricula and textbooks, for instance. The most authoritarian regimes had provoked "a culture of revenge" in the 1970s (Bayart (1983:a,b; Éla, 1990:155). The groups that were most likely to take revenge were youths marginalized from production: women; peasants that had been exploited by the state; and Muslims.

SAPs came to be a means not only for economic liberalization and the implementation of market mechanisms in the economy but also for restructuring of the state (Herbst, 1990' Saine, 1995), especially the centralized and socialist state, and "informalization" of a range of state activities and strengthening of civil society (Azarya, 1994; Bangura and Gibbon, 1992:18; Bratton,1994). Different types of states reacted differently to the economic recession and the SAPs in their ability to implement these programs. Authoritarian states that excluded large portions of the population from participation in politics tended to be most able to implement the SAPs and tended to attain the macroeconomic balance required by the IMF and the World Bank, at least until the beginning of the 1990s (Bangura and Gibbon (1992). Apart from the degree of centralization, consensus among a country´s national elites on the necessity of the SAPs and the fulfillment of the conditionalities seem to have been variables that have facilitated the achievement of macroeconomic balance (Jones, 1990; Mosley, Harrigan and Toye, 1991). The SAPs were in many cases followed by political unrest and liberalization. During the first half of the 1990s, more than twenty African countries held multiparty elections (Saine, 1995). In relation to political transitions, Bratton and van de Walle (1997) make a distinction between transition and democratization. A transition from one type of state to another, which has taken place in practically all African countries, is not necessarily accompanied by democratization of society. The latter implies a reinforcement and mobilization of civil society. Practically all states are characterized by clientelism or patrimonialism (Bratton and van de Walle, 1997; Chazan *et al.* 1988). Ergas (1987: 5), for instance, argued that "the paradigmatic African state is a patrimonial one . . . patrimonial states are based on patron-client ties (networks of reciprocity) . . . " (p. 5). The national elites or the ruling party favor certain groups that, in exchange for favors, guarantee the government their support. In several cases, these clientelistic ties have survived the wave of political transitions that occured during the first half of the 1990s (Bratton and de Walle, 1997). Clientelism is one form of inclusion of the individuals into the state sphere and politics. Another form is participation through organizations.

With the spread of neo-Liberalism and the SAPs, civil society came to be an important element not only in societal and state analyses but also in policy-making (Azarya, 1994; Bratton, 1994). Grassroot initiatives came to be seen as legitimate more than ever before (Cheru, 1996; Rothchild and Lawson, 1994). The focus has shifted towards the creation of NGOs similar to these that exist in industrialized countries, however, most of the definitions of civil society exclude a large number of associations that traditionally exist in Africa (Muslim associations, for instance) since they make "totalistic" claims on the individual. Such associations and organizations of African origin in varying degrees affect the state and education but are seldom taken into account in educational analysis. Kinship and territoriality were in the past, and in many cases still are today, closely connected to traditional political institutions and authority structures (Chazan *et al.*, 1988:74,77). Most of the collectivities mentioned were revived or reinforced with the economic and political liberalizations.

The African states also varied and vary in their approach to NGOs. Until the end of the 1980s, there was a tendency to prevent NGOs from establishing themselves or to control them strictly. With the period of structural adjustments and after the Jomtien conference in 1990, the space for NGO activities increased considerably in the South.

RELIGIOUS INFLUENCE AND REVIVAL MOVEMENTS

In order not to create conflicts, European missionaries avoided (or were told to avoid) areas where Islamic influence was strong (Trimingham, 1968). Thus, there is an Islamic-Christian "division" of territories and souls in Africa. The missionaries came to have a leading position in the educational area, and in some countries, that is, Lesotho and Malawi, they maintained their position when the states became independent. In most countries, a large proportion of the schools had been established by the missionaries and they were either nationalized or continued under private control.

The percentage of Christians is highest in the Southern and Eastern parts of Africa and in the coastal areas. The proportion of Muslims varies from nearly one hundred percent in Mauritania and Somalia to smaller numbers in Zaire, Gabon and South Africa. The number of Christians and Muslims is increasing in sub-Saharan Africa, although the world religions often have been only partially assimilated, and in many instances in their utilitarian or instrumental aspects (Laitin, 1986; Mbembe 1988; Sanneh, 1983). Apart from this, a large number of syncretic movements have emerged (Nyang, 1993; Ranger, 1986), such as *Aladura* and *Yan Tasine* in Nigeria (Yoloye, 1983), *Kiang-Kiang* in Guinea-Bissau (Callewaert, 1996; de Jong, 1987) and the African pentecostal churches (van Dijk, 1999).

Religions of African origin as well as world religions are being revived and reinterpreted (Haynes, 1999; Maseuelier, 1999). First the extension of the secular state and then the chaotic conditions emerging from economic crisis and SAPs contributed to

> enfeeblement of secular political structures and a revival of religions and other value systems. . . . The 1980s have also proven to be a breeding ground for the insertion of religious, primarily Islamic, thought patterns into the realm of official African political discourse . . . Recourse to religious or particularistic arguments is another manifestation of the retreat from secularism that has developed in this third and latest wave of ideological experimentation . . . (Chazan et al 1988:155).

Globalization contributes to the processes mentioned (see Chapter 1), not only by challenging local cultures but also by spreading the economistic and technocratic perspective on phenomena, not least of all in education. Educational processes and outcomes are increasingly judged and measured in terms of costs and returns to investment at the expense of a more humanistic and value-oriented criteria (Graham-Brown, 1991; Samoff, 1996).

In all, the African countries differ in a large number of aspects that condition their primary and secondary education: colonial history, religious composition, type of state, mode of production, economic level and type of development strategy applied after independence (Hartwell, 1994; Orivel & Shaw, 1994). In respect to the colonial history, the majority of the former French colonies are situated in the poor Sahel area, which is also more islamized than other areas. For instance, at the end of the 1980s, the rate of primary school enrollment was seventy-seven percent in Anglophone countries and forty-six percent in Francophone countries (Colclough, 1991). Thus, education is to a large extent conditioned by religious and colonial patterns despite the changes that took place when many states and education systems were restructured, often in connection with the implementation of the SAPs. Educational restructuring, that is, decentralization, privatization, introduction of choice, or systemic reform, has been common in SSA and often accompanied SAPs.

EDUCATIONAL DEVELOPMENT

Since independence, there was a tremendous growth in rates of literacy and school enrollment. However, for several countries this trend was broken in the end of the 1970s or in the 1980s. Some countries experienced a stagnation while others even had a decline in their enrollment and pass rates. Educational indicators vary with the *economic level* of the countries (World Bank, 1987a,b; 1999), *the type of state and development strategy* (Carnoy & Samoff, 1990a,b; Groth, 1987); the extent to which *SAPs have been implemented* (Graham-Brown, 1991; Reimers & Tiburcio, 1993; Samoff *et al.*, 1994). Cultural factors such as ethnicity, religion and revival movements, are not considered to the same extent as economic factors when variation in educational indicators is studied. It has been shown in case studies, that such factors, are also of importance for educational development (Daun, 1992; Grindal, 1972; Peil, 1990). In a study (Daun, 2000) using World Bank data, educational indicators were analyzed in relation to the factors mentioned and this data is the basis of the findings that are presented in the sections that follow (see appendix 9.1).

The level of GNP per capita differed considerably between and within countries in the beginning of the 1960s and it still does. Economic recession affected all countries, but especially those with the lowest income. SAPs were implemented by almost all countries and seem to have added to this differentiation; the poorest countries have had most difficulties with these programs (Reimers & Tiburcio 1993; Rodrik, 1998). For the poorest countries it was more difficult than for others to maintain the standard of primary education achieved before the recession and the implementation of SAPs (Mengisteab, 1995).

As to the type of state and development strategy, at least until mid-1980s, there existed three main development strategies in Africa: (i) growth-oriented; (iii) equality-oriented; and (iii) other type, that is, shifting or mixed. Countries applying the first strategy had the embryo of a capitalist class, foreign-owned companies were not nationalized and growth was in focus (Wilson, 1990). In the second strategy, companies were nationalized, and the state apparatus grew more than in the other countries, since attempts were made to build a social welfare system. By 1992, due to the SAPs, no country persisted in following the equality-oriented development strategy.

As to cultural and religious influences, we note an expansion of the number of Christians and Muslims in sub-Saharan Africa (Coulon, 1983, 1993; Haynes, 1999; Mbembe, 1988; Nyang, 1993; Sanneh, 1983). Even if adherence to a religion is not always a matter of complete conversion, it may be assumed to imply at least an overt choice of lifestyle and way of raising children that has implications for primary education. The categories of the populations that converted to Christianity during the first phase of missionary activities were also the first ones to enroll their children in prima- ry school (Bude, 1985; Bray *et al*, 1986; Cabral, 1988; Peil, 1990).

If we are to understand the role of primary education in Africa, we have to take into account the socialization that takes place in local arrangements and in Islamic educa- tion of two types: Koranic schools and post- elementary (Arabic) schools. Some type of Islamic education is in some areas seen as a supplement or an alternative to primary education; Islamic education may be instrumental to careers in the informal sector (Oni, 1988).

Arabic schools of the type that emerged after the second World War may be seen as a modern type of Islamic education, partially substituting Koranic education. During the 1970s they started to spread in sub-Saharan Africa. They have a schedule similar to the one existing in primary schools. In Guinea-Bissau, Mozambique and Senegal, for instance, these schools compete with primary schools for pupils. The Muslims in the Middle Eastern countries support sub-Saharan African countries in many ways: mosques are built, large development projects are financed, and so on. Teachers are sent to these areas to staff the Arabic schools, local teachers are trained with outside support and textbooks are provided from the "core" countries (ISESCO, 1986; UNESCO, 1993). The network of Islamic schools is expanding to new areas such as Mozambique and Kongo (Chinapah and Daun, 1980; Palme, 1991). For instance, the number of pupils in the Arabic schools run by the three largest Islamic associations in Guinea-Bissau increased from 4,800 to 11,200 between 1990 and 1992 (Coloquio Internacional, 1994; Daun, 1998). In some West African countries, a compromise between Islam and Westernism has been found in the form of Franco-Arabic schools, which in principle follow the national curriculum but also teach some religious ele- ments. In 1993, UNESCO organized a conference in Sudan in order to find out if and how Islamic educational institutions can be involved in the struggle for education for all (UNESCO, 1993).

Case studies and statistics from several African countries show the same tendencies (Anderson, 1988; Belloncle, 1984; Blakemore, 1975; Daun, 1992, 1998; Grindal, 1972; McDowell, 1980; Oni, 1988; Peil, 1990). In all countries, despite different colonial background and economic differences (Orivel & Shaw, 1994) educational indicators vary with religious composition.

Finally, there is interaction between economic level, type of state and religious dis- tribution. Equality-oriented states tended to be formed in the poorest countries (except Congo and Zimbabwe). The most Christianized countries tend to be countries with the highest GNP per capita south of the Sahara, while the opposite applies to islamized countries. In most cases, there is an "inverse" relationship between Christianity and Islam. Countries with a high percentage of Christians have a low percentage of Muslims and vice versa. In the tables and figures that are presented here, only the most Islamized and most Christianized countries are included. However, it is worth mentioning that countries with comparatively small percentages of Muslims and Christians fall in between these two categories on the educational indicators studied here.

Private education

Private schools were common in Africa when most countries became independent around 1960. In 1965, thirty-eight percent of all primary school pupils where enrolled in private schools in the twenty-four sub-Saharan countries for which longitudinal data on this enrollment is available. The percentage was largest in the countries with the highest income, countries with the largest percentage of Christians and countries that came to apply a growth-oriented strategy. A number of countries combine these three features. During the 1970s, the proportion of pupils enrolled in private schools decreased considerably due to nationalization of schools and rapid expansion of public schools. However, the countries mentioned have to a large extent maintained their pattern; they have one third enrolled in private schools.

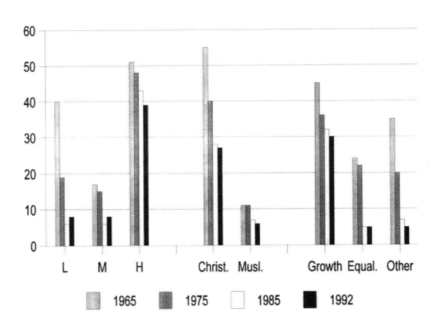

FIGURE 9.1 ENROLLMENT IN PRIVATE PRIMARY EDUCATION IN SUB-SAHARAN AFRICA, SELECTED YEARS 1965–1992
NOTE: L: LOW INCOME, M: MEDIUM INCOME, H: HIGH INCOME. CHRIST: HIGHLY CHRISTIAN-IZED, MUSL: HIGHLY ISLAMIZED. GROWTH: GROWTH-ORIENTED STATE, EQUAL: EQUALITY-ORI-ENTED STATE, OTHER: OTHER TYPE OF STATE.

The equality-oriented states initially had lower rates of enrolled in private schools and then they nationalized such schools to a larger extent than other states during the first decade of independence. Due to liberalization and restructuring in the 1980s and 1990s, they came to allow the establishment of private schools; Guinea-Bissau, Mozambique and Tanzania may be mentioned as examples. Many other countries also came to relax the regulations with which private education was restricted. In many cases, however, more generous attitudes towards state subsidies to private education were not decided upon. Since such subsidies are also needed in order for ordinary children to be able to attend private schools, such schools established in sub-Saharan Africa in the 1980s or 1990s tend to be either low quality schools established and owned by local communities and associations or elite schools that charge fees (Graham-Brown, 1991; Kitaev, 1999; Samoff, 1990). Community-run schools have increased rapidly during the 1990s (Kitaev, 1999). The fact that enrollment in private schools increases somewhat in low and medium income countries indicates this process.

Rate of Literacy

Overall, the percentage of literacy increased from fifteen in 1965 to forty-nine in 1995 in the thirty-two countries studied. Literacy rates vary with economic level but still more with religious composition in 1965 as well as in 1995 (see figure 9.2). In 1995, the differences related to religious pattern were larger than differences related to economic level. When combining economic level and religious composition, we find, for instance, that among low income countries, strongly Christian countries had a rate of literacy of twenty-eight in 1965 and sixty-six in 1995, while strongly Muslim countries had three and twenty-nine respectively. Stagnation occurs between 1985 and 1995 in the Muslim countries.[2]

In regard to the type of state, one might expect that equality-oriented states had higher levels of literacy or at least the largest increase because they organized massive literacy campaigns during the 1970s (Groth, 1987; Lind, 1988). The results support this expectation; in 1960, states that later became equality-oriented initially had the among the lowest rates, but subsequently experienced a larger increase in literacy thanother states. The literacy rate has in fact declined in countries with shifting or unclear development strategies. Some of these countries were "other" state types and were defined by Shaw (1985) as "near-anarchy countries." Adjusting countries had a continuous increase in their literacy rates, while non-adjusting countries experienced a stagnation in the 1970s and then again in the beginning of the 1990s. Most of the decline among the latter countries can be attributed to the Ethiopian case.

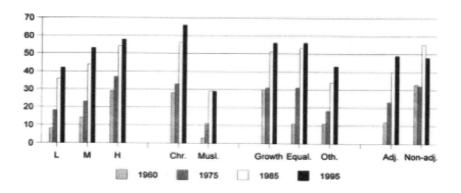

FIGURE 9.2 RATE OF LITERACY IN RELATION TO ECONOMIC LEVEL, RELIGIOUS COMPOSITION, TYPE OF STATE AND STRUCTURAL ADJUSTMENT, 1965, 1975, 1985 AND 1995

Primary school enrollment

In 1960, there were considerable differences between enrollment rates according to economic level, degree of Christianization and type of state. High income countries, and countries with a large percentage of Christians and/or a growth-oriented development strategy have higher rates in 1960 than other countries and they experienced a larger increase. The gaps are maintained despite the immense expansion that has taken place in most countries, and the gap between strongly Muslim and strongly Christian countries was still as wide as that related to the economic level. When religious composition and economic categories are combined, it becomes evident that the religious factor cuts across economic categories and types of state; it makes a significant difference in all economic and state categories, in 1960 as well as in 1992.

The rates stagnate from the 1970s in the low income countries and Muslim countries. Equality-oriented countries have a decline, while a stagnation occurs in "other" types of states as well. Ethiopia and Tanzania account for most of the decrease in the category of equality-oriented states.

Female enrollment

Rates of female enrollment follow to a large extent the same pattern as the general enrollment rates. The highest numbers are found in strongly Christian countries, high

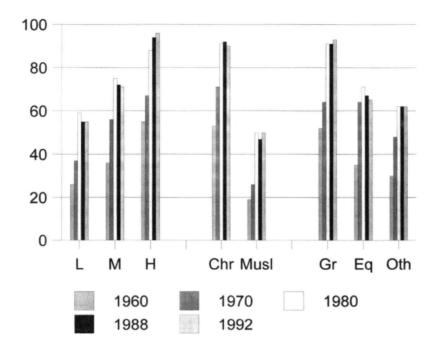

FIGURE 9.3 RATES OF ENROLLMENT IN PRIMARY EDUCATION IN RELATION TO ECO-
NOMIC LEVEL, RELIGIOUS COMPOSITION, AND TYPE OF STATE IN SUB-SAHARAN
AFRICA, SELECTED YEARS 1960–1992
ADJ: ADJUSTING COUNTRIES, NON-ADJ: NON-ADJUSTING COUNTRIES.

income countries and growth-oriented states. An analysis of the rates within each economic category shows that the religious composition makes significant difference in all
economic categories. The difference related to religion is maintained from the 1960s to
the 1990s in low income countries but has to some extent been reduced in the other economic categories. Countries that later come to implement SAPs have a lower rate than
those not implementing such programs.

All the factors studied here make more difference for girls than for boys throughout
the period. Economic level as well as religious pattern has an influence on the rates and
the differences related to religious pattern in the low income category were larger in
1992 than thirty years earlier.

EDUCATION AND STRUCTURAL ADJUSTMENT

Economic recession and SAPs had negative effects on the rates of enrollment. The year
or years of implementation of SAPs and the number of programs implemented differ

between the countries but due to the limited number of cases, it was not possible to differentiate the countries according to the number of SAPs. Countries that implemented SAPs (especially those implementing several programs) started from a lower level of enrollment and lagged behind other countries in the end of the 1970s, that is, before the implementation of SAPs.

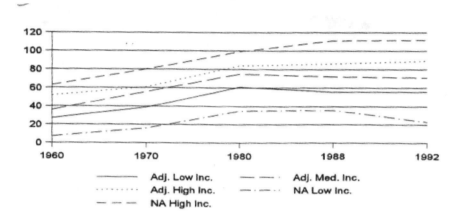

FIGURE 9.4 RATES OF PRIMARY SCHOOL ENROLLMENT IN RELATION TO ECONOMIC
LEVEL AND STRUCTURAL ADJUSTMENT PROGRAM

In the poorest countries there was a decline in expenditures, enrollments, and so on, from the beginning of the 1980s (Reimers and Tiburcio, 1993). Some countries have a continuous decline from the beginning of the 1980, while in other countries the decline starts during the 1980s, followed by a recovery. Countries that were first to adjust had already at independence a lower rate of primary school enrollment and experienced a stagnation from the beginning of the 1980s. The rates of enrollment are presented in relation to SAPs in combination with economic level, religious composition and type of state/development strategy (see figures 9.4, 9.5 and 9.6).

Low-income and medium-income countries that adjusted have a deterioration from 1980, while high income countries continue their increase regardless of whether they implement SAPs or not.

The patterns that emerge when adjustment is analyzed in relation to religious composition are far from clear. Highly Christian non-adjusting countries maintain a high (the highest) level of gross enrollment and adjusting Muslim countries have an increase from the end of the 1980s. Adjusting Christian countries experience a decline. The only highly islamized non-adjusting country is Ethiopia, that sees its enrollment rates more or less collapse.

When enrollment rates are combined with type of state and adjustment policy, it becomes evident that non-adjusting growth-oriented states (which are governing the richest countries) are the only ones that succeed in maintaining in the pattern of increase. Adjusting growth-oriented states have a decline during the first half of the 1980s and then they recover. Other types of state have a decline or stagnation regardless of whether they adjust or not (see figure 9.6).

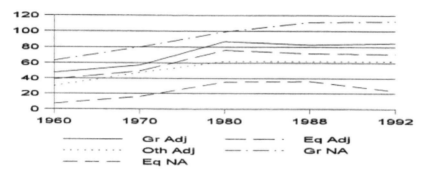

FIGURE 9.5 RATES OF PRIMARY SCHOOL ENROLLMENT IN RELATION TO TYPE OF
STATE AND STRUCTURAL ADJUSTMENT PROGRAMS

Ethiopia accounts for this stagnation among non-adjusting countries. For the poorest countries there was no option while other countries could redistribute funds between different sectors and between different levels within the education system (Ogbu and Gallagher, 1991).

How, then, does adjustment affect enrollment with regard to gender? Data indicates that girls' enrollment rates do not suffer a decline relative to that of boys in adjusting countries. In non-adjusting countries, girls are initially "over-enrolled" (108 girls per 100 boys) and their rates declined from the beginning of the 1980s. Among adjusting countries, girls' rates decline only in equality-oriented states (Tanzania, for instance).

CASE STUDIES

Senegal

Senegal, once a French colony in West Africa, had at independence in 1960, an economy based on groundnut production, a per capita income that was among the lowest in Africa; a society that to a large extent was organized for extraction of resources (from inland to the coast and the capital); a population that was primarily Muslim; and a rate

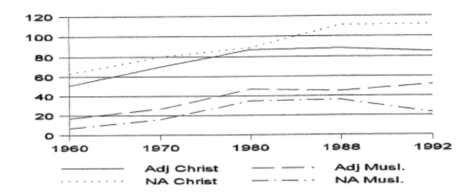

FIGURE 9.6 RATES OF ENROLLMENT IN RELATION TO ADJUSTMENT AND RELIGIOUS COMPOSITION

of school enrollment that was in the middle among the African countries (MINED, 1962; Legum, 1969). Today, the country is to a large extent incorporated into the global economy but it does not have any "strategic" natural resources.

Eighty percent of the population live on activities in the agriculture sector. A larger percentage of the population is employed in service, administration, etc. than in the industrial sector. The industrial sector is of importance mainly in the region of the capital. Eighty percent of all industrial employments are situated in this region (Kasse 1990). From having been self-sufficient on rice still at the end of the 1950s, Senegal is now heavily dependent on rice imports.

After independence, the policies were based on a combination of Catholicism, Socialism and Negritude (Rideout and Bagayoko, 1994; Senghor, 1971, 1976). Clientilistic structures of political control and loyalty were developed. The *Marabuts* (the Muslim leaders) were an important party in these structures. However, in time they made themselves more independent from the state, not always remaining loyal to thenstitutione (Boone, 1989; Villalone, 1995).

Since no national bourgoisie existed, the state took the initiatives to modernize the country. The development strategy that was formulated by the dominating party at independence, was conditioned by the existing circumstances, on the one hand, and a socialist ideology on the other. Trade, commerce and transport were dominated by a few companies, owned by immigrants from France or the Middle East and a large number of smaller tradesmen. The development strategy had the following aims: to eliminate the foreign dominance in trade, to become less dependent on export of groundnuts and on import of manufactured goods, and to create better conditions for the rural population.

In the beginning of the 1980s, the foreign debt was so big that the international lenders required an adjustment of the Senegalese economy. The country had the lowest growth rate among all sub-Saharan countries not having been affected by war although, during the period 1979-1988, Senegal received approximately three times the per capita assistance given to other SSA countries (Rideout & Bagayoko, 1994:222). The explanations for this critical economic situation were, according to the World Bank: the size of the public sector; stagnated export; non-rentable investments; and disequilibrium in the balance of payment (Kasse, 1990:16). The inequalities between socioeconomic categories of the population and between rural and urban areas had not decreased and the situation of the farmers had not improved. The state's foreign debt was very high, and the value of the import exceeded that of the export annually (Kasse, 1990; UNICEF, 1985).

With the pressure from the World Bank and the IMF, the government decided, among other things, to liberalize and privatize the economy and diminish public expenditures, partly by lowering the number of employments in the public sector. The number of employments outside the primary sector was at its maximum in 1985 and then decreased. Employment in services had increased, while those in other sectors (mainly in industry) had decreased (Ndir, 1990). Yet the country did not implement the adjustment programs to the extent or at the rhythm that had been agreed upon. The delay seemed to be tacitly accepted by the international bodies (Vengroff & Creevey, 1997). Among the reasons for the delay, Carton, N'Diaye Diouf and Comelian (1994:122) mention: " . . . a process of corporatist defence by different social groups threatened by structural adjustment, for example the teaching profession; the game of 'cat and mouse' played by civil servants . . . " Some important state enterprises scheduled for privatization were not sold out still in 1999. They had been for sale for a long time but no appropriate buyer had appeared (Nouvel Horizon, 1999).

From the 1970s, the formal rights and liberties have been more extended in Senegal than in most of the other African countries. For instance, the state has permitted multiparty elections, which continue to be relatively fair, and a rather high degree of freedom of speech is also evident. In the spring 2000, the Socialist Party ruling the country since independence, lost the elections and were replaced in the government. Apart from these rights and liberties, the great majority of the population (the farmers) have not been able to articulate their interests through the State (Coulon, 1993; Vengroff & Creevez, 1997). There is a hierachy of Marabuts, from the national level down to sections of villages or towns. This arrangement functions as a buffer and mediator between the population (Villalon, 1995).

Eighty to eighty-five percent of the population are Muslims, ten to fifteen percent have maintained a religion of African origin and about one percent are Catholics. The Muslims belong to four major brotherhoodsare: Tijaniyya sixty percent, Qadiriyya thirty percent and Muridiyya ten percent. In all the brotherhoods, the ordinary believer has to work for his *Marabut* and in the Murid brotherhood, the work may substitute for prayer and Koranic education. The *Grands Marabuts* generally have a negative attitude towards Western education; they are against Western schooling for the masses of children[3].

Islamic education

Almost all areas of the country are covered by Koranic schools. It was estimated in the 1970s that 60,000–70,000 children participated in Koranic education full-time, while some ten thousand attended such schools part-time (Mbaye, 1977). In the Koranic schools (*daara*), children learn the basics of Islam and to recite the Koran. They also work for the Marabut and in Dakar they spend time on begging, especially in the Murid brotherhood. An expansion of a more advanced type of Muslim schools, Arabic schools, took place from the beginning of the 1970s without the intervention of the state. It seems to be a response to at least two different factors. The internal criticism of the Islamic education system has increased. Younger students and teachers (reformists or modernists) are discontent with the Koranic schools, which they see as a 'deformation' of Islam and Islamic education as an instrument for the Marabuts in their struggle to maintain their power. Secondly, other countries (the oil-producing Arab countries, for example) started to support Arabic schools economically and technically in the 1970s. In Arabic schools, the pupils should learn the 'theory' of Islam, the Arabic language and some natural science and history in addition to the religious subjects. Education in the Arabic school is divided into grades or stages, and the duration of education varies from four years in some schools and six years in others.

An investigation was made by the Ministry of Education in 1980 in response to a demand from the Muslim leaders that Koranic schools be supported economically by the government, like the Catholic schools. The principal conclusion of this investigation was that most of the Koranic schools did not live up to any of the requirements which the government made. Some years later, the Ministry of Education decided to include Arabic schools in the general educational system and to give them subsidies if they fulfilled the following requirements: the same structure as the public primary schools; the same curriculum in the most important subjects; accepted government control and inspection; competent teachers; and buildings of an accepted standard. These schools are allowed to teach Arabic and use this language as the language of instruction during a certain amount of hours per week (MINED, 1981).

Arabic schools which applied for subsidies were given two different statuses: (a) authorized Franco-Arabic schools, and (b) recognized Franco-Arabic schools. The former were integrated into the formal educational system, which implied that their pupils were allowed to continue in lower secondary education of the general educational system (if they passed the entrance examinations), but these schools were not given subsidies. The latter type of school was subsidized by the government, and had to meet the same requirements as the former.

The *Marabuts* have for a long time made investments in industry, commerce and service, and during the 1990s, they introduced computers and IT and the *daaras* in Dakar. These *daaras* function as boarding schools where the pupils (mostly older than 14-15 years) learn, among other things, how to use the computers and to contact other Muslims all over the world.

After the Jomtien conference in 1990 and the increasing discourse on civil society, Islamic education has become a legitimate object for development assistance. UNICEF, for instance, supports Islamic schools through Muslim NGOs (Coloquio Internacional, 1994).

Western education

The Catholic and the colonial schools had the same structure and the same curricula as the French. Smaller changes were made (mainly of the content) when Senegal became independent in 1960: six years of primary education, four years of lower secondary and four years of upper secondary education. The elite did not have any interest in changing the education system radically but massive efforts were made during the first years of independence to increase the enrollment, since mass education was one of the cornerstones in the first development plans (MINED, 1962; Rideout and Bagayoko, 1994; Senghor, 1971, 1976). The system that to a large extent is a "reproduction of the French system" and it is is very selective (Rideout & Bagayoko, 1994:207) and the rate of repetition is comparatively high (Barrier et al, 1997).

Until 1980, the enrollment hardly kept pace with the population growth, but during the 1980s, the percentage of enrolled children increased. Apart from the fact that the capital region has the highest rate of enrollment, the rates accompany religious composition; in areas where the Muslim influence is strongest, the rates are lowest. Between 1968 and 1996, the rate of net enrollment in the country increased from thirty-one percent to fifty-one percent (MINED, 1962; MINEC, 1997). In the region of Diourbel, where the centre of the *Murid* brotherhood is situated, the enrollment rate was thirty-one percent (15.5 among the girls) in 1996 (MINED, 1998). The percentage of primary school pupils enrolling in private (Catholic) schools has, since independence, been around ten percent.

At the end of the 1970s and in the beginning of the 1980s, there was a series of strikes among the teachers. Their trade unions demanded a change of the education system and of the teachers' situation. The Prime Minister and the Minister of Education called the teachers for general meetings in 1981, and a number of committees were formed for the elaboration of a proposal for a new education system. This proposal was published in 1985 (Mined, 1986). Some of the principal points in this document may be summarized in the following way: implementation of a comprehensive system of ten years of education for all; introduction of new subjects such as religious/moral education and the Arabic language; abolition of the approach to teaching French; vocational

TABLE 9.3 RATE OF NET ENROLLMENT IN PRIMARY EDUCATION IN SENEGAL, SELECTED YEARS 1962-1996

	1960	1962	1968	1974	1980	1986	1992	1996
No. of pupils	...	149,175	248,749	297,560	392,541	610,541	666,950	854,976
Rate	...	...	31	31	35	46.5	44.9	50.9
Female rate	27	...	...	...	41	41	38	45

Sources: MINED (1962), MINEC (1973,1979,1987,1997).

training in work places in the last grades; automatic promotion; and national languages instead of French as the languages of instruction (MINED, 1986; Sylla 1985). In the mid-1990s, only the sixth theme had been realized to some extent in that experimental classes using mother tongue existed. The government was criticized by teachers for not being willing to reform the education system.

According to Rideout & Bagayoko (1994:214), the structural adjustment in 1986 was "intended to improve access to primary education by making more teachers available and by increasing class sizes to achieve more efficient use of teachers". Associate teachers were upgraded and teachers performing administrative functions returned to teaching. Also, multi-grade classes were introduced in more schools and teaching double shifts started.

Senegal had among the lowest rates of enrollment in Africa in the 1980s. During the past ten years, however, these rates have increased. It seems to be due, at least partially, to tacit compromises with the Muslim community. Part of the increase is due to the growing number of Muslim and Franco-Arabic schools that teach according to the national curriculum and are inspected by the state.

Mozambique

Mozambique, situated in East Africa, has approximately 15 million inhabitants. The population is distributed across some ten principal ethnic groups. The majority adhere to a religion of African origin, while Islam is spreading in the whole country, especially in the north. Around one-fifth of the population are Catholics. The country is one of the poorest in the world. The GNP per capita decreased from 140 US dollars in 1978 to 90 in 1993.

At the end of the colonial period, ninety percent of the population in Mozambique lived on agricultural activities while the small sectors of industry and commerce were controlled by foreigners. No nation-wide network for health care and basic education existed. The rate of illiteracy was 90–95 percent. At independence, the state was taken over by FRELIMO,[4] the party that had led the armed struggle against the Portuguese colonial power. Major parts of the economy were placed under state control and state farms were established mainly on the large agricultural units that had been owned by foreigners. Attempts were made to reorganize society for nation-building, economic growth, elimination of inequality and poverty. Immense investments were made in the creation of a nation-wide network for primary education and primary health.

The enrollment in primary education and literacy campaigns increased rapidly between 1975 and 1980. The rate of illiteracy is estimated to have dropped by about twenty percent during this period. However, insurgent activities backed up by South Africa were started by RENAMO[5] at the end of the 1970s and within just a few years, schools, hospitals, and roads had been attacked and destroyed in many places all over the country. By the mid-1980s, the number of refugees was more than 2 million in neighboring countries or in urban areas within the country.

All this resulted in an economic crisis that began to take a distinct shape by the beginning of the 1980s. Mozambique received support mainly from the COMECON countries but this was found to be insufficient. The volume and value of the aid that was given by the Soviet Union and other socialist countries from independence and onwards is not known (Carrilho, 1991). The socialist countries were, however, not able or willing to increase their contribution. Mozambique also suffered severely from periods of natural disaster during the 1970s and 1980s (Hermele, 1992).

During the FRELIMO party congress in 1983, a Programme of Action for the recovery of the economy was taken, and it implied to some extent liberalization of the economy. However, the effects of the war became even more severe, and hit not only the social services but also production. The economy, by then, was at near collapse (Hermele, 1992; Johnston, 1990; Johnston et al., 1988; UNHCR, 1991). The centralized system made communication between the national center and local communities difficult. Also, state representatives were ambitious to develop the new society which caused them to neglect the economic costs and efficiency of various projects (Nhavoto, 1990).

The re-orientation of the development strategy in 1983 also included an educational reform, which was gradually implemented. The structure of the system and the curricula were determined. The educational policies were formulated in the following way by FRELIMO: educate citizens with a solid political, ideological, scientific, technical, cultural and physical preparation and an elevated patriotic and civil education; eradicate illiteracy in a such that all people have access to scientific knowledge and a full development of capacities; utilize the Portuguese language for the consolidation of the national unity; and make the educational institutions revolutionary bases for the consolidation of popular power, profoundly integrated into the community (SNE, 1982, as quoted in Golias, 1995:312).

The system became very centralized, and the four years of primary education were prolonged to seven years (two cycles: five and two years) and less emphasis than before was given to literacy campaigns. The rate of net enrollment was about fifty percent during the first years of the 1980s and then dropped drastically, especially between 1986 and 1987.

In 1984, the government applied for membership in the IMF and it was agreed that credits be given on the condition that a series of changes were made in the economy. It became evident that the conditionalities would radically alter the core of the development strategy, in particular the social aspects of it, if they were fulfilled, so the government tried as long as possible to save what had been built. The government wanted to maintain at least the social services at the level it had during the the latter half of the 1970s and suggested a longer time perspective for the implementation of the changes (Gibbon, 1992; Hermele, 1992). However, the country had to finally succumb to the conditionalities. The main features of the new strategy were: sale of many of the parastatal bodies; liberalization of the economy; compression of the public sector; weakened price control on consumer goods and agricultural products; and stimulation of exports.

Economic balance and growth and stimulation of production for export were the principal objectives. Ceilings for the public expenditures were set for each sector, and the expenditures on social sectors (which were the core of the FRELIMO strategy) were drastically and abruptly cut in 1987. Between 1986 and 1987, for instance, the government expenditures on education dropped from 12.8 to 4.4 percent and educational costs of the GNP from 3.1 to 2.3 (see table 9.5).

TABLE 9.4 EDUCATIONAL EXPENDITURE IN MOZAMBIQUE AS PERCENTAGE OF GNP, SELECTED YEARS 1980–1992

	1980	1983	1986	1987	1988	1990	1992
%	3.7	4.5	3.1	2.3	3.7	4.5	6.1

Source: MINECM, 1990a; MINEDU, 1998.

The conditionalities were formulated as if the war did not exist. The effects of the adjustment program are impossible to isolate from other influences, and they also differ for various groups and categories (Green, 1991).

Mozambique was (by all possible criteria and indicators) in need of emergency aid from the beginning of the 1980s. The volume of aid coming from the Western countries doubled, when Mozambique started to implement the adjustment program in 1987 (Carrilho, 1991).The total amount of aid to education grew five times between 1986 and

1988 and then more than doubled between 1988 and 1990. Emergency aid started in 1989. Of all aid, the percentage dedicated to education increased from four percent in 1986 to fifty-seven percent in 1990 (Carrilho, 1991; Nhavoto, 1991).

In 1990 a new constitution allowing for a multi-party system, and organization freedom and a free press were introduced, the World Bank gave credits to a reform program; and the new adjustment program came to have at least some orientation towards the social sectors (Hermele 1992). When these decisions were taken, the flow of external economic support began to increase once again. Peace negotiations between FRELIMO and RENAMO resulted in the move of the latter's headquarter to the capital and general and free elections in 1994.

In the plan for the period 1990-1992, emphasis was made on rural development and investment in infrastructures. Education should be provided for all and it should serve rural development and curricula should be adapted to the cultural, economic and social realities of the country (MINEDU, 1990a:37). Many of the imbalances and inequalities inherited from the colonial period were reduced or eliminated during the first five years of independence. However, due to the war, the economic crisis, and the implementation of the SAPs these inequalities re-emerged or were reinforced.

The influence from the international agencies also made it difficult for the MINED not only to handle and implement the projects but also to set its own priorities and follow them. The handling of external aid often requires staff with more competence than is available, an increase in the number of staff (which contradicts the adjustment policy), and consequently, more costs to be covered from internal sources. The GDP decreased by six percent annually between 1982 and 1985. After fifteen years of decline, the country has experienced rapid economic growth from mid-1990s (Rodrik, 1998).

Although the rate of literacy has increased, the rate for women lags far behind that of men (Cabral, 1992). The percentage of girls being enrolled in the first grade is only a little smaller than that of the boys. However, girls drop out much more than boys, especially in grades 5-6 (Palme, 1991; Passos, 1992; Zucula, 1991).

During the whole period (pre-SAP, SAP and the first years of the 1990s), the pass rates and the rates of repetition did not change, the rate of enrollment decreased and the dropout rate increased until 1990 (World Bank 1990b). After 1990, educational indicators have improved substantially; for instance, the rate of enrollment had in 1996 attained the same level as in the beginning of the 1980s (see table 9.6).

Before the general elections in 1994, representatives of the political parties were interviewed by Golias (1995). FRELIMO mentioned socialist development and socialist schooling neither in the election campaign, nor in this interview. In addition, it is not mentioned in the Master Plan for a new educational policy and a new education system (MINEDU, 1994). The largest opposition party, RENAMO mentions to some extent the same items as those mentioned by FRELIMO but they also state that Church involvement in community affairs, among them education, should be encouraged.

TABLE 9.5 PRIMARY SCHOOL ENROLLMENT IN MOZAMBIQUE

	1979	1980	1983	1986	1989	1991	1996
Net enr.	48.5 (1)	51.3 (2)	48.2 (2)	35.3 (2)	36.3 (3)	42 (4)	50 (5)

Sources: (1) Johnston 1986; (2) World Bank 1990b; (3) MINEDU 1990a,b; (4) UNDP, 1995; (5) MINEDU, 1998.

The plans produced by the FRELIMO government in 1994 and 1998 make it clear that the educational policies and the educational system should be reformed. New objectives shall be defined and a curriculum reform will be made, while decentralization is already taking place. It is stated, among other things, that basic education promotes individuality and liberty, that it is relevant for the needs of the family, the local community and the society; that it the involvement of local communities is also implied in the planning and administration of education (MINEDU, 1994). These features are also emphasized in a plan from 1998 (MINEDU, 1998).

During the 1990s, decentralization of some economic affairs at the regional (provincial) level has taken place, and private schools have been established, especially in the capital.

Cameroon

Cameroon is often referred to as "Africa in miniature." It is a country with great diversity and variety (geographic, climatic, ecological, ethnic, cultural, religious and linguistic).The population is extremely diversified ethnically, with over 160 ethnic groups, of which the largest are: Cameroon Highlanders, thirty-one percent, Equatorial Bantu, nineteen percent, and Fulani, eleven percent. Indigenous beliefs are adhered to by 40 per cent of the population, with forty percent Christians, and twenty percent Muslims. The country is a medium-income country although life expectancy, literacy and per capita income are above average for Africa south of the Sahara.

The population is about 13 million people (1992) and a growth rate of 2.7 percent in 1990–1991 was unevenly distributed, like in many other developing countries, with an estimated forty percent residing in urban centers. Since one part of the country was administered by the French and the other by the British, both French and English languages are official languages. In addition to the general use of one or more local languages, many people are conversant in the pidgin English known as Wes Cos. French is spoken by about eighty percent of the population; English by about twenty percent. The northern Fulanis speak Arabic.

Following independence in1960, Cameroon's development strategy was structured on five-year development plans based on a policy of territorial as well as socio-economic development geared towards export crop promotion. Economic growth was the primary concern, and up to 1985, a mix of policies allowed for a steady real economic growth. Agriculture remained up to 1987, the main source of growth and foreign exchange earnings. From 1989, oil production started and became the main source of economic growth

Since 1986, the country has been experiencing a large-scale economic crisis due to a sharp decline in export prices of its key primary commodities: petroleum, cocoa and coffee. This caused Cameroon's earnings to fall by more than fifty percent. The level of per capita GDP in 1990–1991 was almost the same as that of 12 years earlier, in 1979–1980. In 1988–1989, the government launched a SAP. GDP has declined annually and the county's debt has increased. Today, the government faces considerable public finance deficit, high foreign and domestic debt and rising unemployment. Government action has focused on cuts in public expenditure, structural adjustment, a degree of privatization and the rescheduling of external debts (World Bank, 1995c).

Since independence, the country has been ruled by two regimes. After a UN plebiscite in 1961, the country became a federal republic in 1961, with both components retaining their local parliaments. In 1972, the country became a unitary republic. Political liberalisation, which began in 1990, is underway but the process still suffers from hiccups and governance questions still pose a threat to the revival of economic activities. Multiple political parties became legal again in 1990. Since then there have been three sets of elections. There will also be a constitutional council, regional assemblies and a financial administrative organ.

Since independence, education has been a key element of government development programs. Cameroon's rate of literacy is among the highest in Africa. In the Francophone provinces in Cameroon, education is compulsory for six years, while in the Anglophone provinces it is compulsory for seven years from the ages five to twelve. This difference is typical of the dual education system prevalent in the country. A distinctly British system operates in the Southwest and Northwest provinces, while a Gallic system operates in the eight French-speaking provinces. The Anglophone system consists of a two-year nursery school followed by a seven-year primary, a five year secondary education and a further two-year course leading to GCE "A" level examinations. The main difference in the Francophone system lies in the duration of the primary and the nature of the secondary examinations.

There is also a well developed private education sector, which receives a substantial subsidy from the government and is estimated to account for some forty-five percent of educational resources (MINEDUC, 1995). Private, mostly religious, schools continue to play a dominant role in the primary system. The overwhelming majority of primary schools as well as eighty-five percent of secondary schools are in private hands in the former West Cameroon. In the eastern sector, public schools are more numerous, and private-school enrollments have been dropping for years. Approved private schools receive grants-in-aid to pay teacher salaries and help in the provision of learning/teaching materials, which are disbursed through the schools authorities, mainly district councils. However both types of school follow the same curriculum and are subject to the same regulations regarding methods of instruction and qualifications of teachers.

Over the last thirty years, two major evolutions have marked primary school education: firstly, it has become common practice to enroll a child at nursery school at age three, secondly, the average time spent in primary school has gradually decreased. In the area of primary education, focus has been on the expansion of both access to education and the improvement of quality. These efforts did yield success, particularly in the 1970s to the late 1980s. At all levels of education, enrollment rose, and especially at the primary level, it more than tripled. By 1987, the rate of gross enrollment was recorded at 103 percent. Gender equity of access was fully realized at the primary. The general pattern is that girls are nearly on a par with boys in the lower levels of the system, whereas they are considerably under-represented at higher levels. In the first four grades, girl pupils constitute more than forty-nine percent of the total and there has been little change over the years. In the upper grades, however, girls drop out more than boys and their share has fallen. The protracted economic crisis in the late 1980s however brought a reversal of the upwards trends both in enrollment rates The proportion of girls dropping out varies considerably across the regions (MINEDUC, 1995).

A government report of mid-1994 put the percentage of school-age children attending school at 86.4 percent. There is, however, a wide geographical diversity with, for example, 93.4 percent of school-age children in the anglophone Southwest Province attending school but only 47.5 percent in the predominantly Muslim far North Province —which also houses the largest proportion of nomadic people.

About a third of the children in Cameroon are failing to complete even four years of primary education, either because they drop out of school early, or because they never enroll in school at all. Immediately after the Jomtien Conference in 1990, UNESCO adopted Cameroon as a test-case for follow up activities. Technical back up was provided in view of a plan of action for the promotion of primary education. They found out that the annual growth of 13.2 percent was recorded in pre-school education that enrolled one fifth of children aged between three and five years in 1994. There was no discrimination in access to education in gender terms but pre-school was concentrated in the urban areas (UNESCO, 1994).

According to UNESCO, primary education was on the decline during the first half of the 1990s. The number of pupils dropped by 2.3 percent per year. The proportion of girls dropping out from school varies considerably across the regions. According to UNESCO figures, whereas in urban areas only 8.5 percent of girls drop out from primary education, the corresponding figure for the rural areas is very high (UNESCO, 1994). For other levels of education, the situation was more positive in quantitative terms. In post-primary education, the number of students went up between 1993 and 1994. The internal efficiency of the educational system is poor,. because the country has been seriously affected by the difficult economic situation. Conscious of the gravity of the problem, authorities tried to find a solution by organizing a National Conference on the General State of Education in 1995.

In northern Cameroon, instruction provided by Koranic schools predates the modern system. Although without a centrally organized administration, these schools find unity in common structure, content and religious ideology. They use rote methods for teaching the Koran, and memory work is done in Arabic. The usual length of the elementary course is three to five years. Advanced work may last several years or a whole lifetime, delving into Islamic law, history, literature and the Arabic language. State primary and secondary schools have made some inroads into the Islamic strongholds, with some towns reporting large-scale departures of boys from the Koranic schools (Benson, 1985).

The many languages and dialects, twenty-four of them of major importance, pose a major problem for educators. Each of the country's three colonial masters left their language as a legacy to the country, creating tenacious linguistic loyalties (Folon, 1969).

The curriculum in both primary and secondary schools has changed little since colonial days. The curricula are sustained by an examination system similarly oriented to bookish knowledge and rote learning.

Since the late 1980s, the SAPs have led to the impoverishment of millions of people in Cameroon. Internal purchasing power has collapsed, famines have erupted, health clinics and schools have been closed down, and many children have been denied the right to primary education. The crises and the profound changes which have characterised the period from 1987 until present day have had serious repercussions on the educational system. The education sector has not been spared; basic education is in decline. Primary school tuition has been free for a long time and attendance is formally compulsory for all children of primary school age. Parents are expected to pay general purpose fees, building, sports and other fees charged by the school. Although these additional fees are not supposed to be compulsory, many schools press for payment and this is difficult for the poorer families. Primary school attendance appears to be influenced also by such factors as the availability of schools, motivation, cultural and religious considerations and socioeconomic factors within the family and the local community.

The requirements that families must outfit their children in uniforms and provide exercise books and pencils is a big burden. In addition, many families need children to help with farming and other chores. The financial burden has a particularly harmful effect on the schooling of girls. While most parents recognize that it is important for a girl to be educated, many feel that the benefits of a girl's education will be enjoyed by others, since a daughter, typically, leaves her family after marriage.

The establishment of regional education offices in every Provincial capital, Divisional headquarters and District offices in each of the districts in the country has helped to streamline and decentralize the management and administration of primary and secondary school education. Although there has been a quantitative expansion in education since independence, the demand for education at all levels far outstrips the supply. While the government's aim is to harmonize the English and French educational systems, they still remain discrete in respect to language of instruction, structure, curriculum content and examinations.Qualitatively, the classrooms are generally crowded, with as many as 100 children to one teacher, and there is also a problem of shortage of textbooks and equipment.

Tanzania

The republic of Tanzania consists of Tanganyika and Zanzibar. Before the union, Tanganyika had been a colony under German rule from 1885-1918 and after 1945 became a UN Trusteeship. Territory under the British until 1961 when the country became independent. Despite separate political entities in the two countries, their history is closely connected through the mercantilist and later modern imperialist relations (New Africa Year Book, 1997–1998).

Mainland Tanzania is one of the most diversified ecological systems in Africa. Agriculture is the backbone of the economy. Four fifths of the active population is engaged in subsistence farming, of which women form the majority. In 1986, the agricultural sector contributed with almost sixty percent of the GDP. About seventy-five percent of Tanzania's export is made up of agricultural products, the main items being coffee, cotton, tea, sisal, pyrethrum, tobacco, coconut, sugar, cardamon, groundnuts, and cashew nuts. Minerals and tourism also form part of the economy. The agro-ecological conditions vary widely. Both the well-watered highlands and the areas of the high rainfall around Lake Victoria along the fringes of the country account for a high share of the total population and production of market food and export crops (Havnevik *et al*, 1988). These are also the areas with high population densities.

In many parts of the country, the increased population pressure has already contributed to considerable wearing down of natural resources (ibid.). There has been a tremendous increase in population since independence. In 1964, mainland had a population of 12 million and Zanzibar 300,000. With an annual growth rate of 2.8 percent, today the country has a population estimated at 31 million. Ninety percent of the population live in rural areas.

Over 120 tribes of Bantu origin, with different cultures, have enjoyed a sense of cohesiveness in Tanzania. Kiswahili, a Bantu language, has been the main contributor to the unity. Tanzania can be classified as a multi-religious country, where half of the mainland population are of the Christian faith, forty percent are Muslims and the rest have remained with their traditional faith. On the island of Zanzibar, ninety-eight percent of the population are Muslims.

Political development after independence is popularly divided into three phases, in relation to the presidency: Nyerere, 1961–1985; Mwinyi, 1985–1995; and Mkapa, 1995–present. The country has had only one party for 30 years, from 1965 when TANU was declared the only ruling party to 1992 when the doors were opened for other parties. In 1977 Tanganyika African National Union (TANU) of the mainland and Afro

Shirazi Party (ASP) of Zanzibar united to form one party, Chama cha Mapinduzi (CCM).The first multi-party elections were held in 1995 where four parties contested and CCM won by a majority.

Socialism has been the guiding policy, based on the African brotherhood. Respect for human dignity, sharing of the resources, work by everyone and exploitation by none, as stipulated by the Arusha declaration (1967). This declaration contained a policy of *Ujamaa* (Socialism and Self–Reliance) and has been the blueprint behind all development strategies until present time. This is known as the "Basic needs oriented development strategy," in which education and health are free. The Arusha declaration stated the desire to create a society of workers and peasants, and social progress and economic development was to take place under the principles of equality. Education for Self Reliance (ESR) was one important component of this policy. Since independence social services have been provided and delivered mainly by the state.

With the declining economic performance in the 1980s, the government was unable to sustain the quality provision of the essential services which it had supported for many years. The government finally had to withdraw as a key actor in the areas of health and education. The communities were asked to share the costs of education and health at all levels. The national government went from a central planned economy inspired by a vision of African Socialism based on a one party state, self-sufficiency and economic independence, towards a market-oriented economic policy. Private organizations and individuals were encouraged to invest in education and health services as they had been at independence. Some health and education institutions, nationalized in 1967, returned to the previous owners and private initiative. The result was the mushrooming up of private schools from the nursery school to the university level with a major thrust at secondary schools. The interests of stakeholders in education has thus become a critical issue as the government is no longer the sole provider of education.

In 1986, attempts to restructure the economy brought the social services, especially education and health, under severe pressures (Samoff & Sumra, 1994): cuts in public sector budgets which reduced resources available for financing education and training; and declining level and changing distribution of employment affecting work opportunities and, ultimately, the incentive to invest in education and training. Little effort was made by the government to educate the people in the practical implications of a liberalized economy, especially in the provision of basic social services like education and health services. Analysis of the effects of economic liberalization have been done at macro level (World Bank, 1995b) but little has been done to address the effects of liberalization in areas such as education and health.

The liberalization of education services came at a time when Tanzania's real income was declining drastically thus making education more expensive than ever before. The Tanzanian currency was drastically devaluated and the net effect on the household was higher food prices, school fees, health care and other contributions leading ultimately to reduced real incomes which especially affected the low income families in both rural and urban areas (Mbussa & Mlelwa,1991).

The situation of educational funding aggravated by the economic decline of the 1980s, prompted the intervention of IMF and the World Bank. The government was advised to reduce spending on education in various ways and to shift the cost to communities and families by encouraging private schools and by increasing private contributions and to rely upon foreign support.

The SAPs reorganized the economy and brought the social services under severe pressures especially education and health. Specifically the effect of austerity and adjustment policies put on education has been felt through four pressures (Samoff and Sumra, 1994). From the World Bank, among others, certain measures were proposed to be implemented, such as: privatization (communities, organizations and individuals were encouraged to open and run their own schools and colleges and other tertiary); shortening of pre-service teacher training; reduction of expenditure per pupil (Adult Education and Day Secondary Schools); raising funds directly and indirectly from people. In addition, labor provision. and material for school construction were also required. Although private secondary schools charge officially accepted fees, there have sometimes been other contributions, which have made them much more expensive than public schools, especially those considered to be of good quality; schools were expected to establish economic projects to generate funds to support school activities.

Of great concern is the falling standards of education as confirmed by studies (Komba *et al*, 1995; Omari and Mosha, 1987; Omari *et al*, 1994). The consequences on education and training include: overcrowded classrooms, inadequately supplied students, and underpaid teachers. School attendance and participation in disadvantaged areas seems to have been affected drastically. Education lost its importance to parents and their children as a guarantor of salaried employment.

There is a general consensus that, under SAPs, the social sector, that is education and health, has been the main sector affected (Mwanza, 1993; Psacharopolos, 1988; Tibaijuka, 1995; Shayo, Kiwara & Makusi,1993; World Bank. 1991b). This has meant a change in the country's development strategy as stipulated by the Arusha declaration. The quality of public education and health services dropped over the last years of the crisis, with gradual erosion in public provision of free service (Havnevik *et al* 1988). Access to basic education in Tanzania is considered a fundamental right for all school age children since the declaration of the Universal Primary Education (UPE) in 1977. During the first years of UPE, enrolment in primary education increased tremendously. National resources available for funding education became seriously strained so the government was forced to seek for both internal and external assistance to meet the costs of education.

During the 1960s and 1970s, educational funding was a combination of both local sources and foreign assistance, the latter considered just transitional. However, events of the late 1970s and early 1980s changed the relationship between internal and external funding of education by tilting it toward external dependence. In the 1980s, foreign aid provided sixty percent of most elements of the educational system. After the economic difficulties of the 1980s, there was very little money allocated to investments in or maintenance of educational institutions.

TABLE 9.6 EDUCATIONAL EXPENDITURES AS PERCENTAGE OF GDP IN TANZANIA, SELECTED YEARS, 1980–1995

	1980	1982	1984	1986	1989/90	1990/91	1992/93	1993/94	1996/97
%	11.7	13.3	6.5	7.9	2.2	2.3	2.6	3.6	2.7

Source: MoE, 1998.

The share of basic education in the GDP from the 1980s to the 1990s shrank systematically. Donor funding has substantively supported the advancement and maintenance of higher education institutions.

The national objective of providing basic education to every child of school age has also been hit by privatization and commercialization of the social services. Indicators of the crisis in education can been seen in the rates of enrollment and drop- out, absenteeism and in the falling standards of education. Teachers like all low income employees have also been in search for alternative income sources. This has led to tuition, private lessons given after school hours and paid for by the parents. The general consensus is that quantitative expansion has led to qualitative deterioration, hence the recent statement of intent by the government to rectify the situation. Drop out rates sometimes range between twenty and forty-seven percent and there is underachievement in the primary school, especially in maths and languages (Komba, 1995).

In 1995, the Education and Training Policy (ETP) was introduced in response to the structural adjustment policies. The ETP does not provide the guidance needed on how problems of access, equity, quality and affordability of education for all citizens can be enhanced under the competitive cost sharing approach. The policy mentioned crystallized the proposals into: (i) unrestricted liberalization of trade rather than modifications of the systems; (ii) increased private sector participation in the economy; (iii) provision of essential resources to priority areas other than the social sector; (iv) increased investment in infrastructure and social development sectors; and (iv) reduction of subsidies and introduction of cost recovery and cost sharing measures, where applicable, especially in the social services in education and health. As a result, the government was required to encourage privatization of educational institutions at all levels and ensure that school and tuition fees were based on actual unit cost of providing education and training. District councils were called upon to institute a tax rate to finance basic education and training in their respective areas. Schools were encouraged to participate in income generating activities to supplement the financing of education.

Differential school fees and tuition fees were to be introduced depending on how much was contributed by local communities, district councils, donors and income generating activities undertaken by each school. ETP implementation results in differentiation at both family, ethnic group and area levels. The implications for access seems to be that children from poor family backgrounds are unable to meet the cost for education. In general, the ETP seems to contradict the government's guarantee of education for all citizens since parents have to pay for everything except teacher salaries. In practice, it is impossible for the government to ensure equitable distribution of educational institutions and resources in such a large country with its ethnic, district, and regional disparities.

The standard of living in the low-income bracket of the population has continued to deteriorate. A household survey done in 1990 indicated that household earnings had deteriorated by fifty percent due to cuts in government subsidies. There are signs of the widening gap, between those who can afford the services and those who cannot, exactly the opposite of the policies of the Arusha Declaration.

TABLE 9.7 NET ENROLLMENT IN PRIMARY EDUCATION IN TANZANIA, SELECTED YEARS 1962- 1998, NUMBERS IN THOUSANDS

	1962	1970	1980	1985	1990	1993	1996	1998
% enr.	..	..	..	..	54.2	53.7	57.5	..
Numbers	519	828	3,361	3,160	3,379	3,736	3,942	4,042

Source: MoE, 1998.

The highest enrollment rates in primary schools were witnessed during the declaration of Universal Primary Education (UPE) in 1977 when around ninety-five percent of all school age children were enrolled in primary education. The numbers of pupils have remained constant while the age cohorts have become bigger. This means that net enrollment has declined whereas secondary education has expanded. Even with the present low enrolment rates, the problem of retention in school has become a critical issue as many children drop out of school before completion of class seven. The proportion of pupils who dropped out from school increased soon after the UPE began to be implemented in 1977. A study conducted in five regions in the country in confirms this. The enrollment rate has gone down from 91 percent in 1981 to 72 percent in 1996. Evidence has shown that on the average, Tanzanian children start school much later than the statutory age of seven years. From the 1992 Standard I enrollment data, only fourteen percent of the children were seven years old and thirty-eight percent were ten years old, while the rest (forty-eight percent) were eight and nine years old (Sumra, 1997).

The gender differences in primary education still persist despite the almost equal proportion of boys and girls enrolled. Inequality continues because girls are less likely than boys to complete primary education and those who complete primary school generally score lower than boys in the School Leaving Examinations (Malekela, 1995), a fact that lowers their chances for selection into government secondary schools.

Several attempts were made to improve secondary education provision and financing since the UPE years. Fees had been abolished in the late 1960s. In 1984 secondary school fees were reintroduced. Private secondary schools were encouraged in earnest in 1986. Private primary schools, though not directly encouraged, began to emerge. By 1996 Tanzania had more than 11,000 public primary schools and twenty officially registered private primary schools.

In a report, (HRDS, 1993–1994) it was observed that pupils from poor households started school later and left school earlier than children of the rich. By the age of 15 years about 66 percent of the children from the lowest twenty percent of income groups were out of school. Most of these children left school to engage in farm work, family chores and money earning petty businesses. Girls mainly dropped out to start family life and sometimes due to early pregnancies. The enrollment rate is higher for boys than girls in some grades. Discussions with parents and teachers in this study indicated that they preferred daughters to start school early and complete primary school before puberty due to the risk of early pregnancy. Sons start school later in order to complete when they are old enough to enter the labour market. Children from lower income households also start school later than those from better off families. Drop out rates increased from twenty-eight percent soon after the UPE (the 1978/84 cohort) to forty-seven percent (1983–1989 cohort) and forty-two percent (1984–1990 cohort). The opportunity cost of children's time at home was quite significant in influencing school enrolments.

CONCLUSIONS

In a context of different economic, cultural, and political characteristics most countries in sub-Saharan Africa have implemented SAPs and restructured their education system in a similar fashion, principally through decentralization and deregulation of private education. The degree of implementation of these policies varies with the economic level, type of state and managerial competence, among other things. Until now, features of education systems and the levels of educational indicators vary according to the combination of colonial background, economic level, type of state and religious composition.

The poorest countries suffered first from economic crisis and then from the SAPS and they have not been able to implement the restructuring policies to any large extent. The result has been that the populations have taken initiatives and withdrawn from schooling or established their own schools. Religious composition continues to play an important role in enrollment rates. When seen from a holistic perspective, the factors studied constitute horizontal and vertical networks that are sustained by the informal sector. Employment in this sector does not always require formal education of the Western type. The stagnation or even decline of rates of enrollment in most of the poorest countries, at least until mid-1990s, should be seen against this background. There are a few exceptions, such as Mozambique. The richest of the SSA countries, on the other hand, maintained a high level of enrollment.

APPENDIX 9.1 CLASSIFICATION OF ECONOMIC LEVELS, RELIGIOUS PATTERN, TYPE OF STATE AND SAPs IN SUB-SAHARAN AFRICA

Rate of literacy, rate of gross enrollment in primary education, rate of female gross enrollment in primary education and rate of enrollment in private primary schools during the period 1960–1992 were analyzed in relation to societal factors. The countries south of the Sahara were classified according to (i) economic level (GNP per capita); (ii) percentage of Christians; (iii) percentage of Muslims; (iv) type of state from the end of the 1960s and (v) implementation or not of SAPs. Three economic levels were used: low, medium and high in the context of sub-Saharan Africa. "High", for instance, is high relative to other Sub-Saharan countries. The percentage of Christians was classified into low and high. Countries with more than twenty percent (the median) of Christians in the population were placed in the "high" category and others in the "low" category. The same procedure was used for the classification of degree of Islamization: countries with more than forty percent Muslims were placed in the "high" category of Muslims, while others were placed in the "low" category (Legum, 1969; Nicolas, 1981; Coulon, 1983). The states were divided into (i) growth-oriented; (ii) equality-oriented; and (iii) other. The classification of the states applies to the period until the SAPs started to be implemented. Growth-oriented states are Botswana, Cameroon, Côte d'Ivoire, Kenya, Lesotho, Malawi, Nigeria, and Senegal. Equality-oriented states are Angola, Congo, Ethiopia, Guinea-Bissau, Mozambique, Tanzania, and Zambia. All other countries belong to the category "other" (Bratton, 1994; Bratton and Walle, 1997; Chazan et al. 1998; Cocquery-Vidrovitch, 1985).

The years were selected so as to mirror different phases in the educational development in sub-Saharan Africa: the period of independence of most African states (1960), the period before economic recession (1970), during the economic recession but before the implementation of SAPs (1980), after a period of SAPs (1988) and the latest year for which data was available (1992 or 1993).

Data for all selected years was available for thirty-two of the thirty-nine countries included in the study. The trends and patterns that appear for these twenty- two countries are, however, similar to the ones obtained when the analysis is conducted separately year by year with all the countries for which data is available for each respective year. The reports from the World Bank were used as sources for economic and educational data, (see World Bank: Development Reports 1975, 1979, 1981, 1986, 1990–1995), while a broad range of sources were used for data on degree of Islamization/Christianization as well as type of state and development strategy.

APPENDIX 9.2 RATE OF ENROLLMENT IN RELATION TO ECONOMIC LEVEL, RELIGIOUS COMPOSITION, TYPE OF STATE AND STRUCTURAL ADJUSTMENT

	Adjusting before 1992						Not adjusting before 1992					
	1960	1970	1980	1988	1992	N	1960	1970	1980	1988	1992	N
All	37	51	72	70	70	28	49	64	83	93	90	4
Low inc.	27	39	61	56	56	11	7	16	35	36	23	1*
Med. inc.	36	56	75	72	71	10	-	-	-	-	-	0
High inc.	52	61	84	86	89	7	63	80	99	111	112	3
Strongly Christ.	51	70	87	88	85	14	63	80	99	111	112	3
Strongly Muslim	17	27	47	45	52	8	7	16	35	36	23	1*
Growth-or. State	48	57	87	83	85	7	63	80	99	111	112	3
Equality-or. State	39	50	76	72	71	7	7	16	35	36	23	1*
Other State	30	48	62	62	62	14	-	-	-	-	-	0

* Ethiopia

NOTES

[1]   The author wants to thank Cresantus Biamba, Dinah Mbaga Eurén and Wycliffe Odiwor at the Institute of International Education, Stockholm University, for their contribution to this chapter.

[2]   However, Ethiopia is, according to the definitions used here, a low income country with a large percentage of Muslims, and it had an equality-oriented development

strategy during the 1980s. This country had an extreme decline in its literacy and enrollment rates, a fact that severely affects the results in the categories mentioned.

[3] This does not make the *Marabuts* abstain from enrolling at least some of their children in public schools, Catholic as well as public schools (See, Magassouba, 1985).

[4] Frente de Libertacao de Mocambique (The Liberation Front of Mozambique).

[5] RENAMO (Resistencia Nacional de Mocambique): National Resistance of Mozambique.

REFERENCES CITED

Abededji, A. (1995). "Economic Progress: what Africa needs." In K. Mengisteab and B. K. Logan (eds.). *Beyond Economic Liberalization in Africa: Structural Adjustment and Alternatives*. London: Zed Books.

Azarya, V. (1988). "State–Society Relations: Incorporation and Disengagement." In D. Rotchild and N. Chazan (eds.). *The Precarious Balance: State and Society in Africa*. London: Westview Press.

Bangura, Y. and P. Gibbon (1992). "Adjustment, Authoritarianism and Democracy in Sub-Saharan Africa. An Introduction to Some Conceptual and Empirical Issues." In P. Gibbon, Y. Bangura and A. Ofstad (es.). *Authoritarianism, Democracy and Adjustment. The Politics of Economic Reform in Africa*. Uppsala: The Scandinavian Institute of African Studies.

Barrier, R. E. H. Ngom and A. Tall (1997). *Évaluation du système éducatif sénégalais*. Dakar: Institut national d´études et d´action pour le développement d´éducation.

Bayart, J.-F. (1983a). "Les sociétés africaines face à l'état." *Pouvoirs*, vol. 25.

Bayart, J.-F. (1983b). "La revance des sociétés africaines." *Politique africaine*, vol. 11.

Belloncle, G. (1984). *La question éducative en Afrique noire*. Paris: Karthala.

Bgoya, W. and G. Hydén (1987). "The State and the Crisis in Africa. In Search of a Second Liberation." *Development Dialogue*, Vol 2.

Bienen, H. And J. Waterbury (1989). "The Political Economy of Privatization in Developing Countries." *World Development*, vol. 17.

Blakemore, K. P. (1975). "Resistance to Formal Education in Ghana: Its Implications for the Status of School Leavers." *Comparative Education Review*, vol. 19.

Boone, C. (1989). "State Power and Economic Crisis in Senegal." *Comparative Politics*, pp. 341-359 .

Bratton, M. (1994). "Civil Society and Political Transitions in Africa." In J. W. Harbeson, D. Rothchild and N. Chazan (eds.). *Civil Society and the State in Africa*. London: Boulder.

Bratton, M. and N. de Walle (1997) *Democratic Experiments in Africa. Regime Transitions in Comparative Perspective* London: Cambridge University Press.

BREDA (1995). *Education de base et éducation coranique au Sénégal*. BREDA Series No 10. Dakar: UNESCO.

Bude, U. (1985) *Primary Schools, Local Community and Development in Africa* (Baden- Baden: Nomos.)

Cabral, V. (1988) "Colonizacão e religião: da primeira evangelizacão à colonizacão dos povos da Guiné." *Soronda*, vol. 5.

Cabral, Z. (1992). *Gender e educacão em Mocambique - que oportunidade para a mulher.* Seminar Paper, Licenciatura Programme, IIE-Stockholm/ISP-Maputo,1992.

Callaghy, T. M. (1987). "The State as Lame Leviathan: The Patrimonial Administrative State and Africa." In Z. Ergas (ed.). *The African State in Transition.* London: Macmillan Press.

Callewaert, I. (1996). *Fyere Yaabte: Women Healing Movement in Balanta Society of Guinea-Bissau.* Seminar Paper. Lund: University of Lund, Department of History of Religion.

Carnoy, M. and J. Samoff (1990a). "The State and Social Transformation." In M. Carnoy and J. Samoff (eds.). *Education and Social Transition in the Third World.* New Jersey: Princeton University Press.

Carnoy, M. and J. Samoff (1990b). "Education and the Transition State." In M. Carnoy and J. Samoff (eds.). *Education and Social Transition in the Third World.* New Jersey: Princeton University Press.

Carrilho, F. (1991). *Mocambique face à cooperacao em materia de educacao.* Tese de licenciatura ISP-Maputo/IIEP-Paris, 1991.

Carton, M., P. N'Diaye Diouf and C. Comelian (1994). "Budget Cuts in Education and Training in Senegal. An Analysis of Reactions." In J. Samoff and Taskforce (eds.). *Coping with Crisis. Austerity, Adjustment and Human Resources.* London: Castell/Unesco.

Chazan, N. R. Mortimer, J. Ravenhill and D. Rothchild (1988) *Politics and Society in Contemporary Africa.* London: Macmillan.

Cheru, F. (1996). "New Social Movements: Democratic Struggles and Human Rights in Africa." In J. H. Mittelman. (ed.). *Globalization: Critical Reflections.* London: Bouldner.

Chinapah, V. And H. Daun (1981) *Swedish Missions and Education in the Republic of Zaire: A Description and Diagnosis.* Report No 53 from the Institute of International Educaion (Stockholm: Stockholm University).

Coquery-Vidrovitch, C. (1985). *Afrique noire. Permanences et Ruptures.* Paris.

Colclough, C. (1991). "Structuralism versus Neo-Liberalism: An Introduction." In C. Colclough and J.Manor (eds.). *States or Markets? Neo-Liberalism and the development Policy Debate.* Oxford: Clanderon Press.

Coloquio Internaciona.l (1993) *Sobre expenriencias alternativas no ensino de base* Bissau: Ministry of Education/Unicef.

Coulon, C. (1983). *Les musulmans et le pouvoir en Afrique noire* Paris: Karthala.

Coulon, C. (1993). "Les nouveaux oulémas et le nouveau islamique au Nord-Nigeria." In R. Otayek (ed.). *Le radicalisme islamqiue au Sud du Sahara.* Paris: Karthala.

Daun, H. (1992) *Childhood Learning and Adult Life. The Functions of Indigenous, Islamic and Western Education in an African Context.* Stockholm: Institute of International Education, Stockholm University.

Daun, H. (1998) "Educational Development in Guinea-Bissau in the Light of Liberalization and Islamic Revitalization." In H. Daun and N. Ruiz de Forsberg, *Political-Economic Shifts and Educational Restrucuring. A Comparative Sudy of Education in Guinea-Bissau and Nicaragua.* Report No 108 from the Institute of International Education Stockholm: Stockholm University.

Daun, H. (2000). "Primary Education in Sub-Saharan Africa—a Moral Issue, an Economic Matter, or Both?" *Comparative Education*, vol. 2

De Jong, Joop, T. V. M. (1987). *A Descent into African Psychiatry*. Amsterdam: Royal Tropical Institute.

Desjeux, D. (1987). *Strategies paysannes en Afrique noire*. Paris: Harmattan

Dumont, R. (1986). *Pour l'Afrique j'accuse.* Paris: PLON

Éla, J. -M. (1990) *Quand l'État pénètre en brousse. Les rispostes paysannes à la crise.* Paris: Karthala.

Ergas, Z. (ed) (1987). *The African State in Transition* London: Macmillam Press.

Gibbon, P. (1992). "Strucutral Adjustment and Pressures toward Multipartyism in Sub-Saharan Africa." In P. Gibbon, Y. Bangura and A. Ofstad (eds.). *Authoritarianism, Democracy and Adjustment. The Politics of Economic Reform in Africa.* Uppsala: The Scandinavian Institute of African Studies.

Glickman, H. (1987). "Reflections on State-Centrism as Ideology in Africa." In Z. Ergas (ed.). *The African State in Transition.* London: Macmillan Press.

Golias, M. (1995). "Democracia e Educacao em Mocambique." In B. Mazula (ed.). *Mocambique. Eleicoes, democracia e desenvolvimento.* Maputo: Inter-Africa Group.

Graham-Brown, S. (1991) *Education in the Developing World. Conflict and Crisis.* London: Longman.

Green, R.H. (1991). "Neo-Liberalism and the Political Economy of War: Sub-Saharan Africa as a Case-Study of a Vacuum." In C. Colclough and J. Manor (eds.). (1991). *States or Markets? Neo-Liberalism and the Development Policy Debate.* Oxford: Clanderon Press

Grindal, B. (1972). *Growing Up in Two Worlds: Education and Transition Among the Sisala of Northern Ghana.* New York: Holt, Rinehart & Winston.

Groth, A. J. (1987). "The World Marxism-Leninism: the case of education." *Comparative Education*, vol. 23, no. 3.

Harbeson, J. W. (1994). "Civil Society and Political Renaissance in Africa." In J. W. Harbeson, D. Rothchild and N. Chazan (eds.). *Civil Society and the State in Africa.* London: Boulder.

Hartwell, A. (1994). Education Policy Formation in Anglophone Africa. In D.R. Evans (ed.). *Education Policy Formation in Africa. A Comparative Study of Five Countries.* New York: USAID.

Havnesvik, K.J. et al (1988). *Tanzania, Country Study and Norwegian Aid Review.* University of Bergen Centre for Development Studies. Bergen:

Haynes, J. (1999). "Introduction." In J. Haynes (ed.). *Religion, Globalization and Political Culture in the Third World.* London: Macmillam Press Ltd.

Herbst, J. (1990). "Adjustment of Politics in Africa." *World Development*, vol. 18.

Hermele, K. (1992). "Political Alliances and Nascent Capitalism in Mozambique." In P. Gibbon, Y. Bangura and A. Ofstad (es.). *Authoritarianism, Democracy and Adjustment. The Politics of Economic Reform in Africa*. Uppsala: The Scandinavian Institute of African Studies.

Higgot, R.(1986). "Africa and the New International Division of Labour." In J.Ravenhill (ed.). *Africa in Economic Crisis*. London: MacMillan

Hoerner, J.- M. (1995). *Le tiers-monde. Entre la survie et l informel*. Paris: L'Harmattan.

Hydén, G. (1988). "State and Nation Under Stress." In *Sida: Recovery in Africa. Challenges for Development Cooperation in the 1990s*. Stockholm: Sida.

Johnston, A. (1990). "The Mozambican State and Education." In M. Carnoy and J. Samoff (eds.). *Education and Social Transition in the Third World*. New Jersey: Princeton University Press

Johnston, A. *et al.* (1988). *Education and Economic Crisis - the case of Mozambique and Zambia*. Stockholm: SIDA.

Jones, P. W. (1990). *World Bank Financing of Education. Lending, learning and development*. London: Routledge.

Kabeer, N. and J. Humphrey (1991) "Neo-Liberalism, Gender and the Limits of the Market." In C. Colclough and J.Manor (eds.). *States or Markets? Neo-Liberalism and the development Policy Debate*. Oxford: Clanderon Press.

Kassé, M. (1990). *Sénégal: Cris économique et ajustement structurel*. Ivry-sur-Seine: Editions Nouvelles du Sud.

Kitaev, I. (1999). *Privat education in sub-Saharan Africa: a re-examination of theories and concepts related to its development and finance*. Paris: UNESCO.

Komba, D. 1995: *Declining Enrollment and the Quality of Primary Education in Tanzania Mainland. An analysis of Key data and documents and review of explanatory factors*. A report of A MOE/UNICEF- Sponsored study. Dar es Salaam: University of Dar-es-Salaam, Faculty of Education.,

Krugman, H. (1995). "Overcoming Africa's Crisis: Adjusting Structural Adjustment Towards Sustainable Development in Africa." In K. Mengisteab and B. K. Logan (eds.). *Beyond Economic Liberalization in Africa: Structural Adjustment and Alternatives*. London: Zed Books.

Laitin, D. D. (1986). *Hegemony and Culture: Politics and Religious Change among the Yoruba*. London: University of Chicago Press.

Legum, C. (ed.). (1969). *Africa Handbook*. Harmondsworth: Penguin.

Lind, A. (1988). *Adult Literacy Lessons and Promises: Mozambican Literacy Campaigns 1978-1982*. Stockholm: Institute of International Education, Stockholm University

Lubeck, P.M. (1985). "Islamic Protest under Semi-Industrial Capitalism: 'Yan Tasine' Explained." *Africa*, vol. 55 , nos 3- 4.

Malekela, G.A. (1995). "Equity and Equality in Primary Education." *Papers in Education and Development*. No. 16. Dar-es-Salaam: Faculty of Education.

Marenin, O. (1987) "The Managerial State in Africa: A Conflict Coalition Perspective." In Z. Ergas (ed.). *The African State in Transition* London: Macmillam.

Maseuelier, A. (1999). "Debating Muslims, Disputed Practices: Struggles for the Realization of an Alternative Moral Order in Niger." In J. L. Comaroff and J. Comaroff (eds.). *Civil Society and the Political Imagination in Africa*. Chicago: The University of Chicago Press.

Magassouba, M. (1985). *L'islam au Sénégal. Demain les mollahs?* Paris: Karthala.

Marenin, O. (1987) "The Managerial State in Africa: A Conflict Coalition Perspective." In Z. Ergas (ed.). *The African State in Transition* London: Macmillam.

Mbyae, El Hadj R. (1977). "Les foyers de l enseignement." *Bulletin de l Institut Islamique*, No 1, Dakar.

Mbembe, A. (1988) *Afriques indociles. Christianisme, pouvoir et Etat en société postcoloniale.* Paris: Karthala.

Mbussa, E. .L. and R, N, Mlelwa (1991). *The Provision of Income Safety nets for the Poor and Vulnerable During the Adjustment.* Paper for the Social Sector Review. Ministry of Planning, Dar es Salaam.

McDowell, D. (1980) "The Impact of the National Policy on Indigenous Education in Nigeria", *International Review of Education*, vol. XXVI.

Mengisteav, K. (1995) "A Partnership of the State and the Market in African Development. What Is an Appropriate Strategy Mix?" In K. Mengisteab and B. K. Logan (eds.). *Beyond Economic Liberalization in Africa: Structural Adjustment and Alternatives.* London: Zed Books.

MINEC (1973). *Situation économique du Sénégal*, 1973. Dakar: Ministry of Economy and Finance.

MINEC (1979). *Situation économique du Sénégal*, 1979. Dakar: Ministry of Economy and Finance.

MINEC (1987). *Situation économique du Sénégal*, 1987. Dakar: Ministry of Economy and Finance.

MINEC (1997). *Situation Économique du Sénégal* 1997. Dakar: Ministry of Economy and Finance.

MINECM (1990a) Plano triennal de investimento publico, 1991-93. Vol I. *Comissao Nacional de Plano*, Maputo 1991.

MINECM (1990b).Plano triennal de investimento publico 1990-92. Vol II. Educacao. *Comissao Nacional de Plano.* Maputo: Ministry of Finance

MINED (1962). *Renseignements statistiques sur la situation de l enseignement du 1er degré et de l enseignement secondaire.* Dakar: Ministry of Education

MINED (1981). Communication de M. le Ministre de l Education Nationale sur la réorganisation des écoles coranique en conseil interministeriel. Dakar: Ministry of Education.

MINED (1986). *L école nouvelle.* Dakar: Ministry of Education.

MINED (1998). *Statistiques scolaires, 1998.* Dakar: Ministry of Education

MINEDU (1990a). *A Educacao em Mocambique. Problemas e Perspectivas.* Maputo, 1990

MINEDU (1990b). Taxas de admissao bruta, de admissao aparante aos 7 anos e taxa bruta e liquidade escolarizacao. Maputo 1990

MINEDU (1994). Plano director para a educacão básica em Mocambique. Maputo: Ministry of Education.

MINEDU (1998). *Plano estatégico da educacão (Mocambique)*. Maputo: Ministry of Education

MINEDUC (1995). Educational Stastistics, Cameroon. Douala: Ministry of Education.

MoE (1992). The Tanzanian Education System for the 21st Century. Report of the Task Force. Dar es Salaam: Ministry of Education, Culture and Science.

MoE (1997). Basic Education Statistics in Tanzania. Dar es Salaam: Ministry of Education, Culture and Science.

MoE (1998). *Tanzania Education System*. Dar es salaam: Ministry of Education, Culture and Science.

Mosley, P., J. Harrigan and J. Toye (1991). *Aid and Power. The World Bank & Policy-based Lending. Vol 1*. London: Routledge

Mwanza, M. (1993): "Structural Adjustment Programs in SADC: Experiences and Lessons from Malawi, Tanzania, Zambia and Zimbabwe." *In: Southern African Political economy series*

Munene, J. C. (1995). "Structural adjustment, labour commitment and cooperation in the Ugandan service sector." In K. Mengisteab and B. K. Logan (eds.). *Beyond Economic Liberalization in Africa: Structural Adjustment and Alternatives*. London: Zed Books.

Ndiaye, M. (1985). *L'enseignement arabo-islamique au Sénégal*. Istanbul: Centre de recherches sur l'histoire, l'art et culture islamique.

Ndir, B. (1990). Etude preliminaire des statistiques SUCI pour les projections de l emploi moderne. Dakar: Ministry of Economy and Finance.

New Africa Year Book 1997/98. Johannesburg: ANC.

Nhavoto, A. (1991). *Despesas e custos de ensino em Mocambique: A busca duma racionalidade*. Tese de licenciatura, IIEP/Unesco, Paris

Nicolas, G. (1981) *Dynamiques de l'islam au sud du Sahara*. Paris: Publications Orientalistes de France.

Nouvel Horizon (1999). February, 1999.

Nyang, S.S. (1993). Islamic revivalism in West Africa: Historical perspectives and recent development. In J.K. Olupona and S. S. Nyang (eds.). *Religious Plurality in Africa: Essays in Honour of John S. Mbiti*. New York: Mouton de Gruyter.

Ogbu, O.M. and M. Gallagher. (1991). "On Public Expenditures and Delivery of Education in Sub- Saharan Africa." *Comparative Education Review*, vol. 35 , no. 2.

Omari, I. W. (1994). Cost Sharing and Student Loans in Higher Education in Tranzania. In *Papers in Education and Development*, vol. 15. Dar es Salaam: University of Dar es Salaam, Facultry of Education.

Omari, I. W. et al (1983). *Universal Primary Education in Tanzania*. Ottawa: IDRC.

Omari, I. W. and H. J. Mosha (1987). *The quality of Primary Education in Tanzania*. Nairobi, Mangraphics.

Omari, I. W., S. Sumra and R. Levine (1994). Availability, Quality and Utilisation of Social Services: Preliminary Results from Focused Area Studies Technique. Paper on the World Bank Workshop "Investing in Human Capital," Arusha, Tanzania.

Oni, B. (1988) "Education and Alternative Avenues of Mobility. A Nigerian Study." *Comparative Education Review*, vol. 32.

Orivel, F. and C. Shaw (1994). Education Policy Formation in Francophone Sub-Saharan Africa. In D.R. Evans (ed.). *Education Policy Formation in Africa. A Comparative Study of Five Countries*. New York: USAID.

Palme, M. (1991) *Repetition and drop-out in Mozambique's primary schools*. Research report Stockholm-Maputo: School of Education/SIDA-INDE.

Parpart, J. P. (1988) "Women and the State in Africa." In D. Rotchild and N. Chazan (eds.). *The Precarious Balance: State and Society in Africa*. London: Westview Press

Passos, A. (1992). *Disparidades Regionais no EP1 em Mocambique*. Seminar Paper, Licenciatura Programme, IIE-Stockholm/ISP-Maputo, 1992

Peil, M. (1990). "Intergenerational Mobility Through Education: Nigeria, Sierra Leone and Zimbabwe." *International Journal of Educational Development*, vol. 10.

Psacharopoulos, G. (1988). The Planning of Education: Where Do We Stand? *Comparative Education Review*, vol. 30.

Ranger, T. O. (1986). "Religious Movements and Politics in Sub-Saharan Africa." in *African Studies Review*, vol. 19.

Ravenhill, J. (1986) "Africa's Continuing Crisis: The Elusiveness of Development." In J.Ravenhill (ed.). *Africa in Economic Crisis*. London: MacMillan.

Reimers, F. and L. Tiburcio (1993) *Education, Adjustment and Reconstruction: Options for Change*. A Unesco Discussion Paper. Paris: Unesco.

Rideout, W.M. and M. Bagayoko (1994). "Education Policy Formation in Senegal. Evolutionary Not Revolutionary." In *USAID: Education Policy Formation in Africa. A Comparative Study of Five Countries*. Technical paper no 12. New York: USAID

Rodrik, D. (1998). *Trade Policy and Economic Performance in Sub-Saharan Africa*. Harvard: Harvard University.

Rothchild, D. and L. Lawson (1994) "The Interactions Betweeen State and Civil Society in Africa: From Deadlock to New Routines." In J. W. Harbeson, D. Rothchild and N. Chazan (eds.). *Civil Society and the State in Africa*. London: Boulder.

Saine, A. S. M. (1995) "Democracy in Africa: Constraints and Prospects." In K. Mengisteab and B. K. Logan (eds.). *Beyond Economic Liberalization in Africa: Structural Adjustment and Alternatives*. London: Zed Books.

Samoff, J. (1990). "The Politics of Privatization in Tanzania." *International Journal of Educational Development*, vol. 10, no. 1.

Samoff, J. (1996). "Limiting Horizons. The World Bank Priorities and Strategies for Education." Paper presented at the Annual Conference of the Comparative and International Education Society, Williamsburg, Virginia, 6-10 March 1996

Samoff, J. and S. Sumra. (1994). "From Planning to Marketing: Making Education and Training Policy in Tanzania." In J. Samoff and Taskforce (eds.). *Coping with Crisis. Austerity, Adjustment and Human Resources.* London: Castell/Unesco.

Sanneh, L. (1983) *West African Chrisianity. The Religious Impact.* London: C. Hurst & Co.

Senghor, L. (1971). *Liberté 2. Nation et voie africaine du socialisme.* Paris: Editions du Seuil.

Senghor, L. (1976). *Pour une société socialiste et démocratique.* Paris: Editions du Seuil.

Shaw, T. (1985) *Towards a Political Economy for Africa* (London: Macmillan).

Shayo, F. I. , D. A. Kiwara and G. Makusi.(1995). "Structural Adjustment in a Socialist Country. A case of Tanzania; Structural Adjustment Programmes in the SADC. Experience and Lessons from Malawi, Tanzania, Zambia. In M. A. Mwanza (ed.). Southern Africa Political Economy

SNE (1982). *Sistema novo do ensino.* Maputo: Ministry of Education.

Streeten, P. (1987). "Structural Adjustment: A Survery of the Issus and Options.". *World Development*, vol. 15, no. 12.

Sumra, A.S. (1995). "Enrollment Trends in Education in Tanzania." Paper presented to "Education Conference on Quality" in Arusha, March 1997.

Sylla, A. (1985). *L école future, pour qui?* Dakar: Sankoré.

Tanzania: "Unsurpassed Africa" (1997). *Newsweek, Special Advertising Section*, June, 1997.

Tibaijuka, A. (1995). "The social Economic Dimension; Social Effects of Adjustment Programmes." In W.G. Ström (Ed.). *Changes in Tanzania (1980-1994). Political and Economic Reforms as Observed by Four Tanzanian Scholars.* Stockholm: Sida.

Trimingham, J. S, (1968) *The Influence of Islam Upon Africa* (London: Longmans).

Tripp, A. M. (1994). "Rethinking Civil Society: Gender Implications in Contemporary Tanzania." In J. W. Harbeson, D. Rothchild and N. Chazan (eds.). *Civil Society and the State in Africa.* London: Boulder.

UNDP (1995). *Human Development Report 1995.* New York: Oxford University Press.

UNESCO (1993). *Regional Seminars of Experts on Quranic Schools and Their Roles in the Universalization and Renewal of Basic Education.* Karthoum/Paris: The Sudanese National Committee/Unesco

UNESCO (1995) *World Education Report 1995.* Paris: Unesco.

UNHCR (1991). Programme and Technical Support Section. Mozambique, Malawi and Zimbabwe. Maputo 1991

UNICEF (1985). *Un sénégalais sur deux. Analyse de situation de l enfance.* Dakar: Unicef.

Van de Walle, N. (1989). "Privatization in Developing Countries: A Review of the Issues.". *World Development*, vol. 17, no. 5.

Van Dijk, R. (1999). Pentecostalism, Gerontocratic Rule and Democratization in Malawi: the Changing Position of the Young in Political Culture. In J. Haynes (ed.). *Religion, Globalization and Political Culture in the Third World.* London: Macmillam Press Ltd.

Vengroff, R. and L.Creevy (1997). "Senegal: The Evolution of a Quasi Democracy.". In J. F. and D.E. Gardinier (eds.). *Political Reform in Francophone Africa.* London: Westview Press

Villalón, L.A. (1995). *Islamic Society and State Power in Senegal. Disciples and Citizens in Fatick*. Cambridge: Cambridge University Press.

Wilson, E.J. (1989). "Strategies of State Control of the Economy. Nationalization and Indigenization in Africa.". *Comparative Politics*, vol. 1989.

World Bank (1979) *World Development Report 1979*. Washington, D.C.: World Bank.

World Bank (1980) *World Development Report 1980*. Washington, D.C.: World Bank.

World Bank (1981) *World Development Report 1981*. Washington, D.C.: World Bank.

World Bank (1984) *Toward Sustained Development in Sub-Saharan Africa*. Washington, D.C.: World Bank.

World Bank (1986) *World Development Report 1986*. Washington, D.C.: World Bank.

World Bank (1987) *Education Policies for Sub-Saharan Africa: Adjustment, Revitalization and Expansion* Report No 6934. Washington, D.C.: World Bank.

World Bank (1989) *Sub-Saharan Africa. From Crisis to Sustainable Growth*. Washington, D.C.: World Bank.

World Bank (1990a) World Development Report 1990. Washington, D.C.: World Bank.

World Bank (1990b). *Staff appraisal report. Mozambique. Second Education Project*. Washington, D.C.: World Bank.

World Bank (1991a) *World Development Report 1991*. Washington, D.C.: World Bank.

World Bank (1991b). *Improving the Quality of Primary Education in Developing Countries*. Washington DC: World Bank.

World Bank (1992) *World Development Report 1992*. Washington, D.C.: World Bank.

World Bank (1993) *World Development Report 1993*. Washington, D.C.: World Bank.

World Bank (1994) *World Development Report 1994*. Washington, D.C.: World Bank.

World Bank (1995a) *World Development Report 1995* . Washington, D.C.: World Bank.

World Bank (1995b). *The Tanzania Social Sector Review*. Washington, D.C.: World Bank.

World Bank (1995c). *The Cameroon Social Sector Review*. Washington, D.C.: World Bank.

World Bank (1999) *World Development Report 1999*. Washington: World Bank.

Yoloye, E. A. (1986) "The Relevance of Educational Content to National Needs in Africa." *International Review of Education*, vol. 32.

Young, C. (1988). "The African Colonial State and Its Colonial Legacy." In D. Rotchild and N. Chazan (eds.). *The Precarious Balance: State and Society in Africa*. London: Westview Press.

Zucula, C. (1991). *Socio-Cultural aspects of School Attendance of Girls at Primary Level in Mozambique*. Maputo: Unicef.

CHAPTER 10

Latin America

The New Dependency and Educational Reform

MARTIN CARNOY

INTRODUCTION

With the economic crisis, Latin American countries implemented SAPs and restructured their education systems. Decentralization, privatization and introduction of choice have been principal elements of educational reforms in Latin America during the past two decades. This has resulted in a segmentation of the education systems and differential access to quality education.

BACKGROUND

After a long period of rapid import-substitution growth, Latin America entered a decade of economic crisis in the 1980s. The crisis was precipitated by over-borrowing during the high–inflation oil-boom 1970s and the restrictive monetary policies of the U.S. Federal Reserve beginning in 1980. Most Latin American countries in the early 1980s found themselves in a double bind of falling price for their commodity exports and a sudden rise in interest payments on foreign debt. This resulted in huge foreign account deficits, rising interest rates at home, falling exports, and domestic economic crisis. In some countries that tried to finance domestic public deficits through printing money, it also eventually led to hyperinflation (Argentina and Brazil, for example). The import- substitution development process, so successful in industrializing the larger economies, such as Argentina, Brazil, Chile, Colombia, Mexico, Peru, and Venezuela, in the 1950s, 1960s, and early 1970s, simply ground to a halt.

All but a few countries in the region, notably Chile, Colombia, Uruguay, and parts of the English-speaking Caribbean had negative or very low per capita growth rates over the twelve years, 1980-1992 (table 10.1). Ironically, because of the flow of payments on its debt, Latin America in the 1980s became a net capital exporter to the developed countries even as it went into this long recession.

The crisis could not have come at a worse time for the region. Just as Latin America's economy went into a deep and long recession, the world economy entered a period of accelerated globalization and technological and organizational transformation. Economic competition among nations for markets intensified in the midst of a widespread information and communications revolution, Higher productivity and economic growth became increasingly dependent on knowledge and information applied to production, and such knowledge became increasingly science-based. This was not an entirely new phenomenon, since knowledge has always been a key factor in the organization and fostering of economic growth. But as economies became more complex, as consumption worldwide became more varied and competition increased, knowledge and information became more critical to the production and realization process.

Latin American countries, like those elsewhere in the world, had to adjust to these major changes. However, under the conditions of the debt crisis, this was difficult. Their economies were suffering a drain on capital and negative rates of economic growth in the 1980s, and governments were ill-equipped and lacked sufficient resources to improve infrastructure, support private sector efforts to export and develop new products and processes or attract foreign investment on reasonable terms.

Further, the structural adjustment process imposed by the IMF and the principal Latin American debt holders, especially the United States, was based on a "dominant view" of how economies in crisis should reorganize to resume growth. This view saw the public sector as the most important impediment to rapid economic growth. Hence, it focused on reducing public sector spending rather than on creating a more efficient public administration capable of effective (and socially fair) collection of taxes and investment of public resources. When implemented, then, structural adjustment loans (SALs) were conditioned on the reduction of public sector spending and of government regulation. Not surprisingly, SALs increased the already highly unequal income distribution in Latin America, which made underlying political conditions for structural change more difficult. As table 10.1 indicates, many countries in the region took multiple structural adjustment loans, Mexico at the top of the list.

Table 10.2 presents another way of understanding just how drastic public spending reduction was in Latin America in the 1980s recession. Only a small minority of countries, Brazil, Uruguay, and Venezuela among them, increased their public spending as much or more than GNP growth in the 1980s. Most, including Argentina, Bolivia, Chile, Colombia, Costa Rica, Mexico, and Peru, increased their spending much less than GNP growth. Chile's reduction is particularly noteworthy because it led the way in voluntarily pursuing an aggressive monetarist approach to development, reducing public spending rapidly as its economy was expanding. Argentina, Bolivia, Dominican Republic, El Salvador, Peru, and others did the same. The reduction of public sector spending generally continued into the 1990s, although at a slower rate. First and foremost, almost all countries began selling off their state enterprises in the 1980s and 1990s, and decentralized a number of other central state spending responsibilities, usually with (declining) bloc grants for social services to states or provinces.

Latin American regimes, again led by Chile during the military dictatorship, also implemented a broader "restructuring" policy. They reduced direct subsidies to certain sectors, reduced tariff protection for domestic production, and promoted exports, particularly of new kinds of agricultural and industrial products, from flowers, fish, and wine in Chile, to automobiles in Brazil and Mexico.

In the early 1990s, some major economies, such as Argentina, Brazil, Peru, and to a lesser extent, Mexico, greatly improved their economic performance, mainly for two reasons. First, debt restructuring in the 1980s (which included foreign banks and governments forgiving much of the outstanding Latin American loans) greatly reduced Latin American indebtedness. When combined with lower real interest rates worldwide, outflows of capital from Latin America were sharply reduced. Second, as Latin America began to recover, foreign capital began to flow back into the region. This improvement continued until the 1998 Asian economic crisis, when Brazilian capital flows again reversed, and the IMF again had to step in to halt the spread of the Asian crisis to Latin America.

There is some evidence that this "dominant" view of increasing economic growth by restructuring Latin American economies through reduction of public spending and public intervention and making Latin American economies more "appealing" to private foreign investors works, at least to increase total production. We estimated annual growth of gross product in 1990-1995 as a function of the growth of public expenditures in 1980-1990 (columns 3 and 4 of table 10.2). We found that the relationship was negative, as the dominant view predicts that is, the greater the decline in the rate of public spending in the 1980s, the higher the growth of gross product in the 1990s. But the coefficient of public spending growth is *not* statistically significant, and is not large. For every one percent annual rate of decrease in public spending, the rate of growth of gross product increased by about one-third percent.

It could be argued that Latin American countries had little choice in restructuring their economies. Heavily in debt, it may have been wise to subject themselves to IMF conditions, refinance their debt, and stem their capital outflows. The alternative was to self-destruct economically (Nicaragua is an unusual case because of the U.S.-financed war it endured in the 1980s, but it does provide a glimpse of what can happen to a small economy that does not "cooperate" with globalization; Cuba is another example).

On the other hand, the price of restructuring is also high. In Argentina, for example, even with almost four percent per capita growth in the early 1990s, and even more rapid growth in 1996-1998 (about 5.5 percent per capita growth), privatization of public industries raised unemployment rates into the 15-20 percent range in 1995-97. Now that the new financial crisis has hit, unemployment has shot up again. Similarly in

TABLE 10.1 LATIN AMERICA: ECONOMIC GROWTH, GROWTH OF PUBLIC SPENDING, AND NUMBER OF STRUCTURAL ADJUSTMENT LOANS IN 1980S, 1980–1995 (PERCENT ANNUAL GROWTH)

Country	Economic Growth, Per Capita GNP 1980-92 (%)	Economic Growth, Per Capita GNP 1985-92 (%)	Economic Growth, Per Capita GNP 1990-95 (%)	Growth of Public Expenditures 1980-90(%)	Number of Structural Adjust. Loans (SAL)
Argentina	-0.7	1.4	3.7	-3.8	6
Barbados	1.4	1.1	-0.5	1.0	0
Belize	2.1	5.4	3.1	1.0	0
Brazil	-0.8	-0.5	1.2	2.0	3
Bolivia	-1.7	-0.1	1.4	-2.4	3
Chile	2.7	5.2	5.8	-2.7	3
Colombia	1.4	2.3	2.7	1.4	4
Costa Rica	0	1.8	1.3	-0.3	3
Dom Rep.	-0.1	0.4	2.1	-3.5	0
Ecuador	-0.1	0.1	1.3	0.6	2
El Savador	-0.7	0.7	4.1	-4.4	1
Guatemala	-1.4	0.4	1.4	-1.5	0
Guyana	-2.2	-0.4	6	-0.3	2
Haiti	-3.3	-3.7	-5.4	-2.3	0
Honduras	-0.7	0.2	0.6	-1.2	3
Jamaica	0.9	2.5	0	0.4	10
Mexico	-0.1	0.1	-1.2	0.3	13
Nicaragua	-3.5	-4.4	-1.4	2.0	0
Panama	-0.1	-0.6	3.1	-0.9	2
Paraguay	-0.4	0.4	0.5	-0.4	0
Peru	-2.8	-3.3	3.8	-4.8	0
Suriname	-5	0.3	0.3	3.3	0
Trinidad/Tobago	-2.6	-2.4	0.1	0.9	1
Uruguay	0.1	3.4	2.9	2.3	4
Venezuela	-0.5	1.8	0.9	1.8	5

Source: *United Nations Statistical Yearbook, 1998.*

TABLE 10.2 LATIN AMERICA: ECONOMIC GROWTH AND PUBLIC SPENDING GROWTH, 1980–1992

Country	Annual Growth of Gross Product, 1980-92 (%)	Annual Growth of Gross Product, 1990-95 (%)	Annual Growth of Public Expenditures, 1980-90 (%)
Argentina	0.7	4.9	-3.8
Barbados	1.7	0	1.0
Belize	4.7	5.8	1.0
Brazil	1.2	2.7	2.0
Bolivia	0.4	3.8	-2.4
Chile	4.4	7.4	-2.7
Colombia	3.3	4.4	1.4
Costa Rica	2.8	4.8	-0.3
Dom Rep.	2.1	4.1	-3.5
Ecuador	2.4	3.5	0.6
El Salvador	0.8	6.3	-4.4
Guatemala	1.5	4.3	-1.5
Guyana	-1.7	7.0	-0.3
Haiti	-1.3	-3.4	-2.3
Honduras	2.5	3.7	-1.2
Jamaica	1.9	0.9	0.4
Mexico	2.2	0.6	0.3
Nicaragua	-0.6	1.8	2.0
Panama	2	5.0	-0.9
Paraguay	2.8	3.2	-0.4
Peru	-0.6	5.5	-4.8
Suriname	-3.8	1.2	3.3
Trinidad/ Tobago	-1.3	1.5	0.9
Uruguay	0.7	3.5	2.3
Venezuela	2.1	3.2	1.8

Source: *United Nations Statistical Yearbook, 1998*

Brazil and Mexico, two other economic giants, unemployment and poverty remain high despite "recovery" from the 1980s downturn. Chile's rapid rate of economic growth since the mid-1980s has contributed to a reduction in the poverty rate in the 1990s. But income distribution in Chile remains among the most unequal in Latin America, and Latin American income distribution as a whole is probably the most unequal of any region in the world. Restructuring appears to have contributed to this inequality.

ECONOMIC CRISIS AND EDUCATIONAL CHANGE

The economic crisis plus the conditions placed on SALs also made it difficult to expand and improve education in Latin America. Latin America in the 1980s had to confront the information revolution with declining capacity to increase its human capital base. Probably because of continued political pressure during the crisis to increase access to secondary education, these conditions in the 1980s had their greatest negative impact on the quality of education rather than the quantity.

Despite cuts in public spending on social services, access to formal education in the region continued to expand in the 1980s and 1990s, albeit more slowly than in the 1970s. Such expansion continued to be particularly favorable to Latin America's young women. Pre-primary education reached well over 40 percent of the age cohort in 1996, the highest ratio of any developing region, up from 21 percent in 1980. Enrollment in primary education also rose, so that almost all countries have essentially universal primary enrollment. Secondary gross enrollment increased (from 45 percent in 1980) to include about 56 percent of the age cohort and over 60 percent of young women. Even so, net enrollment rates at the secondary level vary greatly among countries, from the mid-teen percent in some Central American countries and Brazil to the low twenty percent in Bolivia, Dominican Republic, and Venezuela, to the 55-60 percent level in the Southern Cone, and about 70 percent in much of the English- speaking Caribbean and Cuba (Appendix 10.1). Generally, young women have higher enrollment rates than men in secondary schools, and, in recent years, in many countries' universities as well, representing 50 percent or more of the enroll-ment at those two levels (UNESCO 1995).

Although university enrollment rose more slowly than in other regions, Latin American remained a leader among developing countries (although behind the Asian NICs), with about twenty percent of the age cohort enrolled. Again, the proportion varies greatly from country to country. In both the secondary and tertiary levels, Latin America leads the developing world in the percentage of young women enrolled and in the percent of women university graduates. The number of teachers in the region increased rapidly in the 1980s: by 1990, the number of teachers per hundred adult population was as high as in North America. The caveat is that there were many more children per hundred adult population in Latin America than in other regions.

EDUCATIONAL QUALITY

Continued access gains to more schooling in the 1980s did little to improve the quality of education in the region. Repetition in and dropout from basic and secondary education continue to be a serious problem, even accentuated in many countries as education expanded under conditions of fiscal austerity (World Bank, 1993), and student achievement remained low. For example, in the late 1980s, the International Educational Assessment (IEA) studied reading literacy among nine year-olds in twenty-seven of the world's countries, including Venezuela and Trinidad and Tobago. Pupils in Trinidad and Tobago did well, scoring slightly more than one-half a standard deviation below many European countries. But Venezuelan pupils scored 1.5 standard deviations below their European counterparts and were the lowest performers among the twenty-seven countries participating (World Bank 1993). In the early 1990s, two cities in Brazil (Sao Paulo and Fortaleza) participated in the International Assessment of Educational Progress (IAEP) Test of Mathematics and Science. On this test, the Brazilian cities scored far below pupils from the developed countries and the Asian NICs. The top five pecent of children in Brazil scored no higher than the average score in countries such as Korea, Taiwan, Switzerland, the (former) Soviet Union, Hungary, and France.

Another pilot study in the early 1990s of science and mathematics achievement among thirteen year-old students suggests that of five Latin American countries (Argentina, Colombia, Costa Rica, Dominican Republic, and Venezuela, only Costa Rican students achieve average scores that are comparable with national averages in the low/mid-range of developed and Asian NIC countries (the United States and Thailand). Pupils in the other four LAC countries score far below except for those pupils in elite private schools, a group that corresponds to less than five percent of the national pupil population. This is confirmed by a recent study of fourth graders' performance in seven LAC countries (OREALC 1994). According to that study, Costa Rican students perform far better in math and language than those in Bolivia, Ecuador, and the Dominican Republic, somewhat better than those in Argentina and Chile, and about as well as those in Venezuela (OREALC 1994). Surveys in other countries such as Uruguay also suggest that the great majority of students (those who are not in elite private schools) are learning only a small fraction of the basic minimum expected by the schools (Rama, 1992).

The Distribution of Educational Quality

These data indicate that not only is the level of educational quality in Latin America low by developed country standards, but that there is considerable inequality both *among* Latin America's national educational systems and *within* countries. In the seven countries surveyed by ORLEAC researchers in the early 1990s, low SES pupils averaged forty-four percent on a test of mathematics, and high SES pupils scored fifty-nine percent. In a test of language, the corresponding scores were forty-eight percent and seventy-two percent. These results reflect not only the home environment, but the high variation in school quality within countries. The system of education can be characterized as highly segmented. Even though some students continue to be excluded from basic education altogether, especially in the low income countries of the region, the segmentation of the 1990s is mainly one of *differential access to quality education.* The mass of pupils generally go to very low quality schools, and the poor are especially excluded from anything approaching high quality education.

The one exception to this rule seems to be Cuba. In a recently completed survey of third and fourth graders in fifteen Latin American countries, OREALC researchers found that Cuban children scored one standard deviation higher than children in the next highest performing countries—Argentina, Chile, and Brazil, and two standard deviations higher than students in low-income countries such as Honduras (OREALC 1999). Although Cuban third and fourth graders in rural schools scored slightly lower than those in urban schools, they, too, performed at about one standard deviation higher than children in Chilean and Argentine *urban* schools. The fact that Cuba, a relatively poor country compared to the three countries with the next highest performance levels, continues to provide such high quality education raises serious issues about the nature of the educational effort in the rest of the region.

As important, there is some evidence that even in the best of Latin America's education systems, quality stagnated or may have even declined in the 1980s. Promotion rates in Costa Rican schools fell substantially, especially at the secondary level. According to data from the Ministry of Education, after reaching highs of 88 percent promotion rates in the first cycle of primary school and 68 percent promotion in secondary school (third cycle) in 1981, these rates fell to 80 percent and 52 percent, respectively, by 1989 (MINEP 1991).

Typology of Educational Reform

Changes in the world economy in the late 1970s and 1980s forced most Latin American countries to find ways to reduce public spending—particularly central government public spending—on education and training while trying to increase enrollment, as we showed. This provoked reforms intended mainly to cut central government public sector budgets—these can be called *"finance-driven reforms."* In practice, the reforms reduced the total public and private resources available for financing education and training. But, at the same time, these reforms (and other, less global efforts) were intended to organize the production of educational achievement and work skills in new, more productive ways, mainly with the objective of producing higher quality human capital to make Latin American countries more "competitive" in the world economy. That aspect of the reforms (where it appeared) can be considered as *"competitiveness-driven."* Finally, some reforms attempted to improve educa-tion's important political role as a source of social mobility and social equalization. These can be called *"equity-driven reforms."* No educational reform in this period can be classified in only one of these categories, since all, at least rhetorically, claimed that they were aimed at producing higher quality education equitably at lower public resource cost. However, as this typology suggests, the outcomes of reforms can best be understood by understanding their principal purpose (as revealed by their princi-pal practice), rhetoric notwithstanding.

The lesson of this reform process, as it now proceeds toward the end of the 1990s is that finance-driven reforms in the 1980s reduced the cost of education to the cen-tral government in the short run and did bring forth new local public and private resources, but also may have reduced educational quality and increased the inequal-ity of educational quality (see Prawda 1993). Primary education in the lowest capac-ity regions and schools was least able to adapt, either financially or technically, to the reduction of public financing and technical assistance from the central government. The quality of secondary education may have suffered even more in such financially reforms, reducing mobility for low-income pupils and increasing educational inequal-ity.

Indeed, the experience of the 1980s and the first half of the 1990s suggest that even when finance-driven reforms contained apparent elements of competitiveness-driven reform, namely attempts at reducing educational bureaucracy and introducing market incentives, quality did not improve until the *capacity* of schools and adminis-trative districts to improve quality were increased. The main focus of the reform process had to change from reducing the central government's financial role to enhancing pupil performance, particularly among the mass of low-income pupils in basic education. Increasing capacity has required more central government resources going to education, highly focused programs aimed at improving teacher pre-service training, the provision of in-service training for teachers and administrators, curricu-lum development, establishing higher standards, and installing regional or national evaluation systems for assessing pupil (and school) performance—all this requiring central or regional government attention and intervention.

A good example of a finance-driven reform *without* any major accompanying com-petitiveness-driven reform took place in Costa Rica. The process of reform is inter-esting because of the highly democratic context of Costa Rican society. The Costa Rican case had its own peculiarities, but illustrates the pitfalls of attempting to reduce the costs of education by posing teachers as the barrier to educational change, and attempting to maintain educational quality while ignoring the declining capacity of the educational system to meet standards. The ultimate result in Costa Rica of such oppositional politics was that one of Latin America's best educational systems prob-ably deteriorated, especially at the secondary level.

DECENTRALIZATION AND PRIVATIZATION

Latin American educational reforms in the 1980s and 1990s focused mainly on decentralizing responsibility for educational decision-making and for financing education. The reforms were intended to increase resources for education coming from local sources, both public and private, and to improve the quality of education by reducing centralized bureaucracies and placing more responsibility for schools in the hands of local education users and providers. The reforms did not raise the quality of education and appeared to increase inequality in educational delivery. Low-income students generally suffered most from the decentralization process, largely because decentralization was more concerned with lowering spending by the central government rather than improving educational quality.

The Lessons of Decentralization

The most popular type of reform in the region in the 1980s and the early 1990s has been the attempt to reduce central government spending on education by means of a decentralization, primarily of educational decision-making (management) but, to a lesser extent, also of educational finance. This type of reform was implemented in several Latin American countries in the 1980s (most forcefully in Argentina and Chile, but also in 1989 in Colombia)[1], and is now spreading almost everywhere else (for example, El Salvador, Mexico, Nicaragua, and Peru). Brazil has not needed a decentralization reform because its primary and secondary school systems have always been decentralized both in terms of decision-making and financially.

As outlined above, the primary purpose of most of such decentralization reforms, while certainly intended to reduce the size of the central government educational bureaucracy and to shift educational management to states and municipalities, was driven mainly by the desire to reduce central government financial responsibility for primary and secondary education. The experience with this finance- driven version of decentralization strongly suggests that decentralization with reduced financial and technical assistance from the central government to local- and state-run schools achieves financial goals but lowers educational quality, especially for the poor. Countries that have gone through that experience (Argentina, Chile and, in a certain historical sense, Brazil) are now attempting to expand central and state government help to municipalities and, in Chile's case, recentralizing educational improvement efforts. But these efforts have been curtailed at the end of the 1990s because of the new economic difficulties resulting from the Asian financial crisis.

Decentralization has been cast as a competitiveness-driven reform—one that increases productivity in education and hence contributes significantly to improving the quality of a nation's human resources—largely through bringing educational decision- making closer to parents' needs and giving local authorities greater educational decision- making autonomy. By increasing control over curriculum and teaching methods to local communities and the teachers and principals of the schools themselves, it is assumed that the result will be a better fit between educational methods and the clientele served, as well as greater accountability for educational results. If the local educational authorities see themselves and are seen as responsible for educational delivery, reformers reason, educational quality will improve.[2]

Yet, most of the decentralization reforms in Latin America in the 1980s followed some version of a "finance-driven" pattern. "Control" of schools was decentralized to the provincial or municipal level with block grants for education to the local authorities, but with increased pressure on them to raise money locally as central government funds were cut. In Argentina and Chile, two countries that undertook major decentralization reforms in the 1980s, overall real spending on education from the central government fell, although in the Chilean case, public spending per pupil on primary education rose and then only declined in the second half of the decade (World Bank 1993).

The Latin American experience suggests that the finance-driven version of decentralization may evoke educational improvement at the local level, but its positive effects are more than offset if educational spending and central government technical expertise are reduced (or in the Brazilian case, not forthcoming); that is, if the reform is finance-driven. Inequality of educational outcomes also increases (in Brazil, remains high) because poor localities have less of their own financial, technical/human resources to invest in education than better off localities. For decentralization to increase quality and reduce inequality, the decentralization reform needs to be specifically competitiveness–and equality-driven. In effect, this means continued central government commitment to providing the resources required to raise quality throughout the system and especially in its weakest components.

Some countries have already understood that finance-driven reforms do not work to increase school quality, but that a direct emphasis on higher achievement and the resources required to produce it, do increase school quality. As the region democratized and economic growth rates in the late 1980s and 1990s intensified, efforts to improve educational quality also changed. In the context of political democratization and improved economic performance, the Chilean central government in the 1990s, for example, shifted reform gears into higher Ministry spending per pupil and specifically focus on schools that performed poorly in terms of productivity and equality enhancement. Although not as systematically as in Chile, Argentina's central and state Ministries also began to take a more active role in pushing productivity-enhancing programs and spending more. In Brazil's long decentralized system, competitiveness–and equality-driven reforms have begun at the state and municipal levels. Reforms in other countries, such as Colombia shifted gears quickly, but for a different reason. Without waiting to learn the lessons of the finance-driven educational reform, municipalities and teachers changed the decentralization reform to

make it more competitiveness– and equality-driven. Yet, reformers in other countries, such as Mexico and El Salvador, are still hoping that finance-driven decentralization will be the mechanism to improve schooling, save public resources, or
both.

THE CHILEAN DECENTRALIZATION/PRIVATIZATION REFORM

The "model" case of a privatization reform was implemented in Chile in 1981, when
the central government turned primary and secondary education over to the municipalities and financed the formation of private schools through a nationwide voucher plan.[3] Thus, most of public finance was still centralized, but control over funds
was turned over to municipalities in the case of public schools and, in the case of
private schools, to the school authorities themselves. Decisions over the delivery of
education were also largely turned over to the municipalities and the schools.

In Chile, the decentralization reform was dictated from the top by the military
regime, with the objective of privatizing—to the greatest degree possible—the management of education. Even so, decentralization occurred in stages. Preceding the
1980 educational reform, Chilean government bureaucracy was devolved in the
1970s to the provinces and to municipalities run by appointed mayors and municipal councils. The teachers' union was also disbanded. In the reform itself, privatization was organized around a voucher plan and the privatization of teachers' contracts, transforming teachers from civil service employees into privately employed
workers without union representation. Both municipal and privately-managed subsidized schools received the same funding per student, and curriculum was dereg-
ulated.

The Chilean reform certainly achieved the decentralization of decision-making
to local communities and to schools (in the case of private schools). It was also
largely successful in privatizing Chilean education. By 1993, 40 percent of primary and 50 percent of secondary school pupils attended privately managed schools
(Comite Tecnico 1994). By 1996, approximately 42 percent of primary school pupils
attended private schools, 34 percent, voucher schools, and another 8 percent, private paid schools that do not accept vouchers. The reform was also successful financially, but only if success is measured in terms of reducing central government contribution. After an initial increase in government spending on education, caused
mainly by the need to pay teachers' severance as part of privatizing their contracts,
the central government's financial contribution to education was reduced sharply,
from 4.6 percent of GDP in 1980 to 2.5 percent in 1990.[4] The private contribution
to secondary and university education rose but not enough to offset the decline in
government spending. Not surprisingly, teachers' salaries fell in the 1980s.

In quality terms, however, the reform had little, if any, success in the 1980s, and
pupils from the lowest socioeconomic strata probably lost ground. Pupil performance overall did not rise despite the alleged greater efficiency of private schools.

New private and local public resources flowing into secondary and higher education did not match reductions in central government spending, creating a crisis of access for lower income students and a crisis of quality for all but those in the highest socioeconomic groups. Poorer municipalities were also not very good at running schools, since the government provided no capacity building as part of the reform. The reform did promote innovative programs in technical education, particularly for the 8 percent of students in schools run by private companies, but the rest of the system did worse.

With a return to democracy in 1990, these shortcomings were officially recognized. Moreover, the tensions and conflicts between teachers and the government emerged despite the new regime's willingness to implement large salary increases and to make considerable improvements in teaching conditions in the public schools. It also became clear that many municipalities simply did not, acting alone, have the resources or the technical capacity to manage education (as well as health care) at the municipal level.5 An evaluation of the 1980 reform conducted in 1994 suggested that a much more integrated approach was needed, one that recognized the need to increase teacher skills and one in which financial incentives were to be provided to schools as a reward for innovation and school improvement. Teacher salaries were raised as part of a commitment to increase government resources going to education, there was an increased emphasis on improving the quality of recruits in teaching and their pre-service training, and increased emphasis placed on in-service teacher training, with teachers who do particularly well to be rewarded with study abroad and public recognition (Comite Tecnico 1994).

The new Chilean government, with external assistance first from Scandinavia, then from the World Bank, also began a major equity-driven reform. Chile's P-900 program was designed to improve the quality of education in the nation's poorest performing primary schools with the most poverty (UNESCO 1993). Begun in 1990 with nine hundred schools, it has steadily expanded to several thousand schools into a general program to raise achievement. On the one hand, it differs from the Escuela Nueva in Colombia, which was and is intended to spread access and increase the quality of education in difficult-access rural areas. P-900 was and is organized on the basis of improving achievement in poorly performing schools. On the other hand, the two programs are similar in the systemic approaches they use in simultaneously raising teacher capacity with recurrent in-service training, improving the textbooks and other teaching material used in the schools, and using outreach programs to increase parent involvement in pupils' academic achievement. In addition, P-900 schools made larger achievement gains than the average of all subsidized schools, private and municipal. According to the SIMCE national test results, pupils in P-900 schools made large gains on Spanish and mathematics tests in 1990-1992 (Comite Tecnico 1994). But the program, like the Escuela Nueva, is not cheap. For example, the World Bank has lent Chile approximately $375 million dollars for the school-based projects portion of a larger primary education improvement program (World Bank 1991), and this was destined to five thousand schools, or $75,000 per school (over five years). Given a cost of about $200 per pupil per year in Chilean primary schools in 1989 (World Bank 1993), this implies an increase of about of about fifteen percent just in external assistance. The Comite Tecnico Asesor del Dialogo Nacional Sobre la Modernizacion del la Educacion Chilena recommended a one hundred percent increase in the public spending per pupil in basic and secondary education to improve quality to acceptable standards (Comite Tecnico, 1994).

Recent studies of the Chilean voucher plan show that vouchers did little, if anything, to improve the quality of education in Chile. When socioeconomic background of students is accounted for, Catholic voucher schools, attended by about ten percent of primary school students are somewhat more effective than municipal, publicly-run schools, but they are also somewhat more costly per student, since they collect fees in addition to the voucher. Commercial private voucher schools are slightly less effective than municipal schools, but are also less costly per student, since they tend to have larger class sizes and pay teachers less. The assumption that increased competition among schools would improve student performance in both private and public schools is not borne out by the data. Districts with a higher percentage of private schools did not improve relative to districts with fewer or no private schools. The only major impact on effectiveness over time was by the P-900 program: the longer schools were in that program, the better their students did relative to the average Chilean student (McEwan & Carnoy, 1999a; McEwan & Carnoy, 1999b).

The voucher plan did produce one change, however. Privatization increased the inequality of the distribution of students among schools. Higher socioeconomic class, higher-scoring students tended to become more concentrated in private schools and higher socioeconomic class students in public schools. Not surprisingly, private schools "skimmed" the better students from the public schools. Also public schools tended to concentrate in higher socioeconomic class municipalities where families with greater demand for private schooling lived (McEwan and Carnoy, 1999b).

There are two points to be made here: the first is that decentralization itself did not produce the answer to educational improvement even in the Chilean "ideal marketization" case; and the second is that, although decentralization is clearly desirable in highly bureaucratized LAC education systems, it needs to be accompanied by a host of other measures focused on capacity building, standard setting, and policy coherence, most of which have usually been the responsibility of central or state governments (for example, in the highly decentralized U.S. educational system) rather than schools or municipalities. These other measures required to improve educational quality also imply that even with decentralization of school management, central governments need to devote more, not less resources to education.

COLOMBIAN DECENTRALIZATION/RECENTRALIZATION

A decentralized education system has obvious advantages *if* capacity at the local level is adequate to the task of producing high quality education, *and* enough resources are available either from the central government or from the local jurisdiction or both. When decentralization reforms have been implemented in Argentina, Chile, and Mexico, however, these conditions of success have been less important than the shift of financial responsibility from central to provincial, departmental, or municipal authorities. For those pushing the reform, decentralization itself is viewed as the key to educational improvement; those opposing the reform (generally, teachers' unions, as in Argentina, Chile, Mexico, and more recently in Nicaragua) base their opposition on financial interests and, in the case of teachers' unions, on the conditions of employment contracts. Although decentralization proponents characterize such opposition as necessarily harmful to educational improvement, if the decentralization is primarily financially-driven (not educational- productivity), the political compromises reached through local authority and teacher opposition may not necessarily be all bad. In some cases, they may actually increase the possibility that the reform will improve educational outcomes.

The history of the recent Colombian reform is instructive in this regard. Colombia had already made a major educational innovation in developing the highly autonomous Escuelas Nuevas in the mid-1970s. But the latest round of the Colombian decentralization reform began in 1989, and was intended to be systemic rather than solving a particular educational access and quality problem. Colombian decentralization occurred in a democratic context, under very different political conditions than in Chile in 1981, and thus took on a different shape than the initial Chilean reform. As in Chile, the pressure for educational decentralization was part of a larger push for political decentralization. In 1985, the Colombian Congress approved the popular election of mayors, immediately raising expectations that social services, such as education and health, would be managed by municipalities. In 1989 a law was passed that increased the role of municipalities in educational administration, effectively giving them control over hiring teachers and making a number of educational resource allocation decisions, while the central government continued to pay teachers and other bills (Montenegro, 1995). But in 1991–1992, as part of a general move to restructure the Colombian economy, the government proposed to give municipalities control over managing local schools, with money supplied by bloc grants from the central government, but these bloc grants implied cuts in central government spending. In this same proposal, departments would be in charge of technical support and teacher training, and schools themselves would have autonomy over managing and selecting school personnel. To increase choice for parents and competition among schools, vouchers were to be created for poor students, and private eduction expansion was to be encouraged.

The debate in the Constitutional Assembly over the reform package showed that municipal governments viewed the decentralization proposal as motivated mainly by a desire to reduce central government spending on education. The municipalities wanted larger monetary transfers and smaller local responsibilities for raising resources in return for taking on the job of providing educational services. Ultimately, the central government did increase the resource transfer package as part of the New Constitution even though this meant raising the fiscal cost of the reform. But once the Constitution was enacted, the Congress had to propose specific legal changes in the way education was run, and this brought on a new round of opposition, this time from the teachers' union, FECODE (Montenegro 1995). The union drafted its own legislation in direct opposition to the reform. After a lengthy and painful debate, both Reform Laws were approved. As a result, full responsibility for schools was transferred only to departments and the larger municipalities, schools did not get the autonomy to select, hire, fire, or sanction teachers or administrative personnel, the evaluation of student achievement was to become a part of the reform but was not to be a basis for teacher promotion, vouchers were approved for poor students, as were incentives to build new private and public schools and the possibility for education services to be contracted with private suppliers. In addition, teachers and education managers' pay was guaranteed to come out of the central government transfers to department and the larger municipalities.

The debate and political maneuvering over the Colombian reform suggest that in a democratic context, central governments have to be realistic about what decentralization of education will cost, since local authorities and teachers' unions are hardly likely to accept a devolution of managerial responsibility to the locality under financial conditions that leave local officials "holding the bag." Reformers also have to be realistic with regard to teachers' unions. The unions are likely to see decentralization reforms—particularly ones that want to "privatize" the contract between the teacher and the school—as a direct threat to teachers' job security. Teachers are not particularly well paid in Latin America and are bound to take a defensive position on a reform that seeks to reduce their bargaining position further. In Colombia, as in other countries, teachers' union leadership is often narrow-minded, sometimes distant from the majority of teachers, often resistant to reforms that might improve teacher productivity, usually overly focused on one issue—teacher pay—and usually too inflexible on changing diploma/seniority-based pay scales. But unions are also a major political force for increasing funds going to education, not only for teacher salaries, but for school supplies, free textbooks for pupils, improved school buildings, and free lunches for children from low-income families.

The compromise reached in the Colombian reform in some ways incorporated at the beginning of the process where the Chilean reform is headed after a reaction to the worst deficiencies of the privatization model. Although Colombian schools will not have the autonomy of Chilean schools, and the bureaucracy in the Colombian system will remain greater, the problems faced by the poorest and lowest technical capacity municipalities in Chile will not be confronted in Colombia, where departments can still maintain much of the responsibility for making educational decisions for those municipalities. Also, thanks partly to municipality and teacher union confrontation over the reform, Colombian schools also will get relatively more public funds than Chilean schools in the 1980s, and privatization will evolve more slowly, allowing public schools to adapt more effectively.

Neither is the assumption that teachers' unions' demands are inherently at odds with parents' and children's interests as obvious as implied (for example, in Montenegro 1994). In the Chilean reform, parents got a choice of private or municipal schools, but, on average, the achievement of low-income children did not rise in the 1980s as a result of the reform. In Colombia, some municipalities may have gotten less autonomy as a result of teacher union intervention, but as a whole municipalities got more funding, and low-income families got vouchers for secondary education. For families living in low-income municipalities, the results of the compromise may on the whole have been more positive than the original proposed reform.

MEXICAN DECENTRALIZATION: AN INCOMPLETE REFORM

The Mexican decentralization reform, put in place in 1992–1993, also transferred the vast majority of responsibility for preschool, primary, secondary, and teacher training away from the federal government—in this case, to the states (Ornelas 1995). But the accord (the National Agreement for the Modernization of Basic Education) reached regarding the reform, and which allowed it to proceed, contained three crucial elements that are similar to the types of compromises reached in Colombia: the first, with the teachers' union (the SNTE), commits resources and political support to the union's bargaining rights and the "revaluation of the teaching profession" through formation of new teachers, higher teacher salaries, and social appraisal of teachers' work; the second is the guarantee to the states that the federal government will keep a high level of educational funding flowing to the states; and the third, a vague commitment by both federal and state governments to make the educational decision process more participative—the creation of Social Participation Councils at the school, municipal, state, and national levels (Ornelas 1995). In addition, the reform increased compulsory education to nine years, eliminated the ban on religious education, and assigned the development of new standards of school curriculum and the curriculum of teachers' education institutions to the federal government.

A more recent evaluation of the reform (Ibarrola 1995), however, casts doubts on the practical meaningfulness of the accord. For one, the economic crisis that began in December, 1994, put teachers' salaries back in steep decline. The reform left unclear responsibility for many of the most important aspects of curriculum reform and teacher training reform. And, finally, one of the most important aspects of teacher incentives, the large proportion of salary that is subject to internal evaluation, is largely in limbo because the national system to assess student outcomes appears far from being implemented.

The Privatization of Higher Education

The clearest example of a finance-driven reform in this period was the generally increased privatization of both secondary and tertiary level education in the region. Although the level of privatization at these levels varies widely among countries (see table 10.3), the tendency in a majority of countries is to rely increasingly on private education to absorb at least some, and in many countries, most of the increased demand for higher levels of schooling.

TABLE 10.3 LATIN AMERICA: PRIVATE ENROLLMENT AS PERCENTAGE OF
TOTAL UNIVERSITY ENROLLMENT, 1960-1990S (PERCENT)

Year	Brazil	Colombia	Dominican Republic	Mexico	Peru	Venezuela
1960				10	10	13
1965				14	16	15
1970			17	14	25	7
1975		54	43	12	30	11
1980		58	44	16	29	10
1985			56	18	36	15
1988				17		16
1989	62			17		
1990						
1991		61			34	
1993					36	
1994	56					
1996					34	

Source: Burton Clark and Guy Neave (eds.) *The Encyclopedia of Higher Education.* Oxford, England: Pergamon Press, 1994, Volume 1. Brazil, Colombia: Statistical Annuals. Peru, 1993, 1996: *Peru en Cifras, 1996.*

The rationale behind this move is that higher secondary and tertiary education students tend to come from relatively higher socioeconomic backgrounds, so can "afford" to pay for higher education. Since the costs of higher levels of education are also much higher than basic education costs, governments trying to reduce public spending can more easily make students that can work part-time bear a significant fraction of their educational costs. Many of these privately run schools and universities are partially subsidized by the government, but they also rely heavily on fees to meet their costs. Many of these private schools and universities also tend to be diploma mills, especially if they cater to lower-income students that work during the day and go to school at night.

The two best-known examples of university privatization are in Brazil and Chile. In Brazil, the military began a tentative private higher education sector in the 1970s. Some elite private institutions already existed, but when the new, commercial private higher education sector expanded rapidly in the 1980s and 1990s, it was largely to absorb lower middle-class students that worked part-time and could not get into the free, more prestigious public universities. In Chile, the military also stimulated the growth of private, for profit universities by limiting the expansion of the public, left-leaning, University of Chile. The government also closed all public teacher-training colleges. By the early 1980s, the entire expansion of higher education was private, with little subsidy from the government. Hence, mostly well-off Chileans could attend university, and like in Brazil, the very best students attended the free, elite University of Chile, because they were the only ones with test scores high enough to enter. Even teacher training colleges were privatized.

A Brief Summation of Decentralization/Privatization Reforms

Educational reforms—including decentralization of educational management and finances—can have a positive impact on educational quality, but the impact is largest when key actors, including teachers, buy into the reforms, and when an important part of the reform is increasing the technical capacity of administrators, teachers, and parents to raise pupil achievement. The initial decentralization- privatization reforms in, for example, Argentina, Chile, and Colombia and the recent reforms in El Salvador and Nicarargua took little or no account of the fact that teachers need to buy into them for maximum impact, nor did they build in capacity-raising measures at the provincial, municipal and school levels. Rather, they relied primarily on "market" incentives for teachers and administrators (fear of unemploymment, parent control of teacher salaries, competition among schools) to produce higher pupil achievement. This on the assumption that school administrators and teachers know how to produce higher pupil achievement but do not exert the effort to do so because they lack incentives. The Mexican reform went forward on a formal buy- in from the teachers' union, but in practice, the commitment to increase the quality of teacher training and to develop a coherent and stable system of teacher evaluation and reward has not yet been put in place.

What these reforms suggest, in the wake of the failure of decentralization and privatization *per se* to improve educational quality (or even efficiency), is that deregulation alone, even in the Chilean reform, with its privatized teacher contracts and no teacher union, did not solve the quality problem. Without skilled teachers well-steeped in knowledge of subject matter and relevant teaching technologies, a deep commitment to increasing pupil achievement and working in schools with clear objectives and organizations that reflect those objectives, this is not likely to change, deregulation/decentralization or not. This implies strategies that focus on (i) clarifying the accountability of the educational system, down to the school, particularly in terms of the outcomes expected; and (ii) increasing the capacity of the system, down to the school, to produce those outcomes. Clarifying accountability may be accomplished by a school's management and teachers, but it may also result from raising standards nationally, based on national examinations and a national curriculum. Increasing capacity may involve innovation on the part of teachers and administrators at the local level, but it also may mean better teacher preparation, pre-service and in-service, using methods developed by centralized organizations.

But predictably, privatization reforms did increase inequality in access to education, especially to quality education, hence contributing to the increased income and wealth inequality associated with the economic structural adjustment that dominated this period in Latin America.

TEACHER SALARIES AND STRUCTURAL ADJUSTMENT

Teachers' salaries, like the wages paid to all workers and professionals, are subject to the pressures of supply and demand. In almost all countries of the world, the vast majority of teachers are government employees. The demand for them is determined by the availability of government revenue and public sector decisions about spending on education compared to other claims on government revenues. Even though private and public schools generally coexist, teacher pay in Latin America's private schools tends to follow the government rate (ILO 1991a; McEwan and Carnoy 1999a). Teacher supply is also a function of spending decisions on education, since teachers are usually prepared according to requirements set by government. Except for countries such as Chile where there is a significant proportion of education students in private higher education, both the demand and the potential supply of teachers is therefore determined largely by government educational spending and regulatory policies.

Teachers' salaries are generally set solely on the basis of formal educational qualifications and years of experience in teaching. There is enormous variation among countries and, within countries, among levels of schooling, in pre-service requirements, in the number of years needed to attain the highest point in the pay scale, and in the ratio of highest pay to starting pay (for data on Latin America, see Reimers, 1990; general, see ILO 1991, table IX). The distribution of teachers among pay categories also varies greatly across countries, influencing the average salary level.

Because data are not available as generally for teacher salaries as for the numbers of teachers employed and public spending on education, a somewhat more selective set of estimates has to serve as the basis of analyzing the impact of structural adjustment on teachers' economic position in absolute terms and relative to other groups. Earlier studies of changes in teacher salaries in Latin America show generally rapid declines in real salaries for 1980-1985. Many of these declines began before 1980, in the 1970s (Tibi 1989). In Latin America, various studies of educational conditions (Reimers 1990; Corvalan 1990; Dewees, Klees, and Quintana 1994) suggest that with cuts in public spending and continued inflation in most countries, teachers' salaries corrected for inflation fell substantially in the 1980s.

Data on changes in teacher salaries from 1980 to the early 1990s show that teachers in structurally-adjusting developing countries generally suffered sharp decreases in real incomes and decreases relative to wages in the private sector. Teachers in Colombia, a country with relatively low indebtedness, positive economic growth, and relatively free from SAPs, did better than teachers in Mexico or Argentina, with high indebtedness, negative per capita economic growth, and forced to implement forcefully structural adjustment policies. In general, salaries at the secondary and university level fell even more than at the primary level. This is consistent with the relatively much larger cuts (or smaller increases) in spending per pupil in universities than in primary and secondary education in most, but not all, Latin American countries. It suggests that the salaries of university professors in developing countries have been a major target of public spending cuts.

Table 10.4 shows how teachers' salaries have changed relative to other salaries in each economy. The better comparison is between teacher salaries and manufacturing wages or salaries of government employees in general. But when such wage series are not available, per capita income changes are used for comparison. The danger of using per capita income as a referrent is that it can change as a result of shifts in the composition of the population between income earners and non-income earners. But over a short period of time, such as the ten years used in this study, per capita income does give some idea of how teachers' salaries changed compared to overall economic conditions. The most important finding in table 10.5 is that teacher incomes in most structurally-adjusting countries declined in the 1980s, whether manufacturing wages or per capita income declined, and that in those cases where incomes fell generally, teachers' incomes dropped much more. Thus, in Latin American countries, teachers' material conditions declined, and they declined most in those countries focusing on reducing public spending or increasing access to education without increasing the budget for education.

The earlier series developed by Tibi (1989) suggests that factors other than SAPs can produce sharp declines in teacher salaries. Negative economic growth for a decade almost necessarily means that a country's teachers be paid less. But the fact that teacher salaries fell so sharply in the 1980s and fell relatively to other workers' incomes in countries implementing SAPs makes a strong case that SAPs contributed to the conditions attached to SALs and to sector loans for education legitimized the view teachers (and all public employees) were paid too much or worked too little or

both, so reducing their wages and increasing their work load were rational responses to a squeeze.

TABLE 10.4. LATIN AMERICA: CHANGES IN PRIMARY TEACHERS SALARIES RELATIVE
TO CHANGES IN NATIONAL AVERAGE WAGES, 1980-EARLY 1990S
(INDEX)

Country	1980	1982	1985	1988	1990-1992
Argentina	100	82	77		58
Chile		100	120		52
Colombia		100	96	93	
Costa Rica		100	79	77	91
Mexico	100	87	83	39	47
Venezuela	100			116	

Source: ILO. *Impact of structural adjustment on the employment and training of teachers.*
Geneva, JMEP/1996/II, 1996, Table 9.

Understanding how SAPs contributed to the decline of teacher salaries requires a
clear picture of the process of salary cuts, especially relative to average wages and
to wages in the public sector as a whole. Data from several Latin American countries
suggest that the recession of the early 1980s, which hit Latin America particularly
hard because of their large indebtedness and U. S. credit cuts, was mainly responsible for major drops in all wages during that period, including teacher salaries. But
where governments found it politically possible to do so, they held teacher salaries
down for much longer in response to the drive to reduce public spending, including
education spending. Thus, it is the second part of the period that is most interesting
in assessing the impact of structural adjustment on teacher salaries (Carnoy and Torres 1995; Imaz 1995; Reimers 1990).

After the early 1980s, teacher salaries behaved differently in various Latin American countries. The clearest example of close adherence to IMF/World Bank structural adjustment policies was Chile, whose government already began to reduce public social spending after the military coup in 1973. In 1980, the government implemented a major reform in education, decentralizing management of central government education grants to municipal governments, which obtained total control of
local public schools. In addition, the government implemented a fully-subsidized
voucher plan, in which a private school could accept full public funding on a per student basis almost without public regulation (Prawda 1993; McEwan and Carnoy
1999).The central government increased per pupil spending for two years, but then
began to cut back (World Bank 1991). Teachers' salaries rose sharply in 1980–1982,
then fell rapidly in the rest of the decade, at double the rate of manufacturing wages.
The salary cuts enabled municipalities to increase teacher employment at the primary level by 2.4 percent annually in 1980–1990 and reduce the average pupil

teacher, ratio while reducing education spending. Through the early 1990s, with the re-establishment of democracy in 1990 and rapid economic growth, the government raised teacher salaries sharply in 1990–1993 almost back to 1982 levels. In 1996, salaries were raised sharply again. The salary increases by the new government were part of an overall effort to correct the general failure of the structural adjustment policies to improve educational outcomes (McEwan & Carnoy 1999a).

Mexico is a second example of rapid and forceful application of structural adjustment policies throughout the economy. According to Imaz (1995), the Mexican federal education budget fell sharply in 1983, to less than 70 percent of its 1982 level, as the Mexican economy went through a severe recession. The budget then leveled off until 1985, fell again to less than 60 percent of its 1982 level by 1988, and then began to rise until, in 1993 it was back to 1982 in real terms. Teacher salaries (Imaz used salaries for Mexico City teachers), however, declined almost continuously from 1981 to 1988, reaching a bottom of 22 percent of their 1981 levels. In 1988-1993, salaries increased substantially, but were still only 42 percent of 1981 levels. Teachers' salaries not only dropped in absolute terms, but also relative to the changes in average wages and average government salaries. According to Lustig (1995), the Mexican government enjoyed the freedom to manage fiscal retrenchment because it did not have to deal wth strong independent unions within its public service. Yet, the government still had to make political choices, and it decided to cut wages and public investment rather than employment in the public sector, possibly because it was safer to socialize the cost of austerity among public employees. This applied much more forcefully to education than the public sector as a whole, where at the bottom of the trough (1988) salaries in the public sector had fallen 55 percent compared to 78 percent for teachers. The number of employed primary school teachers increased 2.5 percent annually in the 1980s, secondary teachers, by 4.3 percent annually, and university teachers, by 5.6 percent annually.Increasing the work force in education enabled the government to keep expanding schooling, including preschools and rural primary schools, and to reduce the pupil-teacher ratio in primary school. But lowering salaries so drastically had the effect of demoralizing teachers, forcing many to seek additional sources of employment, and possibly lowering the quality of education (Carnoy & Torres 1995; Imaz 1995).

In contrast with the "tight" implementation of SAPs by the Chilean and Mexican governments, Argentina, Costa Rica, and other countries of Central America represent cases of looser structural adjustment as applied to teachers, although under very different conditions. Costa Rica was plunged into a deep recession in 1980-1982, and teachers' salaries fell an average 27 percent at the primary level and 39 percent at the secondary level in three years, 1979-1982. With the implementation of World Bank SAPs after 1983, teacher salaries did fall another few percent, especially for unqualified teachers ("aspirantes"), the main effect of SAP pressure in 1983-1988 was to keep teachers' real wages from rising even as GDP per capita, average government wages, and the worker market wage all rose (3.4 percent, 21 percent, and 31 percent, respectively). Three consecutive Costa Rican administrations focused on holding down teacher salaries and shifting the direct cost of school supplies to parents. But teachers fought back through threatened strikes and the courts to raise their salaries almost back to 1970s levels. In the meantime, however, even if the required government reduction of salaries was not successful, the attempt to hold them down and the teachers' reaction had important negative implications for education expansion, notably at the secondary level. Unlike Mexico and Chile, the student-teacher ratio did not decline in the 1980s, and the absolute number of teachers employed increased slowly at the primary level and not at all in secondary.

The situation in other countries of Central America, which suffered economically as much as or more than other Latin American countries, confirms the drastic declines in teacher renumeration. Teachers' salaries in Nicaragua are only four percent of what they were in 1980, and, on average, only one-half of what other Ministry of Education staff earn. this has created a crisis in recruiting and holding teachers, especially since double shifts (and therefore double income) are prohibited (Arnove 1994). Salaries also fell sharply in El Salvador and Guatemala.

In Argentina, society resisted adjustment in the 1980s, and, for part of the decade was successful. But eventually, adjustment occurred by default (Lustig 1995). Real manufacturing wages fell by about fourteen percent in 1980–1990, less than in Chile and Mexico, but substantially, nonetheless. The government encountered serious difficulties in cutting the public deficit and reforming the public sector. One of the major obstacles to cuts in educational spending was the power of the teachers' union. The union engaged in a series of strikes, which during certain periods of the 1980s, were successful in keeping wages from falling further. Yet, after some wage recovery in 1982–1985, especially for primary teachers wages, the adjustment of government spending began, and teachers' salaries declined rapidly to forty percent of 1980 levels. The fall was even greater for university professors.

These case-by-case reviews show that whereas structural adjustment in Latin America almost universally had a significant negative effect on teacher salaries, there were differences among countries (see also Subirats and Nogales 1989 for Bolivia, and Tovar, et. al., 1989 for Peru). Debt overhang and continued economic difficulties meant that teachers' real wages were likely to fall. More often than not (especially at secondary and higher levels of schooling), they fell much more than the general level of wages or per capita income.

GLOBALIZATION AND TESTING LATIN AMERICA

The measurement of quality linked to improving educational efficiency cannot be separated from the financially driven reforms discussed above. Much of the discussion of student performance is in the context of educational spending and how to reduce it without impacting "quality." The implication is that public educational delivery is inefficient and part of its inefficiency can be picked up by measuring student performance to make the "system" aware of well or badly students are doing.

With increased economic competition and the increased availability of information technology, data takes on increased value and increased use. Performance in real time is enhanced as an outcome, quantitative measurement appears easier, and its results become increasingly the means of communication about performance. An important element of such performance is linked to "efficiency." The application of this thinking, part and parcel of globalized thinking, to education takes the form of tracking the quantity and quality of education through data collection. The notion has been stimulated by the spread of a science and math culture (Schofer et.al., 1997), and also the strong effort by many countries to attract foreign high-tech investment and to build up domestic high tech industries.

The new emphasis on measuring and comparing school outcomes across countries and within countries has not occurred spontaneously. Rather, it has been pushed by international organizations such as the International Educational Assessement (IEA), the OECD, and the World Bank. All these organizations share a globalized view of education and efficiency, which includes a highly quantitative view of progress. They also share an explicit understanding that "better" education can be measured and that better education translates directly into higher economic and social productivity. With more intensive economic competition among nation-states, the urgency of improving productivity is translated by these organizations into spreading the acceptance of inter- and intra-national comparisons on standardized tests of student knowledge.

Students in every country are evaluated annually or more often by their teachers (and their school). These evaluations measure, on the basis of teacher- or school-designed examinations, whether a student has "learned" the prescribed curriculum. Except in those countries where there is automatic promotion, they determine whether students repeat the grade or move on to the next one. In addition to such "in-house" evaluations, some countries also have "life-chances" tests, usually at the end of secondary school (O- and A-levels in Africa, the English Caribbean, Malaysia; the Baccalaureat in former French colonies) and others, examinations that rank students for entry into different kinds of universities and university departments (for example, the *vestibular* in Brazil).

Although all these examinations measure student competencies in terms of curricular goals (computation, basic reading and writing skills), they are designed primarily to compare individual students with other students for the purpose of "sorting." For example, teacher-examination evaluations are often characterized as minimum standards that deny promotion to students who perform inadequately. But such standards vary widely from school to school, and the fact that they are usually a function of the number of places available at the next level of schooling suggests that they act more as a sorter than as a standard. The more places available in secondary school, for example, the lower the percentage of failures in primary school.

An increasing number of Latin American countries are moving from what is now almost universal in-school individual student evaluation and end of school level exams with almost no diagnostic implications, toward system/school assessment exams that are intended to identify poorly performing municipalities/schools and suggest directions for school improvement. Tests are given to a sample or an entire population of students at a given level of schooling in a nation, state, province, or municipality to assess the amount of learning against some absolute standard (criterion-referenced tests) taking place in schools, municipalities, states, or nations, and compare the level of student performance in a particular grade among schools. Chile, which has the longest history of such examinations, originally tested a national sample of schools in 1958, again in the late 1960s and early 1970s, and, beginning in 1982, with the PER exam, and then the SIMCE in 1988, has tested students in the fourth and eighth grades for the past fifteen years. Other Latin American countries, such as Argentina, Mexico, and Uruguay have also implemented such tests.

Latin American countries are also increasingly participating in international comparisons of their students' performance. The most recent, mentioned above, it the OREALC survey of third and fourth grade performance of fifteen countries. Although Peru refused to allow publication of its results, the fourteen other countries in the survey did allow themselves to be compared, some with disappointing outcomes.

Comparative testing, whether national or international, does raise the issue of how the results should be employed beyond making them available to analysts in central Ministries or in International agencies. In Chile, Costa Rica, and in Minas Gerais, test results by school are circulated both publicly and in individual schools. In Argentina, recent evaluations are published for the national level divided into socioeconomic class groups, but not for individual schools. Neither are schools informed of their results. In this latter case, then, the test are used as surveys for assessing reform policies, even though in their present form, they are not particularly useful for that purpose, since Ministry does not collect data on school characteristics. The movement toward testing children in every country is spreading rapidly, pushed hard by the World Bank and the Inter-American Development Bank (see Wolff 1998).

The tests enable countries or regions to assess how much of the prescribed curriculum students are learning by school, region, and socioeconomic group. When applied over a period of time, they also give an indication whether improvement is taking place or not, and whether certain policies are working or not. For example, the effects of Chile's P-900 project, begun in May, 1990, in which the Ministry of Education provided educational materials, teacher training, and other student interventions to the lowest performing schools in the country, could be charted by comparing the test scores of the schools that were involved in the project with other schools.

The tests also make teachers, administrators, and parents much more aware of student performance and more sensitive to the need to raise performance, especially if the scores on the tests are systematically publicized. Interviews in Chilean schools, for example, suggest that all these groups know how their school is performing on the SIMCE test, and how performance changes from test to test. Since (urban) parents in every Latin American country have some degree of choice in their children's school, and middle class parents have a high degree of choice, publicizing test scores could influence school choice and competition among schools even in a largely public system.

But while the testing may provide much useful information for teachers, administrators, and parents, the underlying assumptions of the testing may be off the mark. The way tests are applied and their results used is also highly political, and may not be producing the outcomes intended. A comparison of the politics of testing in Argentina, Chile, and Uruguay suggests that each of these countries employs testing for different, political goals (Benveniste 1999). In Argentina, testing as implemented seems to be a means for the central government to retain some regulatory power over primary and secondary education even as administrative and financial decision-making has been ceded to the provinces. By publishing test scores, the Ministry in Buenos Aires can deem which provinces are doing "well" and which "badly." In turn, provinces are developing their own testing and evaluation systems to regain "power" over the definition of school quality. Testing is therefore part of the struggle over control of the educational system and credit from its improvement. At the same time, both federal and provincial administrations push blame for poor performance down to the level below. The federal officials blame the provinces and the teachers and the provinces blame the schools and the teachers. No wonder that teachers in Argentina are vehemently opposed to testing.

In Chile, as argued above, the Ministry of Education publishes results as part of "informing" consumers of education about the quality of individual schools, under the assumption that competition will produce better results for all. Although this assumption has never been realized in practice, it continues to form the basis for the testing system.

Again, the responsibility for improvement lies with the individual school, although the central government has increased its role in technical assistance to schools. Since, for all the rhetoric about the decentralized Chilean model, the Chilean educational system remains relatively centralized, the relation between regulation and responsibility remains less divided than in Argentina. Increasingly, the Ministry of Education takes *de facto* responsibility for improving education in Chile, although under the 1980 decentralization/privatization reform, *de jure* schools bear responsibility for improvement. The national tests therefore continue to play a complex role at the local level, both pressuring schools to teach the test so that they look "good" in any comparisons with other schools, and pressuring the Ministry to take steps that will improve educational quality overall. For example, the latest reform pushed by the

Ministry would increase all schools to full day, ending double shifts. This is an enormously expensive reform, and falls completely outside the model of increasing efficiency through competition. It comes from a concern that the voucher reforms and increased competition have failed to raise educational quality.

In Uruguay, the most centralized education system among these three, testing is implemented not to increase the power of the Ministry, but to meet pressures from the World Bank to use evaluation *without* trying to create competition among schools. The Ministry implemented a testing system with the total "buy-in" of the teachers' union, under the expressed condition that the test results would be used to identify and remediate the problem of lower performance of lower social class students. Hence, the Ministry seems to be using the test results as part of a national project to improve the performance of the poorest-performing social groups. In some sense, this corresponds closely to the present, post 1990 project in Chile, except that the Uruguayans have none of the voucher/competition model in Chile inherited from the 1980s (Benveniste 1999).

The fact that testing can be used for such different purposes politically makes clear that student evaluation has different meaning in different political contexts and applications.

SUMMARY OF LATIN AMERICAN EDUCATIONAL REFORMS UNDER STRUCTURAL ADJUSTMENT

Latin America went through a major economic restructuring in the 1980s and 1990s, and with that, backed into educational reforms. The most important manifestation of globalization in Latin America's educational system was deep cuts in the growth of public spending, hence educational spending, in most countries of the region in the 1980s, and only partial recovery in the 1990s. This meant declining relative salaries for teachers in many of the countries, a shift to more private education at the upper secondary and tertiary education levels, and a relative decline in the quality of education, particularly at the secondary and higher levels.

Economic restructuring did not mean that educational access stopped expanding in Latin America in this period. To the contrary, almost every country was able to continue expanding secondary and higher education even during the financial crisis of the 1980s, and has continued that expansion in the 1990s. Apparently political pressure for continued expansion forced governments to find ways to provide more school places even as they often sacrificed the quality of education in order to do that.

In the 1990s, positive economic growth enabled most countries to interpret the exigencies of globalization as demanding improved educational quality. The World Bank and Inter-American Development Bank have pushed for particular reforms that focus on improving the efficiency of education, namely decentralization, increased competition through vouchers/privatization, and testing and evaluation. There is little evidence that any of these reforms contribute to higher quality education, but they continue to dominate the reform movement in Latin America.

Alternative movements have also sprung up. In Brazil, the organized Left has pushed for democratization of schools, where teachers and parents run schools and make decisions about models of teaching and learning. There is little evidence that this form of decentralization has much effect on quality either. The Escuela Nueva reform in Colombia makes an effort to make sustained improvements in isolated rural schools by creating networks of teachers, materials for teaching, and workshops to improve multi- grade teaching. This has seemed to work, largely because government has taken real responsibility for school improvement and has focused directly on improving teaching and learning.

APPENDIX 10.1 LATIN AMERICA: PRIMARY, SECONDARY AND HIGHER EDUCATION ENROLLMENT RATES, COUNTRY AND STAGE OF EDUCATIONAL ACCESS, 1980-1995/96 (PERCENT AND NUMBER)

Country / Stage	Primary Enrollment Ratio			Secondary Enrollment Ratio			Tertiary Level Students per 100,000 Population		
	1980	1992	1995—1996	1980	1992	1995—1996	1980	1992	1995—1996
Low Access to Education									
Haiti	38	26	n.a.	14**	22**	n.a.	87	n.a.	n.a.
Universalizing Access to Primary Education									
Bolivia	79	91	n.a.	16***	29***	n.a.	1,557	2,214	n.a.
Brazil	81	90	117**	14***	19***	n.a.	1,162	1,179	1,094
Dom. Rep.	73	81	81	n.a.	24	22	n.a.	n.a.	n.a.
El Salvador	n.a.	70	79	24***	26***	21	372	1,512	1,933
Guate-mala	58	70*	84**	13		25**	736	n.a.	755
Hondu-ras	78	90	90	n.a.	21	32	724	852	985
Nicara-gua	73	80	83	23	26	47**	1,106	809	1,231
Para-guay	87	97	91	n.a.	29	38	858	907	1,049
Universalizing Access to Secondary Education									
Argentina	n.a.	95	113*	n.a.	59	77**	1,748	3,268	3,117
Barbados	96	89	n.a.	86	81	n.a.	1,620	1,647	2,602
Chile	n.a.	86	88	n.a.	52	58	1,306	2,145	2,546
Colombia	n.a.	83	89	n.a.	44	72**	1,024	1,554	1,768
Costa Rica	89	87	94	39	37	43	2,433	2,767	2,919
Cuba	95	97	100	81**	82**	77	1,563	1,840	1,013
Ecuador	88	n.a.	97	53**	55**	54**	3,389	2,012	n.a.
Jamaica	96	100	107**	64	64	n.a.	656	976	803
Mexico	n.a.	100	100	n.a.	46	51	1,387	1,477	1,586
Panama	89	91	104**	46	51	68**	2,071	2,398	3,024
Peru	91	88	122**	46	46	70**	1,769	4,188	3,268
Trin &Tob.	92	88	88	64	65	72**	522	593	771
Uruguay	n.a.	93	96	62**	83**	85**	1,339	2,396	2,487
Venezu-ela	83	88	84	14***	20***	22	2,035	2,853	n.a.

Source: UNESCO, *World Education Report, 1995, Tables 4, 6, and 8. UNESCO, Statistical Annual, 1999.* Notes: *Estimated from gross rates. **Gross enrollment rates. ***Net rate refers to higher secondary only: 4 yrs. Boliva; 3, Brazil; 3, El Salvador; 2, Venezuela.

NOTES

[1]   Brazil's primary and secondary education was historically highly decentralized to states and municipalities, with no obvious impact on quality, but considerable impact on inequality and politicization of resource allocation (Amadeo et.al., 1994). That said, in today's climate of educational reform, it can be argued that in those states and municipalities led by politicians intent on educational reform, it is probably easier in the decentralized context to implement reforms.

[2]   Although decentralizing the management and financing of highly bureaucratic, centralized systems of education should lead to more innovativeness and efficiency of educational service delivery, with more accountability to parents, there is little evidence that educational quality improves as a result. For example, in the U.S., where there has been a concerted push to move control of educational decisions down to individual schools, extensive evaluation shows that school autonomy itself has produced no significant student achievement gains (Malen, Ogawa, and Krantz, 1989; Hannaway and Carnoy, 1993).

[3]   "Private" schools are defined here as those that are *managed* privately, either for profit or by religious organizations, even in the case that privately managed schools are financed mainly by government funds and are required to conform to certain government legal requirements. Even though public financing and public regulation suggest that privately-managed schools are not entirely "private," this definition conforms to the generally-held conception of what is a private educational institution, and indeed to the definition of a private business. For example, aerospace companies in the United States are highly dependent on government contracts and, like all private business, subject to government regulations. Yet, they are considered private corporations because they are owned privately and their management is responsible to private shareholders, not the government.

[4]   This has risen in the 1990s, as the democratic government began spending more on education. It reached 3.1 percent of GDP in 1996.

[5]   The democratic government continues a commitment to the process of decentralization. Its major recent recommendations in the 1990s have been for educational management of financial resources in municipal schools to shift to the schools themselves (1994) and for a lengthening of the school day to 6 hours (complete day). The assumption is based on the allegedly greater efficiency of subsidized private schools, which *do* manage finances at the school level. There is a convincing evidence that children of low socioeconomic background do not do as well in for profite voucher schools as in municipal schools (Parry Rounds, 1994; McEwan & Carnoy, 1999a. but that for profit schools spend less per student. This suggests that decision-making handed over to the most decentralized level does not necessarily produce better results for those children requiring the greatest amount of innovativation and technical knowledge to improve their learning, although privately managed schools may be able to save resources.

REFERENCES CITED

Amadeo, E., J. Marcio Camargo, A. E. S. Marques; C. Gomes (1994). Fiscal Crisis and Asymmetries in the Education System in Brazil. In J. Samoff and Taskforce (eds.). *Coping with Crisis: Austerity, Adjustment, and Human Resources*. Paris: ILO-UNESCO.

Arnove, R. (1994). *Education as Contested Terrain: Nicaragua, 1979-1993*. Boulder: Westview Press.

Benveniste, L. (1999). "The Politics of Educational Testing in the Southern Cone: A Comparison of Student Testing Policies in Argentina, Chile, and Uruguay." Unpublished Ph.D. dissertation, School of Education, Stanford University.

Carnoy, M. and C. A. Torres (1995). "Educational Change and Structural Adjustment: A Case Study of Costa Rica." In J. Samoff and Taskforce (eds.). *Coping with Crisis*, ILO-UNESCO.

Carnoy, M. and P. McEwan (1999). "Privatization Through Vouchers in Developing Countries: The Cases of Chile and Colombia," Stanford University School of Education (mimeo).

Comité Técnico Asesor del diálogo nacional sobre la modernización del la educación chilena. (1994). *Los desafíos del la educación chilena frente al Siglo XXI*. Santiago de Chile: Editorial Universitaria.

Corvalan, A. M. (1990). "El financiamento de la educacion en periodo de austeridad presupuestaria," UNESCO/OREALC, Santiago de Chile.

Dewees, A., S. Klees, and J. Quitana (1994). *Diagnostico del Systema de Desarrollo de Recursos Humanos de El Salvador*, Harvard Institute for International Development, January, Chapter 3.

Hannaway, J. and M Carnoy (1993). *Decentralization and School Improvement*. San Francisco: Jossey- Bass.

Ibarrola, M. de. (1995). "Dinamicas de transformacion en el sistema educacativo Mexicano." In Puryear, J. and Brunner, J.J. (eds.). *Educacion, Equidad y Competitividad Economica en Las Americas: Un Proyecto del Dialogo Interamericano, Vol. II*. Washington, D.C.: OEA/OAS, pp. 253-288.

Imaz, C. (1995). "Inertia and Change in the Pedagogy and Politics of Teachers," unpublished Ph.D. dissertation, Stanford University School of Education.

International Labour Organization (1991).*Teachers: Challenges of the 1990s: Second Joint Meeting on Conditions of Work of Teachers, Geneva, 1991*. Geneva: International Labour Office.

Laboratorio Latinoamericano de Evaluación de la Calidad de la Educación (LLECE). 1998. *Primer Estudio Internacional Comparativo sobre Lenguaje, Matemática y Factores Asociados en Tercero y Cuarto Grado*. Santiago: UNESCO.

Lustig, Nora (ed.). (1996). *Coping With Austerity: Poverty and Inequality in Latin America*. Washington, D.C.: The Brookings Institution.

Malen, B. R.T. Ogawa, and J. Krantz. (1989). "What Do We Know About School-Based Management." School of Education, University of Utah, May (mimeo).

McEwan, P. and Carnoy, M. (1999). "The Effectiveness and Efficiency of Private Schools in Chile's Voucher System." Stanford University School of Education (mimeo).

MINEP. (1991). *Indicadores Sociodemograficos.* San Jose, Costa Rica, August.

Montenegro, A. (1995). *An Incomplete Educational Reform: The Case of Colombia,* HCO Working Paper 60 . Washington, D.C.: World Bank.

OREALC (1994). *Medición de la Calidad de la Educación. Resultados.* Santiago de Chile: UNESCO-OREALC.

Ornelas, C. (1995). *El Sistema Educativo Mexicano.* (Mexico : Centro de Investigacion y Docencia Economicas.

Prawda, J. (1993). Educational Decentralization in Latin America: Lessons Learned. *International Journal of Educational Development,* 13, no, 3: 253-64.

Rama, G. (1992). *Aprenden los estudiantes en el Ciclo Básico de Educación Media?* CEPAL, Montevideo.

Reimers, F. (1990). "Education for All in Latin America in the XXI Century: The Challenges of the Stabilization, the Adjustment, and the Fulfillments of Jomtien." UNESCO-OREALC Bulletin, 23 (December): 7-25.

Rounds P. T. (1994). The Impact of Decentralization and Competition on the Quality of Education: An Assessment of Educational Reforms in Chile. University of Georgia. Unpublished paper.

Schofer, E., Francisco Ramirez, John Meyer.1997. "Effects of Science on Economic Development," paper presented at the annual meetings of the American Sociological Association, Toronto.

Subirats, J. and Y. Nogales (1989). *Maestros, Escuelas, Crisis Educativa: Condiciones del trabajo docente en Bolivia.* Santiago, UNESCO/PREALC.

Tibi, C. (1989). "Conditions in the Teaching Profession: A Current Problem." *IIEP Newsletter.* Paris: International Institute of Educational Planning.

Tovar, T. L. Gorriti and E. Morillo (1989). *Ser Maestro: Condiciones del trabajo docente en Peru.* Santiago, UNESCO/PREALC.

UNESCO (1993). *World Education Report, 1993.* Paris: UNESCO.

UNESCO (1995). *World Education Report, 1995.* Paris: UNESCO.

Wolff, L. (1998). *Educational Assessments in Latin America: Current Progress and Future Challenges.* Occasional Paper Series. Washington, D.C.: Inter-American Dialogue.

World Bank (1991). "Staff Appraisal Report, Primary Education Improvement Project," (Chile) September.

World Bank (1993). "Improving the Quality of Primary Education in Latin America and the Caribbean: Towards the 21st Century." Washington, D.C., March.

Name Index

China Daily, 195, 199
Chubb, J. E., 34, 82, 84, 91, 98
Ciborra, C. U., 9
Cohen, D., 34, 75, 95, 125, 127, 130
Cohen, S. S., 7
Colclough, C., 12, 253
Collot, A., 47, 118
Coombs, P., 18
Cornia, G. A., 8
Corvalan, A. M., 313
Coulby, D., 17
Coulon, C., 254, 264
Cox, R., 5, 6, 11–13
Creevy, L., 264
Cummings, W. K., 20
Cvetkovich, A., 5

Dahllöf, U., 18, 116
Dale, R., 15, 19, 38–41, 44, 77, 81
Daun, H., 44, 80, 87, 90, 91, 100, 115, 117,
    188, 254, 255
Desjeux, D., 250
Didier, G., 47, 118
Dodge, B., 207, 214
Dumont, R., 250
Dupree, L., 239

Edwards, R., 5, 9, 88–90, 98
Eickelmann, D. F., 210, 214
Éla, J. -M., 50, 251
El-Garh, M. S., 206
Elham, M. R., 241
Ergas, Z., 252
Escudero, M., 16
Esping-Andersen, G., 9, 11, 13

Featherstone, M., 17
Flacks, R., 14, 46
Freeman, C., 4, 8, 11, 16, 123, 149

Gallagher, H., 37
Gellner, E., 49, 213
Gennaoui, A., 222
Ghai, D., 5
Gibbon, P., 50, 250, 251
Giddens, A., 16, 17, 46, 53
Gill, S., 8, 12, 13
Ginsburg, M. B., 20
Glickman, H., 248

Goontilake, S., 7
Gopinathan, G., 20
Graham-Brown, S., 20, 72, 100, 253, 254, 256
Grindal, B., 254
Groth, A. J., 248, 254, 256

Habermas, J., 14, 16, 41, 42, 53–55
Halsey, A. H., 35–37, 43, 44, 46
Hamilton, C., 8, 11, 72
Hann, C., 4
Hansson, G, 6, 8, 10, 75, 79, 80, 83
Harbeson, J. W., 48–50, 250
Harding, S., 14. 15. 17
Harrigan, J., 7, 12
Havnevik, K. J., 274, 275, 277
Haynes, J., 209
Herbst, J., 15, 251
Hermele, K., 268, 269
Héthy, J., 162–164
Henderson, J, 4
Higgot, R, 39
Hirst, P., 3, 15
Hirth, M., 241
Hjärpe, J., 206
Hoerner, J-M., 7, 11, 16, 17, 250
Hogan, D., 17, 102, 127
Hu, R. W., 189
Humphrey, J., 38, 250
Hurst, H, 214
Hussein, M. G., 216

IMF, 166, 169, 170, 222, 250, 251, 263, 268,
    276, 294, 295, 314
Inglehart, R., 15, 17
Iordanescu, M., 171

Jarrar, S. A., 97, 208, 211, 217
Jigau, M., 160, 170
Johnston, B. J., 34, 73, 126
Jones, P. W., 251

Kabeer, N., 38, 250
Kanaev, A., 84
Ka-ho Mok, 197
Kassé, M., 263
Kellner, D., 17
Kern, H., 9
Kitaev, I., 93, 95, 100, 256
Kiwara , D. A., 277

Subject Index

ROUTLEDGEFALMER STUDIES IN INTERNATIONAL
AND COMPARATIVE EDUCATION
EDWARD R. BEAUCHAMP, *SERIES EDITOR*